HLM 6: Hierarchical Linear and Nonlinear Modeling

HLM 6:

Hierarchical Linear and Nonlinear Modeling

4 5 6 7 8 9 0   09 08 07

Published by:

Scientific Software International, Inc.
7383 North Lincoln Avenue, Suite 100
Lincolnwood, IL 60712-1747
Tel: +1.847.675.0720
Fax: +1.847.675.2140
URL: http://www.ssicentral.com

ISBN: 978-0-89498-054-1 (paper)

Preface

New features in HLM 6 for Windows

HLM 6 greatly broadens the range of hierarchical models that can be estimated. It also offers greater convenience of use than previous versions. Here is a quick overview of key new features and options:

1. All new graphical displays of data: group-specific scatter plots, line plots, and cubic splines that can be color coded by values of predictor variables; box-plots displayed for overall data and data grouped within higher-level units.
2. Greatly expanded graphics for fitted models: graphing of group-specific equations, box-plots of level-1 residuals for each group, plots of residuals by predicted values for each group, posterior credibility intervals for random coefficients. For three-level models, level-1 trajectories are displayed in separate graphs or grouped by level-3 unit. Graphs can be color coded by values of predictor variables.
3. Model equations displayed in hierarchical or mixed-model format with or without subscripts - easy to save for publication. Distributional assumptions and link functions are presented in detail.
4. Cross-classified random effects models for linear models and non-linear link functions with convenient Windows interface.
5. High-order Laplace approximation with EM algorithm for stable convergence and accurate estimation in two-level hierarchical generalized linear models (HGLM).
6. Multinomial and ordinal models for three-level data.
7. New flexible and accurate sample design weighting for two- and three-level HLMs and HGLMs.
8. Easier automated input from a wide variety of software packages, including the current versions of SAS, SPSS, and STATA.
9. Residual files can be saved directly as SPSS (*.sav) or STATA (*.dta) files.
10. Completely revised manual and online Help documentation. Analyses are based on MDM files, replacing the older, less flexible SSM format.

Contents

1 Conceptual and Statistical Background for Two-Level Models

Behavioral and social data commonly have a nested structure. For example, if repeated observations are collected on a set of individuals and the measurement occasions are not identical for all persons, the multiple observations are properly conceived as nested within persons. Each person might also be nested within some organizational unit such as a school or workplace. These organizational units may in turn be nested within a geographical location such as a community, state, or country. Within the hierarchical linear model, each of the levels in the data structure (e.g., repeated observations within persons, persons within communities, communities within states) is formally represented by its own sub-model. Each sub-model represents the structural relations occurring at that level and the residual variability at that level.

This manual describes the use of the HLM computer programs for the statistical modeling of two- and three-level data structures, respectively. It should be used in conjunction with the text *Hierarchical Linear Models: Applications and Data Analysis Methods* (Raudenbush, S.W. & Bryk, A.S., 2002: Newbury Park, CA: Sage Publications)[1]. The HLM programs have been tailored so that the basic program structure, input specification, and output of results closely coordinate with this textbook. This manual also cross-references the appropriate sections of the textbook for the reader interested in a full discussion of the details of parameter estimation and hypothesis testing. Many of the illustrative examples described in this manual are based on data distributed with the program and analyzed in the Sage text.

We begin by discussing the two-level model below and the use of the HLM2 program in Chapter 2. Building on this framework, Chapters 3 and 4 introduce the three-level model and the use of the HLM3 program. Chapters 5 and 6 consider multivariate models that can be estimated from incomplete data. Chapters 7 and 8 discuss use of hierarchical modeling for non-normal level-1 errors. Chapter 9 describes several special features of HLM2 and HLM3, including analyses involving latent variables, multiply-imputed data, and known level-1 variances, as well as the procedure for graphing data and equations. Chapters 10 and 11 introduce cross-classified random effects models that are applicable for analyses of models that do not have a strictly hierarchical data structure. Finally, Chapter 12 illustrates HLMs ability to produce data- and model-based graphs.

1.1 The general two-level model

As the name implies, a two-level model consists of two submodels at level 1 and level 2. For example, if the research problem consists of data on students nested within schools, the level-1 model would represent the relationships among the student-level variables and the level-2 model would capture the

---

[1] Also available from SSI.

influence of school-level factors. Formally, there are $i = 1,..., n_j$ level-1 units (*e.g.*, students) nested within $j = 1,..., J$ level-2 units (*e.g.*, schools).

1.1.1 Level-1 model

We represent in the level-1 model the outcome for case i within unit j as:

$$
\begin{aligned}
Y_{ij} &= \beta_{0j} + \beta_{1j} X_{1ij} + \beta_{2j} X_{2ij} + \cdots + \beta_{Qj} X_{Qij} + r_{ij} \\
&= \beta_{0j} + \sum_{q=1}^{Q} \beta_{qj} X_{qij} + r_{ij},
\end{aligned}
\tag{1.1}
$$

where

β_{qj} $(q = 0,1,..., Q)$ are *level-1 coefficients*;

X_{qij} is the *level-1 predictor* q for case i in unit j;

r_{ij} is the level-1 random effect; and

σ^2 is the variance of r_{ij}, that is the level-1 variance.

Here we assume that the random term $r_{ij} \sim N(0, \sigma^2)$.

1.1.2 Level-2 model

Each of the level-1 coefficients, β_{qj}, defined in the level-1 model becomes an outcome variable in the level-2 model:

$$
\begin{aligned}
\beta_{qj} &= \gamma_{q0} + \gamma_{q1} W_{1j} + \gamma_{q2} W_{2j} + \cdots + \gamma_{qS_q} W_{S_q j} + u_{qj} \\
&= \gamma_{q0} + \sum_{s=1}^{S_q} \gamma_{qs} W_{sj} + u_{qj},
\end{aligned}
\tag{1.2}
$$

where

γ_{qs} $(q = 0,1,..., S_q)$ are *level-2 coefficients*;

W_{sj} is a level-2 predictor; and

u_{qj} is a level-2 random effect.

We assume that, for each unit j, the vector $(u_{0j}, u_{1j},..., u_{Qj})'$ is distributed as multivariate normal, with each element of u_{qj} having a mean of zero and variance of

$$
Var(u_{qj}) = \tau_{qq}.
\tag{1.3}
$$

For any pair of random effects q and q',

$$Cov(u_{qj}, u_{q'j}) = \tau_{qq'}.$$ (1.4)

These *level-2 variance* and *covariance components* can be collected into a dispersion matrix, $\mathbf{T}$, whose maximum dimension is $(Q+1) \times (Q+1)$.

We note that each level-1 coefficient can be modeled at level-2 as one of three general forms:

1. a *fixed level-1 coefficient*; e.g.,

$$\beta_{qj} = \gamma_{q0},$$ (1.5)

2. a *non-randomly varying level-1 coefficient*, e.g.,

$$\beta_{qj} = \gamma_{q0} + \sum_{s=1}^{S_q} \gamma_{qs} W_{sj},$$ (1.6)

3. a *randomly varying level-1* coefficient, e.g.,

$$\beta_{qj} = \gamma_{q0} + u_{qj}$$ (1.7)

or a level-1 coefficient with both non-random and random sources of variation,

$$\beta_{qj} = \gamma_{q0} + \sum_{s=1}^{S_q} \gamma_{qs} W_{sj} + u_{qj}$$ (1.8)

The actual dimension of $\mathbf{T}$ in any application depends on the number of level-2 coefficients specified as randomly varying. We also note that a different set of level-2 predictors may be used in each of the $Q+1$ equations of the level-2 model.

1.2 Parameter estimation

Three kinds of parameter estimates are available in a hierarchical linear model: empirical Bayes estimates of randomly varying level-1 coefficients; generalized least squares estimates of the level-2 coefficients; and maximum-likelihood estimates of the variance and covariance components.

1.3 Empirical Bayes ("EB") estimates of randomly varying level-1 coefficients, β_{qj}

These estimates of the level-1 coefficients for each unit j are optimal composites of an estimate based on the data from that unit and an estimate based on data from other similar units. Intuitively, we are borrowing strength from all of the information present in the ensemble of data to improve the level-1 coefficient estimates for each of the J units. These "EB" estimates are also referred to as "shrunken estimates" of the level-1 coefficients. They are produced by HLM as part of the residual file output (see

Section 2.5.4, *Model checking based on the residual file*). (For further discussion see *Hierarchical Linear Models*, pp. 45-51; 85-95.)

1.4 Generalized least squares (GLS) estimates of the level-2 coefficients, γ_{qs}

Substitution of the level-2 equations for β_{qj} into their corresponding level-1 terms yields a single-equation linear model with a complex error structure. Proper estimation of the regression coefficients of this model (*i.e.*, the γ's) requires that we take into account the differential precision of the information provided by each of the J units. This is accomplished through generalized least squares. In the program output, the final generalized least squares estimates for the γs are represented by Gqs. (For further discussion see *Hierarchical Linear Models*, pp. 38-44.)

1.5 Maximum likelihood estimates of variance and covariance components, σ^2 at level 1, and T at level 2

Because of the unbalanced nature of the data in most applications of hierarchical linear models (*i.e.*, n_j varies across the J units and the observed patterns on the level-1 predictors also vary), traditional methods for variance-covariance component estimation fail to yield efficient estimates. Through iterative computing techniques such as the EM algorithm and Fisher scoring, maximum-likelihood estimates for σ^2 and **T** can be obtained. (For further discussion, see *Hierarchical Linear Models*, pp. 51-56; also Chapters 13, 14). In the program output, these estimates are denoted by SIGMA-SQUARED and TAU respectively.

1.6 Some other useful statistics

Based on the various parameter estimates discussed above, HLM2 and HLM3 also compute a number of other useful statistics. These include:

1. *Reliability of* $\widehat{\beta}_{qj}$.

The program computes an overall or average reliability for the least squares estimates of each level-1 coefficient across the set of J level-2 units. These are denoted in the program output as RELIABILITY ESTIMATES and are calculated according to Equation 3.58 in *Hierarchical Linear Models*, p. 49.

2. *Least squares residuals,* $(\widehat{u}_{qj})$.

These residuals are based on the deviation of an ordinary least squares estimate of a level-1 coefficient, $\widehat{\beta}_{qj}$, from its predicted or "fitted" value based on the level-2 model, *i.e.*,

$$\widehat{u}_{qj} = \widehat{\beta}_{qj} - \left(\widehat{\gamma}_{q0} + \sum_{s=1}^{S_q} \widehat{\gamma}_{qs} W_{sj} \right). \tag{1.9}$$

10

These ordinary least square residuals are denoted in HLM residual files by the prefix OL before the corresponding variable names.

3. *Empirical Bayes residuals* (u_{qj}^*)

These residuals are based on the deviation of the empirical Bayes estimates, β_{qj}^*, of a randomly varying level-1 coefficient from its predicted or "fitted" value based on the level-2 model, *i.e.,*

$$u_{qj}^* = \beta_{qj}^* - \left(\hat{\gamma}_{q0} + \sum_{s=1}^{S_q} \hat{\gamma}_{qs} W_{sj} \right). \tag{1.10}$$

These are denoted in the HLM residual files by the prefix EB before the corresponding variable names. (For a further discussion and illustration of OL and EB residuals see *Hierarchical Linear Models,* pp. 47-48; and 76-95).

1.7   Hypothesis testing

Corresponding to the three basic types of parameter estimates based on a hierarchical linear model (EB estimates of random level-1 coefficients, GLS estimates of the fixed level-2 coefficients, and the maximum-likelihood estimates of the variance and covariance components), are single-parameter and multi-parameter hypothesis-testing procedures. (See *Hierarchical Linear Models,* pp. 56-65). The current HLM programs execute a variety of hypothesis tests for the level-2 fixed effects and the variance-covariance components. These are summarized in Table 1.1.

1.8   Restricted versus full maximum likelihood

By default, two-level models are estimated by means of restricted maximum likelihood (REML). Using this approach, the variance-covariance components are estimated via maximum likelihood, averaging over all possible values of the fixed effects. The fixed effects are estimated via GLS given these variance-covariance estimates. Under full maximum likelihood (ML), variance-covariance parameters and fixed level-2 coefficients are estimated by maximizing their joint likelihood (see *Hierarchical Linear Models,* pp. 52-53). One practical consequence is that, under ML, any pair of nested models can be tested using a likelihood ratio test. In contrast, using REML, the likelihood ratio test is available only for testing the variance-covariance parameters, as indicated in Table 1.1.

1.9   Generalized Estimating Equations

Statistical inferences about the fixed level-2 coefficients, γ_{qs}, using HLM are based on the assumption that random effects at each level are normally distributed; and on the assumed structure of variation and covariation of these random effects at each level. Given a reasonably large sample of level-2 units, it is possible to make sound statistical inferences about γ_{qs} that are not based on these assumptions by using the method of generalized estimating equations or "GEE" (Zeger & Liang, 1986). Comparing these GEE inferences to those based on HLM provides a way of assessing whether the HLM inferences about γ_{qs} are sensitive to the violations of these assumptions. The simplest GEE model assumes that the outcome Y_{ij} for case i in unit j is independent of the outcome $Y_{i'j}$ for some other case, i', in the same unit; and that these outcomes have constant variance. Under these simple assumptions, estimation of the γ coefficients by ordinary least squares (OLS) would be justified. If these OLS assumptions are incorrect, the OLS estimates of γ_{qs} will be consistent (accurate in large samples) but not efficient. However, the standard error estimates produced under OLS will generally be inconsistent (biased, often badly, even in large samples).

Table 1.1 Hypothesis tests for the level-2 fixed effects and the variance-covariance components

Type of hypothesis	Test statistic	Program output
Fixed level-2 effects		
Single Parameter: $H_0 : \gamma_{qs} = 0$ $H_1 : \gamma_{qs} \neq 0$	t-ratio[1]	Standard feature of the Fixed Effects Table for all level-2 coefficients
Multi-parameter: $H_0 : C'\gamma = 0$ $H_1 : C'\gamma \neq 0$	general linear hypothesis test (Wald test), chi-square test[2]	Optional output specification (see Section 2.8)
Variance-covariance components		
Single-Parameter: $H_0 : \tau_{qq} = 0$ $H_1 : \tau_{qq} > 0$	Chi-square test[3]	Standard feature of the Variance Components Table for all level-2 random effects
Multi-parameter: $H_0 : \mathbf{T} = \mathbf{T}_0$ $H_1 : \mathbf{T} \neq \mathbf{T}_0$	Difference in deviances, likelihood ratio test.[4]	Optional output specification (see Section 2.8)

[1]See Equation 3.83 in *Hierarchical Linear Models*.
[2]See Equation 3.91 in *Hierarchical Linear Models*.
[3]See Equation 3.103 in *Hierarchical Linear Models*.
[4]Here $\mathbf{T}_0$ is a reduced form of $\mathbf{T}_1$.

Version 6 of HLM produces the following tables, often useful for comparative purposes:

- A table of OLS estimates along with the OLS standard errors.
- A table including the OLS estimates, but accompanied by robust standard errors, that is, standard errors that are consistent even when the OLS assumptions are incorrect.
- A table of HLM estimates of γ_{qs}, based on GLS, and standard errors based on the assumptions underlying HLM.
- A table of the same HLM estimates, but now accompanied by robust standard errors, that is, standard errors that are consistent even when the HLM assumptions are mistaken.

By comparing these four tables, it is possible a) to discern how different the HLM estimates and standard errors are from those based on OLS; and b) to discern whether the HLM inferences are plausibly distorted by incorrect assumptions about the distribution of the random effects at each level. We illustrate the value of these comparisons in Chapter 2 (for further discussion, see *Hierarchical Linear Models*, pp. 276-280). The GEE approach is very useful for strengthening inferences about the fixed level-2 coefficients but does not provide a basis for inferences about the random, level-1 coefficients or the variance-covariance components. Cheong, Fotiu, and Raudenbush (2001) have intensively studied the properties of HLM and GEE estimators in the context of three-level models. GEE results are also available for three-level data.

2 Working with HLM2

Data analysis by means of the HLM2 program will typically involve three stages:

1. construction of the "MDM file" (the multivariate data matrix);
2. execution of analyses based on the MDM file; and
3. evaluation of fitted models based on a residual file.

We describe each stage below and then illustrate a number of special options. Data collected from a High School & Beyond (HS&B) survey on 7,185 students nested within 160 US high schools, as described in Chapter 4 of *Hierarchical Linear Models*, will be used for demonstrations.

2.1 Constructing the MDM file from raw data

We assume that a user has employed a standard computing package to clean the data, make necessary transformations, and conduct relevant exploratory and descriptive analyses. We also recommend exploratory graphical analyses within HLM prior to model building as described in detail in Section 12.1 of this manual.

The first task in using HLM2 is to construct the Multivariate Data Matrix (MDM) from raw data or from a statistical package. We generally work with two raw data files: a level-1 file and a level-2 file. Both files must be sorted by the level-2 ID (It is possible, however, to build the MDM file from the level-1 file above, though this option is not suggested when the level-1 file is very large. The level-1 file must be sorted by level-2 ID. The level-1 file name will be selected as both the level-1 and level-2 file).

For the HS&B example, the level-1 units are students and the level-2 units are schools. The two files are linked by a common level-2 unit ID, school id in our example, which must appear on every level-1 record. In constructing the MDM file, the HLM program will compute summary statistics based on the level-1 unit data and store these statistics together with level-2 data.

The procedure to create a MDM file consists of three major steps. The user needs to

- Inform HLM of the input and MDM file type.
- Supply HLM with the appropriate information for the data, the command and the MDM files.
- Check if the data have been properly read into HLM.

2.2   Executing analyses based on the MDM file

Once the MDM file is constructed, all subsequent analyses will be computed using the MDM file as input. It will therefore be unnecessary to read the larger student-level data file in computing these analyses. The efficient summary of data in the MDM file leads to faster computation. The MDM file is like a "system file" in a standard computing package in that it contains not only the summarized data but also the names of all of the variables.

Model specification has three steps:

- Specifying the level-1 model, which defines a set of level-1 coefficients to be computed for each level-2 unit.
- Specifying a level-2 structural model to predict each of the level-1 coefficients.
- Specifying the level-1 coefficients to be viewed as random or non-random.

The output produced from these analyses includes:

- Ordinary least squares and generalized least squares results for the fixed coefficients defined in the level-2 model.
- Estimates of variance and covariance components and approximate chi-square tests for the variance components.
- A variety of auxiliary diagnostic statistics.

Additional output options and hypothesis-testing procedures may be selected.

2.3   Model checking based on the residual file

After fitting a hierarchical model, it is wise to check the tenability of the assumptions underlying the model:

- Are the distributional assumptions realistic?
- Are results likely to be affected by outliers or influential observations?
- Have important variables been omitted or non-linear relationships been ignored?

These questions and others can be addressed by means of analyses of the HLM residual files. A level-1 residual file includes:

- The level-1 residuals (discrepancies between the observed and fitted values).
- Fitted values for each level-1 unit (that is, values predicted on the basis of the model).
- The observed values of all predictors included in the model.
- Selected level-2 predictors useful in exploring possible relationships between such predictors and level-1 residuals.

A level-2 residual file includes:

- Fitted values for each level-1 coefficient (that is, values predicted on the basis of the level-2 model).
- Ordinary least squares (OL) and empirical Bayes (EB) estimates of level-2 residuals (discrepancies between level-1 coefficients and fitted values).
- Empirical Bayes coefficients, which are the sum of the EB estimates and the fitted values.
- Dispersion estimates useful in exploring sources of variance heterogeneity at level 1.
- Expected and observed Mahalanobis distance measures useful in assessing the multivariate normality assumption for the level-2 residuals.
- Selected level-2 predictors useful in exploring possible relationships between such predictors and level-2 residuals.
- Posterior variances.

For HLM2 FML analyses, there is an additional set of posterior variances. See Chapter 9 in *Hierarchical Linear Models* for a full discussion of these methods.

2.4   Windows, interactive, and batch execution

Formulation and testing of models using HLM programs can be achieved via Windows, interactive, or batch modes. Most PC users will find the Windows mode preferable. This draws on the visual features of Windows while preserving the speed of use associated with a command-oriented (batch) program. Non-PC users have the choice of interactive and batch modes only. Interactive execution guides the user through the steps of the analysis by posing questions and providing a menu of options. In this chapter, we employ the Windows mode for all the examples. Descriptions and examples on how to use HLM2 in interactive and batch modes are given in Appendix A.

2.5   An example using HLM2 in Window mode

Chapter 4 in *Hierarchical Linear Models* presents a series of analyses of data from the HS&B survey. A level-1 model specifies the relationship between student socioeconomic status (SES) and mathematics achievement in each of 160 schools; at level-2, each school's intercept and slope are predicted by school sector (Catholic versus public) and school mean social class. We reproduce one analysis here (see Table 4.5 in *Hierarchical Linear Models*, p. 82).

2.5.1 Constructing the MDM file from raw data

PC users may construct the MDM file directly from different types of input files including SPSS, ASCII, SAS, SYSTAT, and STATA, or indirectly from many additional types of data file formats through the third-party software module included in the HLM program.

Non-PC users may construct the MDM file with one of the following types of input files: ASCII data files, SYSTAT data files, or SAS V5 transport files.

In order for the program(s) to correctly read the data, the IDs need to conform to the following rules:

1. For ASCII data the ID variables must be read in as character (alphanumeric). These IDs are indicated by the A field(s) in the format statement. For all other types of data, the ID may be character or numeric.

2. The level-1 cases must be grouped together by their respective level-2 unit ID. To assure this, sort the level-1 file by the level-2 ID field prior to entering the data into HLM2.

3. If the ID is numeric, it must be in the range $-(10^{13}+1)$ to $+(10^{13}+1)$ (*i.e.* 12 digits). Although the ID may be a floating point number, only the integer part is used.

4. If the ID variable is character, the length must not exceed 12 characters. Furthermore, the IDs at a given level must all be the same length. *This is often a cause of problems.* For example, imagine your data has IDs ranging from "1" to "100". You will need to recreate the IDs as "001" to "100". In other words, all spaces (blank characters) should be coded as zeros.

5. For non-ASCII files, the program can only properly deal with numeric variables (with the exception of character ID variables). Other data types, such as a "Date format", will not be processed properly.

6. For non-ASCII files with missing data, one should only use the "standard" missing value code. Some statistical packages (SAS, for example) allow for a number of missing value codes. The HLM modules are incapable of understanding these correctly, thus these additional missing codes need to be recoded to the more common "." (period) code.

2.5.1.1   SPSS file input

We first illustrate the use of SPSS file input and then consider input from ASCII data files. Data input requires a level-1 file and a level-2 file.

Level-1 file. For our HS&B example data, the level-1 file (HSB1.SAV) has 7,185 cases and four variables (not including the SCHOOL ID). The variables are:

- MINORITY, an indicator for student ethnicity ($1 =$ minority, $0 =$ other)
- FEMALE, an indicator for student gender ($1 =$ female, $0 =$ male)
- SES, a standardized scale constructed from variables measuring parental education, occupation, and income
- MATHACH, a measure of mathematics achievement

Data for the first ten cases in HSB1.SAV are shown in Fig. 2.1.

Note: level-1 cases must be grouped together by their respective level-2 unit ID. To assure this, sort the level-1 file by the level-2 unit ID field prior to entering the data into HLM2.

	id	minority	female	ses	mathach
1	1224	0	1	-1.528	5.876
2	1224	0	1	-.588	19.708
3	1224	0	0	-.528	20.349
4	1224	0	0	-.668	8.781
5	1224	0	0	-.158	17.898
6	1224	0	0	.022	4.583
7	1224	0	1	-.618	-2.832
8	1224	0	0	-.998	.523
9	1224	0	1	-.888	1.527
10	1224	0	0	-.458	21.521

Figure 2.1   First ten cases in HSB1.SAV

Level-2 file. At level 2, the illustrative data set HSB2.SAV consists of 160 schools with 6 variables per school. The variables are:

- SIZE (school enrollment)
- SECTOR (1 = Catholic, 0 = public)
- PRACAD (proportion of students in the academic track)
- DISCLIM (a scale measuring disciplinary climate)
- HIMNTY (1 = more than 40% minority enrollment, 0 = less than 40%)
- MEANSES (mean of the SES values for the students in this school who are included in the level-1 file)

The data for the first ten schools are displayed in Fig 2.2.

	id	size	sector	pracad	disclim	himinty	meanses
1	1224	842	0	.350	1.597	0	-.428
2	1288	1855	0	.270	.174	0	.128
3	1296	1719	0	.320	-.137	1	-.420
4	1308	716	1	.960	-.622	0	.534
5	1317	455	1	.950	-1.694	1	.351
6	1358	1430	0	.250	1.535	0	-.014
7	1374	2400	0	.500	2.016	0	-.007
8	1433	899	1	.960	-.321	0	.718
9	1436	185	1	1.000	-1.141	0	.569
10	1461	1672	0	.780	2.096	0	.683

Figure 2.2   First ten cases in HSB2.SAV

As mentioned earlier, the construction of an MDM file consists of three major steps. This will now be illustrated with the HS&B example.

To inform HLM of the input and MDM file type

1. At the **WHLM** window, open the **File** menu.
2. Choose **Make new MDM file...Stat package input** (see Figure 2.3). A **Select MDM type** dialog box opens (see Figure 2.4).
3. Select **HLM2** and click **OK**. A **Make MDM - HLM2** dialog box will open (see Figure 2.5).

To supply HLM with appropriate information for the data, the command, and the MDM files:

1. Select **SPSS/Windows** from the **Input File Type** pull-down menu (see Figure 2.5).
2. Click **Browse** in the **Level-1 Specification** section to open an **Open Data File** dialog box.
3. Open a level-1 SPSS system file in the HLM folder (HSB1.SAV in our example). The **Choose Variables** button will be activated.
4. Click **Choose Variables** to open the **Choose Variables - HLM2** dialog box and choose the ID and variables by clicking the appropriate check boxes (See Figure 2.6). To deselect, click the box again.
5. Select the options for missing data in the level-1 file (there is no missing data in HSB1.SAV; see Section 2.6 for details).
6. Click the selection button for **measures within persons** for the **type of nesting of input data** if the level-1 data consist of repeated measures or item responses. With this selection, WHLM will use in its displays and output model notations that match those used in *Hierarchical Linear Models* for studies on individual change and latent variables (Chapters 6 and 11). The default type is **persons within groups**. It is generally used when the level-1 data are comprised of cross-sectional measures. With this option, WHLM will use model notations that correspond to those used for applications in organization research (Chapters 4 and 5).
7. Click **Browse** in the **Level-2 specification** section to open an **Open Data File** dialog box.
8. Open a level-2 SPSS system file in the HLM folder (HSB2.SAV in our example). The **Choose Variables** button below **Browse** will be activated.
9. Click **Choose Variables** to open the **Choose Variables - HLM2** dialog box and choose the ID and variables by clicking the appropriate check boxes (see Figure 2.7).
10. Enter a name for the MDM file in the **MDM file name** box (for example, HSB.MDM).
11. Click **Save mdmt file** in the **MDM template file** section to open a **Save MDM template file** dialog box. Enter a name for the MDMT file (for example, HSBSPSS.MDMT). Click **Save** to save the file. The command file saves all the input information entered by the user. It can be re-opened by clicking the **Open mdmt file** button (see Figure 2.5). To make changes to an existing MDMT file, click the **Edit mdmt file** button.
12. Note that HLM will also save the input information into another file called CREATMDM.MDMT when the MDM is created.
13. Click the **Make MDM** button. A screen displaying the prompts and responses for MDM creation will appear.

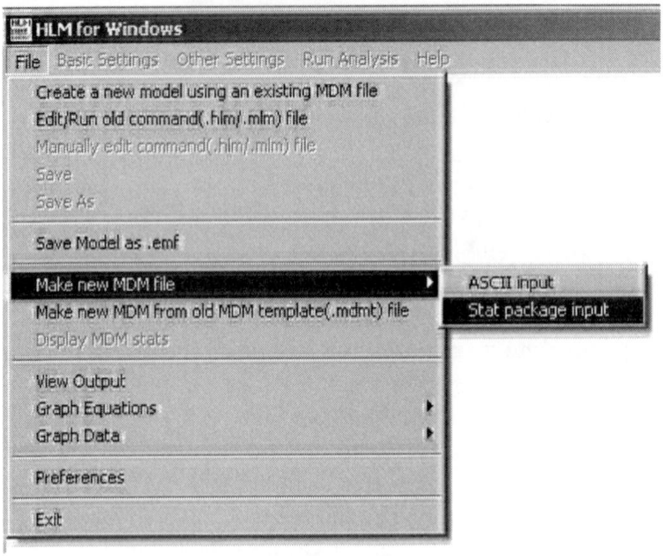

Figure 2.3   **WHLM window**

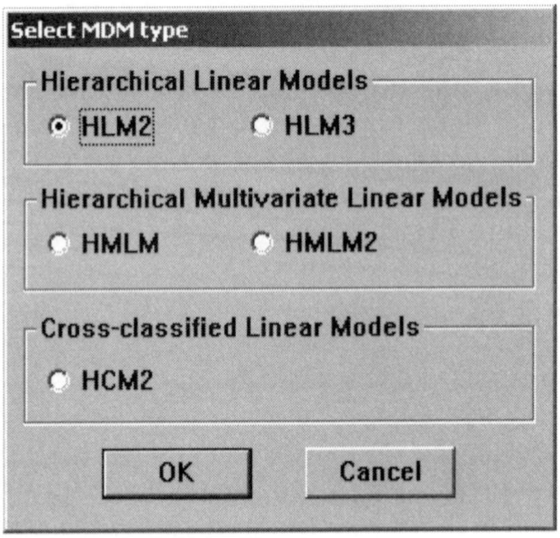

Figure 2.4   **Select MDM type dialog box**

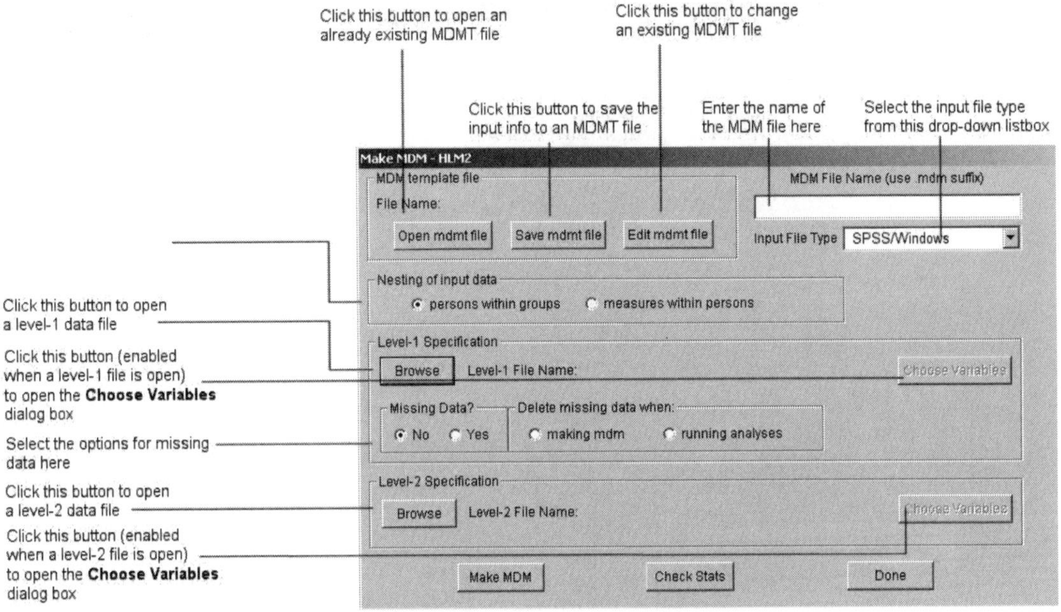

Click this button to open an
already existing MDMT file

Click this button to change
an existing MDMT file

Click this button to save the
input info to an MDMT file

Enter the name of
the MDM file here

Select the input file type
from this drop-down listbox

Make MDM - HLM2

MDM template file

File Name:

MDM File Name (use .mdm suffix)

| Open mdmt file | Save mdmt file | Edit mdmt file |

Input File Type SPSS/Windows

Nesting of input data

    ○ persons within groups   ○ measures within persons

Click this button to open
a level-1 data file

Level-1 Specification

Click this button (enabled
when a level-1 file is open)
to open the **Choose Variables**
dialog box

| Browse | Level-1 File Name:

Choose Variables

Select the options for missing
data here

Missing Data?   Delete missing data when:

    ● No ○ Yes   ○ making mdm   ○ running analyses

Click this button to open
a level-2 data file

Level-2 Specification

Click this button (enabled
when a level-2 file is open)
to open the **Choose Variables**
dialog box

| Browse | Level-2 File Name:

Choose Variables

| Make MDM | Check Stats | Done |

Figure 2.5   Make MDM - HLM2 dialog box

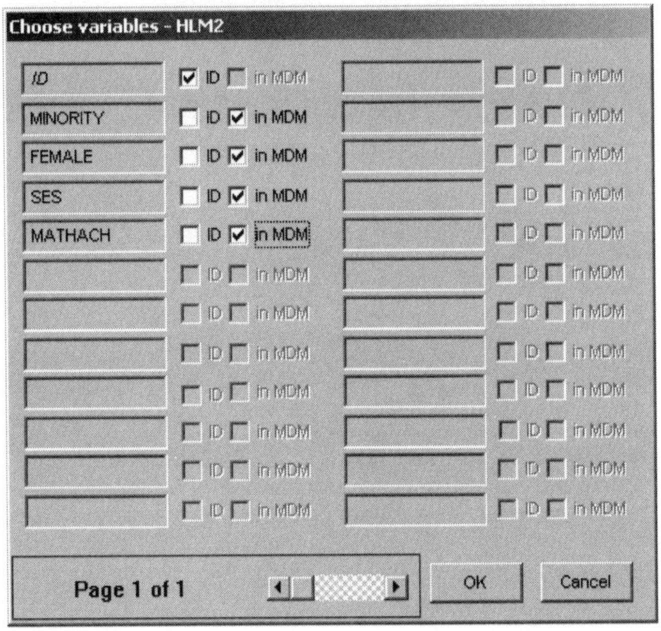

Choose variables - HLM2

ID	☑ ID ☐ in MDM		☐ ID ☐ in MDM
MINORITY	☐ ID ☑ in MDM		☐ ID ☐ in MDM
FEMALE	☐ ID ☑ in MDM		☐ ID ☐ in MDM
SES	☐ ID ☑ in MDM		☐ ID ☐ in MDM
MATHACH	☐ ID ☑ in MDM		☐ ID ☐ in MDM
	☐ ID ☐ in MDM		☐ ID ☐ in MDM
	☐ ID ☐ in MDM		☐ ID ☐ in MDM
	☐ ID ☐ in MDM		☐ ID ☐ in MDM
	☐ ID ☐ in MDM		☐ ID ☐ in MDM
	☐ ID ☐ in MDM		☐ ID ☐ in MDM
	☐ ID ☐ in MDM		☐ ID ☐ in MDM
	☐ ID ☐ in MDM		☐ ID ☐ in MDM

Page 1 of 1   ◄ � ► | OK | Cancel |

Figure 2.6   Choose Variables - HLM2 dialog box for the level-1 file, HSB1.SAV

21

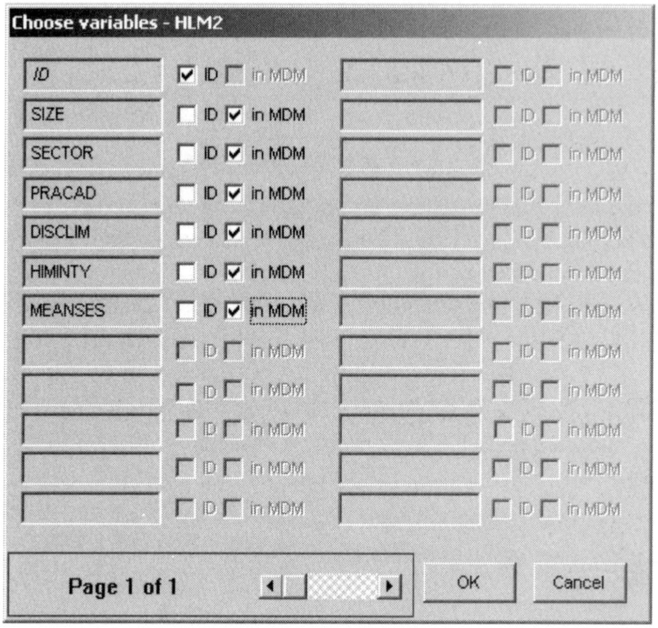

Figure 2.7 Choose variables - HLM2 dialog box for the level-2 file, HSB2.SAV

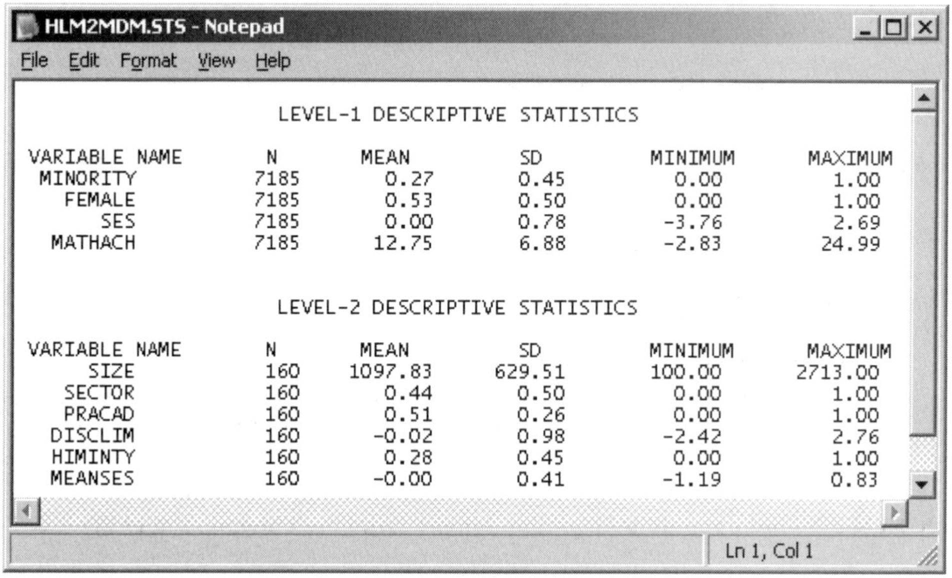

LEVEL-1 DESCRIPTIVE STATISTICS

VARIABLE NAME	N	MEAN	SD	MINIMUM	MAXIMUM
MINORITY	7185	0.27	0.45	0.00	1.00
FEMALE	7185	0.53	0.50	0.00	1.00
SES	7185	0.00	0.78	-3.76	2.69
MATHACH	7185	12.75	6.88	-2.83	24.99

LEVEL-2 DESCRIPTIVE STATISTICS

VARIABLE NAME	N	MEAN	SD	MINIMUM	MAXIMUM
SIZE	160	1097.83	629.51	100.00	2713.00
SECTOR	160	0.44	0.50	0.00	1.00
PRACAD	160	0.51	0.26	0.00	1.00
DISCLIM	160	-0.02	0.98	-2.42	2.76
HIMINTY	160	0.28	0.45	0.00	1.00
MEANSES	160	-0.00	0.41	-1.19	0.83

Figure 2.8 Descriptive Statistics for the MDM file, HSB.MDM

To check whether the data have been properly read into HLM

1. Click **Check Stats** to display and check the level-1 and level-2 descriptive statistics (See Figure 2.8). Pay particular attention to the N column. It is not an uncommon mistake to forget to sort by the ID variable, which can lead to a lot (or most) of the data not being processed. Close the Notepad window when done. Use the **Save As** option to give it a new name if later use of this file is anticipated.

2. Click **Done**. The **WHLM** window displays the type and name on its title bar (**hlm2 &** **HSB.MDM**) and the level-1 variables on a drop-down menu (See Figure 2.9).

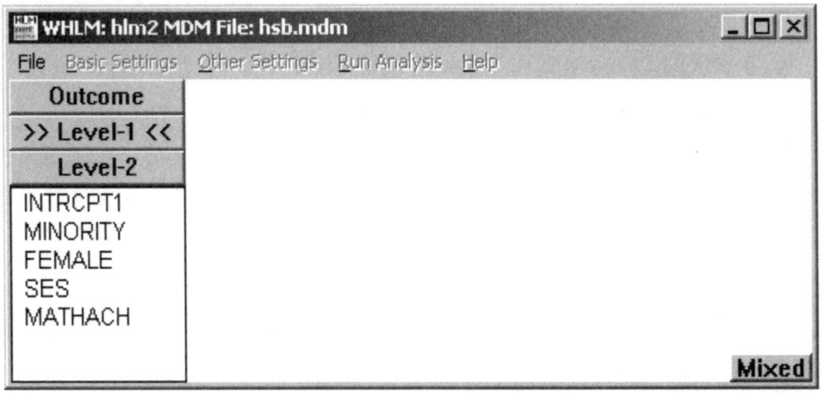

Figure 2.9   WHLM: hlm2 MDM File window for HSB.MDM

2.5.1.2   ASCII file input

Below is the procedure for creating a multivariate data matrix file with input from ASCII files.

To inform HLM of the input and MDM file type

1. At the **WHLM** window, open the **File** menu.
2. Choose **Make new MDM file...ASCII** input. A **Select MDM type** dialog box opens.
3. Select **HLM2** (see Figure 2.4) and click **OK**. A **Make MDM File – HLM2** will open (see Figure 2.10).

To supply HLM with appropriate information for the data, the command, and the MDM files

1. Click **Browse** in the **Level-1 specification** section to open an **Open Data File** dialog box. Open a level-1 ASCII data file in the HLM examples folder (HSB1.DAT in our example). The file name (HSB1.DAT) appears in the **Level-1 File Name** box.
2. Enter the number of variables into the **Number of Variables** box (4 in our example) and the data entry format in the **Data Format** box (A4,4F12.3 in our example).

Note that the ID is included in the format statement, but excluded in the **Number of Variables** box. Rules for input format statements are given in Section A.2 in Appendix A.

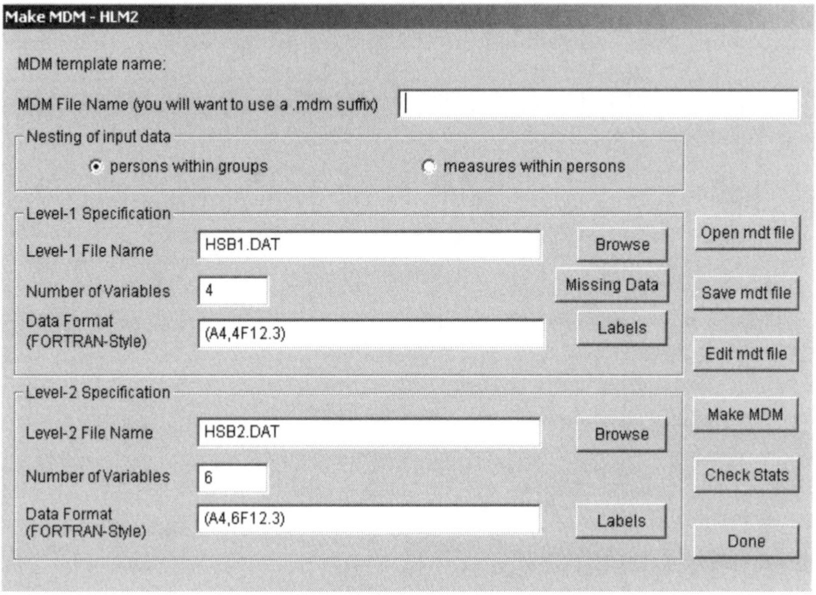

Figure 2.10   Make MDM – HLM2 dialog box

3. Click **Labels** to open the **Enter Variable Labels** dialog box.
4. Enter the variable names into the boxes (MINORITY, FEMALE, SES, MATHACH for our example, see Figure 2.11). Click **OK**.
5. Click the **Missing Data** button to enter level-1 missing data info (there is no missing data in HSB1.DAT; see Section 2.6 for details).
6. Click **Browse** in the **Level-2 specification** section to open an **Open Data File** dialog box. Open a level-2 ASCII data file in the HLM folder (HSB2.DAT in our example). The file name (HSB2.DAT in our example) will appear in the in the **Level-2 File Name** box.
7. Enter the number of variables into the **Number of Variables** box (6 in our example) and the data entry format in the **Data Format** box (A4,6F12.3 in our example).
8. Click **Labels** to open the **Enter Variable Labels** dialog box for the level-2 variables.
9. Enter the variable names into the **Variable** boxes (SIZE, SECTOR, PRACAD, DISCLIM, HIMINTY, MEANSES in our example, see Figure 2.12). Click **OK**.
10. Enter an MDM file name in the **MDM File Name** box (for example, HSB.MDM).
11. Click **Save mdmt file** in the **MDM template file** section to open a **Save MDM template file** dialog box. Enter a name for the MDMT file (for example, HSBASCII.MDMT). Click **Save** to save the file. The command file saves all the input information entered by the user. It can be re-opened or changed by clicking either the **Open mdmt file** or the **Edit mdmt file** button (see Figure 2.10).

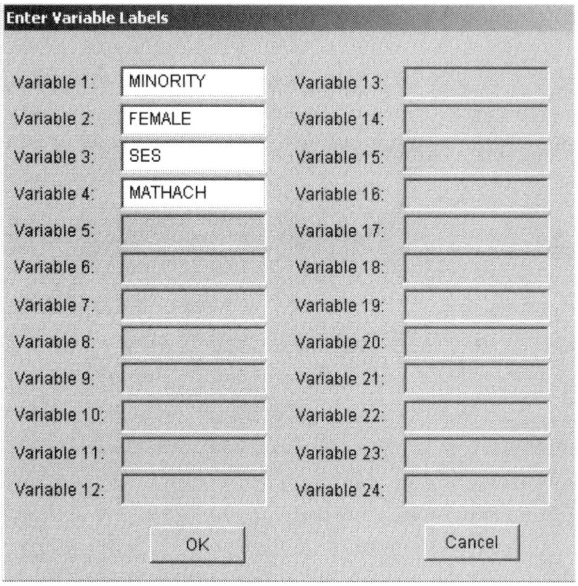

Figure 2.11   Enter Variable Labels dialog box for level-1 file, HSB1.DAT

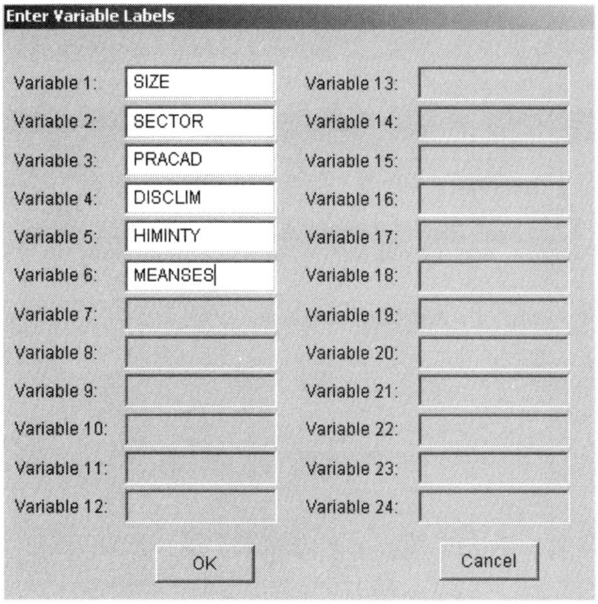

Figure 2.12   Enter Variable Labels dialog box for level-2 file, HSB2.DAT

To check whether the data have been properly read into HLM

The procedure is the same as for SPSS file input (see Section 2.5.1.1 for a complete description).

2.5.1.3 SAS transport, SYSTAT, STATA file input and other formats for raw data

For SAS transport, SYSTAT or STATA file input, a user selects either **SAS 5 transport**, **SYSTAT** or **STATA** from the **Input File Type** drop-down menu as appropriate to open the **Open Data File** dialog box. With the third-party software module included in the current version, HLM will read data from EXCEL, LOTUS and many other formats. Select **Anything else** from the **Input File Type** drop-down menu *before* clicking on the **Browse** button in the input file specifications sections. If the data type is set on the **File**, **Preferences** screen, the program will default to your selected type for both input data and residual files.

2.5.2 Executing analyses based on the MDM file

Once the MDM file is constructed, it can be used as input for the analysis. As mentioned earlier, model specification has three steps:

- Specification of the level-1 model. In our example, we shall model mathematics achievement (MATHACH) as the outcome, to be predicted by student SES. Hence, the level-1 model will have two coefficients: the intercept and the SES-MATHACH slope.
- Specification of the level-2 prediction model. We shall predict each school's intercept by school SECTOR and MEANSES in our example. Similarly, SECTOR and MEANSES will predict each school's SES-MATHACH slope.
- Specification of level-1 coefficients as random or non-random. We shall model both the intercept and the slope as having randomly varying residuals. That is, we are assuming that the intercept and slope vary not only as a function of the two predictors, SECTOR and MEANSES, but also as a function of a unique school effect. The two school residuals (e.g., for the intercept and slope) are assumed sampled from a bivariate normal distribution.

The procedure for executing analyses based on the MDM file is described below.

Step 1: To specify the level-1 prediction model

1. From the **HLM** window, open the **File** menu.
2. Choose **Create a new model using an existing MDM file** to open an **Open MDM File** dialog box. Open an existing MDM file (HSB.MDM in our example). The name of the MDM file will be displayed on the title bar of the main window. A listbox for level-1 variables (**>>Level-1<<**) will appear (see Figure 2.13).
3. Click on the name of the outcome variable (MATHACH in our example). Click **Outcome variable** (see Figure 2.13). The specified model will appear in equation format.

26

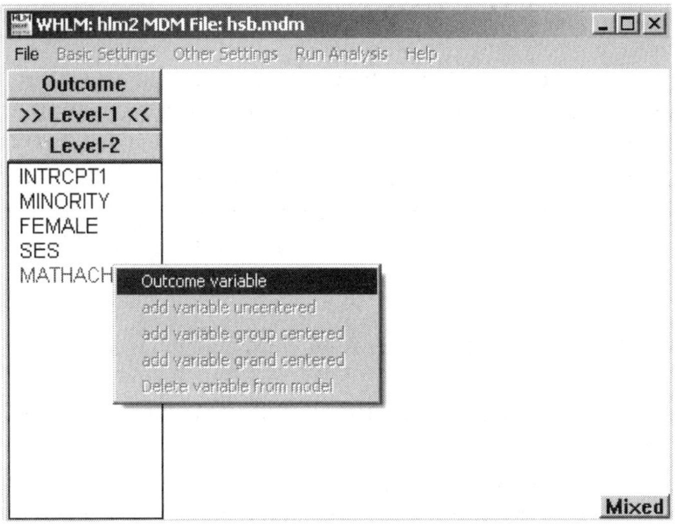

Figure 2.13   Model window for the HS&B example

4. Click on the name of a predictor variable and click the type of centering (SES and **add variable group centered**, see Figure 2.14). The predictor will appear on the equation screen and each regression coefficient associated with it will become an outcome in the Level-2 model (see Figure 2.15).

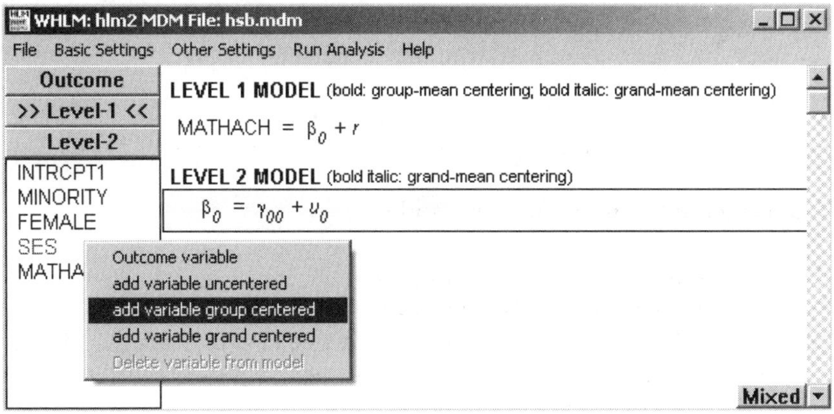

Figure 2.14   Specification of model predictor, SES, for the HS&B example

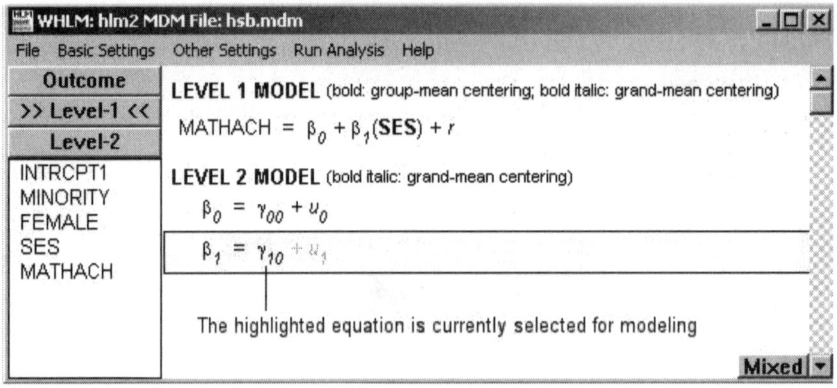

Figure 2.15   Model window for the HS&B example

Step 2: To specify the level-2 prediction model

1. Select the equation containing the regression coefficient(s) to be modeled by clicking on the equation (β_0 (intercept) and β_1 (SES slope) in our HS&B example). A listbox for level-2 variables (**>>LeveL-2<<**) will appear (see Figure 2.16).

2. Click to select the variable(s) to be entered as predictor(s) and the type of centering. For our example, select SECTOR and **add variable uncentered**, and MEANSES and add variable **grand-mean centered** to model β_0 and β_1, see Figure 2.16.

3. HLM allows the model to be displayed in three alternative forms. Figure 2.17 displays the model specified in the default notation familiar to users of previous versions of HLM.

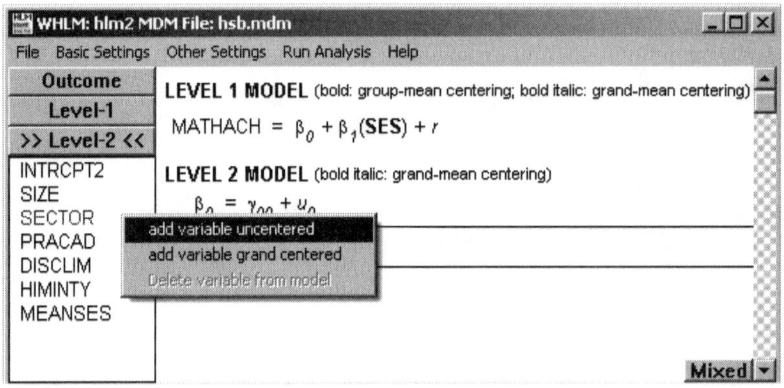

Figure 2.16   Specification of the level-2 model

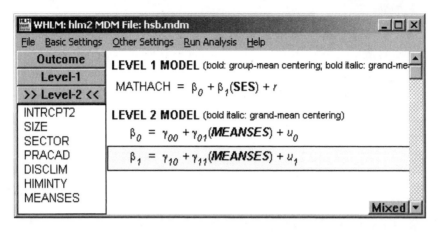

Figure 2.17   Model window for the HS&B example

4. In addition, the model can also be displayed in a mixed model formulation and with complete subscripts for all coefficients present in the model as illustrated in Figure 2.18. The mixed model is obtained by clicking the **Mixed** button at the bottom of the main window. The model is shown as a single equation, obtained by substituting the equations for β_0 and β_1 in the level-1 equation. This notation shows the model in a familiar linear regression format, and also draws attention to any cross-level interaction terms present in the combined model. By using the **Preferences** dialog box accessible via the **File** menu (see details in Section 2.8) both the mixed model formulation and the model with subscripts for all coefficients can be displayed automatically. The model can also be saved as an EMF file for later use in reports or papers.

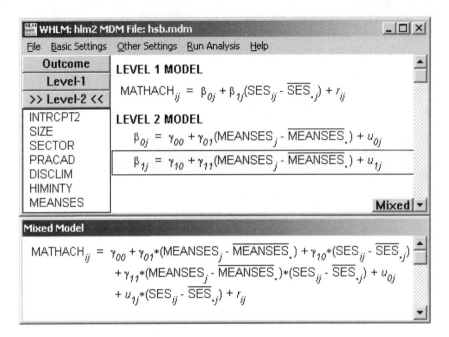

Figure 2.18   Alternative model window for the HS&B example

Step 3: To specify level-1 coefficients as random or non-random

The program begins by assuming that only the intercept (β_0) is specified as random. The u_1 at the end of the β_1 equation is grayed out and constrained to zero (See Figure 2.15), *i.e.* this level-1 coefficient is specified as "fixed". In the HS&B example, both level-1 coefficients, β_0 and β_1, are to be specified as random. To specify the SES slope as randomly varying, click on the equation for β_1 so that the error term u_1 is enabled (see Figure 2.17). Note that one can toggle the error term in any of the three following ways:

- Click on the error term, u_1.
- Type *u*.
- Right-click on the yellow box, which will bring up a single-item menu **toggle error term**. Click on the button.

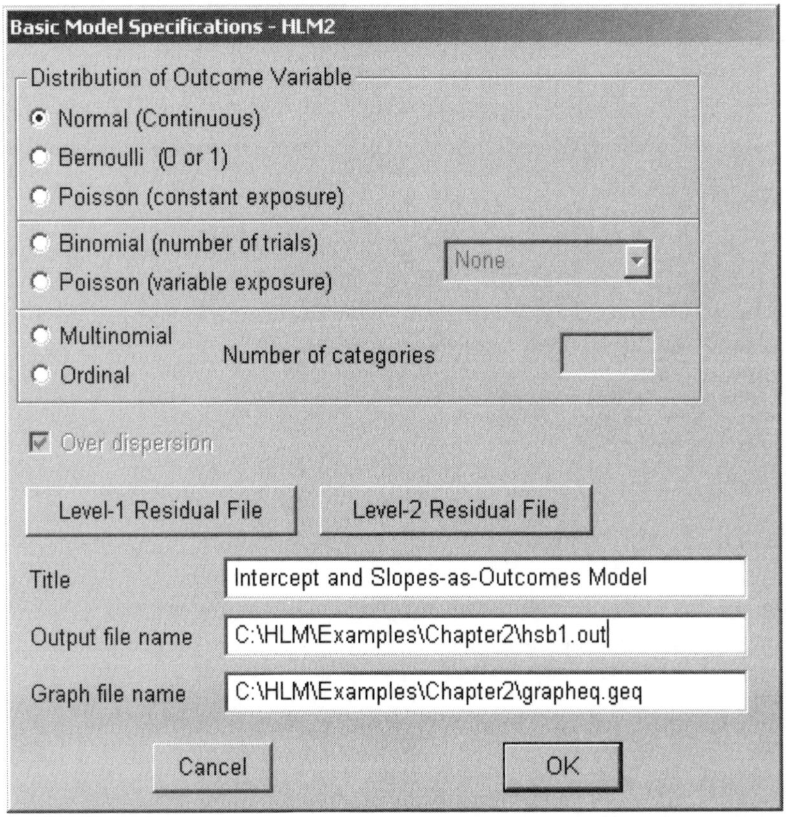

Figure 2.19   Basic Model Specifications – HLM2 dialog box for the HS&B example

Steps 1 to 3 are the three major steps for executing analyses based on the MDM file. Other analytic options are described in Section 2.9. After specifying the model, a title can be given to the output and the output file can be named by the following procedure:

1. Select **Basic Settings** to open the **Basic Model Specifications – HLM2** dialog box. Enter a title in the **Title** field (for example, Intercept and slopes-as-Outcomes Model) and an output file name in **Output file name** field (for example, HSB1.OUT). See Figure 2.19. Click **OK**. See Section 2.8 for the definitions of entries and options in **Basic Model Specifications – HLM2** dialog box.
2. Open the **File** menu and choose **Save As** to open a **Save command file** dialog box.
3. Enter a command file name (for example, HSB1.MDM).
4. Click **Run Analysis**. A dialog box displaying the iterations will appear (see Figure 2.20).

Note: If you wish to terminate the computations early, press the Ctrl-C key combination once. This will stop the analysis after the current iteration and provide a full presentation of results based on that iteration. If you press Ctrl-C more than once, however, computation is terminated immediately and all output is lost.

31

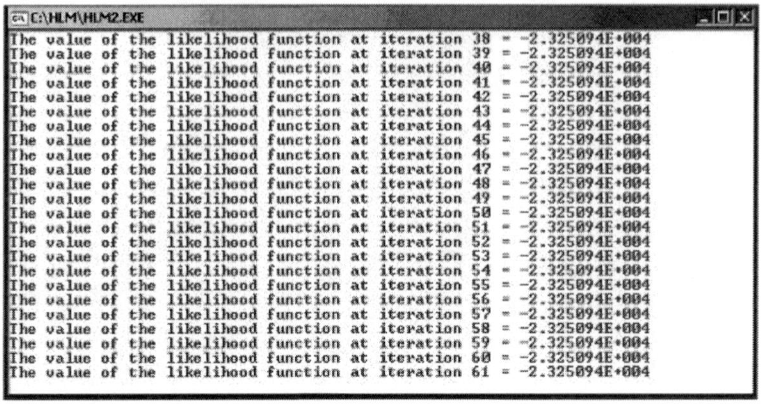

Figure 2.20   Iteration screen

2.5.3 Annotated HLM2 output

Open the **File** menu and choose **View Output** to call up Notepad to look at the results. Here is the output produced by the Windows session described above (see example HSB1.MDM).

```
The data source for this run  = C:\HLM\Examples\Chapter2\hsb.mdm
The command file for this run = C:\HLM\Examples\Chapter2\hsb1.mlm
Output file name             = C:\HLM\Examples\Chapter2\HSB1.OUT
The maximum number of level-1 units = 7185
The maximum number of level-2 units = 160
The maximum number of iterations = 100
Method of estimation: restricted maximum likelihood

The outcome variable is  MATHACH

The model specified for the fixed effects was:
------------------------------------------------------
    Level-1                Level-2
    Coefficients           Predictors
    --------------------   ---------------

         INTRCPT1, B0      INTRCPT2, G00
                             SECTOR, G01
$                            MEANSES, G02
 *      SES slope, B1      INTRCPT2, G10
                             SECTOR, G11
$                            MEANSES, G12

'*' - This level-1 predictor has been centered around its group mean.
'$' - This level-2 predictor has been centered around its grand mean.

The model specified for the covariance components was:
------------------------------------------------------------
        Sigma squared (constant across level-2 units)

        Tau dimensions
            INTRCPT1
                SES slope
```

32

```
Summary of the model specified (in equation format)
-------------------------------------------------

Level-1 Model

    Y = B0 + B1*(SES) + R

Level-2 Model
    B0 = G00 + G01*(SECTOR) + G02*(MEANSES) + U0
    B1 = G10 + G11*(SECTOR) + G12*(MEANSES) + U1
```

The information presented on the first page or two of the HLM2 printout summarizes key details about the MDM file (e.g., number of level-1 and level-2 units, whether weighting was specified), and about both the fixed and random effects models specified for this run. In this particular case, we are estimating the model specified by Equations 4.14 and 4.15 in *Hierarchical Linear Models*.

```
Level-1 OLS regressions
-----------------------
Level-2 Unit    INTRCPT1        SES slope
---------------------------------------------------------------------
        1224     9.71545         2.50858
        1288    13.51080         3.25545
        1296     7.63596         1.07596
        1308    16.25550         0.12602
        1317    13.17769         1.27391
        1358    11.20623         5.06801
        1374     9.72846         3.85432
        1433    19.71914         1.85429
        1436    18.11161         1.60056
        1461    16.84264         6.26650
```

When first analyzing a new data set, examining the OL equations for all of the units may be helpful in identifying possible outlying cases and bad data. By default, HLM2 does not print out the ordinary least squares (OL) regression equations, based on the level-1 model. The OLS regression equations for the first 10 units, as shown here, were obtained using optional settings on the **Other Settings** menu.

```
The average OLS level-1 coefficient for INTRCPT1 =      12.62075
The average OLS level-1 coefficient for       SES =       2.20164
```

This is a simple average of the OLS coefficients across all units that had sufficient data to permit a separate OLS estimation.

```
Least Squares Estimates
-----------------------

 sigma_squared =     39.03409

Least-squares estimates of fixed effects
---------------------------------------------------------------------
                              Standard
Fixed Effect      Coefficient  Error     T-ratio    d.f.    P-value
---------------------------------------------------------------------
For      INTRCPT1, B0
  INTRCPT2, G00    12.083837   0.106889   113.050     7179    0.000
    SECTOR, G01     1.280341   0.157845     8.111     7179    0.000
   MEANSES, G02     5.163791   0.190834    27.059     7179    0.000
```

```
For       SES slope, B1
  INTRCPT2, G10            2.935664    0.155268    18.907    7179    0.000
    SECTOR, G11           -1.642102    0.240178    -6.837    7179    0.000
   MEANSES, G12            1.044120    0.299885     3.482    7179    0.001
---------------------------------------------------------------------------

Least-squares estimates of fixed effects
(with robust standard errors)
---------------------------------------------------------------------------
                                      Standard
Fixed Effect           Coefficient    Error       T-ratio   d.f.    P-value
---------------------------------------------------------------------------
For       INTRCPT1, B0
  INTRCPT2, G00           12.083837    0.169507    71.288    7179    0.000
    SECTOR, G01            1.280341    0.299077     4.281    7179    0.000

   MEANSES, G02            5.163791    0.334078    15.457    7179    0.000
For       SES slope, B1
  INTRCPT2, G10            2.935664    0.147576    19.893    7179    0.000
    SECTOR, G11           -1.642102    0.237223    -6.922    7179    0.000
   MEANSES, G12            1.044120    0.332897     3.136    7179    0.002
---------------------------------------------------------------------------
```

The first of the fixed effects tables are based on OLS estimation. The second table provides robust standard errors. Note that the standard errors associated with G00, G01, and G12 are smaller than their robust counterparts.

```
The least-squares likelihood value = -23362.111334
Deviance =  46724.22267
Number of estimated parameters =     1

  STARTING VALUES
  ---------------
  sigma(0)_squared =      36.72025

  Tau(0)
  INTRCPT1,B0     2.56964          0.28026
       SES,B1     0.28026         -0.01614

  New Tau(0)
  INTRCPT1,B0     2.56964          0.28026
       SES,B1     0.28026          0.43223
```

The initial starting values failed to produce an appropriate variance-covariance matrix (Tau(0)). An automatic fix-up was introduced to correct this problem (New Tau(0)).

```
Estimation of fixed effects
(Based on starting values of covariance components)
---------------------------------------------------------------------------
                                      Standard              Approx.
Fixed Effect           Coefficient    Error       T-ratio   d.f.    P-value
---------------------------------------------------------------------------
For       INTRCPT1, B0
  INTRCPT2, G00           12.094864    0.204326    59.194    157     0.000
    SECTOR, G01            1.226266    0.315204     3.890    157     0.000
   MEANSES, G02            5.335184    0.379879    14.044    157     0.000
```

```
For        SES slope, B1
  INTRCPT2, G10          2.935219   0.168674    17.402      157    0.000
    SECTOR, G11         -1.634083   0.260672    -6.269      157    0.000
   MEANSES, G12          1.015061   0.323523     3.138      157    0.002
---------------------------------------------------------------------
```

Above are the initial estimates of the fixed effects. These are not to be used in drawing substantial conclusions.

```
The value of the likelihood function at iteration 2 = -2.325182E+004
The value of the likelihood function at iteration 3 = -2.325174E+004
The value of the likelihood function at iteration 4 = -2.325169E+004
The value of the likelihood function at iteration 5 = -2.325154E+004
                                    .
                                    .
The value of the likelihood function at iteration 59 = -2.325094E+004
The value of the likelihood function at iteration 60 = -2.325094E+004

Iterations stopped due to small change in likelihood function
```

Below are the estimates of the variance and covariance components from the final iteration and selected other statistics based on them.

```
******* ITERATION 61 *******

Sigma_squared =     36.70313              Level-1 variance components

Tau                                       Level-2 variance-covariance
  INTRCPT1,B0    2.37996      0.19058              components
     SES,B1      0.19058      0.14892

Tau (as correlations)                     Level-2 variance-covariance
  INTRCPT1,B0  1.000   0.320                 components expressed as
     SES,B1    0.320   1.000                        correlations
----------------------------------------------------
   Random level-1 coefficient Reliability estimate
----------------------------------------------------
     INTRCPT1, B0                  0.733      These are average reliability
                                              estimates for the random
         SES, B1                   0.073      level-1 coefficients

The value of the likelihood function at iteration 61 = -2.325094E+004
```

The next three tables present the final estimates for: the fixed effects with GLS and robust standard errors, variance components at level-1 and level-2, and related test statistics.

```
The outcome variable is  MATHACH
Final estimation of fixed effects:
---------------------------------------------------------------------
                                   Standard         Approx.
Fixed Effect          Coefficient  Error    T-ratio  d.f.   P-value
---------------------------------------------------------------------
For        INTRCPT1, B0
  INTRCPT2, G00         12.095006   0.198717    60.865      157    0.000
    SECTOR, G01          1.226384   0.306272     4.004      157    0.000
   MEANSES, G02          5.333056   0.369161    14.446      157    0.000
```

35

```
For        SES slope, B1
  INTRCPT2, G10         2.937787    0.157119     18.698        157      0.000
    SECTOR, G11        -1.640954    0.242905     -6.756        157      0.000
   MEANSES, G12         1.034427    0.302566      3.419        157      0.001
----------------------------------------------------------------------------
```

Final estimation of fixed effects
(with robust standard errors)

```
----------------------------------------------------------------------------
                                  Standard                 Approx.
Fixed Effect           Coefficient  Error     T-ratio      d.f.      P-value
----------------------------------------------------------------------------
For        INTRCPT1, B0
  INTRCPT2, G00        12.095006    0.173688     69.637        157      0.000
    SECTOR, G01         1.226384    0.308484      3.976        157      0.000
   MEANSES, G02         5.333056    0.334600     15.939        157      0.000
For        SES slope, B1
  INTRCPT2, G10         2.937787    0.147615     19.902        157      0.000
    SECTOR, G11        -1.640954    0.237401     -6.912        157      0.000
   MEANSES, G12         1.034427    0.332785      3.108        157      0.003
----------------------------------------------------------------------------
```

The first table provides model-based estimates of the standard errors while the second table provides robust estimates of the standard errors. Note that the two sets of standard errors are similar. If the robust and model-based standard errors are substantively different, it is recommended that the tenability of key assumptions should be investigated further (see Section 4.3 on examining residuals).

Final estimation of variance components:

```
----------------------------------------------------------------------------
Random Effect          Standard    Variance    df     Chi-square  P-value
                       Deviation   Component
----------------------------------------------------------------------------
INTRCPT1,   U0          1.54271     2.37996    157     605.29503    0.000
SES slope,  U1          0.38590     0.14892    157     162.30867    0.369
level-1,    R           6.05831    36.70313
----------------------------------------------------------------------------
```

Statistics for current covariance components model
```
-------------------------------------------------------------
Deviance                        = 46501.875643
Number of estimated parameters = 4
```

2.5.4 Model checking based on the residual file

HLM2 provides the data analyst with a means of checking the fit and distributional assumptions of the model by producing residual files for the level-1 and level-2 models. These files may be requested using the **Basic Model Specifications – HLM2** dialog box (see Fig. 2.19). The level-1 and level-2 residual files will be written as SPSS, SAS, STATA, SYSTAT or ASCII data files. In the case of SPSS and STATA, the residual files will be written out so that the respective packages may use them immediately. The other forms of raw data will require submitting them as command streams.

2.5.4.1 The level-1 residual file

2.5.4.1.1 Structure of the level-1 residual file

The level-1 residual file will contain level-1 residuals (the differences between the observed and fitted values), the fitted values, the square root of σ^2, the values of the level-1 and level-2 predictors entered in the model, and those of other level-1 and level-2 variables selected by the user. To illustrate, we show how to prepare SPSS residual files.

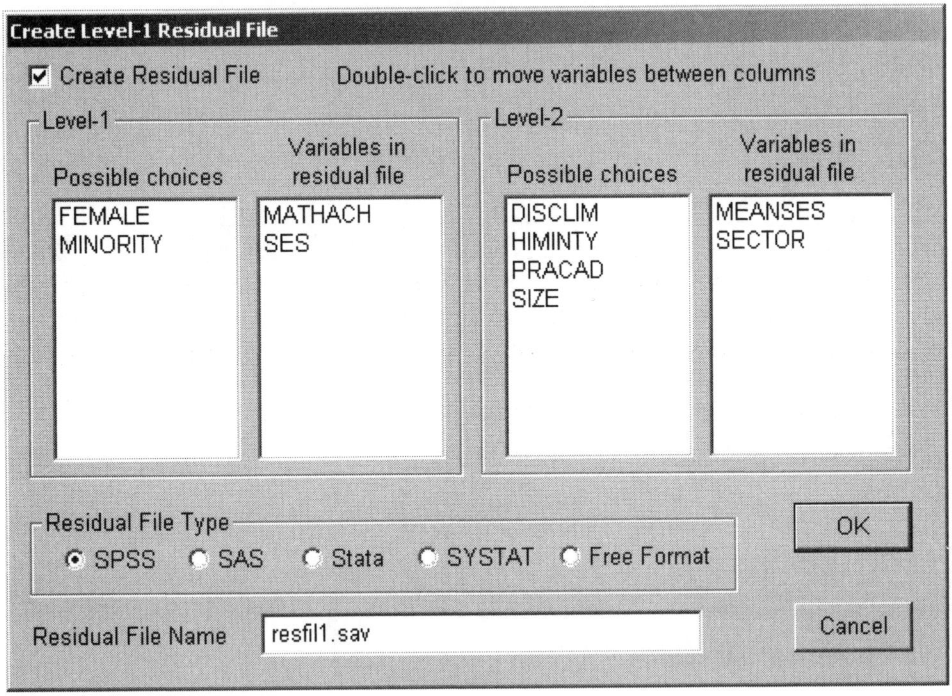

Figure 2.21   Create Level-1 Residual File dialog box

To create the SPSS level-1 residual file type

1. Select **Basic Settings** to open the **Basic Model Specifications – HLM2** dialog box.
2. Click **Level-1 Residual File** to open a **Create Level-1 Residual File** dialog box (see Figure 2.21).
3. For the level-1 and level-2 variables, the box displays two columns of variables. The predictor variables in the model are in the **Variables in residual file** column. Others are listed in the **Possible choices** column. To include any of them in the residual file for exploratory purposes, double-click on their labels.
4. Select **SPSS residual file type** (default).
5. Enter a name for the residual file in the **Residual File Name** box (for example, RESFIL1.SAV, see Figure 2.21). Click **OK**.

Data for the first ten cases in RESFIL1.SAV are shown in Figure 2.22. The file consists of the level-2 ID, L2ID, and the following variables:

- L1RESID: the difference between the fitted and observed value for each level-1 unit.
- FITVAL: the fitted value for each level-1 unit.
- SIGMA: the square root of σ^2.

The variables SES, MATHACH, SECTOR, and MEANSES are described in Section 2.5.1.1.

	l2id	l1resid	fitval	sigma	ses	mathach	sector	meanses
1	1224	-1.516	7.392	6.060	-1.094	5.876	.000	-.428
2	1224	10.246	9.462	6.060	-.154	19.708	.000	-.428
3	1224	10.755	9.594	6.060	-.094	20.349	.000	-.428
4	1224	-.505	9.286	6.060	-.234	8.781	.000	-.428
5	1224	7.489	10.409	6.060	.276	17.898	.000	-.428
6	1224	-6.223	10.806	6.060	.456	4.583	.000	-.428
7	1224	-12.228	9.396	6.060	-.184	-2.832	.000	-.428
8	1224	-8.036	8.559	6.060	-.564	.523	.000	-.428
9	1224	-7.274	8.801	6.060	-.454	1.527	.000	-.428
10	1224	11.772	9.749	6.060	-.024	21.521	.000	-.428

Figure 2.22   Level-1 Residual File

2.5.4.1.2 Some possible residual analyses

We illustrate a possible use of a residual file in examining the tenability of the assumption of normal distribution of level-1 errors, whose violations could adversely influence the estimated standard errors for the estimates of the fixed effects and inferential statistics (see *Hierarchical Linear Models* p. 266). Figure 2.23 displays a normal Q-Q plot of the level-1 residuals for the 7,185 students based on the final fitted model. The plot is approximately linear, suggesting there is not a serious departure from a normal distribution and that the assumption is tenable.

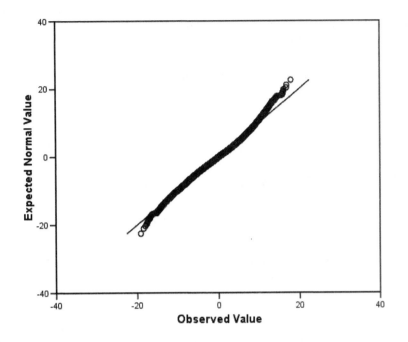

Figure 2.23   Q-Q plot of level-1 residuals

2.5.4.2   The level-2 residual file

This file will contain the EB residuals (see Equation 1.10 above), OL residuals (see Equation 1.9 above), and fitted values, *i.e.*,

$$\hat{\gamma}_{q0} + \sum \hat{\gamma}_{qs} W_{sj}$$

for each level-1 coefficient. By adding the OL residuals to the corresponding fitted values, the analyst can also obtain the OL estimate of the corresponding level-1 coefficient β_{qj}. The file also produces the EB estimate β_{qj}^{*} of each level-1 coefficient, β_{qj}.

In addition, the file will contain Mahalanobis distances (which are discussed below), estimates of the total and residual standard deviations (log metric) within each unit, the values of the predictors used in the level-2 model, and any other level-2 prediction variables selected by the user.

To create the SPSS level-2 residual file type

1. Select **Basic Settings** to open the **Basic Model Specifications – HLM2** dialog box.
2. Click **Level-2 Residual File** to open a **Create Level-2 Residual File** dialog box.
3. Double-click the variables to be entered into the residual file (for our example, select DISCLIM, PRACAD, HIMINTY and SIZE, see Figure 2.24).

4. Select **SPSS** as **Residual File Type**. Note that SYSTAT, STATA or SAS file type can be created as well, or the residuals written to file in free format. By default, a SYSTAT file will be created. To set the default file type created to one of the other formats, the **Preference** dialog box (see Section 2.8) can be used.
5. Enter a name for the residual file in the **Residual File Name** box (for example RESFIL2.SPS, see Figure 2.24). Click **OK**.

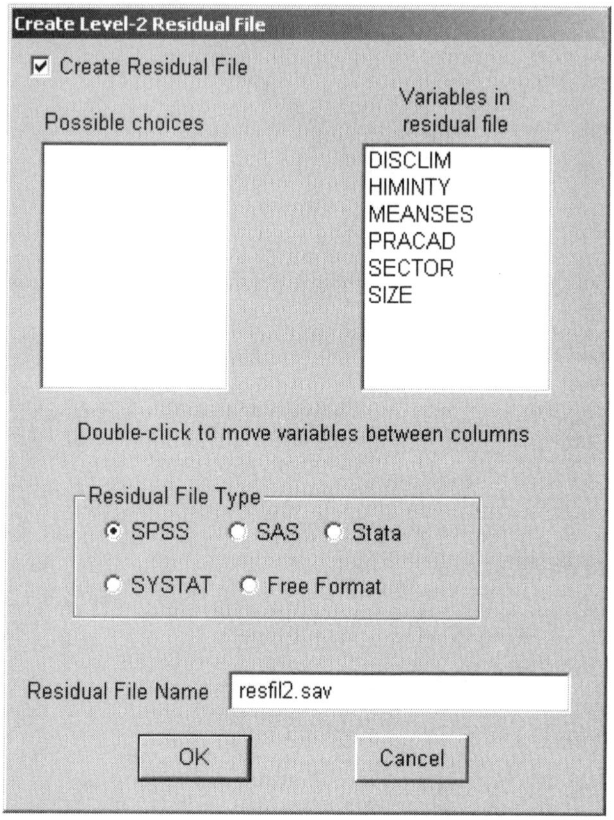

Figure 2.24   Create Residual File dialog box

An example of an SPSS version of a level-2 residual file is shown in Figure 2.25. Only the data from the first ten units and the first 8 variables are reproduced here. This file can be used to construct various diagnostic plots.

2.5.4.2.1   Structure of the level-2 residual file

The residual file contains a single record per unit (see Figure 2.25 and the output listed on page 43). The first variable in this file is the level-2 unit ID (here named l2ID), followed by the number of level-1 units within that level-2 unit (denoted by nj), and various summary statistics (chipct through mdrsvar explained below). These are followed by the two EB residuals (ebintrcp and ebses); the two OLS residuals (olintrcp and olses); and the fitted values, that is, the predicted values based on the estimated

40

level-2 model (fvintrcp and fvses). Next are the EB coefficients (ecintrcp and ecses), which are the sum of the fitted values and the EB residuals. The posterior variances and covariances of the level-2 residuals are given next (pv00 for the posterior variance of the intercept residual, pv10 for the posterior covariance between the intercept residual and the slope residual, and pv11 for the posterior variance of the slope residual). Next are the corresponding posterior variances and covariances of the random intercept and coefficient (pvc00 for the posterior variance of the random intercept, pvc10 for the posterior covariance between the random intercept and the random slope, and pv11 for the posterior variance of the random slope). Finally, the level-2 predictors used in the analysis plus those additional level-2 predictors requested by the user for inclusion in the file are given (see output listed on page 43).

While most of this is straightforward, the information contained in the first set of variables for each unit merits elaboration. nj is the number of cases for level-2 unit j. It is followed by two variables, chipct and mdist. If we model q level-1 coefficients, mdist would be the Mahalanobis distance (*i.e.*, the standardized squared distance of a unit from the center of a v-dimensional distribution, where v is the number of random effects per unit). Essentially, mdist provides a single, summary measure of the distance of a unit's EB estimates, β_{qj}^*, from its "fitted value," $\hat{\gamma}_{q0} + \sum \hat{\gamma}_{q0} W_{sj}$.

	I2id	nj	chipct	mdist	Intotvar	olsrsvar	mdrsvar	ebintrcp
1	1224	47	.019	.003	2.027	2.016	2.005	-.073
2	1288	25	.119	.148	1.949	1.920	1.899	.456
3	1296	48	2.739	2.460	1.678	1.680	1.684	-1.710
4	1308	20	.256	.396	1.811	1.838	1.820	.031
5	1317	48	1.392	1.341	1.698	1.701	1.691	-1.531
6	1358	30	1.711	1.824	1.771	1.595	1.618	-.492
7	1374	28	1.891	1.880	2.123	2.087	2.072	-1.478
8	1433	35	1.987	2.009	1.356	1.329	1.314	1.776
9	1436	44	1.031	1.037	1.515	1.506	1.495	1.292
10	1461	33	3.567	3.136	1.939	1.707	1.745	.814

Figure 2.25   SPSS version of residual file

Note that the units in the residual file are sorted in ascending order by mdist. If the normality assumption is true, then the Mahalanobis distances should be distributed approximately $\chi^2_{(v)}$. Analogous to univariate normal probability plotting, we can construct a Q-Q plot of mdist vs. chipct. chipct are the expected values of the order statistics for a sample of size J selected from a population that is distributed $\chi^2_{(v)}$. If the Q-Q plot resembles a 45 degree line, we have evidence that the random effects are distributed v-variate normal. In addition, the plot will help us detect outlying units (*i.e.*, units with large mdist values well above the 45 degree line). It should be noted that such plots are good diagnostic tools only when the level-1 sample sizes, nj, are at least moderately large. (For further discussion see *Hierarchical Linear Models*, pp. 274-280.)

After mdist, three estimates of the level-1 variability are given:

- The natural logarithm of the total standard deviation within each unit, lntotvar.
- The natural logarithm of the residual standard deviation within each unit based on its least squares regression, olsrsvar. Note, this estimate exists only for those units which have sufficient data to compute level-1 OLS estimates.
- The mdrsvar, the natural logarithm of the residual standard deviation from the final fitted fixed effects model.

The natural log of these three standard deviations (with the addition of a bias-correction factor for varying degrees of freedom) is reported (see *Hierarchical Linear Models*, p. 219). We note that these statistics can be used as input for the V-known option in HLM2 in research on group-level correlates of diversity (Raudenbush & Bryk, 1987; also see Sections 2.8.9 and 9.3).

Steps 1 to 3 are the three major steps for executing analyses based on the MDM file. Other analytic options are described in Section 2.9. After specifying the model, a title can be given to the output and the output file can be named by the following procedure:

1. Select **Basic Settings** to open the **Basic Model Specifications - HLM2** dialog box. Enter a title in the **Title** field (for example, Intercept and slopes-as-Outcomes Model) and an output file name in **Output file name** field (for example, HSB1.OUT). See Figure 2.19. Click **OK**. See Section 2.8 for the definitions of entries and options in **Basic Model Specifications - HLM2** dialog box.
2. Open the **File** menu and choose **Save As** to open a **Save command file** dialog box.
3. Enter a command file name (for example, HSB1.MDM).
4. Click **Run Analysis**. A dialog box displaying the iterations will appear (see Figure 2.20).

Note: If you wish to terminate the computations early, press the Ctrl-C key combination once. This will stop the analysis after the current iteration and provide a full presentation of results based on that iteration. If you press Ctrl-C more than once, however, computation is terminated immediately and all output is lost.

2.5.4.2.2   Some possible residual analyses

We illustrate below some of the possible uses of a level-2 residual file in examining the adequacy of fitted models and in considering other possible level-2 predictor variables. (For a full discussion of this topic see Chapter 9 of *Hierarchical Linear Models*.) Here are the basic statistics for each of the variables created as part of the HLM2 residual file.

	N	Minimum	Maximum	Mean	Std. Deviation
nj	160	14	67	44.91	11.855
chipct	160	.006	11.537	1.99115	1.967047
mdist	160	.003	13.218	2.00727	2.144775
lntotvar	160	1.265	2.138	1.82057	.150434
olsrsvar	160	1.272	2.087	1.78983	.137449
mdrsvar	160	1.314	2.072	1.79039	.134968
ebintrcp	160	-3.718	4.162	.00000	1.312584
ebses	160	-.378	.438	.00000	.141577
olintrcp	160	-7.714	5.545	-.01079	1.847386
olses	160	-3.560	3.803	-.01823	1.460555
fvintrcp	160	5.760	17.754	12.63155	2.490807
fvses	160	.515	3.650	2.21987	.775690
ecintrcp	160	4.710	18.928	12.63155	2.815492
ecses	160	.288	3.845	2.21987	.788504
pv00	160	.486	1.255	.66785	.140621
pv10	160	.036	.098	.05033	.011378
pv11	160	.121	.138	.12900	.003583
pvc00	160	.449	1.257	.63936	.147741
pvc10	160	.030	.097	.04682	.011911
pvc11	160	.138	.247	.16255	.017345
size	160	100.000	2713.000	1097.82500	629.506431
sector	160	.000	1.000	.43750	.497636
pracad	160	.000	1.000	.51394	.255897
disclim	160	-2.416	2.756	-.01513	.976978
himinty	160	.000	1.000	.27500	.447916
meanses	160	-1.188	.831	.00000	.413973
Valid N (listwise)	160				

Examining OL and EB residuals. Figure 2.27 shows a plot of the OL vs EB residuals for the SES slopes. As expected, the EB residuals for the slope are much more compact than the OL residuals. While the latter ranges between ($-4.0, 4.0$), the range for the EB residuals is only ($-0.5, 0.5$). (For a further discussion see *Hierarchical Linear Models*, pp. 76-82.)

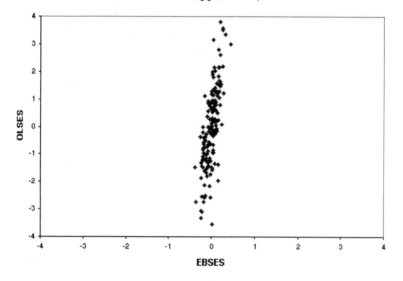

Figure 2.27   OL versus EB residuals for the SES slopes

Exploring the potential of other possible level-2 predictors. Figure 2.27 shows a plot of EB residuals against a possible additional level-2 predictor, PRACAD, for the intercept model. Although the relationship appears slight (a correlation of 0.15), PRACAD will enter this model as a significant predictor. (For a further discussion of the use of residual plots in identifying possible level-2 predictors see *Hierarchical Linear Models*, pp. 267-270.)

Next, in Figure 2.28, we see a plot of the OL vs EB residuals for the intercepts. Notice that while the EB intercepts are "shrunk" as compared to the OL estimates, the amount of shrinkage for the intercepts is far less than for the SES slopes in Figure 2.27.

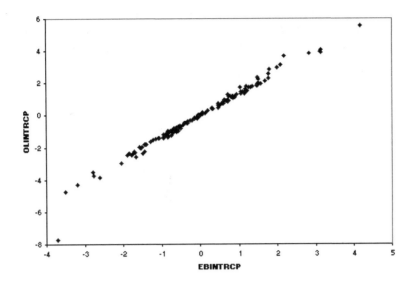

Figure 2.28   OL versus EB residuals for the intercepts

Examining possible nonlinearity of a level-2 predictor's relationship to an outcome. Next, in Fig.2.30, is an example of a plot of EB residuals, in this case the SES slope, against a variable included in the model. This plot suggests that the assumption of a linear relationship between the SES slope and MEANSES is appropriate. (That is, the residuals appear randomly distributed around the zero line without regard to values of MEANSES.)

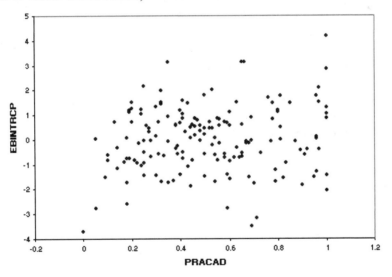

Figure 2.29   EB residuals against a possible additional level-2 predictor, PRACAD, for the intercept model

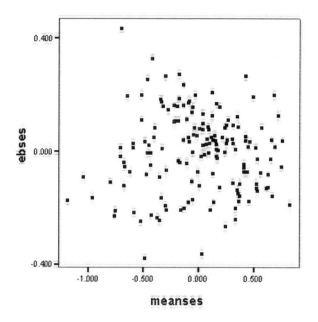

Figure 2.30   EB residuals for SES slope against MEANSES

2.6   Handling of missing data

HLM2 provides three options for handling missing data at level 1: listwise deletion of cases when the MDM file is made, listwise deletion of cases when running the analysis (See Figure 2.3), and analysis of multiply-imputed data (see Section 9.2). These follow the conventional routines used in standard statistical packages for regression analysis and the general linear model. Listwise deletion of cases when the MDM file is made is based on the variables selected for inclusion in the MDM file, while listwise deletion when running the analysis only takes the variables included in the model into account.

At level 2, HLM2 assumes complete data. If you have missing data at level 2, you should either impute a value for the missing information or delete the units in question, or preferably use methods described in Section 9.2. **Failure to do so will cause the automatic liswise deletion of level-2 units with missing data when the MDM file is created.**

For ASCII file input, click **Missing Data** in the **Make MDM – HLM2** dialog box. The dialog box displayed in Fig. 2.31 will open.

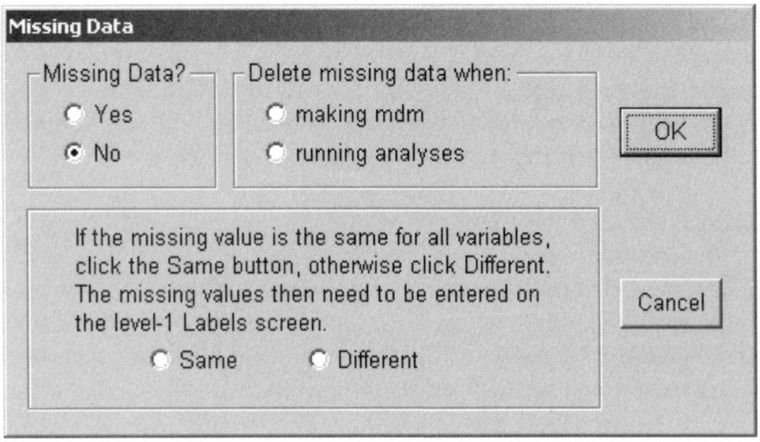

Figure 2.31   Missing Data dialog box

Assuming you have missing data, you should click **Yes** in the **Missing Data?** box, and select deletion when making the MDM file or when running analyses. Then, if you have coded all of your missing values for all of the variables to the same number, click the **Same** button. When you specify the variable names, enter this number in the box to right of the first variable in the **Enter Variable Labels** dialog box (see Fig. 2.32). If you have more than one missing value code, check the **Different** button, and enter these codes for each respective variable on the **Enter Variable Labels** screen.

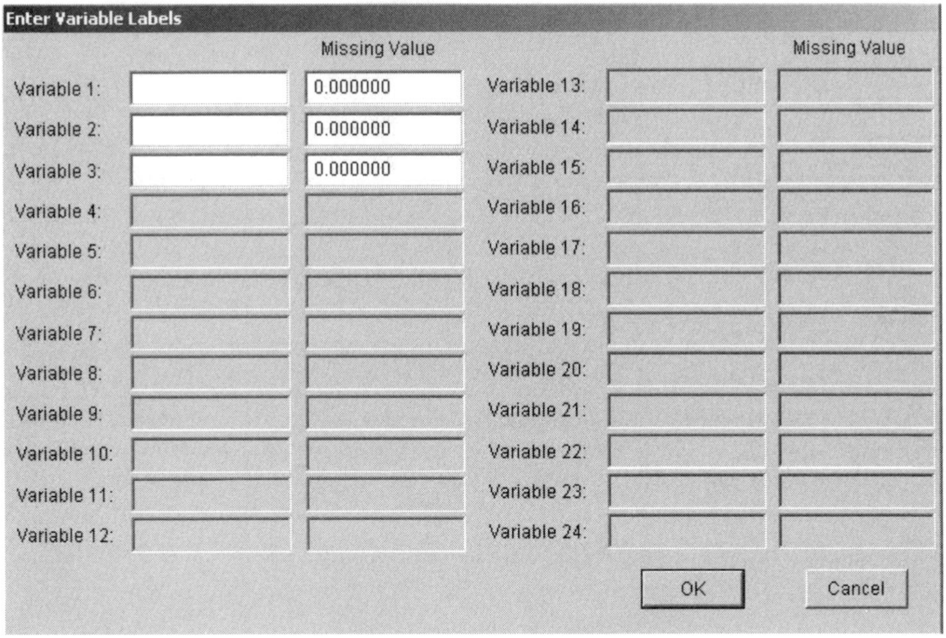

Figure 2.32   Enter Variable Labels dialog box for missing ASCII data

For non-ASCII data at level 1, you should click **Yes** in the **Missing Data?** field, and select when you want to implement the listwise deletion by selecting one of the two options in this groupbox. Then, when HLM2 encounters values coded as missing, it will recognize these properly. It is important to note that some statistics packages (*e.g.* SAS) allow for more than one kind of missing data code. HLM2 (and HLM3, etc.) will recognize only the standard, "system-missing" code.

How HLM2 handles missing data differs a bit in the ASCII and non-ASCII cases. *For ASCII data, it is very important that you don't have any missing data codes or blanks in the level 2 file.* HLM2 will read these as valid data; missing data codes as they are coded, and blanks will be read as zeros. For non-ASCII data, the program will skip over cases that have missing data in them, essentially performing listwise deletion on the level-2 data file. Note: For non-ASCII file input, the user has to either prepare system-missing values or missing value codes for the missing data.

2.7   The Basic Model Specifications - HLM2 dialog box

The **Basic Model Specifications – HLM2** dialog box (see Fig. 2.33) is used to indicate the distribution of the outcome variable, to request residual files and to provide a title and the locations and names of output files.

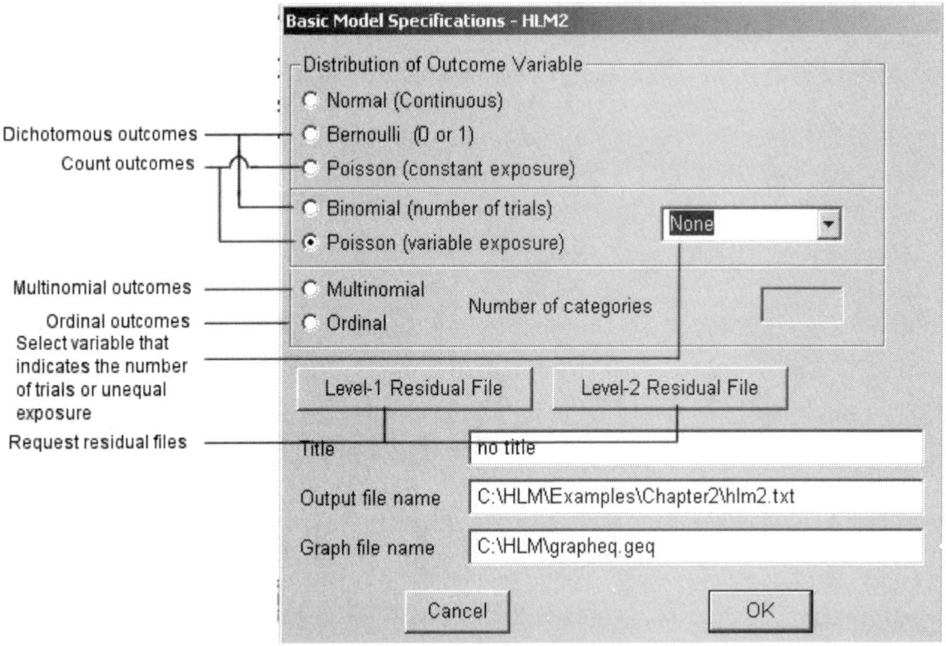

Figure 2.33   Basic Model Specifications - HLM2 dialog box

2.8   Other analytic options

2.8.1   Controlling the iterative procedure

The iterative procedure settings can be changed by opening the **Iteration Control – HLM2** dialog box. To do so, select the **Iteration Settings** option from the **Other Settings** menu. Table 2.1 lists the definitions and options in the **Iteration Control – HLM2** dialog box. See Fig. 2.34; note the linking numbers in figure and table.

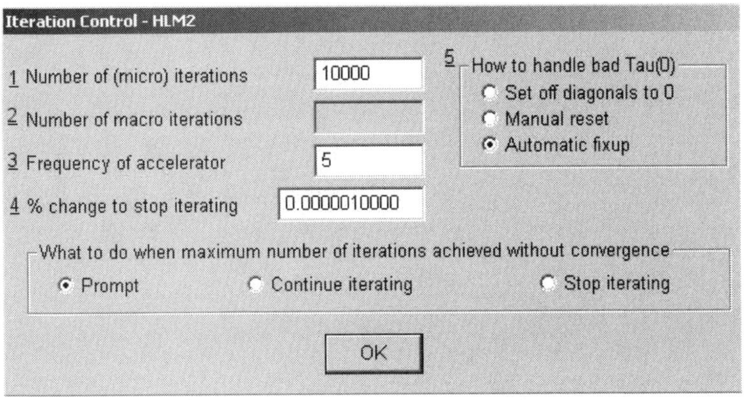

Figure 2.34   Iteration Control - HLM2 dialog box

Table 2.1 Table of definitions and options in Iteration Control - HLM2 dialog box

Key Terms	Function	Option	Definition
1, 2 Number of iterations	Maximum number of iterations	positive integer	
3 Frequency of accelerator	Controls frequency of use of acceleration	integer ≥ 3	Selects how often the accelerator is used. Default is 10.
4 % change to stop iterating	Convergence criterion for maximum likelihood estimation	positive real number	Default: 0.000001. Can be specified to be more (or less) restrictive
5 How to handle bad Tau(0)	Method of correcting unacceptable starting values	3 choices	1. Set off-diagonal to 0 2. Manual reset (starting values) 3. Automatic fix-up (default)

2.8.2 Estimation control

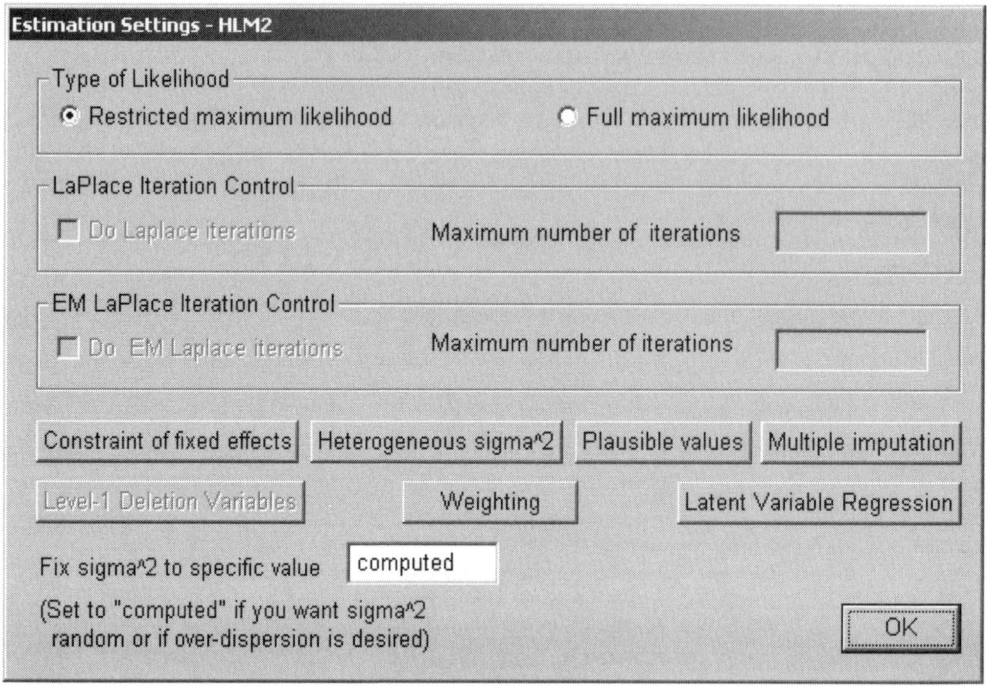

Figure 2.35 Estimation Settings – HLM2 dialog box

The **Estimation Settings – HLM2** dialog box, accessed via the **Estimation Settings** option on the **Other Settings** menu, offers additional control over the iterative procedure.

HLM2 will use restricted maximum likelihood estimation by default. The type of likelihood used is set in the **Type of Likelihood** group box (see Fig. 2.35), where full maximum likelihood estimation may alternatively be requested (see *Hierarchical Linear Models*, pp. 52-53.)

LaPlace and EM LaPlace iterations may be requested when nonlinear (HGLM) models are fitted. The maximum number of iterations required, which has to be a positive integer, should be entered in the **LaPlace Iteration Control** or **EM LaPlace Iteration Control** group box (see Fig. 2.35).

The **Estimation Settings – HLM2** dialog box may also be used to access dialog boxes used in defining special analyses, *e.g.* latent variable regression, applying HLM to multiply-imputed data, and plausible value analysis.

These special features, associated with the **Plausible values**, **Multiple imputation** and **Latent Variable Regression** buttons in the **Estimation Settings – HLM2** dialog box, are discussed in Chapter 9.

2.8.3 Constraints on the fixed effects

A user may wish to constrain two or more fixed effects to be equal. For example, Barnett, Marshall, Raudenbush, & Brennan (1993) applied this approach in studying correlates of psychological distress in married couples. Available for each person were two parallel measures of psychological distress. Hence, for each couple, there were four such measures (two per person). At level-1 these measures were modeled as the sum of a "true score" plus error:

$$Y_{ij} = \beta_{1j}X_{1ij} + \beta_{2j}X_{2ij} + r_{ij},$$

where X_{1ij} is an indicator for females, X_{2ij} is an indicator for males, and r_{ij} is a measurement error. Hence β_{1j} is the "true score" for females and β_{2j} is the "true score" for males. At level 2, these true scores are modeled as a function of predictor variables, one of which was marital role quality, W_j, a measure of one's satisfaction with one's marriage. (Note that this is also a model without a level-1 intercept.) A simple level-2 model is then:

$$\beta_{1j} = \gamma_{10} + \gamma_{11}W_j + u_{1j}$$
$$\beta_{2j} = \gamma_{20} + \gamma_{21}W_j + u_{2j}.$$

The four coefficients to be considered are $\gamma_{10}, \gamma_{11}, \gamma_{20}, \gamma_{21}$. We may, for instance, wish to specify some constraints of fixed effects.

2.8.4 To put constraints on fixed effects

1. Open the **Other Settings** menu.
2. Click the **Constraint of fixed effects** button to open the **Constrain Gamma** dialog box. Enter **1** in the Sector boxes (see Figure 2.36 for an example). Click **OK**. The constraint imposed is $\gamma_{11} = \gamma_{21}$.

Coefficients with 0s are not constrained, and those with 1s are. A user is allowed to impose multiple constraints up to 5. Each set of the constrained coefficients will share the same value from 1 to 5.

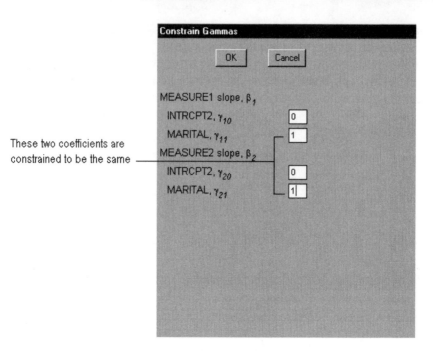

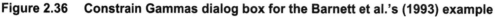

These two coefficients are
constrained to be the same

Figure 2.36 Constrain Gammas dialog box for the Barnett et al.'s (1993) example

2.8.5 Modeling heterogeneity of level-1 variances

Users may wish to estimate models that allow for heterogeneous level-1 variances. A simple example (see HSB3.HLM) using the HS&B data would be a model that postulates that the two genders have different means in and variances of math achievement scores. To specify a model that hypothesizes different central tendency and variability in math achievement for the two genders, the model displayed in Fig. 2.37 must first be set up.

To model heterogeneity of level-1 variances

1. Open the **Other Settings** menu and select the **Estimation Settings** option to open the **Estimation Settings – HLM2** dialog box.
2. Click the **Heterogeneous sigma^2** button to open the **Heterogeneous sigma^2 Predictors of level-1 variance** dialog box. Double-click FEMALE to enter as a variable in the **Predictors of level-1 variance** box (see Figure 2.38 for an example). Click **OK**.

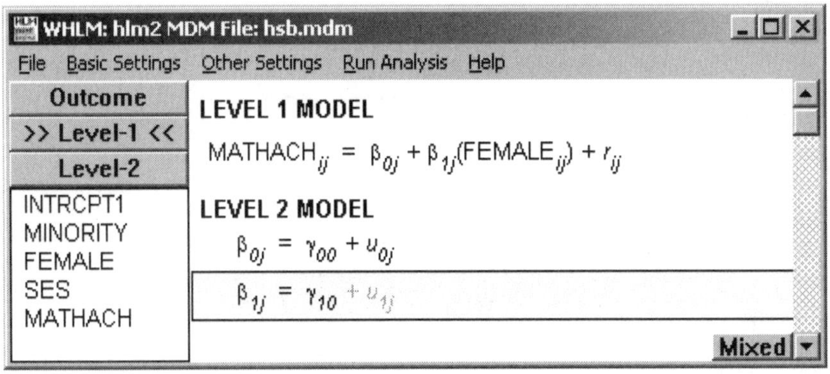

Figure 2.37   Model window for the modeling heterogeneity of level-1 variances example

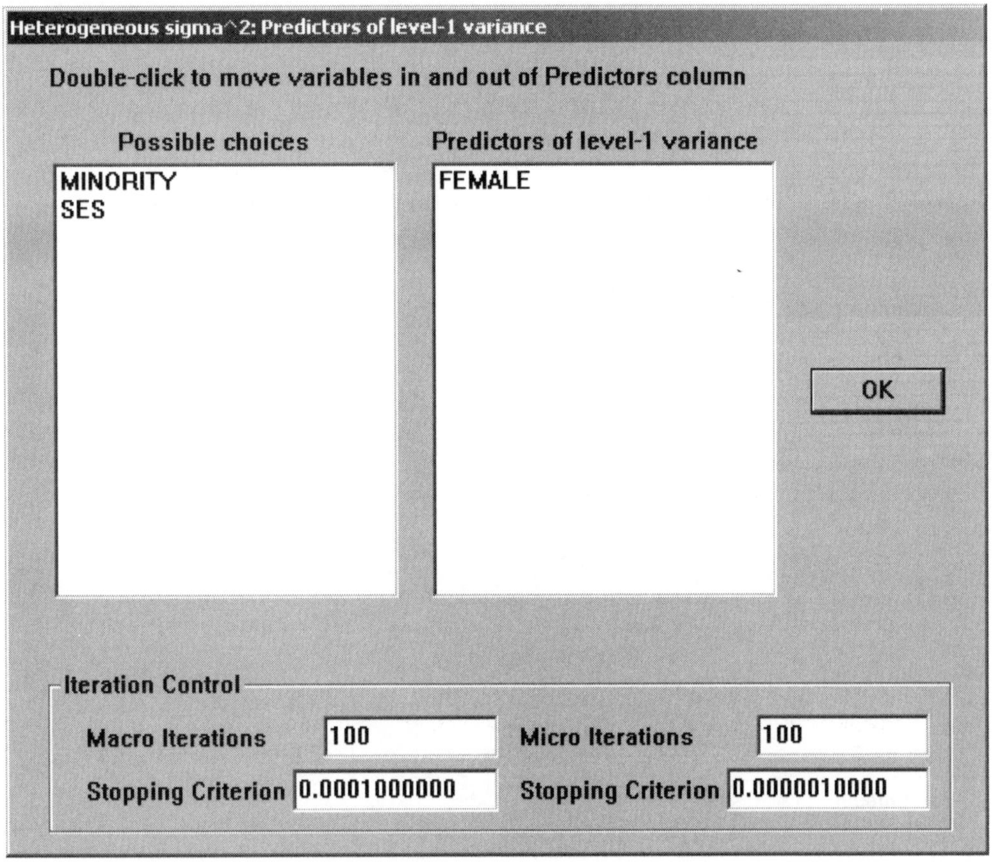

Figure 2.38   Heterogeneous sigma^2: Predictors of level-1 variance dialog box

The model estimated is a log linear-model for the level-1 variances, which can be generally stated as:

$$\sigma_{ij}^2 = \exp\left\{\alpha_0 + \alpha_1 \text{FEMALE}_{ij}\right\}$$

The following is a selected annotated output of the model run.

```
The outcome variable is  MATHACH

Final estimation of fixed effects:
---------------------------------------------------------------------
                                     Standard          Approx.
Fixed Effect          Coefficient    Error    T-ratio  d.f.    P-value
---------------------------------------------------------------------
For      INTRCPT1, B0
   INTRCPT2, G00        13.345654    0.261011  51.131      159   0.000
For    FEMALE slope, B1
   INTRCPT2, G10        -1.381355    0.185852  -7.433      159   0.000
---------------------------------------------------------------------


Final estimation of fixed effects
(with robust standard errors)
---------------------------------------------------------------------
                                     Standard          Approx.
   Fixed Effect       Coefficient    Error    T-ratio  d.f.    P-value
---------------------------------------------------------------------
For        INTRCPT1, B0
  INTRCPT2, G00        13.345654     0.261027  51.127      159   0.000
For    FEMALE slope, B1
  INTRCPT2, G10        -1.381355     0.185897  -7.431      159   0.000
---------------------------------------------------------------------

RESULTS FOR HETEROGENEOUS SIGMA-SQUARED
(macro iteration 4)

Var(R) = Sigma_squared and
log(Sigma_squared) = alpha0 + alpha1(FEMALE)


Model for level-1 variance
---------------------------------------------------------------------
                                   Standard
    Parameter        Coefficient   Error     Z-ratio  P-value
---------------------------------------------------------------------
INTRCPT1    ,alpha0    3.70390     0.024798  149.365   0.000
   FEMALE   ,alpha1   -0.09122     0.034089   -2.676   0.008
---------------------------------------------------------------------

Summary of Model Fit
---------------------------------------------------------------------
Model                             Number of        Deviance
                                  Parameters
---------------------------------------------------------------------
1. Homogeneous sigma_squared          6           47049.46273
2. Heterogeneous sigma_squared        7           47042.27641
---------------------------------------------------------------------

Model Comparison                  Chi-square       df    P-value
---------------------------------------------------------------------
Model 1 vs Model 2                  7.18633          1    0.007
```

The Z-ratio for γ_0 (Z = -7.433) and Z-ratio for γ_1 (Z =-2.677) for FEMALE indicate that the math achievement scores of males are on average higher as well as more variable than those for females. Furthermore, a comparison of the fits of the models suggests that the model with heterogeneous within-school variances appears appropriate (χ^2 = 7.18547, df = 1). See Chapter 7 for details on model comparison.

2.8.6 Specifying level-1 deletion variables

If, when making the MDM file, "Delete missing data when running analyses" was specified, this feature may be used to alter the default behavior of the programs. By default, the programs will delete missing data on the basis of the level-1 variables actually in the model. While in many cases this is the desired behavior, in other situations it may not be. For instance, one might be running and comparing analyses that have different level-1 models. With many datasets, this can lead to comparing results that have a different number of level-1 records used. To solve this problem, this feature may be used to specify a deletion list for all of the runs to compare.

2.8.7 Using design weights

In many studies, data arise from sample surveys in which units have been selected with known but unequal probabilities. In these cases, it will often be desirable to weight observations in order to produce unbiased estimates of population parameters. According to standard practice in such cases, the information from each unit is weighted inversely proportional to its probability of selection.

Suppose, for instance, that in a pre-election poll, ethnic minority voters are over-sampled to insure that various ethnic groups are represented in the sample. Without weighting, the over-sampled groups would exert undue influence on estimates of the proportion of voters in the population favoring a specific candidate. Use of design weights can yield unbiased estimates of the population parameters.

Design weights are also commonly used to correct for differential non-response of sub-groups. Response rates are estimated for relevant sub-groups, and information from each respondent is weighted inversely proportional to the probability of response. That way, respondents who are over-represented in a sample as a function of non-response are appropriately weighted down.

2.8.7.1   Design weighting in the hierarchical context

Hierarchical data can be described as arising from a multi-stage sampling procedure. For example, schools might be sampled from a national frame of schools and then, within each school, students might then be sampled from a list of all students attending the school. Probabilities at each level might be known but unequal. For example, one might over-sample private schools and then over-sample minority students within each school. Weights might be constructed at each level to be inversely proportional to the probability of selection at that level. In some cases, weights might be available at only one level. For example, in a two-level design with students nested within schools, one might compute the marginal probability that a student is selected as the product of the probability that student's school is selected multiplied by the conditional probability that the student is selected given that his or her school is selected. In another context, suppose persons are selected with known probability and then followed longitudinally over time. In this case, we have occasions at level 1 nested within persons at level 2. The only weight may be a level-2 weight, inversely proportional to the probability of selection of that person. It is, of course, possible to include level-1 weights as well, but it is common to have weights only at level-2 in such longitudinal studies.

HLM 6 uses a method of computation devised by Pfefferman et al. (1998) for hierarchical data. This method, based on weighting the information of each case in the framework of maximum likelihood, is more appropriate than the method of weighting in earlier versions of HLM, which used a more conventional approach of weighting observations.

2.8.7.2 Weighting in two-level designs

In the two-level context, weights might be available at level 1, at level 2 or at both levels. If weights are available at level-1 only, the methodology used in HLM 6 assumes that these weights are inversely proportional to P_{ij}, the marginal probability of that student i in school j is selected into the sample. HLM 6 will then normalize the weight to have a mean of 1.0. Thus we have

$$w_{ij} = \frac{N / P_{ij}}{\sum_{j=1}^{J} \sum_{i=1}^{n_j} 1/ P_{ij}} \tag{2.1}$$

in which case

$$\sum_{J=1}^{J} \sum_{i=1}^{n_j} w_{ij} = N \tag{2.2}$$

where N is the total sample size of level-1 units. In contrast, if weights are available only at level 2, the methodology assumes that these weights are inversely proportional to P_j the probability of selection of the level-2 unit. In this case, HLM 6 will again normalize the weight to have a mean of 1.0, yielding

$$w_j = \frac{J/P_{ij}}{\sum_{j=1}^{J} 1/ P_{ij}}, \tag{2.3}$$

in which case

$$\sum_{j=1}^{J} w_j = J. \tag{2.4}$$

where J is the total number of level-2 units. If weights are available at both level-1 and level-2, the methodology assumes that the level-1 weight is $P_{i|j}$, the conditional probability of selection of unit i

given that unit j was selected, so that $P_{i|j} = P_{ij} | P_j$. The level-2 weight is assumed to be inversely proportional to P_j. In this case, HLM will normalize the level-1 weight within level-2 units:

$$w_{i|j} = \frac{n_j / P_{i|j}}{\sum_{i=1}^{n_j} 1 / P_{i|j}}$$ (2.5)

so that the sum of these weights within a level-2 unit will be

$$\sum_{i=1}^{n_j} w_{i|j} = n_j$$ (2.6)

where n_j is the sample size of level-1 units in level-2 unit j.

2.8.7.3   Weighting in three-level designs

In the three-level context, weights might be available at any one of the three levels, at any pair of them, or at all three levels. Normalization proceeds in a fashion completely analogous to that in the case of two levels. If weights are available only at level 1, we assume these are inversely proportional to P_{ijk}, the marginal probability of selection of unit ijk. Similarly, if weights are available only at level 2 or only at level 3, the corresponding probabilities are P_{jk} or P_k, respectively. If the weights are at levels 1 and 2 but not 3, the corresponding probabilities are $P_{i|jk}$ and P_{jk}; if at levels 2 and 3 (but not 1), the corresponding probabilities are $P_{j|k}$ and P_k; if the weights are at levels 1 and 3 (but not 2), the corresponding probabilities are $P_{i|k}$ and P_k. If weights are present at all three levels, the probabilities are $P_{i|jk}$, $P_{j|k}$ and P_k .

To apply weights for both levels

In HLM6, weights are selected at the time of analysis, not when the MDM file is made:

1. Select the **Estimation Settings** option from the **Other Settings** menu.
2. Use the pull down menus to select the weighting variables at any level.

Note that the cover sheet of each HLM2 output reminds the user of the weighting specification chosen. Note that there are no model-based standard errors for the fixed effect estimates when weighting is employed. Rather, the appropriate standard errors are the robust standard errors, and these are printed out.

2.8.8 Hypothesis testing

2.8.8.1 Multivariate hypothesis tests for fixed effects

HLM allows multivariate hypothesis tests for the fixed effects. For instance, for the model displayed in Fig. 2.40, a user can test the following composite null hypothesis:

$$H_0 : \gamma_{01} = \gamma_{11} = 0,$$

where γ_{01} is the effect of SECTOR on the intercept and γ_{11} is the effect of sector on the SES slope.

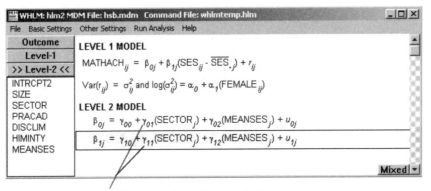

Test if these two fixed effects are both zero

Figure 2.40   Model window

Below is a procedure that illustrates a Windows execution of the hypothesis test.

To pose a multivariate hypothesis test among the fixed effects

1. Open the **Other Settings** menu and select the **Estimation Settings** option to open the **Hypothesis Testing – HLM2** dialog box (See Figure 2.41).
2. Click "1" to open the the **General Linear Hypothesis: Hypothesis 1** dialog box and to specify the first hypothesis (see Fig 2.42 for the contrast comparing the effect of SECTOR on the intercept and on the SES slope). Click **OK**.

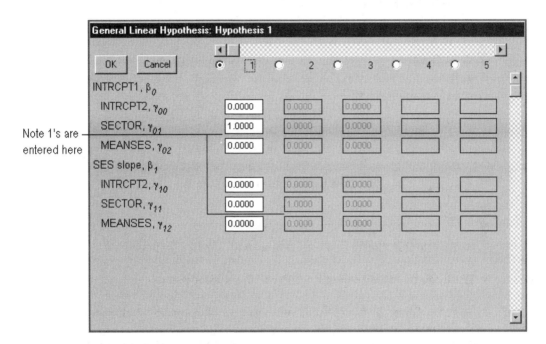

Click here to implement multivariate hypothesis tests using Wald tests

Enter deviance statistic and number of parameters here to compute likelihood ratio tests

Click here to implement test of homogeneity of variance

Figure 2.41   Optional Hypothesis Testing/Estimation dialog box

Note 1's are entered here

Figure 2.42   General Linear Hypothesis: Hypothesis 1 dialog box

The HLM2 output associated with this test appears in Section 2.8.8.3 below. (For a further discussion of this multivariate hypothesis test for fixed effects see *Hierarchical Linear Models*, pp. 58-61, 81-85).

2.8.8.2   Testing homogeneity of level-1 variances

By default, HLM2 assumes homogeneity of residual variance at level 1. That is, it specifies a common σ^2 within each of the J level-2 units. As an option, HLM2 tests the adequacy of this assumption.

To test homogeneity of level-1 variances

1. Click the **Test homogeneity of level-1 variance** box (Figure 2.41).
2. The HLM2 output associated with this test also appears in Section 2.8.8.3 below. (For a further discussion of this test see *Hierarchical Linear Models*, pp. 263-267. We advise that users review these pages carefully before using this procedure.)

2.8.8.3 Multivariate tests of variance-covariance components specification

HLM2 also provides, as an option, a multi-parameter test for the variance-covariance components. This likelihood-ratio test compares the deviance statistic of a restricted model with a more general alternative. The user must input the value of the deviance statistic and related degrees of freedom for the alternative specification. Below we compare the variance-covariance components of two Intercept-and-Slope-as-Outcome models. One treats β_1 as random and the other does not.

To specify a multivariate test of variance-covariance components

Enter the deviance and the number of parameters in the **Deviance Statistics** box and in the **Number of Parameters** box (see Fig. 2.41) respectively (the two numbers for our example are 46512.978000 and 4, obtained in Section 2.5.3).

The HLM2 output associated with this test appears in the section below. (For a further discussion of this multi-parameter test see *Hierarchical Linear Models*, pp. 63-65, 83-85). Below is an example of a selected HLM2 output that illustrates optional hypothesis testing procedures.

```
Weighting Specification
-----------------------
                              Weight
                              Variable
                 Weighting?   Name          Normalized?
   Level 1          no
   Level 2          no


  The outcome variable is  MATHACH

The model specified for the fixed effects was:
---------------------------------------------------------
   Level-1                 Level-2
   Coefficients            Predictors
---------------------      ----------------
        INTRCPT1, B0          INTRCPT2, G00
                                SECTOR, G01
                               MEANSES, G02

#*      SES slope, B1         INTRCPT2, G10
                                SECTOR, G11
                               MEANSES, G12

'#' - The residual parameter variance for this level-1 coefficient has been set to zero.
'*' - This level-1 predictor has been centered around its group mean.
```

```
The model specified for the covariance components was:
----------------------------------------------------------------
        Sigma squared (constant across level-2 units)

        Tau dimensions
            INTRCPT1

  Summary of the model specified (in equation format)
  --------------------------------------------------------
```

```
Level-1 Model
    Y = B0 + B1*(SES) + R

Level-2 Model
    B0 = G00 + G01*(SECTOR) + G02*(MEANSES) + U0
    B1 = G10 + G11*(SECTOR) + G12*(MEANSES)
```

Note, the middle section of output has been deleted. We proceed directly to the final results page.

```
Final estimation of fixed effects:
----------------------------------------------------------------------
                                Standard            Approx.
Fixed Effect        Coefficient Error     T-ratio   d.f.    P-value
----------------------------------------------------------------------
 For        INTRCPT1, B0
   INTRCPT2, G00      12.096251  0.198643  60.894     157    0.000
     SECTOR, G01       1.224401  0.306117   4.000     157    0.000
     MEANSES, G02      5.336698  0.368978  14.463     157    0.000
 For      SES slope, B1
   INTRCPT2, G10       2.935860  0.150705  19.481    7179    0.000
     SECTOR, G11      -1.642102  0.233097  -7.045    7179    0.000
     MEANSES, G12      1.044120  0.291042   3.588    7179    0.001
----------------------------------------------------------------------
Final estimation of fixed effects
 (with robust standard errors)
----------------------------------------------------------------------
                                Standard            Approx.
Fixed Effect        Coefficient Error     T-ratio   d.f.    P-value
----------------------------------------------------------------------
 For        INTRCPT1, B0
   INTRCPT2, G00      12.096251  0.173691  69.642     157    0.000
     SECTOR, G01       1.224401  0.308507   3.969     157    0.000
     MEANSES, G02      5.336698  0.334617  15.949     157    0.000
 For      SES slope, B1
   INTRCPT2, G10       2.935860  0.147580  19.893    7179    0.000
     SECTOR, G11      -1.642102  0.237223  -6.922    7179    0.000
     MEANSES, G12      1.044120  0.332897   3.136    7179    0.002
----------------------------------------------------------------------
Final estimation of variance components:
----------------------------------------------------------------------
Random Effect      Standard     Variance    df    Chi-square  P-value
                   Deviation    Component
----------------------------------------------------------------------
 INTRCPT1,  U0      1.54118      2.37524    157    604.29895   0.000
 level-1,   R       6.06351     36.76611
----------------------------------------------------------------------
```

```
Statistics for current covariance components model
-------------------------------------------------------
Deviance                      = 46502.952743
Number of estimated parameters = 2
```

For the likelihood ratio test, the deviance statistic reported above is compared with the value from the alternative model manually. The result of this test appears below.

```
Variance-Covariance components test
-----------------------------------
Chi-square statistic         =     1.07710
Number of degrees of freedom =   2
P-value                      = >.500
```

A model that constrains the residual variance for the SES slopes, B1, to zero appears appropriate. (For a further discussion of this application see *Hierarchical Linear Models*, pp. 83-85.)

```
Test of homogeneity of level-1 variance
----------------------------------------
Chi-square statistic         =   244.08638
Number of degrees of freedom =   159
P-value                      = 0.000
```

These results indicate that there is variability among the ($J = 160$) level-2 units in terms of the residual within-school (*i.e.*, level-1) variance. (For a full discussion of these results see *Hierarchical Linear Models*, pp. 263-267.)

```
              Results of General Linear Hypothesis Testing
--------------------------------------------------------------------
                                    Coefficients      Contrast
--------------------------------------------------------------------
For        INTRCPT1, B0
      INTRCPT2, G00                  12.096251      0.000   0.000
        SECTOR, G01                   1.224401      1.000   0.000
       MEANSES, G02                   5.336698      0.000   0.000
For        SES slope, B1
      INTRCPT2, G10                   2.935860      0.000   0.000
        SECTOR, G11                  -1.642102      0.000   1.000
       MEANSES, G12                   1.044120      0.000   0.000

Chi-square statistic = 60.527852
Degrees of freedom   = 2
P-value              = 0.000000
```

The table above is a reminder of the multivariate contrast specified. The chi-square statistic and associated *p*-value indicate that it is highly unlikely that the observed estimates for G01 and G11 could have occurred under the specified null hypothesis.

2.9   Output options

There are a few options relating to the output that can be selected on the **Other Settings, Output Settings** menu:

- **# of OLS estimates shown** (HLM2 only) – this controls the number of OLS estimates printed in the output. See the output in Section 2.5.3.
- **Print variance-covariance matrices** – see Section A.5.
- **Print reduced output** – if this is checked, only the header page and the final results are printed.

Starting values, OLS estimates (if present), etc. will not be printed.

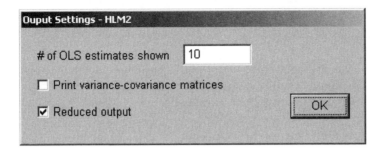

Figure 2.43   Output Settings – HLM2 dialog box

2.10   Models without a level-1 intercept

In some circumstances, users may wish to estimate models without a level-1 intercept. Consider, for example, a hypothetical study in which three alternative treatments are implemented within each of J hospitals. One might estimate the following level-1 (within-hospital) model:

$$Y_{ij} = \beta_{1j} X_{1ij} + \beta_{2j} X_{2ij} + \beta_{3j} X_{3ij} + r_{i_j},$$

where X_{qij} ($q = 1,2,3$) are indicator variables taking on a value of 1 if patient i in hospital j has received treatment q, 0 otherwise; and β_{qj} is the mean outcome in hospital j of those receiving treatment q. At level-2, the treatment means β_{qj} are predicted by characteristics of the hospitals. Of course, the same data could alternatively be modeled by a level-1 intercept and two treatment contrasts per hospital, but users will sometimes find the no-intercept approach is more convenient.

An example of a no-intercept model appears on page 174 of *Hierarchical Linear Models*. The vocabulary growth of young children is of interest. Both common sense and the data indicated that children could be expected to have no vocabulary at 12 months of age. Hence, the level-1 model contained no intercept:

$$Y_{ti} = \pi_{1i} \left(\text{AGE}_{ti} - 12 \right) + \pi_{2i} \left(\text{AGE}_{ti} - 12 \right)^2 + e_{ti}$$

where AGE_{ti} is the age of child i at time t in months and Y_{ti} is the size of that child's vocabulary at that time.

To delete an intercept from a level-1 model

Click INTRCPT1 on the **>>Level-1<<** drop-down list. Click **delete variable from model**.

2.11 Coefficients having a random effect with no corresponding fixed effect

A user may find it useful at times to model a level-1 predictor as having a random effect but no fixed effect. For example, it might be that gender differences in educational achievement are, on average, null across a set of schools; yet, in some schools females outperform males while in other schools males outperform females. In this case, the fixed effect of gender could be set to zero while the variance of the gender effect across schools would be estimated.

The vocabulary analysis in *Hierarchical Linear Models* supplies an example of a level-1 predictor having a random effect without a corresponding fixed effect. For the age interval under study, it was found that, on average, the linear effect of age was zero. Yet this effect varied significantly across children. The level-1 model estimated was:

$$Y_{ti} = \pi_{1i}\left(AGE_{ti} - 12\right) + \pi_{2i}\left(AGE_{ti} - 12\right)^2 + e_{ti}$$

However, the level-2 model was:

$$\pi_{1i} = r_{1i}$$
$$\pi_{2i} = \beta_{20} + r_{2i}$$

Notice that AGE – 12 has a random effect but no fixed effect.

To delete the fixed effect from a level-2 model

1. Select the equation from which the fixed effect is to be removed.
2. Click INTRCPT2 on the **>>Level-2<<** drop-down list. Click **delete variable from model**.

2.12 Exploratory analysis of potential level-2 predictors

The user may be interested in computing "*t*-to-enter statistics" for potential level-2 predictors to guide specification of subsequent HLM2 models. The implementation procedure is as follows.

To implement exploratory analysis of potential level-2 predictors

1. Open the **Other Settings menu** and choose **Exploratory Analysis (level 2)**. A **Select Variables For Exploratory Analysis** dialog box appears.
2. Click the equation associated with a regression coefficient to model the corresponding coefficient. Click to select variables for exploratory analysis. (Figure 2.44 displays the level-2 predictors chosen for our HS&B example).
3. Click **Return to Model Mode** to return to the model window.

The following contains a selected HLM2 output to illustrate exploratory analysis of potential level-2 predictors.

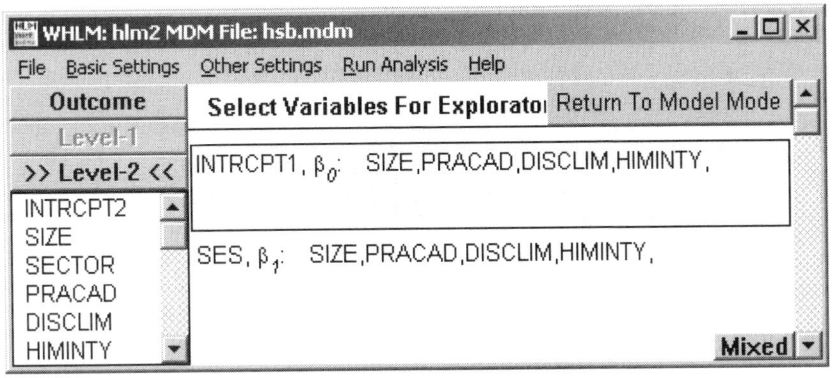

Figure 2.44   Select Variables For Exploratory Analysis dialog box for the HS&B example

```
Exploratory Analysis: estimated level-2 coefficients and their standard errors obtained
by regressing EB residuals on level-2 predictors selected for
possible inclusion in subsequent HLM runs
```

Level-1 Coefficient	Potential Level-2 Predictors			
	SIZE	PRACAD	DISCLIM	HIMNTY
INTRCPT1,B0				
Coefficient	0.000	0.690	-0.161	-0.543
Standard Error	0.000	0.404	0.106	0.229
t value	1.569	1.707	-1.515	-2.372
	SIZE	PRACAD	DISCLIM	HIMNTY
SES,B1				
Coefficient	0.000	0.039	-0.005	-0.058
Standard Error	0.000	0.044	0.012	0.025
t value	1.297	0.899	-0.425	-2.339

The results of this exploratory analysis suggest that HIMINTY might be a good candidate to include in the INTRCPT1 model. The *t*-values represent the approximate result that will be obtained when one additional predictor is added to any of the level-2 equations. This means that if HIMINTY is added to the model for the INTRCPT1, for example, the apparent relationship suggested above for HIMINTY in the

SES slope model might disappear. (For a further discussion of the use of these statistics see discussion in *Hierarchical Linear Models*, p. 270 on "Approximate *t*-to-Enter Statistics.")

3   Conceptual and Statistical Background for Three-Level Models

The models estimated by HLM3 are applicable to a hierarchical data structure with three levels of random variation in which the errors of prediction at each level can be assumed to be approximately normally distributed. Consider, for example, a study in which achievement test scores are collected from a sample of children nested within classrooms that are in turn nested within schools. This data structure is hierarchical (each child belongs to one and only one classroom and each classroom belongs to one and only one school); and there are three levels of random variation: variation among children within classrooms, variation among classrooms within schools, and variation among schools. The outcome (achievement test scores) makes the normality assumption at level 1 reasonable, and the normality assumption at the classroom and school levels will often also be a sensible one.

Chapter 8 of *Hierarchical Linear Models* discusses several applications of a three-level model. The first is a three-level cross-sectional study as described above. A second case involves time-series data collected on each subject where the subjects are nested within organizations. This latter example is from the Sustaining Effects Study, where achievement data were collected at five time points for each child. Here the time-series data are nested within children and the children are nested within schools. A third example in Chapter 8 involves measures taken on each of the multiple classes taught by secondary school teachers. The classes are nested within teachers and the teachers within schools. A final example involves multiple items from a questionnaire administered to teachers. The items vary "within teachers" at level 1, the teachers vary within schools at level 2, and the schools vary at level 3. In effect, the level-1 model is a model for the measurement error associated with the questionnaire. Clearly, there are many interesting applications of a three-level model.

3.1   The general three-level model

The three-level model consists of three submodels, one for each level. For example, if the research problem consists of data on students nested within classrooms and classrooms within schools, the level-1 model will represent the relationships among the student-level variables, the level-2 model will capture the influence of class-level factors, and the level-3 model will incorporate school-level effects. Formally there are $i = 1, ..., n_{jk}$ level-1 units (*e.g.*, students), which are nested within each of $j = 1,...,$ J_k level-2 units (*e.g.*, classrooms), which in turn are nested within each of $k = 1,..., K$ level-3 units (*e.g.*, schools).

3.1.1 Level-1 model

In the level-1 model we represent the outcome for case i within level-2 unit j and level-3 unit k as:

$$Y_{ijk} = \pi_{0jk} + \pi_{1jk}a_{1jk} + \pi_{2jk}a_{2jk} + \ldots + \pi_{pjk}a_{pjk} + e_{ijk}$$

$$= \pi_{0jk} + \sum_{p=1}^{P} \pi_{pjk}a_{pjk} + e_{ijk} \tag{3.1}$$

where

π_{pjk} $(p = 0,1,\ldots, P)$ are *level-1 coefficients*,

a_{pjk} is a *level-1 predictor* p for case i in level-2 unit j and level-3 unit k,

e_{ijk} is the *level-1 random effect*, and

σ^2 is the variance of e_{ijk}, that is the *level-1 variance*.

Here we assume that the random term $e_{ijk} \sim N(0, \sigma^2)$.

3.1.2 Level-2 model

Each of the π_{pjk} coefficients in the level-1 model becomes an outcome variable in the level-2 model:

$$\pi_{pjk} = \beta_{p0k} + \beta_{p1k}X_{1jk} + \beta_{p2k}X_{2jk} + \cdots + \beta_{pQ_pk}X_{Q_pjk} + r_{pjk}$$

$$= \beta_{p0k} + \sum_{q=1}^{Q_p} \beta_{pqk}X_{qjk} + r_{pjk}, \tag{3.2}$$

where

β_{pqk} $(q = 0,1,\ldots,Q_p)$ are *level-2 coefficients*,

X_{qjk} is a *level-2 predictor*, and

r_{pjk} is a *level-2 random effect*.

We assume that, for each unit j, the vector $\left(r_{0jk}, r_{1jk}, \ldots, r_{Pjk}\right)'$ is distributed as multivariate normal where each element has a mean of zero and the variance of r_{pjk} is:

$$\text{Var}(r_{pjk}) = \tau_{\pi pp} . \tag{3.3}$$

For any pair of random effects p and p',

$$\text{Cov}(r_{pjk}, r_{p'jk}) = \tau_{\pi pp'} . \tag{3.4}$$

These level-2 variance and covariance components can be collected into a dispersion matrix, $\mathbf{T}_{\pi}$, with a maximum dimension is $(P+1) \times (P+1)$.

We note that each level-1 coefficient can be modeled at level 2 as one of three general forms:

1. *a level-1 coefficient that is fixed at the same value for all level-2 units; e.g.,*

$$\pi_{pjk} = \beta_{p0k} , \tag{3.5}$$

2. *a level-1 coefficient that varies non-randomly among level-2 units, e.g.,*

$$\pi_{pjk} = \beta_{p0k} + \sum_{q=1}^{Q_p} \beta_{pqk} X_{qjk} , \tag{3.6}$$

3. *a level-1 coefficient that varies randomly among level-2 units, e.g.,*

$$\pi_{pjk} = \beta_{p0k} + r_{pjk} \tag{3.7}$$

or

$$\pi_{pjk} = \beta_{p0k} + \sum_{q=1}^{Q_p} \beta_{pqk} X_{qjk} + r_{pjk}. \tag{3.8}$$

The actual dimension of $\mathbf{T}_{\pi}$ in any application depends on the number of level-1 coefficients specified as randomly varying. We also note that a different set of level-2 predictors may be used in each of the $P+1$ equations that form the level-2 model.

3.1.3 Level-3 model

Each of the level-2 coefficients, β_{pqk}, defined in the level-2 model becomes an outcome variable in the level-3 model:

$$\beta_{pqk} = \gamma_{pq0} + \gamma_{pq1}W_{1k} + \gamma_{pq2}W_{2k} + \cdots + \gamma_{pqS_{pq}}W_{S_{pq}k} + u_{pqk}$$

$$= \gamma_{pq0} + \sum_{s=1}^{S_{pq}} \gamma_{pqs}W_{sk} + u_{pqk},$$

(3.9)

where

γ_{pqs} $(s = 0, 1, ..., S_{pq})$ are *level-3 coefficients*,

W_{sk} is a *level-3 predictor*, and

u_{pqk} is a *level-3 random effect*.

We assume that, for each level-3 unit, the vector of level-3 random effects (the u_{pqk} terms) is distributed as multivariate normal, with each having a mean of zero and with covariance matrix $\mathbf{T}_\beta$, whose maximum dimension is:

$$\sum_{p=0}^{p}(Q_p+1) \times \sum_{p=0}^{p}(Q_p+1),$$

(3.10)

We note that each level-2 coefficient can be modeled at level-3 as one of three general forms:

1. *as a fixed effect, e.g.,*

$$\beta_{pqk} = \gamma_{pq0},$$

(3.11)

2. *as non-randomly varying, e.g.*

$$\beta_{pqk} = \gamma_{pq0} + \sum_{s=1}^{S_{pq}} \gamma_{pqs}W_{sk},$$

(3.12)

3. *as randomly varying, e.g.*

$$\beta_{pqk} = \gamma_{pq0} + u_{pqk}$$

(3.13)

or

$$\beta_{pqk} = \gamma_{pq0} + \sum_{s=1}^{S_{pq}} \gamma_{pqs} W_{sk} + u_{pqk}. \tag{3.14}$$

The actual dimension of $\mathbf{T}_\beta$ in any application depends on the number of level-3 coefficients specified as randomly varying. We also note that a different set of level-3 predictors may be used in each equation of the level-3 model.

3.2   Parameter estimation

Three kinds of parameter estimates are available in a three-level model: empirical Bayes estimates of randomly varying level-1 and level-2 coefficients; maximum-likelihood estimates of the level-3 coefficients (note: these are also generalized least squares estimates); and maximum-likelihood estimates of the variance-covariance components. The maximum-likelihood estimate of the level-3 coefficients and the variance-covariance components are printed on the output for every run. The empirical Bayes estimates for the level-1 and level-2 coefficients may optionally be saved in the "residual files" at levels 2 and 3, respectively. Reliability estimates for each random level-1 and level-2 coefficient are always produced. The actual estimation procedure for the three-level model differs a bit from the default two-level model. By default, HLM2 uses a "restricted maximum likelihood" approach in which the variance-covariance components are estimated by means of maximum likelihood and then the fixed effects (level-2 coefficients) are estimated via generalized least squares given those variance-covariance estimates. In HLM3, not only the variance-covariance components, but also the fixed effects (level-3 coefficients) are estimated by means of maximum likelihood. This procedure is referred to as "full" as opposed to "restricted" maximum likelihood (For a further discussion of this see *Hierarchical Linear Models*, pp. 52-53). Note that full maximum likelihood is also available as an option for HLM2.

3.3   Hypothesis testing

As in the case of the two-level program, the three-level program routinely prints standard errors and *t*-tests for each of the level-3 coefficients ("the fixed effects") as well as a chi-square test of homogeneity for each random effect. In addition, optional "multivariate hypothesis tests" are available in the three-level program. Multivariate tests for the level-3 coefficients enable both omnibus tests and specific comparisons of the parameter estimates just as described in the section *Multivariate hypothesis tests for fixed effects* in this chapter. Multivariate tests regarding alternative variance-covariance structures at level 2 or level 3 proceed just as in the section *Multivariate tests of variance-covariance components specification* in this chapter.

The use of full maximum likelihood for parameter estimation in HLM3 has a consequence for hypothesis testing. For both restricted and full maximum likelihood, one can test alternative variance-covariance structures by means of the likelihood-ratio test as described in the section *Multivariate tests of variance-covariance components specification*. However, in the case of full maximum likelihood, it is also possible to test alternative specifications of the fixed coefficients by means of a likelihood-ratio test.

In fact, any pair of nested models can be compared using the likelihood-ratio test under full maximum likelihood. By nested models, we refer to a pair of models in which the more complex model includes all of the parameters of the simpler model plus one or more additional parameters. Any pair of nested two-level models can be compared using a likelihood ratio test.

4 Working with HLM3

As in the case of the two-level program, data analysis by means of the HLM3 program will typically involve three stages:

- Construction of an MDM file (the multivariate data matrix)
- Execution of analyses based on the MDM file
- Evaluation of fitted models based on residual files

As in HLM2, HLM3 analyses can be executed in Windows, interactive, and batch modes. We describe a Windows execution below. We consider interactive and batch execution in Appendix B. A number of special options are presented at the end of the chapter.

4.1 An example using HLM3 in Windows mode

Chapter 8 in *Hierarchical Linear Models* presents a series of analyses of data from the US *Sustaining Effects Study*, a longitudinal study of children's growth in academic achievement during the primary years. A level-1 model specifies the relationship between age and academic achievement for each child. At level 2, the coefficients describing each child's growth vary across children within schools as a function of demographic variables. At level 3, the parameters that describe the distribution of growth curves within each school vary across schools as a function of school-level predictors.

To illustrate the operation of the HLM3 program, we analyze another data set having a similar structure. The level-1 data are time-series observations on 1721 students nested within 60 urban public primary schools and mathematics achievement is the outcome. These data are provided along with the HLM software so that a user may replicate our results in order to assure that the program is operating correctly.

4.1.1 Constructing the MDM file from raw data

In constructing the MDM file, the user has the same range of options for data input for HLM3 as for HLM2 (see Section 2.5.1). We first describe the use of SPSS file input and then consider ASCII, SYSTAT, SAS, and other data file formats.

4.1.1.1 SPSS input

Data input requires a level-1 file (in our illustration a time-series data file), a level-2 file (child-level file), and a level-3 (school level) file.

Level-1 file. The level-1 file, EG1.SAV, has 7242 observations collected on 1721 children beginning at the end of grade one and followed up annually thereafter until grade six. There are four level-1 variables (not including the schoolid and the childid). Time-series data for the first two children are shown in Figure 4.1.

There are eight records listed, three for the first child and five for the second. (Typically there are four or five observations per child with a maximum of six.) The first ID is the level-3 (*i.e.*, school) ID and the second ID is the level-2 (*i.e.*, child) ID. We see that the first record comes from school 2020 and child 273026452 within that school. Notice that this child has three records, one for each of three measurement occasions. Following the two ID fields are that child's values on four variables:

- YEAR (year of the study minus 3.5)

  This variable can take on values of -2.5, -1.5, -0.5, 0.5, 1.5, and 2.5 for the six years of data collection.
- GRADE

  The grade level minus 1.0 of the child at each testing occasion. Therefore, it is 0 at grade 1, 1 at grade 2, etc.
- MATH

  A math test in an IRT scale score metric.
- RETAINED

  An indicator that a child is retained in grade for a particular year (1 = retained, 0 = not retained).

	schoolid	childid	year	grade	math	retained
1	2020	273026452	.50	2.00	1.15	.00
2	2020	273026452	1.50	3.00	1.13	.00
3	2020	273026452	2.50	4.00	2.30	.00
4	2020	273030991	.50	2.00	2.43	.00
5	2020	273030991	1.50	3.00	2.25	.00
6	2020	273030991	2.50	4.00	3.87	.00
7	2020	273030991	-.50	1.00	.44	.00
8	2020	273030991	-1.50	.00	-1.30	.00

Figure 4.1   First eight cases in EG1.SAV

We see that the first child, child 27306452 in school 2020, had values of 0.5, 1.5, and 2.5 on year. Clearly, that child had no data at the first three data collection waves (because we see no values of

−2.5, −1.5, or −0.5 on year), but did have data at the last three waves. We see also that this child was not retained in grade during this period since the values for GRADE increase by 1 each year and since RETAINED takes on a value of 0 for each year. The three MATH scores of that child (1.146, 1.134, 2.300) show no growth in time period 1.5. Oddly enough, the time-series record for the second child (child 273030991 in school 2020) displays a similar pattern in the same testing.

Note: The level-1 and level-2 files must also be sorted in the same order of level-2 ID nested within level-3 ID, *e.g.*, children within schools. If this nested sorting is not performed, an incorrect multivariate data matrix file will result.

Level-2 file. The level-2 units in the illustration are 1721 children. The data are stored in the file EG2.SAV. The level-2 data for the first eight children are listed below. The first field is the schoolid and the second is the childid. Note that each of the first ten children is in school 2020.

There are three variables:

- FEMALE (1 = female, 0 = male)
- BLACK (1 = African-American, 0 = other)
- HISPANIC (1= Hispanic, 0 = other)

We see, for example, that child 273026452 is a Hispanic male (FEMALE = 0, BLACK = 0, HISPANIC = 1).

	schoolid	childid	female	black	hispanic
1	2020	273026452	.00	.00	1.00
2	2020	273030991	.00	.00	.00
3	2020	273059461	.00	.00	1.00
4	2020	278058841	.00	.00	.00
5	2020	292017571	.00	.00	1.00
6	2020	292020281	.00	.00	.00
7	2020	292020361	.00	.00	.00
8	2020	292025081	.00	.00	.00

Figure 4.2   First eight children in EG2.SAV

Level-3 file. The level-3 units in the illustration are 60 schools. Level-3 data for the first seven schools are printed below. The full data are in the file EG3.SAV. The first field on the left is the schoolid. There are three level-3 variables:

- SIZE, number of students enrolled in the school
- LOWINC, the percent of students from low income families
- MOBILE, the percent of students moving during the course of a single academic year

We see that the first school, school 2020, has 380 students, 40.3% of whom are low income. The school mobility rate is 12.5%.

	schoolid	size	lowinc	mobility
1	2020	380.00	40.30	12.50
2	2040	502.00	83.10	18.60
3	2180	777.00	96.60	44.40
4	2330	800.00	78.90	31.70
5	2340	1133.00	93.70	67.00
6	2380	439.00	36.90	39.30
7	2390	566.00	100.00	39.90

Figure 4.3   First seven schools in EG3.SAV

In sum, there are four variables at level 1, three at level 2 and three at level 3. Note that the ID variables do not count as variables. Once the user has identified the two sets of IDs, the number of variables in each file, the variable names, and the filenames, creation of the MDM file is exactly analogous to the three major steps described in the Section 2.5.1.1. The user first informs HLM that the input files are SPSS systems files and the MDM is a three-level file. Then HLM is supplied with the appropriate information for the data. Note that the three files are linked by level-2 and level-3 IDs here.

Note: In addition, the program can handle missing data at level-1 only, with the same options available as discussed in HLM2. HLM3 will listwise delete cases with missing data at levels two and three. The three level program handles design weights at all three levels.

The response file, EGSPSS.MDMT, contains a log of the input responses used to create the MDM file, EG.MDM, using EG1.SAV, EG2.SAV, and EG3.SAV. Figure 4.4 displays the dialog box used to create the MDM file. Figure 4.5 shows the dialog box for the level-1 file, EG1.SAV.

Note: As in the case of HLM2, after constructing the MDM file, you should check whether the data have been properly read into HLM by examining the descriptive statistics of the MDM file.

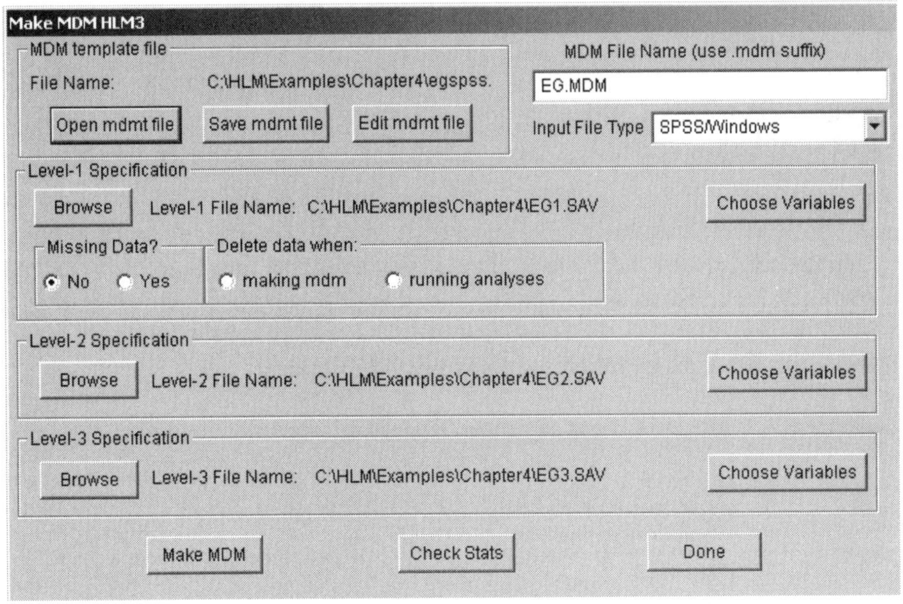

Figure 4.4   Make MDM – HLM3 dialog box for EG.MDM

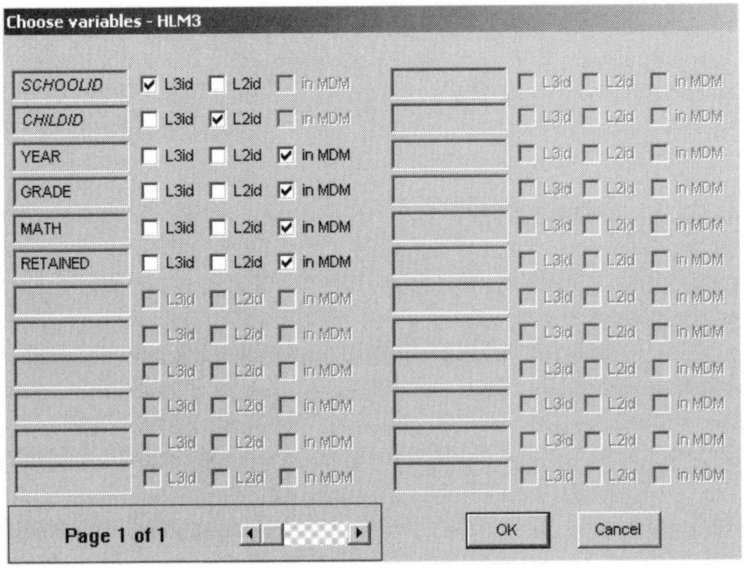

Figure 4.5   Choose Variables – HLM3 dialog box for level-1 file, EG1.SAV

4.1.1.2 ASCII input

The procedure for constructing an MDM file from ASCII data files is similar to that for SPSS file input. The major difference is that the format statements must be entered for the three data files, variable names, and missing value codes, if applicable. Rules about the format are included in the Appendix. An example is included in the response file, EGASCII.MDMT, which constructs the MDM file, EGASCII.MDM, using EG1.DAT, EG2.DAT, and EG3.DAT. Figure 4.6 shows the dialog box for creating the MDM file, displaying the input responses of EGASCII.MDMT.

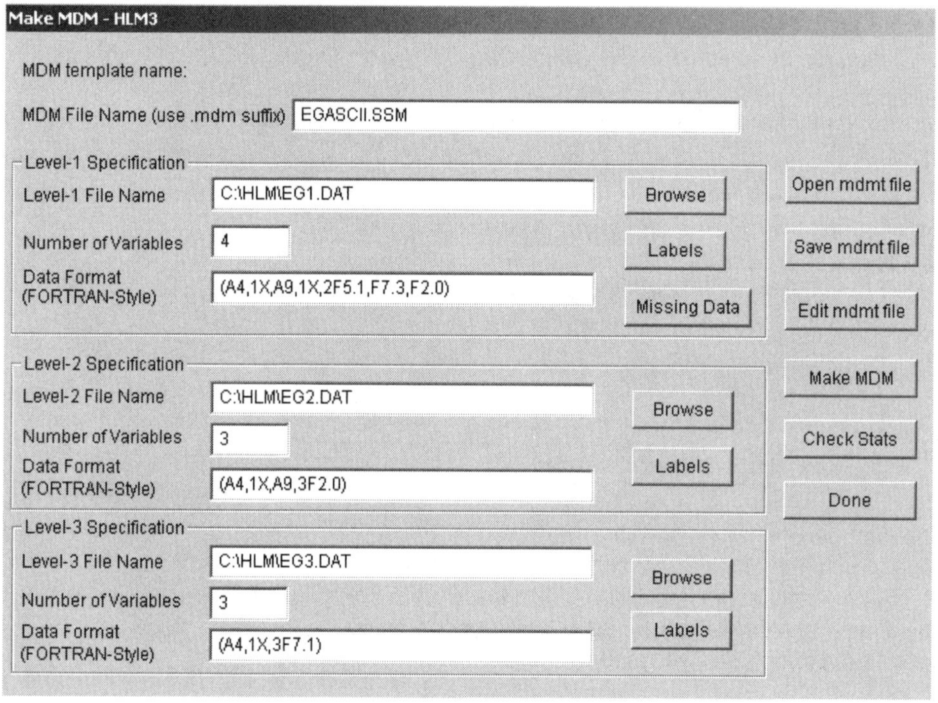

Figure 4.6   Make MDM – HLM3 dialog box for EGASCII.MDM

4.1.1.3 Other file input

For SAS and SYSTAT file input, a user selects either SAS5 transport or SYSTAT from the **Input File Type** drop-down listbox as appropriate before clicking the **Browse** buttons in the file specification sections and follows the same steps for SPSS input type to create MDM files.

4.1.1.4   Other file type input

HLM3 has the same range of options for data input as HLM2. In addition to SYSTAT,SPSS, STATA, free format, and SAS, the Windows version (through a third-party module) allows numerous other data formats from, for example, EXCEL, and LOTUS input. See Section 2.5.1 for details.

4.2   Executing analyses based on the MDM file

Once the MDM file is constructed, it is used as input for the analysis. Model specification via the Windows mode has five steps:

1. Specification of the level-1 model. In our case we shall model mathematics achievement (MATH) as the outcome, to be predicted by YEAR in the study. Hence, the level-1 model will have two coefficients for each child: the intercept and the YEAR slope.
2. Specification of the level-2 prediction model. Here each level-1 coefficient – the intercept and the YEAR slope in our example – becomes an outcome variable. We may select certain child characteristics to predict each of these level-1 coefficients. In principle, the level-2 parameters then describe the distribution of growth curves within each school.
3. Specification of level-1 coefficients as random or non-random across level-two units. We shall model the intercept and the YEAR slope as varying randomly across the children within schools.
4. Specification of the level-3 prediction model. Here each level-2 coefficient becomes an outcome, and we can select level-3 variables to predict school-to-school variation in these level-2 coefficients. In principle, this model specifies how schools differ with respect to the distribution of growth curves within them.
5. Specification of the level-2 coefficients as random or non-random across level-3 units.

Following the five steps above, we first specify a model with no child- or school-level predictors. The Windows execution is very similar to the one for HLM2 as described in Section 2.5.2. The command file, EG1.HLM, contains the model specification input responses. To open the command file, open the **File** menu and choose **Edit/Run old command file**. Figure 4.7 displays the model specified in both standard and mixed model notation.

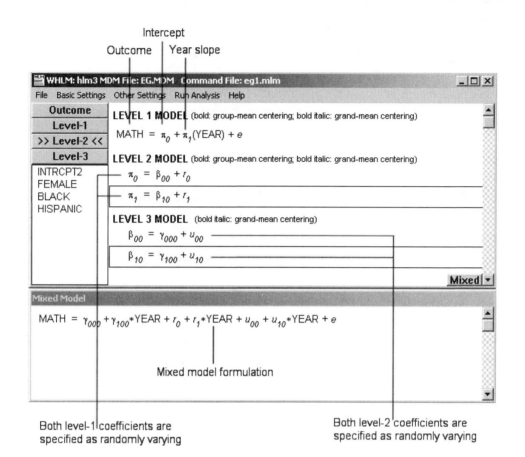

Figure 4.7   Model Window for the public school example

4.2.1 An annotated example of HLM3 output

Here is the output produced by the model described above. The first page of the output gives the specification of the model.

```
SPECIFICATIONS FOR THIS HLM3 RUN

  Problem Title: UNCONDITIONAL LINEAR GROWTH MODEL

  The data source for this run  = EG.MDM                    Name of the MDM file
  The command file for this run = C:\HLM\Examples\Chapter4\eg1.mlm
                                                            Name of the command file
  Output file name              = C:\HLM\Examples\Chapter4\hlm3.txt
                                                            Name of this output file
  The maximum number of level-1 units = 7230          There are 7230 observations
  The maximum number of level-2 units = 1721              There are 1721 children
  The maximum number of level-3 units = 60                   There are 60 schools
  The maximum number of iterations = 100
  Method of estimation: full maximum likelihood
```

The outcome variable is   MATH

The model specified for the fixed effects was:
```
---------------------------------------------------------
    Level-1                 Level-2               Level-3
    Coefficients            Predictors            Predictors
---------------------  ----------------  ----------------
        INTRCPT1, P0    INTRCPT2, B00    INTRCPT3, G000
       YEAR slope, P1   INTRCPT2, B10    INTRCPT3, G100
```

Summary of the model specified (in equation format)
```
---------------------------------------------------------
```
Level-1 Model

    Y = P0 + P1*(YEAR) + E

Level-2 Model

    P0 = B00 + R0
    P1 = B10 + R1

Level-3 Model

    B00 = G000 + U00
    B10 = G100 + U10

Next come the initial parameter estimates or "starting values." Users should not base inferences on these values, the sole purpose of which is to get the iterations started.

For starting values, data from 7230 level-1 and 1721 level-2 records were used

```
STARTING VALUES
---------------
Sigma_squared(0) =      0.29710

Tau(pi)(0)
  INTRCPT1,P0      0.71125        0.05143
       YEAR,P1     0.05143        0.01582

Tau(beta)(0)

   INTRCPT1            YEAR
   INTRCPT2,B00  INTRCPT2,B10
     0.14930         0.01473
     0.01473         0.01196
```

The value of the likelihood function at iteration 1 = -8.169527E+003
The value of the likelihood function at iteration 2 = -8.165377E+003
The value of the likelihood function at iteration 3 = -8.165024E+003
                                ...

Iterations stopped due to small change in likelihood function

******* ITERATION 9 *******

```
Sigma_squared =       0.30142
Standard Error of Sigma_squared =       0.00508
```

Final estimate of the level-1 variance.

```
Tau(pi)
  INTRCPT1,P0      0.64048        0.04678
       YEAR,P1     0.04678        0.01127
```

81

Final estimates of the level-2 variances and covariances.

```
Tau(pi) (as correlations)
 INTRCPT1,P0  1.000  0.551
     YEAR,P1  0.551  1.000
```

Note that the estimated correlation between true status at YEAR = 3.5 (halfway through third grade) and true rate of change is estimated to be 0.551 for children in the same school.

```
Standard Errors of Tau(pi)

 INTRCPT1,P0      0.02514      0.00499
     YEAR,P1      0.00499      0.00191
```

```
-----------------------------------------------------
 Random level-1 coefficient   Reliability estimate
-----------------------------------------------------
 INTRCPT1, P0                        0.839
     YEAR, P1                        0.190
-----------------------------------------------------
```

Reliabilities of child parameter estimates.

```
Tau(beta)
 INTRCPT1        YEAR
 INTRCPT2,B00 INTRCPT2,B10
    0.16532       0.01705
    0.01705       0.01102
```

Final estimates of the level-3 variances and covariances.

```
Tau(beta) (as correlations)
 INTRCPT1/INTRCPT2,B00  1.000  0.399
     YEAR/INTRCPT2,B10  0.399  1.000
```

Notice that the estimated correlation between true school mean status at YEAR = 3.5 and true school-mean rate of change is 0.399.

```
Standard Errors of Tau(beta)
 INTRCPT1        YEAR
 INTRCPT2,B00 INTRCPT2,B10
    0.03641       0.00720
    0.00720       0.00252
```

```
-----------------------------------------------------
 Random level-2 coefficient   Reliability estimate
-----------------------------------------------------
 INTRCPT1/INTRCPT2, B00              0.821
     YEAR/INTRCPT2, B10              0.786
-----------------------------------------------------
```

Reliabilities of school-level parameter estimates. These indicate the reliability with which we can discriminate among level-2 units using their least-squares estimates of β_0 and β_1. Low reliabilities do not invalidate the HLM analysis. Very low reliabilities (e.g., <.10), often indicate that a random coefficient might be considered fixed in subsequent analyses.

```
Final estimation of fixed effects:
-----------------------------------------------------------------
                                  Standard           Approx.
Fixed Effect        Coefficient   Error    T-ratio   d.f.   P-value
-----------------------------------------------------------------
For       INTRCPT1, P0
    For INTRCPT2, B00
      INTRCPT3, G000   -0.779309   0.057829   -13.476    59    0.000
    For    YEAR slope, P1
      For INTRCPT2, B10
      INTRCPT3, G100    0.763029   0.015263    49.993    59    0.000
-----------------------------------------------------------------
```

The above table indicates that the average growth rate is significantly positive at 0.763 logits per year, $t = 49.997$.

```
Final estimation of fixed effects
(with robust standard errors)
-----------------------------------------------------------------
                                  Standard           Approx.
Fixed Effect        Coefficient   Error    T-ratio   d.f.   P-value
-----------------------------------------------------------------
For       INTRCPT1, P0
    For INTRCPT2, B00
      INTRCPT3, G000   -0.779309   0.057830   -13.476    59    0.000
    For    YEAR slope, P1
      For INTRCPT2, B10
      INTRCPT3, G100    0.763029   0.015260    50.000    59    0.000
-----------------------------------------------------------------
```

Note that the results with and without robust standard errors are nearly identical. If the robust and model-based standard errors are substantially different, further investigation of the tenability of key assumptions (see Section 4.3 on examining residuals) is recommended.

```
Final estimation of level-1 and level-2 variance components:
-----------------------------------------------------------------
Random Effect       Standard     Variance    df    Chi-square   P-value
                    Deviation    Component
-----------------------------------------------------------------
INTRCPT1,      R0   0.80030      0.64049     1661   6046.38093   0.000
  YEAR slope,  R1   0.10595      0.01122     1661   2083.62359   0.000
  level-1,     E    0.54907      0.30148
-----------------------------------------------------------------

Final estimation of level-3 variance components:
-----------------------------------------------------------------
Random Effect       Standard     Variance    df    Chi-square   P-value
                    Deviation    Component
-----------------------------------------------------------------
INTRCPT1/INTRCPT2, U00   0.40658   0.16531    59    488.34492    0.000
    YEAR/INTRCPT2, U10   0.10498   0.01102    59    377.40852    0.000
-----------------------------------------------------------------
```

The results above indicate significant variability among schools in terms of mean status at YEAR = 3.5 (chi-square = 488.34499, df = 59) and in terms of school-mean rates of change (chi-square of 377.40852, df = 59).

```
Statistics for current covariance components model
-------------------------------------------------
Deviance                     = 16326.231292
Number of estimated parameters = 9
```

Exploratory Analysis: estimated level-2 coefficients and their standard errors obtained by regressing EB residuals on level-2 predictors selected for possible inclusion in subsequent HLM runs

```
--------------------------------------------------------------
Level-1 Coefficient          Potential Level-2 Predictors
--------------------------------------------------------------

                             FEMALE    BLACK  HISPANIC
     INTRCPT1, P0
        Coefficient          -0.011   -0.362   -0.033
        Standard Error        0.036    0.067    0.070
        t value              -0.312   -5.432   -0.465

                             FEMALE    BLACK  HISPANIC
        YEAR, P1
        Coefficient           0.001   -0.029    0.005
        Standard Error        0.003    0.006    0.006
        t value               0.369   -4.835    0.761
```

Exploratory Analysis: estimated level-3 coefficients and their standard errors obtained by regressing EB residuals on level-3 predictors selected for possible inclusion in subsequent HLM runs

```
--------------------------------------------------------------
Level-2 Predictor            Potential Level-3 Predictors
--------------------------------------------------------------

                             SIZE    LOWINC MOBILITY
INTRCPT1/INTRCPT2, B00
        Coefficient          -0.000   -0.009   -0.016
        Standard Error        0.000    0.002    0.004
        t value              -1.651   -5.100   -4.324

                             SIZE    LOWINC MOBILITY
     YEAR/INTRCPT2, B10
        Coefficient          -0.000   -0.001   -0.002
        Standard Error        0.000    0.000    0.001
        t value              -1.525   -2.871   -1.962
```

Just as in the case of the two-level program, the potential predictors not included in the model to be employed as significant predictors in subsequent models is indicated approximately by the "t-values" given above. Note: because of the metric of school size (100s and 1000s), the actual coefficients and standard errors are too small to be printed. The t-values are not, however.

4.3   Model checking based on the residual files

HLM3 produces three residual files, one each at levels 1 and 2 (see Chapter 2 for a discussion of these files) and one at level-3 (containing estimates of the βs). These files will contain the EB residuals defined at the various levels, fitted values, and OLS residuals, and EB coefficients. In addition, level-2 predictors can be included in the level-2 residual file and level-3 predictors in the level-3 residual file. However, other statistics provided in the residual file of HLM2, for example the Mahalanobis distance measures, are not available in the residual files produced by HLM3. The procedures for requesting level-3 residual files are similar to those for HLM2 as described in Section 2.5.4.

The files in this example are structured as SPSS data files and can be directly opened in SPSS. As with HLM2, the user can also specify STATA, SYSTAT or SAS command file format for the residual file. The result will be STATA, SYSTAT or SAS data files. (For more details see Section 2.5.4.) Alternatively, the data can be obtained in free form (*i.e.*, as a text file) by selecting the **Free Format** option on the **Create Level-3 Residual File** dialog box. These residual files can then be read into any other computing package. The list of variables in the level-3 residual file and their attributes are shown in Figure 4.8, while the first 10 records contained in this file are shown in Figure 4.10.

	Name	Type	Width	Deci	Label	Values	Missing	Columns	Align	Measure
1	l3id	String	12	0		None	None	7	Left	Nominal
2	nk	Numeric	8	0		None	None	5	Right	Scale
3	eb00	Numeric	12	3		None	None	7	Right	Scale
4	eb10	Numeric	12	3		None	None	6	Right	Scale
5	ol00	Numeric	12	3		None	-99.000	6	Right	Scale
6	ol10	Numeric	12	3		None	-99.000	6	Right	Scale
7	fv00	Numeric	12	3		None	None	5	Right	Scale
8	fv10	Numeric	12	3		None	None	5	Right	Scale
9	ec00	Numeric	12	3		None	None	6	Right	Scale
10	ec10	Numeric	12	3		None	None	5	Right	Scale
11	pv30000	Numeric	12	3		None	None	6	Right	Scale
12	pv31000	Numeric	12	3		None	None	5	Right	Scale
13	pv31010	Numeric	12	3		None	None	6	Right	Scale

Data View \ **Variable View**

SPSS Processor is ready

Figure 4.8   List of variables and attributes for level-3 residual file

An example of the level-2 residual file produced in the above analysis is shown in Figure 4.9. Only data from school 2020 are given.

We see that the level-3 ID (l3id) is the first variable and the level-2 ID (l2id) is the second. The third variable is njk, the number of observations associated with child j in school k. The empirical Bayes estimates of the residuals, r_{pjk}, are given next, including, respectively, the intercept (ebintrcp) and the year effect (ebyear). The ordinary least squares estimates of the same quantities (olintrcp and olyear); and the fitted values, that is, the predicted values of the π_{pjk}s for a given child based on the fixed effects (fvintrcp and fvyear) and random school effect, follow. These are followed by the EB coefficients. Finally, the posterior variances and covariances (pv200, pv210, and pv211) of the empirical Bayes estimates are given.

85

	l3id	l2id	njk	ebintrcp	ebyear	olintrcp	olyear	fvintrcp	fvyear	ecintrcp	ecyear	pv200	pv210	pv211
1	2020	273026452	3	.245	.004	.866	-.376	-.205	.953	.039	.957	.106	-.001	.007
2	2020	273030991	5	1.123	.124	1.136	.264	-.205	.953	.918	1.077	.077	.002	.006
3	2020	273059461	5	.644	.058	.685	.085	-.205	.953	.439	1.011	.077	.002	.006
4	2020	278058841	5	1.318	.099	1.451	.079	-.205	.953	1.113	1.052	.077	.002	.006
5	2020	292017571	3	1.301	.124	1.821	.808	-.205	.953	1.096	1.077	.114	.011	.008
6	2020	292020281	6	-.221	-.038	-.228	-.086	-.205	.953	-.426	.915	.070	.004	.006
7	2020	292020361	6	-.368	-.044	-.389	-.082	-.205	.953	-.573	.909	.070	.004	.006
8	2020	292025081	5	.180	.056	.089	.223	-.205	.953	-.026	1.009	.077	.002	.006
9	2020	292026211	5	-.202	-.043	-.151	-.152	-.205	.953	-.408	.910	.077	.002	.006
10	2020	292027291	5	.208	.050	.140	.186	-.205	.953	.002	1.003	.077	.002	.006
11	2020	292027531	5	.045	.015	.019	.062	-.205	.953	-.160	.968	.077	.002	.006
12	2020	292028181	5	-.779	-.055	-.867	-.028	-.205	.953	-.984	.898	.077	.002	.006

Figure 4.9 First 12 children in level-2 residual file

We see that the first child in the data set has schoolid 2020 and childid 273026452. That child has 3 time-series observations. The predicted growth rate for that child (the YEAR effect) is the fitted value .953. That child's empirical Bayes residual YEAR effect is .004. Thus, the EB coefficient ("ebyear") is computed as:

$$\begin{aligned} \pi^*_{1jk} &= \beta^*_{10k} + r^*_{1jk} \\ &= \text{FVYEAR} + \text{EBYEAR} \\ &= 0.953 + 0.004 \\ &= 0.957 \end{aligned} \tag{3.15}$$

The empirical Bayes estimate for the child's intercept, π^*_{0jk} ("ecintrcp"), is computed similarly.

The level-3 residual file, printed below, has a similar structure. Only the data for the first 10 schools are given. We see that the level-3 ID (l3id) is the first value given, and is followed by nk, the number of children in school k. This is followed by the empirical Bayes estimates of the βs, including, respectively, the intercept (eb00) and the *year* effect (eb10). The ordinary least squares estimates of the same quantities (ol00 and ol10); and the fitted values, that is, the predicted values of the βs for a given school based on that school's effect and the fixed effects (fv00 and fv01). The EB coefficients are given next. Finally, the posterior variances and covariances (pv30101, pv30201, and pv30202) of the estimates are given.

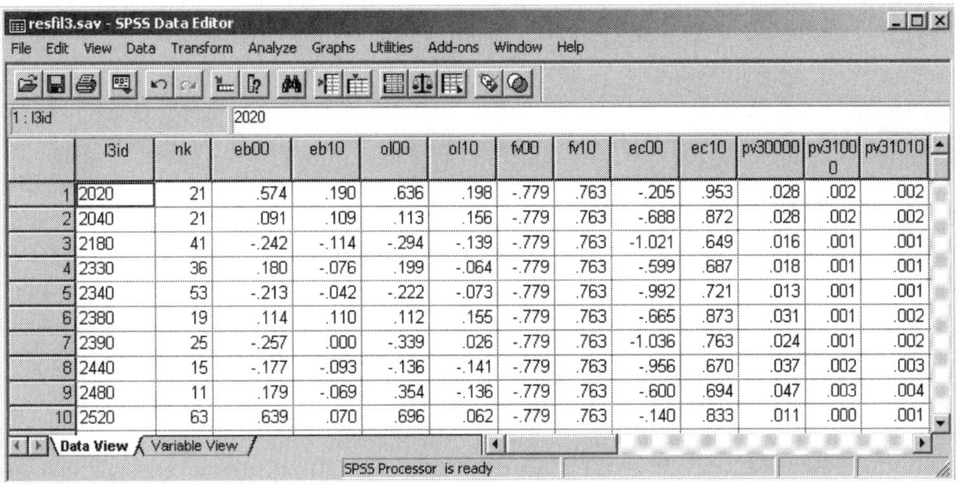
resfil3.sav - SPSS Data Editor

File Edit View Data Transform Analyze Graphs Utilities Add-ons Window Help

1 : l3id 2020

	l3id	nk	eb00	eb10	ol00	ol10	fv00	fv10	ec00	ec10	pv30000	pv31000	pv31010
1	2020	21	.574	.190	.636	.198	-.779	.763	-.205	.953	.028	.002	.002
2	2040	21	.091	.109	.113	.156	-.779	.763	-.688	.872	.028	.002	.002
3	2180	41	-.242	-.114	-.294	-.139	-.779	.763	-1.021	.649	.016	.001	.001
4	2330	36	.180	-.076	.199	-.064	-.779	.763	-.599	.687	.018	.001	.001
5	2340	53	-.213	-.042	-.222	-.073	-.779	.763	-.992	.721	.013	.001	.001
6	2380	19	.114	.110	.112	.155	-.779	.763	-.665	.873	.031	.001	.002
7	2390	25	-.257	.000	-.339	.026	-.779	.763	-1.036	.763	.024	.001	.002
8	2440	15	-.177	-.093	-.136	-.141	-.779	.763	-.956	.670	.037	.002	.003
9	2480	11	.179	-.069	.354	-.136	-.779	.763	-.600	.694	.047	.003	.004
10	2520	63	.639	.070	.696	.062	-.779	.763	-.140	.833	.011	.000	.001

Data View / Variable View

SPSS Processor is ready

Figure 4.10 First 10 schools in level-3 residual file

We see that the first unit, school 2020, has nk = 21 children. The predicted YEAR effect for school 2020 is the fitted value .763, that is, the maximum-likelihood estimate of the school mean growth rate in the case of this unconditional model. That school's empirical Bayes residual YEAR effect is .190. Thus HLM3 constructs the empirical Bayes estimate of that school's YEAR effect (mean rate of growth, "ec10") as

$$\beta^*_{10k} = \gamma^*_{100} + u^*_{1k} \;=\; \text{fv01} + \text{eb10} \qquad (3.16)$$

$$= .763 + .190 = .953.$$

Similarly, HLM3 constructs the empirical Bayes estimate for the school's intercept, β^*_{00k} ("ec00"), using fv00 + eb00.

Note that the empirical Bayes estimate of the school YEAR effect, 0.953, is the fitted value for each child in that school (in the level-2 residual file). This will be true in any model that is unconditional at level 2, that is, any model with no child-level predictors such as race, ethnicity or female. When level-2 predictors are in the model, the level-2 fitted values will also depend on those predictors.

4.4 Specification of a conditional model

The above example involves a model that is "unconditional" at levels 2 and 3; that is, no predictors are specified at each of those levels. Such a model is useful for partitioning variation in intercepts and growth rates into components that lie within and between schools (see *Hierarchical Linear Models*, Chapter 8), but provides no information on how child or school characteristics relate to the growth curves. Figure 4.11 shows a model that incorporates information about a child's race and ethnicity and a school's percent low income. Moreover, we explore the possibility that several other predictors (gender, school enrollment, and percent mobility) might help account for variation in subsequent models.

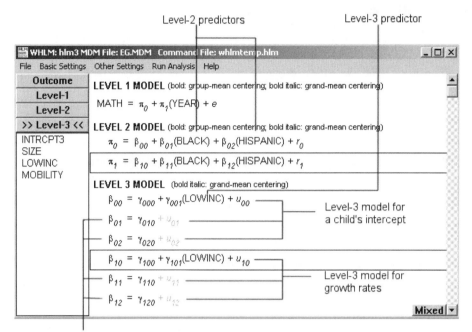

Level-2 predictors   Level-3 predictor

WHLM: hlm3 MDM File: EG.MDM   Command File: whlmtemp.hlm

File   Basic Settings   Other Settings   Run Analysis   Help

Outcome
Level-1
Level-2
>> Level-3 <<

INTRCPT3
SIZE
LOWINC
MOBILITY

LEVEL 1 MODEL (bold: group-mean centering; bold italic: grand-mean centering)

$$MATH = \pi_0 + \pi_1(YEAR) + e$$

LEVEL 2 MODEL (bold: group-mean centering; bold italic: grand-mean centering)

$$\pi_0 = \beta_{00} + \beta_{01}(BLACK) + \beta_{02}(HISPANIC) + r_0$$

$$\pi_1 = \beta_{10} + \beta_{11}(BLACK) + \beta_{12}(HISPANIC) + r_1$$

LEVEL 3 MODEL (bold italic: grand-mean centering)

$$\beta_{00} = \gamma_{000} + \gamma_{001}(LOWINC) + u_{00}$$
$$\beta_{01} = \gamma_{010} + u_{01}$$
$$\beta_{02} = \gamma_{020} + u_{02}$$
$$\beta_{10} = \gamma_{100} + \gamma_{101}(LOWINC) + u_{10}$$
$$\beta_{11} = \gamma_{110} + u_{11}$$
$$\beta_{12} = \gamma_{120} + u_{12}$$

Level-3 model for
a child's intercept

Level-3 model for
growth rates

Mixed ▼

Effects associated with race/ethnicity are assumed to
be invariant across schools (*i.e.*, fixed)

Figure 4.11   Model window for the public school example

The results of the analysis are given below.

```
Problem Title: LINEAR GROWTH OVER GRADE, MINORITY, LOW INCOME
The data source for this run  = EG.MDM
The command file for this run = C:\HLM\Examples\Chapter4\eg2.mlm
Output file name              = C:\HLM\Examples\Chapter4\hlm3.txt
The maximum number of level-1 units = 7230
The maximum number of level-2 units = 1721
The maximum number of level-3 units = 60
The maximum number of iterations = 100
Method of estimation: full maximum likelihood
```

```
The model specified for the fixed effects was:
----------------------------------------------------
    Level-1             Level-2             Level-3
    Coefficients        Predictors          Predictors
--------------------    ---------------     ---------------
        INTRCPT1, P0        INTRCPT2, B00       INTRCPT3, G000
                                                LOWINC, G001
                        #      BLACK, B01       INTRCPT3, G010
                        # HISPANIC, B02         INTRCPT3, G020
YEAR slope, P1          INTRCPT2, B10       INTRCPT3, G100
                                                LOWINC, G101


                        #      BLACK, B11       INTRCPT3, G110
                        # HISPANIC, B12         INTRCPT3, G120
'#' - The residual parameter variance for the parameter has been set to zero
```

Summary of the model specified (in equation format)

Level-1 Model
   Y = P0 + P1*(YEAR) + E

Level-2 Model
   P0 = B00 + B01*(BLACK) + B02*(HISPANIC) + R0
   P1 = B10 + B11*(BLACK) + B12*(HISPANIC) + R1

Level-3 Model
   B00 = G000 + G001(LOWINC) + U00
   B01 = G010
   B02 = G020
   B10 = G100 + G101(LOWINC) + U10
   B11 = G110
   B12 = G120

 STARTING VALUES

 Sigma_squared(0) =   0.29710

Tau(pi)(0)
 INTRCPT1,P0   0.69259   0.04914
      YEAR,P1   0.04914   0.01481

Tau(beta)(0)
 INTRCPT1   YEAR
 INTRCPT2,B00 INTRCPT2,B10
   0.05922   0.00290
   0.00290   0.01057

The value of the likelihood function at iteration 1 = -8.127397E+003
The value of the likelihood function at iteration 2 = -8.121908E+003
The value of the likelihood function at iteration 3 = -8.121269E+003
The value of the likelihood function at iteration 4 = -8.121059E+003
The value of the likelihood function at iteration 5 = -8.120942E+003
                                    ...
The value of the likelihood function at iteration 5 = -8.120942E+003
The value of the likelihood function at iteration 6 = -8.119607E+003
The value of the likelihood function at iteration 7 = -8.119604E+003
The value of the likelihood function at iteration 8 = -8.119604E+003

Iterations stopped due to small change in likelihood function

******* ITERATION 9 *******

Sigma_squared =   0.30162
 Standard Error of Sigma_squared =   0.00660

Tau(pi)
 INTRCPT1,P0   0.62231   0.04657
      YEAR,P1   0.04657   0.01106

```
Tau(pi) (as correlations)
 INTRCPT1,P0  1.000  0.561
     YEAR,P1  0.561  1.000

Standard Errors of Tau(pi)
 INTRCPT1,P0       0.02451      0.00491
     YEAR,P1       0.00491      0.00196


 ----------------------------------------------------
  Random level-1 coefficient   Reliability estimate
 ----------------------------------------------------
  INTRCPT1, P0                      0.835
      YEAR, P1                      0.188
 ----------------------------------------------------

Tau(beta)
 INTRCPT1          YEAR
 INTRCPT2,B00  INTRCPT2,B10
    0.07808       0.00082
    0.00082       0.00798

Tau(beta) (as correlations)
 INTRCPT1/INTRCPT2,B00  1.000  0.033
     YEAR/INTRCPT2,B10  0.033  1.000

Standard Errors of Tau(beta)
 INTRCPT1          YEAR
 INTRCPT2,B00  INTRCPT2,B10
    0.01991       0.00441
    0.00441       0.00194


 ----------------------------------------------------
  Random level-2 coefficient   Reliability estimate
 ----------------------------------------------------
  INTRCPT1/INTRCPT2, B00            0.702
      YEAR/INTRCPT2, B10            0.735
 ----------------------------------------------------
```

The value of the likelihood function at iteration 9 = -8.119604E+003

Final estimation of fixed effects:

Fixed Effect	Coefficient	Standard Error	T-ratio	Approx. d.f.	P-value
For INTRCPT1, P0					
For INTRCPT2, B00					
INTRCPT3, G000	0.140628	0.127486	1.103	58	0.275
LOWINC, G001	-0.007578	0.001691	-4.482	58	0.000
For BLACK, B01					
INTRCPT3, G010	-0.502091	0.077879	-6.447	1718	0.000
For HISPANIC, B02					
INTRCPT3, G020	-0.319381	0.086099	-3.709	1718	0.000
For YEAR slope, P1					
For INTRCPT2, B10					
INTRCPT3, G100	0.874501	0.039144	22.340	58	0.000
LOWINC, G101	-0.001369	0.000523	-2.619	58	0.012
For BLACK, B11					
INTRCPT3, G110	-0.030918	0.022453	-1.377	1718	0.169
For HISPANIC, B12					
INTRCPT3, G120	0.043085	0.024652	1.748	1718	0.080

Final estimation of fixed effects
 (with robust standard errors)

Fixed Effect	Coefficient	Standard Error	T-ratio	Approx. d.f.	P-value
For INTRCPT1, P0					
For INTRCPT2, B00					
INTRCPT3, G000	0.140628	0.113814	1.236	58	0.222
LOWINC, G001	-0.007578	0.001396	-5.428	58	0.000
For BLACK, B01					
INTRCPT3, G010	-0.502091	0.076842	-6.534	1718	0.000
For HISPANIC, B02					
INTRCPT3, G020	-0.319381	0.081918	-3.899	1718	0.000
For YEAR slope, P1					
For INTRCPT2, B10					
INTRCPT3, G100	0.874501	0.037287	23.453	58	0.000
LOWINC, G101	-0.001369	0.000499	-2.744	58	0.009
For BLACK, B11					
INTRCPT3, G110	-0.030918	0.022274	-1.388	1718	0.165
For HISPANIC, B12					
INTRCPT3, G120	0.043085	0.024368	1.768	1718	0.077

Final estimation of level-1 and level-2 variance components:

Random Effect		Standard Deviation	Variance Component	df	Chi-square	P-value
INTRCPT1,	R0	0.78886	0.62231	1659	7983.94604	0.000
YEAR slope,	R1	0.10518	0.01106	1659	2090.47655	0.000
level-1,	E	0.54920	0.30162			

Final estimation of level-3 variance components:

Random Effect	Standard Deviation	Variance Component	df	Chi-square	P-value
INTRCPT1/INTRCPT2, U00	0.27943	0.07808	58	254.98866	0.000
YEAR/INTRCPT2, U10	0.08935	0.00798	58	277.25277	0.000

Statistics for current covariance components model

Deviance   = 16239.207232
Number of estimated parameters = 15

Exploratory Analysis: estimated level-2 coefficients and their standard errors obtained
by regressing EB residuals on level-2 predictors selected for possible inclusion in
subsequent runs

Level-1 Coefficient	Potential Level-2 Predictors

	FEMALE
INTRCPT1, P0	
Coefficient	-0.010
Standard Error	0.036
t value	-0.273
	FEMALE
YEAR, P1	
Coefficient	0.001
Standard Error	0.003
t value	0.454

```
Exploratory Analysis: estimated level-3 coefficients and their standard errors obtained
by regressing EB residuals on level-3 predictors selected for possible inclusion in
subsequent runs

-------------------------------------------------------------------
   Level-2 Predictor              Potential Level-3 Predictors
-------------------------------------------------------------------

                               SIZE  MOBILITY
INTRCPT1/INTRCPT2, B00
     Coefficient             -0.000  -0.007
     Standard Error           0.000   0.002
     t value                 -0.717  -2.824

                               SIZE  MOBILITY
YEAR/INTRCPT2, B10
     Coefficient             -0.000  -0.000
     Standard Error           0.000   0.001
     t value                 -1.155  -0.540
```

4.5   Other program features

The options available for HLM3 are similar to those available with HLM2. The differences are outlined below.

4.5.1 Basic specifications

The level-3 residual files may also be specified. They are specified similarly to the level-2 residuals.

4.5.2 Iteration control

The **Mode of iteration acceleration** section of this screen is primarily intended for people who have data large enough to cause the accelerator (and final) iterations to take a prohibitive amount of time. While for most data the 2nd derivative option is recommended, users with large amounts of data (particularly with large ratios of level-1 to level-2 data) may find the 1st derivative Fisher useful, although this will make the standard errors of σ^2 and the Tau matrices more crude.   If the third option, **No accelerator**, is selected, there will be *no* Fisher iterations will be performed. This will make large MDMs run faster, but will have the side effect of not producing standard errors of σ^2 and the tau matrices. If you want to suppress any Fisher iterations, but do want to have the above mentioned standard errors, choose 1st or 2nd derivative Fisher, and set the value in the **Frequency of accelerator** box to the number of iterations + 1.

4.5.3 Estimation settings

HLM3 has the EM Laplace option for the Bernoulli HGLM models only.

4.5.4 Hypothesis testing

HLM3 does not have the test of level-1 homogeneity.

4.5.5 Output settings

HLM3 output does not include OLS estimates.

5 Conceptual and Statistical Background for Hierarchical Generalized Linear Models (HGLM)

The hierarchical linear model (HLM) as described in the previous four chapters is appropriate for two- and three-level data where the random effects at each level are normally distributed. The assumption of normality at level-1 is quite widely applicable when the outcome variable is continuous. Even when a continuous outcome is highly skewed, a transformation can often be found that will make the distribution of level-1 random effects (residuals) at least roughly normal. Methods for assessing the normality of random effects at higher levels are discussed on page 38 and on page 274 of *Hierarchical Linear Models*.

There are important cases, however, where the assumption of normality at level-1 is clearly not realistic and no transformation can make it so. Examples of a binary outcome, Y, are: the presence of a disease ($Y = 1$ if the disease is present, $Y = 0$ if the disease is absent), graduation from high school ($Y = 1$ if a student graduates on time, $Y = 0$ if not), or the commission of a crime ($Y = 1$ if a person commits a crime during a given time interval, $Y = 0$ if not). The use of the standard level-1 model in this case would be inappropriate for three reasons:

- Given the predicted value of the outcome, the level-1 random effect can take on only one of two values, and therefore cannot be normally distributed.

- The level-1 random effect cannot have homogeneous variance. Instead, the variance of this random effect depends on the predicted value as specified below.

- Finally, there are no restrictions on the predicted values of the level-1 outcome in the standard model: they can legitimately take on any real value. In contrast, the predicted value of a binary outcome Y, if viewed as the predicted probability that $Y = 1$, cannot meaningfully be less than zero or greater than unity. Thus, an appropriate model for predicting Y ought to constrain the predicted values to lie in the interval $(0, 1)$. Without this constraint the effect sizes estimated by the model are, in general, uninterpretable.

Another example involves count data, where Y is the number of crimes a person commits during a year or Y is the number of questions a child asks during the course of a one-hour class period. In these cases, the possible values of Y are non-negative integers 0, 1, 2, ... Such data will typically be positively skewed. If there are very few zeros in the data, a transformation, *e.g.*, $Y^* = \log(1 + Y)$, may solve this problem and allow sensible use of the standard HLM. However, in the cases mentioned above, there will typically be many zeros (many persons will not commit a crime during a given year and many children will not raise a question during a one-hour class). When there are many zeros, the normality assumption cannot be approximated by a transformation. Also, as in the case of the binary outcome, the variance of the level-1 random effects will depend on the predicted value (higher predicted values will have larger variance). Similarly, the predicted values ought to be constrained to be positive.

Another example involves multi-category (≥ 2) data, where the outcome comprises of responses tapping teachers' commitment to their career choice. Teachers are asked if they would choose the teaching profession if they could go back to college and start over again. The three response categories are:

1. yes, I would choose teaching again
2. not sure
3. no, I would not choose teaching again.

Such outcomes can be studied using a multinomial model. Thus, as discussed previously for models with binary outcomes, the use of the standard level-1 model would be inappropriate. Another model one may use is an ordinal model, which treats the categories as ordered.

Within HLM, the user can specify a non-linear analysis appropriate for counts and binary, multinomial, or ordinal data. The approach is a direct extension of the generalized linear model of McCullagh & Nelder (1989) to the case of hierarchical data. We therefore refer to this approach as a "hierarchical generalized linear model" (HGLM). The execution of these analyses is in many ways similar to that in HLM, but there are also important differences.

5.1 The two-level HLM as a special case of HGLM

The level-1 model in the HGLM may be viewed as consisting of three parts: a sampling model, a link function, and a structural model. In fact, the standard HLM can be viewed as a special case of the HGLM where the sampling model is normal and the link function is the identity link.

5.1.1 Level-1 sampling model

The sampling model for a two-level HLM might be written as

$$Y_{ij} \mid \mu_{ij} \sim NID(\mu_{ij}, \sigma^2) \tag{5.1}$$

meaning that the level-one outcome Y_{ij}, given the predicted value, μ_{ij}, is normally and independently distributed with an expected value of μ_{ij} and a constant variance, σ^2. The level-1 expected value and variance may alternatively be written as

$$E(Y_{ij} \mid \mu_{ij}) = \mu_{ij} \qquad Var(Y_{ij} \mid \mu_{ij}) = \sigma^2 . \tag{5.2}$$

5.1.2 Level-1 link function

In general it is possible to transform the level-1 predicted value, μ_{ij}, to η_{ij} to insure that the predictions are constrained to lie within a given interval. Such a transformation is called a link function. In the normal case, no transformation is necessary. However, this decision not to transform may be made explicit by writing

$$\eta_{ij} = \mu_{ij} . \tag{5.3}$$

The *link function* in this case is viewed as the "identity link function."

5.1.3 Level-1 structural model

The transformed predicted value is now related to the predictors through the linear model or "structural model"

$$\eta_{ij} = \beta_{0j} + \beta_{1j} X_{1ij} + \beta_{2j} X_{2ij} + \cdots + \beta_{Qj} X_{Qij} . \tag{5.4}$$

It is clear that combining the level-1 sampling model (5.1), the level-1 link function (5.3), and the level-1 structural model (5.4) reproduces the level-1 model of HLM (1.1). In the context of a standard HLM, it seems silly to write three equations where only one is needed, but the value of the extra equations becomes apparent in the case of binary, count, and multi-categorical data.

5.2 Two- and three-level models for binary outcomes

While the standard HLM uses a normal sampling model and an identity link function, the binary outcome model uses a binomial sampling model and a logit link. Only the level-1 models differ from the linear case.

5.2.1 Level-1 sampling model

Let Y_{ij} be the number of "successes" in m_{ij} trials. Then we write that

$$Y_{ij} \mid \phi_{ij} \sim B\left(m_{ij}, \phi_{ij}\right),$$

(5.5)

to denote that Y_{ij} has a binomial distribution with m_{ij} trials and probability of success ϕ_{ij}. According to the binomial distribution, the expected value and variance of Y_{ij} are then

$$E(Y_{ij} \mid \phi_{ij}) = m_{ij}\phi_{ij} \quad Var(Y_{ij} \mid \phi_{ij}) = m_{ij}\phi_{ij}\left(1 - \phi_{ij}\right).$$

(5.6)

When $m_{ij} = 1$, Y_{ij} may take on values of either zero or unity. This is a special case of the binomial distribution known as the Bernoulli distribution. HGLM allows estimation of models in which $m_{ij} = 1$ (Bernoulli case) or $m_{ij} > 1$ (other binomial cases). The case with $m_{ij} > 1$ will be treated later.

For the Bernoulli case, the predicted value of the binary Y_{ij} is equal to the probability of a success, ϕ_{ij}.

5.2.2 Level-1 link function

When the level-1 sampling model is binomial, HGLM uses the logit link function

$$\eta_{ij} = \log\left(\frac{\phi_{ij}}{1 - \phi_{ij}}\right).$$

(5.7)

In words, η_{ij} is the log of the odds of success. Thus if the probability of success, ϕ_{ij}, is 0.5, the odds of success is 1.0 and the log-odds or "logit" is zero. When the probability of success is less than 0.5, the odds are less than one and the logit is negative; when the probability is greater than 0.5, the odds are greater than unity and the logit is positive. Thus, while ϕ_{ij} is constrained to be in the interval $(0,1)$, η_{ij} can take on any real value.

5.2.3 Level-1 structural model

This will have exactly the same form as (5.4). Note that estimates of the β s in (5.4) make it possible to generate a predicted log-odds (η_{ij}) for any case. Such a predicted log-odds can be converted to an odds by computing odds = exponential (η_{ij}). Similarly, predicted log-odds can be converted to a *predicted probability* by computing

$$\phi_{ij} = \frac{1}{1 + \exp\left(-\eta_{ij}\right)}.$$ (5.8)

Clearly, whatever the value of η_{ij}, applying (5.8) will produce a ϕ_{ij} between zero and unity.

5.2.4 Level-2 and Level-3 models

In the case of a two-level analysis, the level-2 model has the same form as used in a standard 2-level HLM (equations 1.2, 1.3, and 1.4). In the case of a three-level analysis, the level-2 and level-3 models are also the same as in a standard 3-level HLM.

5.3 The model for count data

For count data, we use a Poisson sampling model and a log link function.

5.3.1 Level-1 sampling model

Let Y_{ij} be the number of events occurring during an interval of time having length m_{ij}. For example, Y_{ij} could be the number of crimes a person i from group j commits during five years, so that $m_{ij} = 5$. The time-interval of m_{ij} units may be termed the "exposure." Then we write that

$$Y_{ij} \mid \lambda_{ij} \sim P(m_{ij}, \lambda_{ij})$$ (5.9)

to denote that Y_{ij} has a Poisson distribution with exposure m_{ij} and event rate λ_{ij}. According to the Poisson distribution, the expected value and variance of Y_{ij} are then

$$E(Y_{ij} \mid \lambda_{ij}) = m_{ij}\lambda_{ij} \quad Var(Y_{ij} \mid \lambda_{ij}) = m_{ij}\lambda_{ij}.$$ (5.10)

The exposure m_{ij} need not be a measure of time. For example, if Y_{ij} is the number of bombs dropping on neighborhood i of city j during a war, m_{ij} could be the area of that neighborhood. A common case arises when, for each i and j, the exposure is the same (*e.g.*, Y_{ij} is the number of crimes committed during one year for each person i within each neighborhood j). In this case, we set $m_{ij} = 1$ for simplicity. HGLM allows estimation of models in which $m_{ij} = 1$ or $m_{ij} \geq 1$. (The case with $m_{ij} \geq 1$ will be treated later.)

According to our level-1 model, the predicted value of Y_{ij} when $m_{ij} = 1$ will be the event rate λ_{ij}.

5.3.2 Level-1 link function

HGLM uses the log link function when the level-1 sampling model is Poisson, that is

$$\eta_{ij} = \log(\lambda_{ij}). \tag{5.11}$$

In words, η_{ij} is the log of the event rate. Thus, if the event rate, λ_{ij}, is one, the log is zero. When the event rate is less than one, the log is negative; when the event rate is greater than one, the log is positive. Thus, while λ_{ij} is constrained to be non-negative, η_{ij} can take on any real value.

5.3.3 Level-1 structural model

This will have exactly the same form as (5.4). Note that estimates of the β s in (5.4) make it possible to generate a predicted log-event rate (η_{ij}) for any case. Such a predicted log-event rate can be converted to an event rate by computing

$$\lambda_{ij} = \text{event rate} = \exp(\eta_{ij})$$

Clearly, whatever the value of η_{ij}, λ_{ij} will be non-negative.

5.3.4 Level-2 model

The level-2 model has the same form as the level-2 model for HLM2 (equations 1.2, 1.3, and 1.4), and the level-2 and level-3 models have the same form in the three-level case as in HLM3.

99

5.4 The model for multinomial data

For multi-category nominal data, we use a multinomial model and a logit link function. This is an extension of the Bernoulli model with more than two possible outcomes.

5.4.1 Level-1 sampling model

Let

$$\text{Prob}\left(R_{ij} = m\right) = \phi_{ij},$$

that is, the probability that person i in group j lands in category m is ϕ_{ij}, for categories $m = 1, ..., M$, there being M possible categories.

For example, $R_{ij} = 1$ if high school student i in school j goes on to college; $R_{ij} = 2$ if that student goes on to a job; $R_{ij} = 3$ if that student becomes unemployed. Here $M = 3$. The analysis is facilitated by constructing dummy variables $Y_1, Y_2, ..., Y_M$, where $Y_{mij} = 1$ if $R_{ij} = m$, 0 otherwise. For example, if student ij goes to college, $R_{ij} = 1$, so $Y_{1ij} = 1$, $Y_{2ij} = 0$, $Y_{3ij} = 0$; if student ij goes to work, $R_{ij} = 2$, so $Y_{1ij} = 0$, $Y_{2ij} = 1$, $Y_{3ij} = 0$; if that student becomes unemployed, $R_{ij} = 3$, so $Y_{1ij} = 0$, $Y_{2ij} = 0$, $Y_{3ij} = 1$. This leads to a definition of the probabilities as $\text{Prob}\left(Y_{mij} = 1\right) = \phi_{mij}$. For example, for $M = 3$,

$$\text{Prob}\left(Y_{1ij} = 1\right) = \phi_{1ij}$$
$$\text{Prob}\left(Y_{2ij} = 1\right) = \phi_{2ij} \tag{5.12}$$
$$\text{Prob}\left(Y_{3ij} = 1\right) = \phi_{3ij} = 1 - \phi_{1ij} - \phi_{2ij}$$

Note that because $Y_{3ij} = 1 - Y_{1ij} - Y_{2ij}$, Y_{3ij} is redundant.

According to the multinomial distribution, the expected value and variance of Y_{mij} given ϕ_{mij}, are then

$$E\left(Y_{mij} \mid \phi_{mij}\right) = \phi_{mij} \qquad Var\left(Y_{mij} \mid \phi_{mij}\right) = \phi_{mij}\left(1 - \phi_{mij}\right). \tag{5.13}$$

The covariance between outcomes Y_{mij} and $Y_{m'ij}$ is

$$Cov\left(Y_{mij}, Y_{m'ij}\right) = \phi_{mij}\phi_{m'ij}. \tag{5.14}$$

5.4.2 Level-1 link function

HGLM uses the logit link function when the level-1 sampling model is multinomial. Define η_{mij} as the log-odds of falling into category m relative to that of falling into category M. Specifically

$$\eta_{mij} = \log\left(\frac{\phi_{mij}}{\phi_{Mij}}\right) \tag{5.15}$$

where

$$\phi_{Mij} = 1 - \sum_{m=1}^{M-1} \phi_{mij}. \tag{5.16}$$

In words, η_{mij} is the log odds of being in m-th category relative to the M-th category, which is known as the "reference category."

5.4.3 Level-1 structural model

At level-1, we have

$$\eta_{mij} = \beta_{0j(m)} + \sum_{q=1}^{Q} \beta_{qj(m)} X_{qij}, \tag{5.17}$$

for $m = 1, ..., (M-1)$. For example, with $M = 3$, there would be two level-1 equations, for η_{1ij} and η_{2ij}.

5.4.4 Level-2 model

The level-2 model has a parallel form

$$\beta_{qj(m)} = \gamma_{q0(m)} + \sum_{s=1}^{S_q} \gamma_{qs(m)} W_{sj} + u_{qj(m)}. \tag{5.18}$$

Thus, for $M = 3$, there would be two sets of level-2 equations.

5.5　The model for ordinal data

5.5.1 Level-1 sampling model

Again a person falls into category m and there are M possible categories, so $m = 1, ..., M$. But now the categories are ordered. Given the ordered nature of the data, we derive the M dummy variables $Y_{mij}, ..., Y_{(M-1)ij}$ for case i in unit j as

$$Y_{mij} = 1 \quad \text{if} \quad R_{ij} \leq m, \quad 0 \quad \text{otherwise.} \tag{5.19}$$

For example, with $M = 3$, we have

$$\begin{aligned} Y_{1ij} &= 1 \quad \text{if} \quad R_{ij} = 1 \\ Y_{2ij} &= 1 \quad \text{if} \quad R_{ij} \leq 2 \end{aligned} \tag{5.20}$$

The probabilities $\text{Prob}\left(Y_{mij} = 1\right)$ are thus cumulative probabilities. For example, with $M = 3$,

$$\begin{aligned} \text{Prob}\left(Y_{1ij} = 1\right) &= \text{Prob}\left(R_{ij} = 1\right) = \phi_{1ij} \\ \text{Prob}\left(Y_{2ij} = 1\right) &= \text{Prob}\left(R_{ij} = 1\right) + \text{Prob}\left(R_{ij} = 2\right) = \phi_{2ij} \\ \text{Prob}\left(Y_{3ij} = 1\right) &= \text{Prob}\left(R_{ij} = 1\right) + \text{Prob}\left(R_{ij} = 2\right) + \text{Prob}\left(R_{ij} = 3\right) = 1 \end{aligned} \tag{5.21}$$

Since $Y_{3ij} = 1 - Y_{2ij}$, Y_{3ij} is redundant. We actually need only $M - 1$ dummy variables.

Associated with the cumulative probabilities are the cumulative logits,

$$\eta_{mij} = \log\left(\frac{\text{Prob}\left(R_{ij} \leq m\right)}{\text{Prob}\left(R_{ij} > m\right)}\right) = \log\left(\frac{\phi_{mij}}{1 = \phi_{mij}}\right). \tag{5.22}$$

5.5.2 Level-1 structural model

The level-1 structural model assumes "proportional odds",

$$\eta_{mij} = \beta_{0j} + \sum_{q=1}^{Q} \beta_{qj} X_{qij} + \sum_{m=2}^{M} \delta_m. \tag{5.23}$$

Under the proportional odds assumption, the relative odds that $R_{ij} \leq m$, associated with a unit increase in the predictor, does not depend on m.

Here δ_m is a "threshold" that separates categories $m-1$ and m. For example, when $M = 4$,

$$\eta_{1ij} = \beta_{0j} + \sum_{q=1}^{Q} \beta_{qj} X_{qij}$$

$$\eta_{2ij} = \beta_{0j} + \sum_{q=1}^{Q} \beta_{qj} X_{qij} + \delta_2 \qquad (5.24)$$

$$\eta_{3ij} = \beta_{0j} + \sum_{q=1}^{Q} \beta_{qj} X_{qij} + \delta_2 + \delta_3$$

5.6 Parameter estimation

HGLM uses two approaches to estimation for HGLM. The first method bases inference on the joint posterior modes of the level-1 and level-2 (and level-3) regression coefficients given the variance-covariance estimates. The variance-covariance estimates are based on a normal approximation to the restricted likelihood. Stiratelli, Laird, & Ware (1984) and Wong & Mason (1985) developed this approach for the binary case. Schall (1991) discusses the extension of this approach to the wider class of generalized linear models. Breslow & Clayton (1993) refer to this estimation approach as "penalized quasi-likelihood" or PQL. Extending HLM to HGLM requires a doubly iterative algorithm, significantly increasing computational time. Related approaches are described by Goldstein (1991), Longford (1993), and Hedeker & Gibbons (1994).

The second method of estimation ("Laplace") involves a somewhat more computationally intensive algorithm but provides accurate approximation to maximum likelihood (ML). This approach is currently available for two-level and three-level Bernoulli models and for two-level Poisson models with $m_{ij} = 1$. We consider PQL below in some detail followed by a brief discussion of Laplace.

5.6.1 Estimation via PQL

The approach can be presented heuristically by computing a "linearized dependent variable" as in the generalized linear model of McCullagh and Nelder (1989). Basically, the analysis involves use of a standard HLM model with the introduction of special weighting at level-1. However, after this standard HLM analysis has converged, the linearized dependent variable and the weights must be recomputed. Then, the standard HLM analysis is re-computed. This iterative process of analyses and recomputing weights and linearized dependent variable continues until estimates converge.

We term the standard HLM iterations "micro-iterations." The recomputation of the linearized dependent variable and the weights constitute a "macro iteration." The approach is outlined below for four cases: Bernoulli (binomial with $m_{ij} = 1$), Poisson with $m_{ij} = 1$, binomial with $m_{ij} > 1$, and Poisson with $m_{ij} > 1$.

5.6.1.1   Bernoulli (binomial with $m_{ij} = 1$)

Consider the model

$$Y_{ij} = \phi_{ij} + \varepsilon_{ij} \qquad (5.25)$$

with ϕ_{ij} defined as in Equation 5.8 and

$$E(\varepsilon_{ij}) = 0 \qquad Var(\varepsilon_{ij}) = w_{ij} = \phi_{ij}(1 - \phi_{ij}). \qquad (5.26)$$

We now substitute for ϕ_{ij} its linear approximation with

$$\phi_{ij} \approx \phi_{ij}^{(0)} + \frac{\partial \phi_{ij}^{(i)}}{\partial \eta_{ij}^{(i)}}\left(\eta_{ij} - \eta_{ij}^{(0)}\right) \qquad (5.27)$$

$$\eta_{ij}^{(0)} = \log\left(\frac{\phi_{ij}^{(0)}}{1 - \phi_{ij}^{(0)}}\right), \qquad (5.28)$$

where $\phi_{ij}^{(0)}$ is an initial estimate and

$$\frac{\partial \phi_{ij}}{\partial \eta_{ij}} = w_{ij} = \phi_{ij}(1 - \phi_{ij}). \qquad (5.29)$$

If we evaluate w_{ij} at its initial estimates

$$w_{ij}^{(0)} = \phi_{ij}^{(0)}(1 - \phi_{ij}^{(0)}). \qquad (5.30)$$

(5.25) can be written as

$$Y_{ij} = \phi_{ij}^{(0)} + w_{ij}^{(0)}\left(\eta_{ij} - \eta_{ij}^{(0)}\right) + \varepsilon_{ij}. \qquad (5.31)$$

Algebraically rearranging the equation so that all observables are on the left-hand side yields

$$Z_{ij}^{(0)} = \eta_{ij} + \frac{\varepsilon_{ij}}{w_{ij}^{(0)}}$$

$$= \beta_{0j} + \beta_{1j} X_{1ij} + \beta_{2j} X_{2ij} + \cdots + \beta_{Qj} X_{Qij} + e_{ij},$$

(5.32)

where

$$Z_{ij}^{(0)} = \frac{Y_{ij} - \phi_{ij}^{(0)}}{w_{ij}^{(0)}} + \eta_{ij}^{(0)}$$

(5.33)

is the linearized dependent variable and

$$Var(e_{ij}) = Var\left(\frac{\varepsilon_{ij}}{w_{ij}^{(0)}}\right) \approx \frac{1}{w_{ij}^{(0)}}.$$

(5.34)

Thus, (5.32) is a standard HLM level-1 model with outcome $Z_{ij}^{(0)}$ and level-1 weighting variable $w_{ij}^{(0)}$. The algorithm works as follows.

1. Given initial estimates of the predicted value, ϕ_{ij}, and therefore of the linearized dependent variable, Z_{ij}, and the weight, w_{ij}, compute a weighted HLM analysis with (5.32) as the level-1 model.

2. The HLM analysis from step 1 will produce new predicted values and thus new linearized dependent variables and weights. HLM will now compute a new, re-weighted MDM file with the appropriate linearized dependent variable and weights.

3. Based on the new linearized dependent variable and weights, re-compute step 1.

This process goes on until the linearized dependent variable, the weights, and therefore, the parameter estimates, converge to a pre-specified tolerance. The program then stops.

5.6.1.2 Poisson with $m_{ij} = 1$

The procedure is exactly the same as in the binomial case with $m_{ij} = 1$ except that

$$Var(\varepsilon_{ij}) = w_{ij} = \frac{\partial \lambda_{ij}}{\partial \eta_{ij}} = \lambda_{ij}. \tag{5.35}$$

5.6.1.3 Binomial with $m_{ij} > 1$

In the previous example, Y_{ij} was formally the number of successes in one trial and therefore could take on a value of 0 or 1. We now consider the case where Y_{ij} is the number of successes in m_{ij} trials, where Y_{ij} and m_{ij} are non-negative integers, $Y_{ij} \leq m_{ij}$.

Suppose that a researcher is interested in examining the relationship between pre-school experience (yes or no) and grade retention and wonders whether this relationship is similar for males and females. The design involves students at level 1 nested within schools at level 2. In this case, each school would have four "cell counts" (boys with and without pre-school and girls with and without pre-school). Thus, the data could be organized so that every school had four observations (except possibly schools without variation on pre-school or sex), where each observation was a cell having a cell size m_{ij} and a cell count Y_{ij} of students in that cell who were, in fact, retained. One could then re-conceptualize the study as having up to four level-1 units (cells); the outcome Y_{ij}, given the cell probability ϕ_{ij}, would be distributed as $B(m_{ij}, \phi_{ij})$. There would be three level-1 predictors (a contrast for pre-school experience, a contrast for sex, and an interaction contrast). This problem then has the structure of a $2 \times 2 \times J$ contingency table (pre-school experience by sex by school) with the last factor viewed as random.

The structure of a level-1 file for group 2 might appear as follows.

Group	ID	n_{ij}	Y_{ij}	X_{1ij}	X_{2ij}	X_{3ij}
Girls with pre-school	2	n_{12}	Y_{12}	0.50	0.50	0.25
Girls without pre-school	2	n_{22}	Y_{22}	0.50	-0.50	-0.25
Boys with pre-school	2	n_{32}	Y_{32}	-0.50	0.50	-0.25
Boys without pre-school	2	n_{42}	Y_{42}	-0.50	-0.50	0.25

For example, n_{12} is the number of girls in school 2 with pre-school and Y_{12} is the number of those girls who were retained. The predictor X_{1ij} is a contrast coefficient to assess the effect of sex (0.5 if female, –0.5 if male); X_{2ij} is a contrast for pre-school experience (0.5 if yes, –0.5 if no), and $X_{3ij} = X_{1ij} \times X_{2ij}$ is the interaction contrast.

Estimation works the same in this case as in the binomial case except that

$$Z_{ij} = \frac{Y_{ij} - m_{ij}\phi_{ij}}{w_{ij}} + \eta_{ij} \tag{5.36}$$

with

$$w_{ij} = m_{ij}\phi_{ij}(1-\phi_{ij}). \tag{5.37}$$

5.6.1.4   Poisson with $m_{ij} > 1$

Consider now a study of the number of homicides committed within each of j neighborhoods in a large city. Many neighborhoods will have no homicides. The expected number of homicides in a neighborhood will depend not only on the homicide rate for that neighborhood, but also on the size of that neighborhood as indexed by its number of residents, m_{ij}. Level-1 variables might include characteristics of the homicide (*e.g.*, whether the homicide involved a domestic dispute, whether it involved use of a gun). Each cell (*e.g.*, the four types of homicide as defined by the cross-classification of domestic – yes or no – and use of a gun – yes or no) would be a level-1 unit.

Estimation in this case is the same as in the Poisson case with $m_{ij} = 1$ except that

$$Z_{ij} = \frac{Y_{ij} - m_{ij}\lambda_{ij}}{w_{ij}} + \eta_{ij} \qquad (5.38)$$

and

$$w_{ij} = m_{ij}\lambda_{ij}. \qquad (5.39)$$

5.6.2 Properties of the estimators

Using PQL, HGLM produces approximate empirical Bayes estimates of the randomly varying level-1 coefficients, generalized least squares estimators of the level-2 (and level-3) coefficients, and approximate maximum-likelihood estimators of the variance and covariance parameters. Yang (1995) has conducted a simulation study of these estimators in comparison with an alternative approach used by some programs that sets the level-2 random coefficients to zero in computing the linearized dependent variables. Breslow & Clayton (1993) refer to this alternative approach as "marginalized quasi-likelihood" or MQL. Rodriquez & Goldman (1995) had found that MQL produced biased estimates of the level-2 variance and the level-2 regression coefficients. Yang's results showed a substantial improvement (reduction in bias and mean squared error) in using the approach of HGLM. In particular, the bias in estimation of the level-2 coefficients was never more than 10 percent for HGLM, while the MQL approach commonly produced a bias between 10 and 20 percent. HGLM performed better than the alternative approach in estimating a level-2 variance component as well. However, a negative bias was found in estimating this variance component, ranging between two percent and 21 percent. The bias was most severe when the true variance was very large and the typical "probability of success" was very small (or, equivalently, very large). Initial simulation results under the Poisson model appear somewhat more favorable than this. Breslow & Clayton (1993) suggest that the estimation will be more efficient as the level-1 sample size increases.

5.6.3 Parameter estimation: A high-order Laplace approximation of maximum likelihood

For two- and three-level Bernoulli models and for two-level Poisson models with constant exposure, HGLM provides an alternative to estimation via PQL. The alternative uses a high-order approximation to the likelihood based on a Laplace transform and is therefore called "Laplace 6." Simulations by Yang (1998) and by Raudenbush, Yang, and Yosef (1998) show that this approach produces a remarkably accurate approximation to maximum likelihood (ML) estimates of all parameters. In the case of two-level data, a new implementation of the Laplace method is implemented via the EM algorithm in HLM 6. We find that this EM approach provides more reliable convergence than does the Fisher scoring approach used in HLM 5.

5.7 Unit-specific and population-average models

The models described above have been termed "unit-specific" models. They model the expected outcome for a level-2 unit conditional on a given set of random effects. For example, in the Bernoulli case ($m_{ij} = 1$), we might have a level-1 (within-school) model

$$\eta_{ij} = \beta_{0j} + \beta_{qj} X_{ij}, \tag{5.40}$$

and a level-2 (between-school) model

$$\begin{aligned} \beta_{0j} &= \gamma_{00} + \gamma_{01} W_j + u_{0j} \\ \beta_{1j} &= \gamma_{10} \end{aligned} \tag{5.41}$$

leading to the combined model

$$\eta_{ij} = \gamma_{00} + \gamma_{01} W_j + \gamma_{10} X_{ij} + u_{0j}. \tag{5.42}$$

Under this model, the predicted probability for case ij, given u_{0j}, would be

$$E\left(Y_{ij} \mid u_{0j}\right) = \frac{1}{1 + \exp\left\{-\left(\gamma_{00} + \gamma_{01} W_j + \gamma_{10} X_{ij} + u_{0j}\right)\right\}}. \tag{5.43}$$

In this model γ_{10} is the expected difference in the log-odds of "success" between two students who attend the same school but differ by one unit on X (holding u_{0j} constant); γ_{01} is the expected difference in the log-odds of success between two students who have the same value on W but attend schools differing by one unit on W (holding u_{0j} constant). These definitions parallel definitions used in a standard HLM for continuous outcomes.

However, one might also want to know the average difference between log-odds of success of students having the same X but attending schools differing by one unit on W, that is, the difference of interest *averaging over all possible values of* u_{0j}. In this case, the unit-specific model would not be appropriate. The model that would be appropriate would be a "population-average" model (Zeger, Liang, & Albert, 1988). The distinction is tricky in part because it does not arise in the standard HLM (with an identity link function). It arises only in the case of a non-linear link function.

Using the same example as above, the population average model would be

$$E\left(Y_{ij}\right) = \frac{1}{1 + \exp\left\{-\left(\gamma_{00}^* + \gamma_{01}^* W_j + \gamma_{10}^* X_{ij}\right)\right\}}. \tag{5.44}$$

Notice that (5.41) does not condition on (or "hold constant") the random effect u_{0j}. Thus, γ_{01}^* gives the expected difference in log-odds of success between two students with the same X who attend schools differing by one unit on W – without respect to the random effect, u_{0j}. If one had a nationally representative sample and could validly assign a causal inference to W, γ_{01}^* would be the change in the log-odds of success in the whole society associated with boosting W by one unit while γ_{01} would be the change in log-odds associated with boosting W one unit for those schools sharing the same value of u_{0j}.

HGLM produces estimates for both the unit-specific and population-average models. The population-average results are based on generalized least squares given the variance-covariance estimates from the unit-specific model. Moreover, HGLM produces robust standard error estimates for the population-average model (Zeger, *et al.*, 1988). These standard errors are relatively insensitive to misspecification of the variances and covariances at the two levels and to the distributional assumptions at each level. The method of estimation used in HGLM for the population-average model is equivalent to the "generalized estimating equation" (GEE) approach popularized by Zeger, *et al.* (1988).

The following differences between unit-specific and population-average results are to be expected:

- If all predictors are held constant at their means, and if their means are zero, the population-average intercept can be used to estimate the average probability of success across the entire population, that is

$$\hat{\phi}_{ij} = \frac{1}{1 + \exp(-\gamma_{00}^*)}. \tag{5.45}$$

  This will not be true of unit-specific intercepts unless the average probability of success is very close to .5.
- Coefficient estimates (other than the intercept) based on the population-average model will often tend to be similar to those based on the unit-specific model but will tend to be smaller in absolute value.

Users will need to take care in choosing unit-specific versus population-average results for their research. The choice will depend on the specific research questions that are of interest. In the previous example, if one were primarily interested in how a change in W can be expected to affect a particular individual school's mean, one would use the unit-specific model. If one were interested in how a change in W can be expected to affect the overall population mean, one would use the population-average model.

5.8 Over-dispersion and under-dispersion

As mentioned earlier, if the data follow the assumed level-1 sampling model, the level-1 variance of the Y_{ij} will be w_{ij} where

$$\begin{aligned}
w_{ij} &= m_{ij}\phi_{ij}(1-\phi_{ij}), &&\text{Binomial case, or} \\
w_{ij} &= m_{ij}\lambda_{ij}, &&\text{Poisson case.}
\end{aligned} \tag{5.46}$$

However, if the level-1 data do not follow this model, the actual level-1 variance may be larger than that assumed (over-dispersion) or smaller than that assumed (under-dispersion). For example, if undetected clustering exists within level-1 units or if the level-1 model is under-specified, extra-binomial or extra-Poisson dispersion may arise. This problem can be handled in a variety of ways; HGLM allows estimation of a scalar variance so that the level-1 variance will be $\sigma^2 w_{ij}$.

5.9 Restricted versus full PQL versus full ML

The default method of estimation for the two-level HGLM is restricted PQL, while full PQL is an option. For the three-level HGLM, PQL estimation is by means of full PQL only. All Laplace6 estimates involve full ML.

5.10 Hypothesis testing

The logic of hypothesis testing with HGLM is quite similar to that used in the case of HLM. Thus, for the fixed effects (the γs), a table of approximate t-values is routinely printed for univariate tests; multivariate tests for the fixed effects are available using the approach described earlier in Chapter 2. Similarly, univariate tests for variance components (approximate chi-squares) are also routinely printed out. The one exception is that multivariate tests based on comparing model deviances (-2 log likelihood at convergence) are not available using PQL, because PQL is based on quasi-likelihood rather than maximum-likelihood estimation. These are available using Laplace6.

6 Fitting HGLMs (Nonlinear Models)

There is no difference between HGLM ("nonlinear analysis") and HLM ("linear analysis") in the construction of the MDM file. Thus, the same MDM file can be used for nonlinear and linear analysis.

6.1   Executing nonlinear analyses based on the MDM file

Model specification for nonlinear analyses, as in the case of linear analyses, can be achieved via Windows (PC implementation only), interactive execution, or batch execution. The mechanics of model specification are generally the same as in linear analyses with the following differences:

- Six types of nonlinear analysis are available. With Windows execution, these options are displayed in the **Basic Model Specifications – HLM2** dialog box (See Figure 6.1). This dialog box is accessed by clicking the **Outcome** button at the top of the variable listbox to the left of the main HLM window. There are two choices for dichotomous outcomes, two for count outcomes, one for multinomial outcomes, and one for ordinal outcomes.

- Highly accurate Laplace approximation to maximum likelihood option is available for 2- and 3-level Bernoulli models and for 2-level Poisson models through the **Estimation Settings – HLM2** dialog box shown in Figure 6.3.

- If desired, an over-dispersion option is available for binomial and Poisson models. This option is not available with Laplace (see Figure 6.3). To specify over-dispersion, set the σ^2 value to **computed** in the **Estimation Settings – HLM2** dialog box (see Figure 6.3).

- As mentioned, the nonlinear analysis is doubly iterative so the maximum number of macro iterations can be specified as well as the maximum number of micro iterations. Similarly, convergence criteria can be reset for macro iterations as well as micro iterations.[2] The number of iterations and method of estimation is set through the **Iteration Control – HLM2** dialog box shown in Figure 6.2.

---

[2]The overall accuracy of the parameter estimates is determined by the convergence criterion for macro iterations. The convergence criterion for micro iterations will influence the number of micro iterations per macro iteration. The default specifications stop macro iterations when the largest parameter estimate change is less than 10^{-4}; micro iterations within macro iterations stop when the conditional log likelihood (conditional on the current weights and values of the linearized dependent variable) changes by less than 10^{-6}.

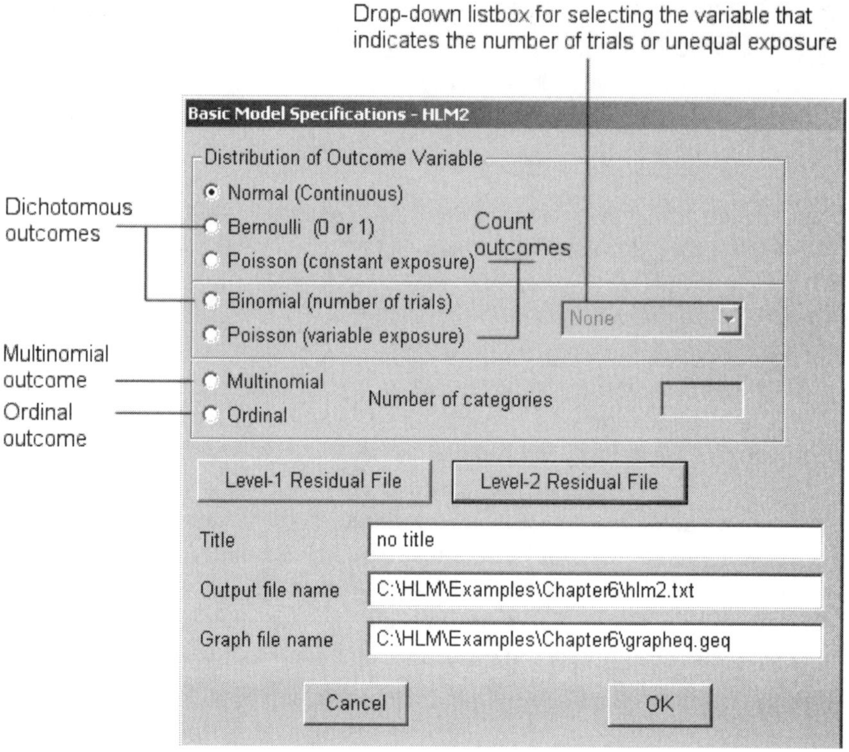

Drop-down listbox for selecting the variable that indicates the number of trials or unequal exposure

Figure 6.1 **Basic Model Specifications – HLM2 dialog box**

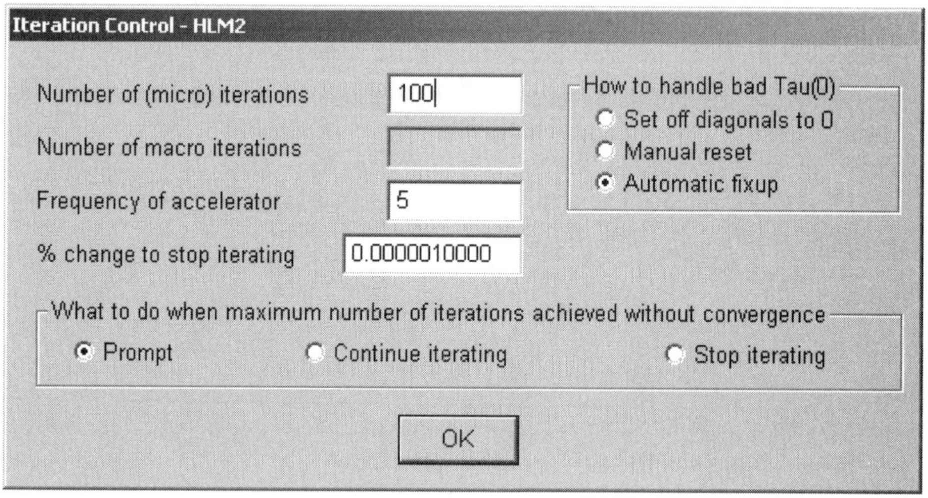

Figure 6.2 **Iteration Control – HLM2 dialog box**

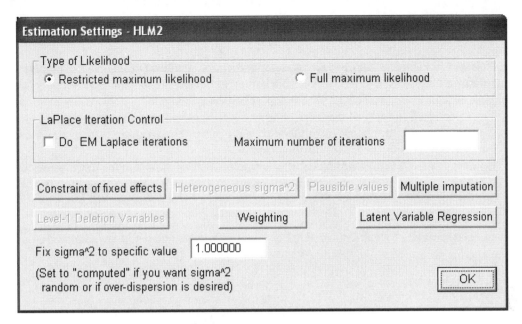

Figure 6.3   Estimation Settings – HLM2 dialog box

Below we provide two detailed examples of nonlinear analyses: the first uses the Bernoulli model, that is, a binomial model with the number of trials, m_{ij}, equal to one. The second example uses a binomial model with $m_{ij} > 1$. The analogs of these two analyses for count data are, respectively, the Poisson model with equal exposure and the Poisson case with variable exposure (some brief notes about these two applications are also included). Finally, we furnish two examples for multi-category outcomes, one for multinomial data and one for ordinal data. Windows mode specification is illustrated. See Appendix C for interactive and batch specification.

6.2   Case 1: a Bernoulli model

Data are from a national survey of primary education in Thailand (see Raudenbush & Bhumirat, 1992, for details), conducted in 1988, and yielding, for our analysis, complete data on 7516 sixth graders nested within 356 primary schools. Of interest is the probability that a child will repeat a grade during the primary years (REP1 = 1 if yes, 0 if no). It is hypothesized that the sex of the child (MALE = 1 if male, 0 of female), the child's pre-primary experience (PPED = 1 if yes, 0 if no), and the school mean SES (MSESC) will be associated with the probability of repetition. Every level-1 record corresponds to a student, with a single binary outcome per student, so the model type is Bernoulli. These data (level-1 and level-2) data files are UTHAIL1.SAV and THAI2.SAV.

Below are the Windows commands for specifying a Bernoulli model.

To specify a Bernoulli model

1. After specifying the outcome in the model specification window (REP1 in our example), click the **Outcome** button at the top of the variable listbox to the left of the main HLM window to open the **Basic Model Specifications – HLM2** dialog box (See Figure 6.1).
2. Select **Bernoulli (0 or 1)** as there is one binary outcome per level-1 unit.
3. (Optional) Specify the maximum number of macro and micro iterations by selecting the **Iteration Settings** option from the **Other Settings** menu.
4. (Optional) Select **Laplace approximation** by selecting this option on the **Estimation Settings – HLM2** dialog box, which is accessed by selecting the **Estimation Settings** options from the **Other Settings** menu (See sections 6.8 and 5.6.3).

The model described above is displayed in Figure 6.4 in both standard and mixed model notation. The command file for the model is THAIU1.HLM.

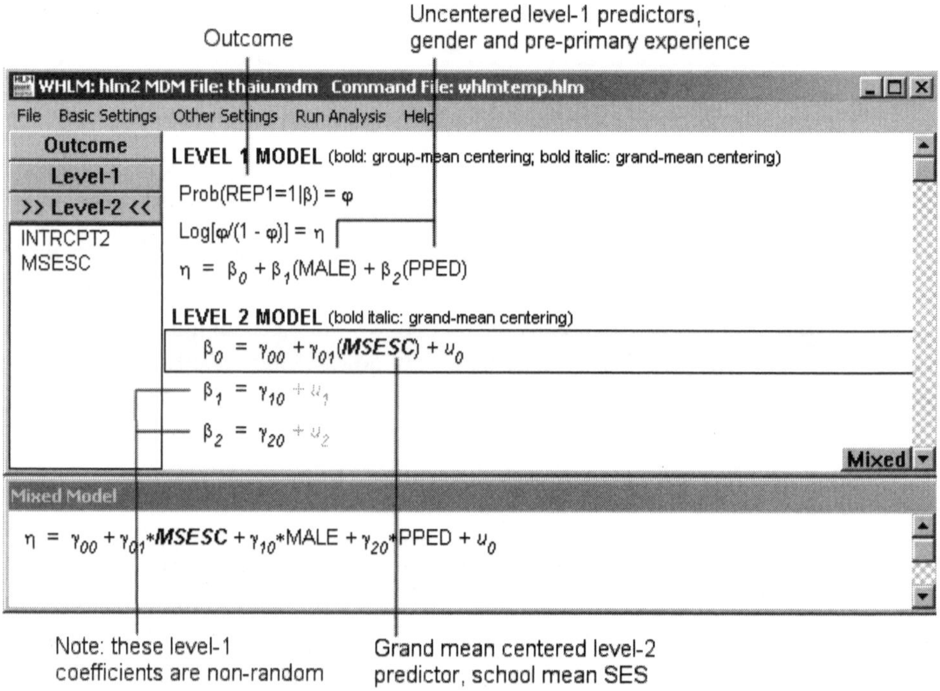

Figure 6.4   Model specification window for the Bernoulli model

Below we provide a transcript of the messages that HLM2 sent to the iteration window during computation of the results.

```
                          MACRO ITERATION 1

Starting values computed.  Iterations begun.
Should you wish to terminate the iterations prior to convergence, enter cntl-c
The value of the likelihood function at iteration 1 = -2.400265E+003
The value of the likelihood function at iteration 2 = -2.399651E+003
The value of the likelihood function at iteration 3 = -2.399620E+003
The value of the likelihood function at iteration 4 = -2.399614E+003
The value of the likelihood function at iteration 5 = -2.399612E+003
The value of the likelihood function at iteration 6 = -2.399612E+003
The value of the likelihood function at iteration 7 = -2.399612E+003
```

Macro iteration number 1 has converged after seven micro iterations. This macro iteration actually computes the linear-model estimates (using the identity link function as if the level-1 errors were assumed normal). These results are then transformed and input to start macro iteration 2, which is, in fact, the first nonlinear iteration.

```
                          MACRO ITERATION 2

Starting values computed.  Iterations begun.
Should you wish to terminate the iterations prior to convergence, enter cntl-c
The value of the likelihood function at iteration 1 = -1.067218E+004
The value of the likelihood function at iteration 2 = -1.013726E+004
The value of the likelihood function at iteration 3 = -1.011008E+004
The value of the likelihood function at iteration 4 = -1.010428E+004
The value of the likelihood function at iteration 5 = -1.010265E+004
The value of the likelihood function at iteration 6 = -1.010193E+004
The value of the likelihood function at iteration 7 = -1.010188E+004
The value of the likelihood function at iteration 8 = -1.010188E+004
The value of the likelihood function at iteration 9 = -1.010187E+004
The value of the likelihood function at iteration 10 = -1.010187E+004
The value of the likelihood function at iteration 11 = -1.010187E+004
The value of the likelihood function at iteration 12 = -1.010187E+004
```

Macro iteration 2, the first nonlinear macro iteration, converged after twelve micro iterations.

```
                          MACRO ITERATION 8

Starting values computed.  Iterations begun.
Should you wish to terminate the iterations prior to convergence, enter cntl-c
The value of the likelihood function at iteration 1 = -1.000374E+004
The value of the likelihood function at iteration 2 = -1.000374E+004
```

Note that macro iteration 8 converged with just 2 micro iterations. Macro iteration 8 was the final "unit-specific" macro iteration. One final "population-average" iteration is computed. Its output is given below.

```
MACRO ITERATION 9

Starting values computed.  Iterations begun.
Should you wish to terminate the iterations prior to convergence, enter cntl-c
The value of the likelihood function at iteration 1 = -1.011638E+004
The value of the likelihood function at iteration 2 = -1.010710E+004
The value of the likelihood function at iteration 3 = -1.010710E+004
```

Next, we examine the output file THAIBERN.OUT.

```
SPECIFICATIONS FOR THIS NONLINEAR HLM RUN

    Problem Title: Bernoulli output, Thailand data
    The data source for this run  = C:\HLM\THAIUGRP.MDM
    The command file for this run = C:\HLM\THAIU1.HLM
    Output file name              = C:\HLM\THAIBERN.OUT
    The maximum number of level-1 units = 7516
    The maximum number of level-2 units = 356
    The maximum number of micro iterations = 20
    Method of estimation: restricted PQL
    Maximum number of macro iterations = 25


    Distribution at Level-1: Bernoulli

    The outcome variable is      REP1

    The model specified for the fixed effects was:
    ----------------------------------------------------------
    Level-1                  Level-2
    Coefficients             Predictors
    ----------------------   ----------------
          INTRCPT1, B0       INTRCPT2, G00
   $                         MSESC, G01
   #      MALE slope, B1     INTRCPT2, G10
   #      PPED slope, B2     INTRCPT2, G20

 '#' - The residual parameter variance for this level-1 coefficient has been set
       to zero.
 '$' - This level-2 predictor has been centered around its grand mean.

    The model specified for the covariance components was:
    ----------------------------------------------------------
          Tau dimensions
              INTRCPT1

 Summary of the model specified (in equation format)
 ----------------------------------------------------------
 Level-1 Model
 Prob(Y=1|B) = P
```

This is the program's way of saying that the level-1 sampling model is Bernoulli; the above equation, written with subscripts and Greek letters, is

$$\mathrm{Prob}(Y_{ij} = 1 \mid \beta_j) = \phi_{ij}.$$

```
log[P/(1-P)] = B0 + B1*(MALE) + B2*(PPED)
```

Thus, the level-1 structural model is

$$\eta_{ij} = \log\left[\frac{\phi_{ij}}{1-\phi_{ij}}\right] = \beta_{0j} + \beta_{1j}\left(\mathrm{MALE}\right)_{ij} + \beta_{2j}\left(\mathrm{PPED}\right)_{ij}$$

```
Level-2 Model
B0 = G00 + G01*(MSESC) + U0
B1 = G10
B2 = G20
```

And the level-2 structural model is

$$\beta_{0j} = \gamma_{00} + \gamma_{01}(\text{MSESC})_{ij} + u_{0j}$$
$$\beta_{1j} = \gamma_{10}$$
$$\beta_{2j} = \gamma_{20}.$$

```
Level-1 variance = 1/[P(1-P)]
```

In the metric of the linearized dependent variable, the level-1 variance is the reciprocal of the Bernoulli variance, $\phi_{ij}(1-\phi_{ij})$.

Three sets of output results appear below: those for the normal linear model with identity link function, those for the unit-specific model with logit link function, and those for the population-average model with logit link. Typically, only the latter 2 sets of results will be relevant for drawing conclusions. The linear model with identity link is estimated simply to obtain starting values for the estimation of the models with logit link.

```
RESULTS FOR LINEAR MODEL WITH THE IDENTITY LINK FUNCTION

 Sigma_squared =        0.12181

 Tau
 INTRCPT1,B0       0.01910

Tau (as correlations)
 INTRCPT1,B0  1.000


-------------------------------------------------------
 Random level-1 coefficient   Reliability estimate
-------------------------------------------------------
 INTRCPT1, B0                        0.750
-------------------------------------------------------
The value of the likelihood function at iteration 6 = -2.414933E+003

 Estimation of fixed effects: (linear model with identity link function)
----------------------------------------------------------------------
                                   Standard          Approx.
 Fixed Effect         Coefficient  Error    T-ratio  d.f.     P-value
----------------------------------------------------------------------
 For        INTRCPT1, B0
 INTRCPT2, G00           0.154789  0.010809  14.320    354    0.000
     MSESC, G01         -0.002865  0.022245  -0.129    354    0.898
 For       MALE slope, B1
 INTRCPT2, G10           0.054209  0.008330   6.507   7512    0.000
 For       PPED slope, B2
 INTRCPT2, G20          -0.066803  0.010832  -6.167   7512    0.000
----------------------------------------------------------------------


RESULTS FOR NON-LINEAR MODEL WITH THE LOGIT LINK FUNCTION: Unit-Specific Model
(macro iteration 8)

 Tau
 INTRCPT1,B0       1.30261
```

```
Tau (as correlations)
INTRCPT1,BO   1.000


------------------------------------------------------
Random level-1 coefficient   Reliability estimate
------------------------------------------------------
INTRCPT1, BO                         0.683
------------------------------------------------------


The value of the likelihood function at iteration 2 = -1.000998E+004

Final estimation of fixed effects: (Unit-specific model)
```

Fixed Effect	Coefficient	Standard Error	T-ratio	Approx. d.f.	P-value
For INTRCPT1, BO					
INTRCPT2, G00	-2.039237	0.093806	-21.739	354	0.000
MSESC, G01	-0.019450	0.192184	-0.101	354	0.920
For MALE slope, B1					
INTRCPT2, G10	0.509358	0.073941	6.889	7512	0.000
For PPED slope, B2					
INTRCPT2, G20	-0.609174	0.095290	-6.393	7512	0.000

Fixed Effect	Coefficient	Odds Ratio	Confidence Interval
For INTRCPT1, BO			
INTRCPT2, G00	-2.039237	0.130128	(0.108,0.156)
MSESC, G01	-0.019450	0.980738	(0.672,1.430)
For MALE slope, B1			
INTRCPT2, G10	0.509358	1.664222	(1.440,1.924)
For PPED slope, B2			
INTRCPT2, G20	-0.609174	0.543800	(0.451,0.655)

```
Final estimation of fixed effects
(Unit-specific model with robust standard errors)
```

Fixed Effect	Coefficient	Standard Error	T-ratio	Approx. d.f.	P-value
For INTRCPT1, BO					
INTRCPT2, G00	-2.039237	0.095106	-21.442	354	0.000
MSESC, G01	-0.019450	0.197203	-0.099	354	0.922
For MALE slope, B1					
INTRCPT2, G10	0.509358	0.075933	6.708	7512	0.000
For PPED slope, B2					
INTRCPT2, G20	-0.609174	0.093749	-6.498	7512	0.000

Fixed Effect	Coefficient	Odds Ratio	Confidence Interval
For INTRCPT1, BO			
INTRCPT2, G00	-2.039237	0.130128	(0.108,0.157)
MSESC, G01	-0.019450	0.980738	(0.666,1.445)
For MALE slope, B1			
INTRCPT2, G10	0.509358	1.664222	(1.434,1.931)
For PPED slope, B2			
INTRCPT2, G20	-0.609174	0.543800	(0.453,0.653)

Final estimation of variance components:
```
--------------------------------------------------------------------------
Random Effect              Standard    Variance    df    Chi-square  P-value
                           Deviation   Component
--------------------------------------------------------------------------
INTRCPT1,        U0        1.14132     1.30261     354   1443.31192  0.000
--------------------------------------------------------------------------
```

RESULTS FOR NON-LINEAR MODEL WITH THE LOGIT LINK FUNCTION:
Population Average Model

The value of the likelihood function at iteration 2 = -1.010986E+004

Final estimation of fixed effects: (Population-average model)
```
----------------------------------------------------------------------------
                                      Standard            Approx.
        Fixed Effect      Coefficient  Error    T-ratio    d.f.    P-value
----------------------------------------------------------------------------
For          INTRCPT1, B0
    INTRCPT2, G00         -1.738257    0.087800  -19.798    354    0.000
       MSESC, G01         -0.006736    0.182496   -0.037    354    0.971
For      MALE slope, B1
    INTRCPT2, G10          0.447045    0.067032    6.669   7512    0.000
For      PPED slope, B2
    INTRCPT2, G20         -0.549532    0.087499   -6.280   7512    0.000
----------------------------------------------------------------------------
```

```
-----------------------------------------------------------------
                                      Odds       Confidence
        Fixed Effect      Coefficient  Ratio      Interval
-----------------------------------------------------------------
For          INTRCPT1, B0
    INTRCPT2, G00         -1.738257    0.175827   (0.148,0.209)
       MSESC, G01         -0.006736    0.993286   (0.694,1.421)
For      MALE slope, B1
    INTRCPT2, G10          0.447045    1.563685   (1.371,1.783)
For      PPED slope, B2
    INTRCPT2, G20         -0.549532    0.577220   (0.486,0.685)
-----------------------------------------------------------------
```

Notice that the results for the population-average model are quite similar to the results for the unit-specific model except in the case of the intercept. The intercept in the population-average model in this case is the expected log-odds of repetition for a person with values of zero on the predictors (and therefore, for a female without pre-primary experience attending a school of average SES). In this case, this expected log-odds corresponds to a probability of $1/(1+\exp\{1.738257\}) = .149$, which is the "population-average" repetition rate for this group. In contrast, the unit-specific intercept is the expected log-odds of repetition rate for the same kind of student, but one who attends a school that not only has a mean SES of 0, but also has a random effect of zero (that is, a school with a "typical" repetition rate for the school of its type). This conditional expected log-odds is -2.039237, corresponding to a probability of $1/(1+\exp\{2.039237\}) = .115$. Thus the probability of repetition is lower in a school with a random effect of zero than the average in the population of schools having mean SES of zero taken as a whole. This is a typical result. Population-average probabilities will be closer to .50 (than will the corresponding unit-specific probabilities).

One final set of results is printed out: population-average results with robust standard errors (below). Note that the robust standard errors in this case are very similar to the model-based standard errors, with a slight increase for the level-2 predictor and slight decreases for level-1 predictors. Results for other data may not follow this pattern.

Final estimation of fixed effects
(Population-average model with robust standard errors)
```
-----------------------------------------------------------------------
                                      Standard           Approx.
     Fixed Effect       Coefficient   Error    T-ratio   d.f.    P-value
-----------------------------------------------------------------------
For         INTRCPT1,  B0
    INTRCPT2,  G00       -1.738257    0.082556  -21.056    354    0.000
       MSESC,  G01       -0.006736    0.174783   -0.039    354    0.970
For      MALE slope,  B1
    INTRCPT2,  G10        0.447045    0.062832    7.115   7512    0.000
For      PPED slope,  B2
    INTRCPT2,  G20       -0.549532    0.079679   -6.897   7512    0.000
-----------------------------------------------------------------------
```

```
-----------------------------------------------------------------------
                                       Odds        Confidence
     Fixed Effect       Coefficient    Ratio       Interval
-----------------------------------------------------------------------
For         INTRCPT1,  B0
    INTRCPT2,  G00       -1.738257    0.175827    (0.150,0.207)
       MSESC,  G01       -0.006736    0.993286    (0.705,1.400)
For      MALE slope,  B1
    INTRCPT2,  G10        0.447045    1.563685    (1.383,1.769)
For      PPED slope,  B2
    INTRCPT2,  G20       -0.549532    0.577220    (0.494,0.675)
-----------------------------------------------------------------------
```

6.3   Case 2: a binomial model (number of trials, $m_{ij} \geq 1$)

A familiar example of two-level binomial data is the number of hits, Y_{ij}, in game i for baseball player j based on m_{ij} at bats. In an experimental setting, a subject j under condition i might produce Y_{ij} successes in m_{ij} trials.

A common use of a binomial model is when analysts do not have access to the raw data at level 1. For example, one might know the proportion of children passing a criterion-referenced test within each of many schools. This proportion might be broken down within schools by sex and grade. A binomial model could be used to analyze such data. The cases would be sex-by-age "cells" within each school where Y_{ij} is the number passing within cell i of school j and m_{ij} is the number of "trials," that is, the number of children in that cell. Sex and grade would be level-1 predictors.

Indeed, in the previous example, although raw level-1 data were available, the two level-1 predictors, MALE and pre-primary experience, were categorical. For illustration, we reorganized these data so that each school had, potentially, four cells defined by the cross-classification of sex and pre-primary experience:

- females without pre-primary experience
- females with pre-primary experience

- males without pre-primary experience
- males with pre-primary experience

Level-1 predictors were the same as before, with MALE = 1 if male, 0 if female; PPED = 1 if pre-primary experience, 0 if not. The outcome is the number of children in a particular cell who repeated a grade, and we created a variable TRIAL, which is the number of children in each cell. In some schools there were no children of a certain type (*e.g.*, no females with pre-primary experience). Such schools would have fewer than four cells. The necessary steps for executing the analysis via the Windows interface are given below.

To specify a Binomial model

1. After specifying the outcome in the model specification window (REP1 in our example), click the **Outcome** button at the top of the variable listbox to the left of the main HLM window to open the **Basic Model Specifications – HLM2** dialog box (See Figure 6.1).

2. Select **Binomial (number of trials)**.

3. Select the variable from the pull down menu in the dialog box which indicates number of trials (TRIAL in our example) (See Figure 6.1).

4. (Optional) Specify the maximum number of macro and micro iterations by selecting the **Iteration Settings** option from the **Other Settings** menu.

5. (Optional) Select the **Over-dispersion** option if appropriate (See section on *Additional Features* at the end of the chapter).

The model described above uses the same predictors at level-1 and level-2 as those in the Bernoulli example (see Figure 6.5). The command file for the example is THAIBNML.HLM.

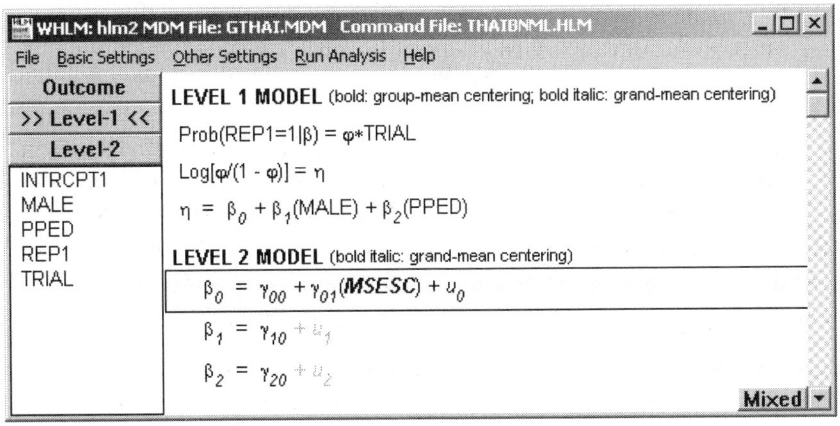

WHLM: hlm2 MDM File: GTHAI.MDM   Command File: THAIBNML.HLM

File   Basic Settings   Other Settings   Run Analysis   Help

| Outcome |
| >> Level-1 << |
| Level-2 |

INTRCPT1
MALE
PPED
REP1
TRIAL

LEVEL 1 MODEL (bold: group-mean centering; bold italic: grand-mean centering)

$\text{Prob(REP1=1}|\beta) = \varphi * \text{TRIAL}$

$\text{Log}[\varphi/(1 - \varphi)] = \eta$

$\eta = \beta_0 + \beta_1(\text{MALE}) + \beta_2(\text{PPED})$

LEVEL 2 MODEL (bold italic: grand-mean centering)

$\beta_0 = \gamma_{00} + \gamma_{01}(\textbf{\textit{MSESC}}) + u_0$

$\beta_1 = \gamma_{10} + u_1$

$\beta_2 = \gamma_{20} + u_2$

Mixed ▼

Figure 6.5   Model specification window for the Binomial model

```
Problem Title: BINOMIAL ANALYSIS, THAILAND DATA
   The data source for this run  = THAIGRP.MDM
   The command file for this run = C:\HLM\thaibnml.hlm
   Output file name              = C:\HLM\thaibnml.out
   The maximum number of level-1 units = 1097
   The maximum number of level-2 units = 356
   The maximum number of micro iterations = 50
   Method of estimation: restricted PQL
   Maximum number of macro iterations = 50


   Distribution at Level-1: Binomial

  The model specified for the fixed effects was:
  -------------------------------------------------------
      Level-1                  Level-2
      Coefficients             Predictors
  ---------------------    ---------------
          INTRCPT1, B0      INTRCPT2, G00
  $                           MSESC, G01
  #       MALE slope, B1    INTRCPT2, G10
  #       PPED slope, B2    INTRCPT2, G20
```

'#' - The residual parameter variance for this level-1 coefficient has been set
      to zero.
'$' - This level-2 predictor has been centered around its grand mean.

```
  The model specified for the covariance components was:
  -------------------------------------------------------
          Tau dimensions
              INTRCPT1

  Summary of the model specified (in equation format)
  -------------------------------------------------------
```

Level-1 Model

```
E(Y|B) = TRIAL*P
V(Y|B) = TRIAL*P(1-P)
```

This is the program's way of saying that the level-1 sampling model is binomial with "TRIAL" indicating the number of trials, so that the above equation, written with subscripts and Greek letters, is

$$E(Y_{ij} \mid \beta_j) = m_{ij}\phi_{ij}$$

$$Var(Y_{ij} \mid \beta_j) = m_{ij}\phi_{ij}(1-\phi_{ij}),$$

where m_{ij} = TRIAL.

```
log[P/(1-P)] = B0 + B1*(MALE) + B2*(PPED)

Level-2 Model
B0 = G00 + G01*(MSESC) + U0
B1 = G10
B2 = G20
```

Notice that the level-1 and level-2 structural models are identical to those in Case 1.

```
Level-1 variance = 1/[TRIAL*P(1-P)]
```

In the metric of the linearized dependent variable, the level-1 variance is the reciprocal of the binomial variance,

$$m_{ij}\phi_{ij}(1-\phi_{ij}).$$

Results for the unit-specific model, population-average model, and population-average model with robust standard errors, are not printed below. They are essentially identical to the results using the Bernoulli model.

6.4   Case 3: Poisson model with equal exposure

Suppose that the outcome variable in Case 1 had been the number of days absent during the previous year rather than grade repetition. This outcome would be a non-negative integer, that is, a count rather than a dichotomy. Thus, the Poisson model with a log link would be a reasonable choice for the model. Notice that the time interval during which the absences could accumulate, that is, one year, would be the same for each student. We call this a case of "equal exposure," meaning that each level-1 case had an "equal opportunity" to accumulate absences. (Case 4 describes an example where exposure varies across level-1 cases.)

This model has exactly the same logic as in Case 1 except that the type of model and therefore the corresponding link function will be different.

To specify a Poisson model with equal exposure

1. After specifying the outcome in the model specification window (REP1 in our example), click the **Outcome** button at the top of the variable listbox to the left of the main HLM window to open the **Basic Model Specifications – HLM2** dialog box (See Figure 6.1).
2. Select **Poisson (constant exposure)** to tell HLM that the level-1 sampling model is Poisson with equal exposure per level-1 case.
3. (Optional) Specify the maximum number of macro and micro iterations by selecting the **Iteration Settings** option from the **Other Settings** menu.
4. (Optional) Select the **Over-dispersion** option if appropriate (See section on *Additional Features* at the end of the chapter).

The HLM output would describe the model as follows

```
Level-1 Model
  E(Y|B) = L
  E(Y|B) = L
```

The above equation, written with subscripts and Greek letters, is

$$E(Y_{ij} \mid \beta_j) = \lambda_{ij}$$

$$Var(Y_{ij} \mid \beta_j) = \lambda_{ij}$$

where λ_{ij} is the "true" rate of absence for child ij.

```
Log(L) = B0 + B1*(MALE) + B2*(PPED)
```

Notice that the log link replaces the logit link when we have count data. In the example above, β_2 is the expected difference in log-absenteeism between two children of the same sex attending the same school. To translate back to the rate of absenteeism, we would expect a child with pre-primary experience to have exp $\{\beta_2\}$ times the absenteeism rate of a child attending the same school who did not have pre-primary experience (holding sex constant). In this particular case, the estimated effect for β_2 is most plausibly negative; exp $\{\beta_2\}$ is less than 1.0 so that pre-primary experience would reduce the rate of absenteeism. Notice that the level-2 structural models are identical to those in Case 1.

```
Level-2 Model
B0 = G00 + G01*(MSESC) + U0
B1 = G10
B2 = G20
```

Notice that the level-1 and level-2 structural models are identical to those in Case 1.

```
Level-1 variance = 1/L
```

In the metric of the linearized dependent variable, the level-1 variance is the reciprocal of the Poisson variance, λ_{ij}.

6.5   Case 4: Poisson model with variable exposure

Suppose that the frequency of a given kind of cancer were tabulated for each of many counties. For example, with five age-groups, the data could be organized so that each county had five counts, with Y_{ij} being the number of cancers in age-group i of county j and m_{ij} being the population size of that age group in that county. A Poisson model with variable exposure would be appropriate, with m_{ij} the variable measuring exposure.

To specify a Poisson model with variable exposure

1. After specifying the outcome in the model specification window (REP1 in our example), click the **Outcome** button at the top of the variable listbox to the left of the main HLM window to open the **Basic Model Specifications – HLM2** dialog box (See Figure 6.1).

2. Select **Poisson (variable exposure)** to tell HLM that the level-1 sampling model is Poisson with variable exposure per level-1 case.

3. Select the variable that indicates variable exposure from the drop-down listbox (See Figure 6.1). (In the illustration below, we use SIZE as the variable to indicate variable exposure to indicate the population size, n_{ij}, for age group i in county j).

4. (Optional) Specify the maximum number of macro and micro iterations by selecting the **Iteration Settings** option from the **Other Settings** menu.

5. (Optional) Select the **Over-dispersion** option if appropriate (See section on *Additional Features* at the end of the chapter).

The HLM output would describe the model as follows:

```
Level-1 Model
E(Y|B) = SIZE*L
E(Y|B) = SIZE*L
```

This is the program's way of saying that the level-1 sampling model is Poisson with variable exposure per level-1 case, so that the above equation, written with subscripts and Greek letters, is

$$E(Y_{ij} \mid \beta_j) = m_{ij}\lambda_{ij}$$
$$Var(Y_{ij} \mid \beta_j) = m_{ij}\lambda_{ij},$$

Notice that the log link replaces the logit link when we have count data.

```
Level-2 Model
B0 = G00 + G01*(MSESC) + U0
B1 = G10
B2 = G20
```

Notice that the level-1 and level-2 structural models are identical to those in Case 1.

```
Level-1 variance = 1/L
```

In the metric of the linearized dependent variable, the level-1 variance is the reciprocal of the Poisson variance, $m_{ij}\lambda_{ij}$.

6.6   Case 5: Multinomial model

Data are from a 1990 survey of teachers in 16 high schools in California and Michigan. In the MDM file, not included with the software, there are a total of 650 teachers. The level-1 SPSS input file is TCHR1.SAV, and the level-2 file is TCHR2.SAV.

An outcome with three response categories tapping teachers' commitment to their career choice is derived from teachers' responses to the hypothetical question of whether they would become a teacher if they could go back to college and start over again. The possible responses are:

- yes, I would choose teaching again
- not sure
- no, I would not choose teaching again.

At the teacher level, it is hypothesized that teachers' perception of task variety is positively associated with greater odds of a teacher choosing the first category relative to the third category, and with greater odds of a teacher choosing the second category relative to the third category. The perception is measured by a task variety scale that assessed the extent to which teachers followed the same teaching routines each day, performed the same tasks each day, had something new happening in their job each day, and liked the variety present in their work (Rowan, Raudenbush & Cheong, 1993).

At the school level, it is postulated that the extent of teacher control has the same relationship to the two log odds as perception of task variety does. The teacher control scale is constructed by aggregating nine-item scale scores of teachers within a school. This scale indicates teacher control over school policy issues such as student behavior codes, content of in-service programs, student grouping, school curriculum, and text selection; and control over classroom issues such as teaching content and techniques, and amount of homework assigned (Rowan, Raudenbush & Kang, 1991).

As a previous analysis showed that there is little between-teacher variability in their log-odds of choosing the second category relative to the third category, the level-1 coefficient associated with it is fixed. Furthermore, the effects associated with perception of task variety are constrained to be the same across teachers for the sake of parsimony.

The general procedure to specify a multinomial logit model is given below. Note that the multinomial and ordinal analyses provide unit-specific estimates only. They do not currently produce population-average estimates.

To specify a multinomial model

1. After specifying the outcome in the model specification window, click the **Outcome** button at the top of the variable listbox to the left of the main HLM window to open the **Basic Model Specifications – HLM2** dialog box (See Figure 6.1).

2. Select **Multinomial** to tell HLM that the level-1 sampling model is multinomial.

3. Enter the number of categories into the **Number of Categories** box.

4. (Optional) Specify the maximum number of macro and micro iterations by selecting the **Iteration Settings** option from the **Other Settings** menu.

Figure 6.6 displays the model discussed above.

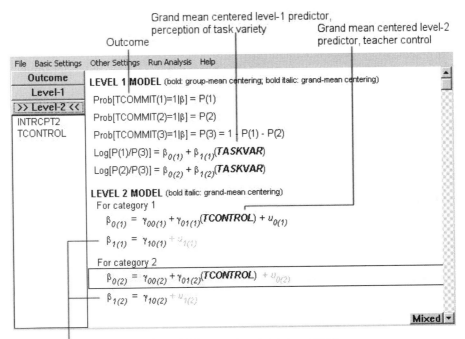

Figure 6.6   Model specification window for the multinomial example

The output obtained for this model follows.

```
SPECIFICATIONS FOR THIS MULTINOMIAL HLM RUN
Problem Title: Multinomial Output, High School Context Data
The data source for this run  = C:\HLM\tchr.MDM
The command file for this run = C:\HLM\tchr1.hlm
Output file name              = C:\HLM\tchr1.out
The maximum number of level-1 units = 650
The maximum number of level-2 units = 16
The maximum number of micro iterations = 14
Number of categories = 3
Method of estimation: restricted PQL
```

The outcome variable is TCOMMIT

The model specified for the fixed effects was:

   Level-1   Level-2
   Coefficients   Predictors
---------------------   ---------------
For category 1:
        INTRCPT1, B0(1)   INTRCPT2, G00(1)
$ SCHTCONT, G01(1)
#% TASKVAR slope, B1(1)   INTRCPT2, G10(1)
For category 2:
INTRCPT1, B0(2)   INTRCPT2, G00(2)
$ SCHTCONT, G01(2)
#   TASKVAR slope, B1(2)   INTRCPT2, G10(2)

'#' - The residual parameter variance for this level-1 coefficient has been set
    to zero.
'%' - This level-1 predictor has been centered around its grand mean.
'$' - This level-2 predictor has been centered around its grand mean.

The model specified for the covariance components was:

       Sigma squared (constant across level-2 units)

       Tau dimensions
           INTRCPT1(1)

Summary of the model specified (in equation format)

Level-1 Model

Prob[Y(1) = 1|B] = P(1)
Prob[Y(2) = 1|B] = P(2)
Prob[Y(3) = 1|B] = P(3) = 1 - P(1) - P(2)

This is the program's way of saying that the level-1 sampling model is multinomial; the above equations, written with subscripts and Greek letters, are

$$\text{Prob}(Y_{ij(1)} = 1 \mid \beta_j) = \phi_{ij(1)}$$

$$\text{Prob}(Y_{ij(2)} = 1 \mid \beta_j) = \phi_{ij(2)}$$

$$\text{Prob}(Y_{ij(3)} = 1 \mid \beta_j) = \phi_{ij(3)} = 1 - \phi_{ij(1)} - \phi_{ij(2)}$$

log[P(1)/P(3)] =B0(1) + B1*(TASKVAR)
log[P(2)/P(3)] =B0(2) + B1*(TASKVAR)

Thus, the level-1 structural models are

$$\eta_{ij(1)} = \log\left[\frac{\phi_{ij(1)}}{\phi_{ij(3)}}\right] = \beta_{0j(1)} + \beta_{1j(1)}(\text{TASKVAR})_{ij}$$

$$\eta_{ij(2)} = \log\left[\frac{\phi_{ij(2)}}{\phi_{ij(3)}}\right] = \beta_{0j(2)} + \beta_{1j(2)}(\text{TASKVAR})_{ij}$$

Level-2 Model

```
B0(1) = G00(1) + G01(1)*(TCONTROL) + U0(1)
B1(1) = G10(1)

B0(2) = G00(2) + G01(2)*(TCONTROL)
B1(2) = G10(2)
```

The level-2 structural models are

$$\beta_{0j(1)} = \gamma_{00(1)} + \gamma_{01(1)}(\text{TCONTROL})_{ij} + u_{0j(1)}$$

$$\beta_{1j(1)} = \gamma_{10(1)}$$

$$\beta_{0j(2)} = \gamma_{00(2)} + \gamma_{01(2)}(\text{TCONTROL})_{ij}$$

$$\beta_{1j(2)} = \gamma_{10(2)}$$

RESULTS FOR MULTINOMIAL ITERATION 198

```
Tau
INTRCPT1(1)       0.00986

Tau (as correlations)
INTRCPT1(1),B0  1.000
```

```
-----------------------------------------------------
  Random level-1 coefficient   Reliability estimate
-----------------------------------------------------
  INTRCPT1(1), B0(1)                  0.083
-----------------------------------------------------
```

The value of the likelihood function at iteration 2 = -1.246191E+003

Final estimation of fixed effects:

Fixed Effect	Coefficient	Standard Error	T-ratio	Approx. d.f.	P-value
For Category 1					
For INTRCPT1, B0(1)					
INTRCPT2, G00(1)	1.079269	0.123439	8.743	14	0.000
TCONTROL, G01(1)	2.090207	0.508369	4.112	14	0.001
For TASKVAR slope, B1(1)					
INTRCPT2, G10(1)	0.398355	0.113650	3.505	644	0.001
For Category 2					
For INTRCPT1, B0(2)					
INTRCPT2, G00(2)	0.091930	0.141643	0.649	644	0.516
TCONTROL, G01(2)	1.057285	0.577673	1.830	644	0.067
For TASKVAR slope, B1(2)					
INTRCPT2, G10(2)	0.030693	0.130029	0.236	644	0.814

131

```
                                             Odds        Confidence
       Fixed Effect         Coefficient      Ratio       Interval
----------------------------------------------------------------------
For Category 1
  For       INTRCPT1, B0(1)
    INTRCPT2, G00(1)          1.079269      2.942528     (2.259,3.834)
    TCONTROL, G01(1)          2.090207      8.086586     (2.720,24.038)
  For   TASKVAR slope, B1(1)
    INTRCPT2, G10(1)          0.398355      1.489373     (1.192,1.861)

For Category 2
  For       INTRCPT1, B0(2)
    INTRCPT2, G00(2)          0.091930      1.096288     (0.830,1.447)
    TCONTROL, G01(2)          1.057285      2.878545     (0.927,8.936)
  For   TASKVAR slope, B1(2)
    INTRCPT2, G10(2)          0.030693      1.031169     (0.799,1.331)
----------------------------------------------------------------------
```

G00(1), the unit-specific intercept, is the expected log-odds of an affirmative response relative to a negative response for a teacher with mean perception of task variety and working in a school with average teacher control and a random effect of zero. It is adjusted for the between-school heterogeneity in the likelihood of an affirmative response relative to a negative response, which is independent of the effect of task variety and teacher control. The estimated conditional expected log-odds is 1.079269.

The predicted probability that the same teacher responds affirmatively (Category 1) is $\exp\{1.079269\}/(1 + \exp\{1.079269\} + \exp\{0.091930\}) = .584$. The predicted probability of responding "not sure" (category 2) is $\exp\{0.091930\}/(1 + \exp\{1.079269\} + \exp\{0.091930\}) = 1 - .584 - .218 = .198$.

The sets of G01 and G10 give the estimates of the change in the respective log-odds given one-unit change in the predictors, holding all other variables constant. For instance, all else being equal, a standard deviation increase in TASKVAR (.32) will nearly double the odds of an affirmative response to a negative response ($\exp\{2.090207 * .32\} = 1.952$). Note that the partial effect associated with perception of task variety is statistically significant for the logit of affirmative versus negative responses but not for the logit of undecided versus negative responses.

Below is a table for the results for the fixed effects with robust standard errors.

```
Final estimation of fixed effects
 (with robust standard errors)
-----------------------------------------------------------------------
                                    Standard           Approx.
       Fixed Effect      Coefficient  Error    T-ratio  d.f.    P-value
-----------------------------------------------------------------------
For Category 1
  For       INTRCPT1, B0(1)
    INTRCPT2, G00(1)       1.079269   0.128263   8.415    14     0.000
    TCONTROL, G01(1)       2.090207   0.409607   5.103    14     0.000
  For   TASKVAR slope, B1(1)
    INTRCPT2, G10(1)       0.398355   0.127511   3.124   644     0.002
```

```
For Category 2
  For       INTRCPT1, B0(2)
    INTRCPT2, G00(2)        0.091930    0.139637    0.658       644     0.510
    TCONTROL, G01(2)        1.057285    0.529606    1.996       644     0.046
  For  TASKVAR slope, B1(2)
    INTRCPT2, G10(2)        0.030693    0.126446    0.243       644     0.808
----------------------------------------------------------------------------
```

```
                                              Odds        Confidence
     Fixed Effect          Coefficient         Ratio       Interval
------------------------------------------------------------------------
For Category 1
  For       INTRCPT1, B0(1)
    INTRCPT2, G00(1)         1.079269         2.942528     (2.235,3.873)
    TCONTROL, G01(1)         2.090207         8.086586     (3.362,19.453)
  For  TASKVAR slope, B1(1)
    INTRCPT2, G10(1)         0.398355         1.489373     (1.160,1.912)

For Category 2
  For       INTRCPT1, B0(2)
    INTRCPT2, G00(2)         0.091930         1.096288     (0.834,1.442)
    TCONTROL, G01(2)         1.057285         2.878545     (1.019,8.132)
  For  TASKVAR slope, B1(2)
    INTRCPT2, G10(2)         0.030693         1.031169     (0.805,1.321)
------------------------------------------------------------------------
```

The robust standard errors are appropriate for datasets having a moderate to large number of level 2 units. These data do not meet this criterion.

Final estimation of variance components:

```
----------------------------------------------------------------------------
Random Effect          Standard      Variance     df    Chi-square  P-value
                       Deviation     Component
----------------------------------------------------------------------------
INTRCPT1(1),    U0(1)   0.09931       0.00986      14    17.87423    0.212
----------------------------------------------------------------------------
```

Note that the residual variance of $\beta_{00(1)}$ is not statistically different from zero. The model may be re-run with the coefficient set to be non-random.

6.7 Case 6: Ordinal model

The same data set, the multi-category outcome, and the same predictors in Case 5 are used here. The procedure for specifying an ordinal model is very similar to that of a multinomial model. Select the **Ordinal** instead of **Multinomial** option in the **Basic Model Specifications – HLM2** dialog box (See Figure 6.1). Figure 6.7 displays the model specified for the example (TCHR2.HLM).

Note: The multinomial and ordinal analyses currently produce unit-specific results only. They do not provide population-average results.

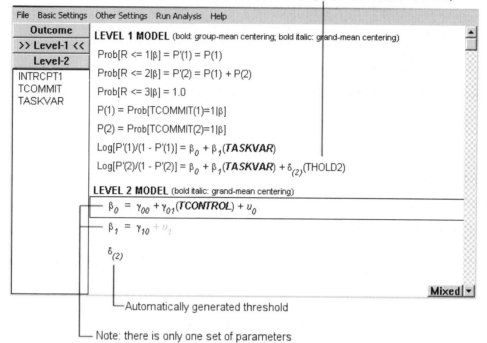

The threshold that separates the two cumulative logits
(automatically generated by the program when "ordinal" is selected)

| File | Basic Settings | Other Settings | Run Analysis | Help |

Outcome
>> Level-1 <<
Level-2

INTRCPT1
TCOMMIT
TASKVAR

LEVEL 1 MODEL (bold: group-mean centering; bold italic: grand-mean centering)

$\text{Prob}[R \le 1|\beta] = P'(1) = P(1)$

$\text{Prob}[R \le 2|\beta] = P'(2) = P(1) + P(2)$

$\text{Prob}[R \le 3|\beta] = 1.0$

$P(1) = \text{Prob}[\text{TCOMMIT}(1)=1|\beta]$

$P(2) = \text{Prob}[\text{TCOMMIT}(2)=1|\beta]$

$\text{Log}[P'(1)/(1 - P'(1)] = \beta_0 + \beta_1(\textbf{\textit{TASKVAR}})$

$\text{Log}[P'(2)/(1 - P'(2)] = \beta_0 + \beta_1(\textbf{\textit{TASKVAR}}) + \delta_{(2)}(\text{THOLD2})$

LEVEL 2 MODEL (bold italic: grand-mean centering)

$\beta_0 = \gamma_{00} + \gamma_{01}(\textbf{\textit{TCONTROL}}) + u_0$

$\beta_1 = \gamma_{10} + u_1$

$\delta_{(2)}$

Mixed ▼

— Automatically generated threshold

— Note: there is only one set of parameters

Figure 6.7   Model specification window for the ordinal model

The output obtained for this model follows.

```
SPECIFICATIONS FOR THIS ORDINAL HLM RUN
Problem Title: Ordinal Output, HIGH SCHOOL CONTEXT DATA
The data source for this run  = TCHR.MDM
The command file for this run = C:\HLM\TCHR2.HLM
Output file name              = C:\HLM\TCHR2.OUT
The maximum number of level-1 units = 650
The maximum number of level-2 units = 16
The maximum number of micro iterations = 14
Number of categories = 3
Method of estimation: restricted PQL


The outcome variable is  TCOMMIT


The model specified for the fixed effects was:
----------------------------------------------------


     Level-1                Level-2
     Coefficients           Predictors
     --------------------   ----------------
      INTRCPT1 slope, B0     INTRCPT2, G00
 $                           TCONTROL, G01
 #%  TASKVAR slope, B1       INTRCPT2, G10
              THOLD2,             d(2)

 '#' - The residual parameter variance for this level-1 coefficient has been set
       to zero.
 '%' - This level-1 predictor has been centered around its grand mean.
 '$' - This level-2 predictor has been centered around its grand mean.
```

134

```
The model specified for the covariance components was:
---------------------------------------------------------------

          Sigma squared (constant across level-2 units)

          Tau dimensions
               INTRCPT1

Summary of the model specified (in equation format)
-------------------------------------------------------------

Level-1 Model

Prob[R = 1|B] = P'(1) = P(1)
Prob[R <= 2|B] = P'(2) = P(1) + P(2)
Prob[R <= 3|B] = 1.0

where

P(1) = Prob[Y(1) = 1|B]
P(2) = Prob[Y(2) = 1|B]
```

This is the programs way of saying that the level-1 sampling model is ordinal; the above equations, written with subscripts and Greek letters, are

$$\text{Prob}(R_{ij} = 1 \mid \beta_j) = \phi'_{ij(1)} = \phi_{ij(1)}$$
$$\text{Prob}(R_{ij} \leq 1 \mid \beta_j) = \phi'_{ij(2)} = \phi_{ij(1)} + \phi_{ij(2)}$$
$$\text{Prob}(R_{ij} \leq 1 \mid \beta_j) = 1$$

where

$$\phi_{ij(1)} = \text{Prob}(R_{ij} = 1 \mid \beta_j)$$
$$\phi_{ij(2)} = \text{Prob}(R_{ij} = 2 \mid \beta_j)$$

```
log[P'(1)/(1 - P'(1)] = B0 + B1*(TASKVAR)
log[P'(2)/(1 - P'(2)] = B0 + B1*(TASKVAR) + d(2)
```

Thus, the level-1 structural models are

$$\eta'_{ij(1)} = \left[\frac{\phi'_{ij(1)}}{1 - \phi'_{ij(1)}} \right] = \beta_{0j} + \beta_{1j}(\text{TASKVAR})_{ij}$$

$$\eta'_{ij(2)} = \left[\frac{\phi'_{ij(2)}}{1 - \phi'_{ij(2)}} \right] = \beta_{0j} + \beta_{1j}(\text{TASKVAR})_{ij} + \delta_{(2)}.$$

```
Level-2 Model

B0 = G00 + G01*(TCONTROL) + U0
B1 = G10
```

135

The level-2 structural model is

$$\beta_{0j} = \gamma_{00} + \gamma_{01}(\text{TCONTROL})_{ij} + u_{0j}$$
$$\beta_{1j} = \gamma_{10}$$

```
RESULTS FOR ORDINAL ITERATION 9152
```

The extremely large number of iterations reflects the fact that the final estimate of the between-school variance, τ_{00}, is near zero, after adjusting for TCONTROL.

```
Tau
INTRCPT1,B0        0.00010

Tau (as correlations)
INTRCPT1,B0   1.000

--------------------------------------------------------
  Random level-1 coefficient   Reliability estimate
--------------------------------------------------------
  INTRCPT1, B0                         0.001
--------------------------------------------------------
```

The value of the likelihood function at iteration 2 = -1.249070E+003

Final estimation of fixed effects:

Fixed Effect	Coefficient	Standard Error	T-ratio	Approx. d.f.	P-value
For INTRCPT1 slope, B0					
INTRCPT2, G00	0.333918	0.089735	3.721	14	0.003
TCONTROL, G01	1.541051	0.365624	4.215	14	0.001
For TASKVAR slope, B1					
INTRCPT2, G10	0.348801	0.087280	3.996	646	0.000
For THOLD2,					
d(2)	1.054888	0.080868	13.045	646	0.000

Fixed Effect	Coefficient	Odds Ratio	Confidence Interval
For INTRCPT1 slope, B0			
INTRCPT2, G00	0.333918	1.396429	(1.152,1.693)
TCONTROL, G01	1.541051	4.669496	(2.133,10.222)
For TASKVAR slope, B1			
INTRCPT2, G10	0.348801	1.417367	(1.194,1.682)
For THOLD2,			
d(2)	1.054888	2.871653	(2.451,3.365)

G00, the unit-specific intercept, is the expected log-odds of an affirmative response relative to an undecided or negative response for a teacher with mean perception of task variety and working in a school with average teacher control and a random effect of zero. It is adjusted for the between-school heterogeneity in the likelihood of an affirmative response relative to a negative response, which is independent of the effect of task variety and teacher control. This conditional expected log-odds, is 0.333918. The expected log-odds for a teacher to give an affirmative or undecided response relative to a negative response is $0.333918 + 1.054888 = 1.388806$. G01 and G10 give the estimates of the change in the respective cumulative logits, holding all other variables constant. For instance, all else being equal, a standard deviation increase in TASKVAR (.32) will increase the odds of an affirmative response to an undecided or negative response as well as the odds of an affirmative or undecided response to a negative response by a factor of 1.637 ($\exp\{1.541051 * .32\} = 1.637$).

Below is a table for the results for the fixed effects with robust standard errors.

```
Final estimation of fixed effects
  (with robust standard errors)
-----------------------------------------------------------------------
                                       Standard           Approx.
    Fixed Effect        Coefficient    Error     T-ratio  d.f.    P-value
-----------------------------------------------------------------------
For INTRCPT1 slope, B0
   INTRCPT2, G00          0.333918     0.092707   3.602    14     0.003
   TCONTROL, G01          1.541051     0.340944   4.520    14     0.000
For  TASKVAR slope, B1
   INTRCPT2, G10          0.348801     0.092285   3.780    646    0.000
For           THOLD2,
        d(2)              1.054888     0.080353  13.128    646    0.000
-----------------------------------------------------------------------
```

```
-----------------------------------------------------------------------
                                        Odds         Confidence
    Fixed Effect        Coefficient     Ratio        Interval
-----------------------------------------------------------------------
For INTRCPT1 slope, B0
   INTRCPT2, G00          0.333918     1.396429     (1.145,1.703)
   TCONTROL, G01          1.541051     4.669496     (2.249,9.696)
For  TASKVAR slope, B1
   INTRCPT2, G10          0.348801     1.417367     (1.183,1.699)
For           THOLD2,
        d(2)              1.054888     2.871653     (2.453,3.362)
-----------------------------------------------------------------------
```

```
The robust standard errors are appropriate for datasets having a moderate to
large number of level 2 units.  These data do not meet this criterion.
```

```
Final estimation of variance components:
-----------------------------------------------------------------------
Random Effect         Standard    Variance    df   Chi-square  P-value
                      Deviation   Component
-----------------------------------------------------------------------
INTRCPT1,      U0      0.01016     0.00010     14   14.57034    0.408
-----------------------------------------------------------------------
```

Note that the residual variance of $\beta_{00(1)}$ is not statistically different from zero. In fact, it is very close to zero, which accounts for the large number of iterations required to achieve convergence. The model may be re-run with the coefficient set to be non-random.

6.8   Additional features

6.8.1 Over-dispersion

For binomial models with $m_{ij} > 1$ and for all Poisson models, there is an option to estimate a level-1 dispersion parameter σ^2 (See Figure 6-1). If the assumption of no dispersion holds, $\sigma^2 = 1.0$. If the data are over-dispersed, $\sigma^2 > 1.0$; if the data are under-dispersed, $\sigma^2 < 1.0$.

6.8.2 Laplace approximation for binary outcome models

For two- and three-level binary outcome models, the highly accurate Laplace approximation to maximum likelihood for binary outcome models (See Figure 6.1) can be selected. When estimating the model parameters, the program will send messages, similar to the following, to the iteration window during computation of the results.

```
.The Laplace-6 likelihood is -9.631409E+003
...
.The Laplace-6 likelihood is -9.627211E+003
```

The following is an example of an output for Laplace6 iterations.

```
RESULTS FOR LAPLACE-6 ITERATION 7

   Tau
   INTRCPT1,BO      1.69946

   Standard Errors of Tau
   INTRCPT1,BO      0.21446

Tau (as correlations)
   INTRCPT1,BO   1.000


----------------------------------------------------
   Random level-1 coefficient   Reliability estimate
----------------------------------------------------
   INTRCPT1, BO                      0.734
----------------------------------------------------

The likelihood at Laplace iteration 8 is -9.628115E+003

   Final estimation of fixed effects
   (Laplace)
   ------------------------------------------------------------------
                                   Standard            Approx.
      Fixed Effect     Coefficient Error     T-ratio   d.f.    P-value
   ------------------------------------------------------------------
   For        INTRCPT1, BO
      INTRCPT2, G00     -2.234807   0.101852  -21.942    354    0.000
         MSESC, G01     -0.014905   0.211040   -0.071    354    0.944
   For     MALE slope, B1
      INTRCPT2, G10      0.536539   0.072595    7.391   7512    0.000
   For     PPED slope, B2
      INTRCPT2, G20     -0.641909   0.100169   -6.408   7512    0.000
   ------------------------------------------------------------------
```

```
-----------------------------------------------------------------
                                         Odds       Confidence
   Fixed Effect          Coefficient     Ratio       Interval
-----------------------------------------------------------------
For        INTRCPT1,  B0
   INTRCPT2,  G00       -2.234807      0.107013    (0.088,0.131)
      MSESC,  G01       -0.014905      0.985206    (0.651,1.491)
For      MALE slope,  B1
   INTRCPT2,  G10        0.536539      1.710078    (1.483,1.972)
For      PPED slope,  B2
   INTRCPT2,  G20       -0.641909      0.526287    (0.432,0.640)
-----------------------------------------------------------------
```

6.8.3 Printing variance-covariance matrices for fixed effects

Files containing variance-covariances for the fixed effects for the unit-specific, population-averaged and Laplace6 estimates can be requested. See Appendix A for more details.

6.9 Fitting HGLMs with three levels

For simplicity of exposition, all of the examples above have used the two-level HGLM. These procedures generalize directly to three-level applications. Again the type of *nonlinear* model desired at level-1 must be specified. There are now, however, structural models at both levels 2 and 3 as in the case of HLM3.

7 Conceptual and Statistical Background for Hierarchical Multivariate Linear Models (HMLM)

One of the most frequent applications of hierarchical models involves repeated observations (level 1) nested within persons (level 2). These are described in Chapter 6 of *Hierarchical Linear Models*. In these models, the outcome Y_{ij} for occasion i within person j is conceived as a univariate outcome, observed under different conditions or at different times. An advantage of viewing the repeated observations as nested within the person is that it allows each person to have a different repeated measures design. For example, in a longitudinal study, the number of time points may vary across persons, and the spacing between time points may be different for different persons. Such unbalanced designs would pose problems for standard methods of analysis such as the analysis of variance.

Suppose, however, that the aim of the study is to observe every participant according to a fixed design with, say, T observations per person. The design might involve T observation times or T different outcome variables or even T different experimental conditions. Given the fixed design, the analysis can be reconceived as a multivariate repeated measures analysis. The multivariate model is flexible in allowing a wide variety of assumptions about the variation and covariation of the T repeated measures (Bock, 1985). In the standard application of multivariate repeated measures, there can be no missing outcomes: every participant must have a full complement of T repeated observations.

Advances in statistical computation, beginning with the EM algorithm (Dempster, Laird, & Rubin, 1977; see also Jennrich & Schluchter, 1986), allow the estimation of multivariate normal models from incomplete data. In this case, the aim of the study was to collect T observations per person, but only n_j observations were collected ($n_j \leq T$). These n_j observations are indeed collected according to a fixed design, but $T - n_j$ data points are missing at random.

HMLM allows estimation of multivariate normal models from incomplete data; HMLM2 allows for study of multivariate outcomes for persons who are, in turn, nested within higher-level units. Within the framework of HMLM, it is possible to estimate models having

1. An unrestricted covariance structure, that is a full $T \times T$ covariance matrix.
2. A model with homogenous level-1 variance and random intercepts and/or slopes at level-2.
3. A model with heterogeneous variances at level 1 (a different variance for each occasion) and random intercepts and/or slopes at level 2.
4. A model that includes a log-linear structure for the level-1 variance and random intercepts and/or slopes at level 2.

5. A model with first-order auto-regressive level-1 random errors and random intercepts and/or slopes at level 2.

We note that applications 2 - 4 are available within the standard HLM2. However, within HMLM, models 2 - 4 can be compared to the unrestricted model (model 1), using a likelihood ratio test. No "unrestricted model" can be meaningfully defined within the standard HLM2; such a model is definable only within the confines of a fixed design with T measurements.

HMLM2 allows the five models listed above to be embedded within a nested structure, *e.g.*, the persons who are repeatedly observed may be nested within schools.

7.1   Unrestricted model

This model is appropriate when the aim of the study is to collect T observations per participant according to a fixed design. However, one or more observations may be missing at random. We assume a constant but otherwise arbitrary $T \times T$ covariance matrix for each person's "complete data."

7.1.1 Level-1 model

The level-1 model relates the observed data, Y, to the complete data, Y^*:

$$Y_{hi} = \sum_{t=1}^{T} m_{thi} Y_{ti}^* \tag{7.1}$$

where Y_{hi} is the r-th outcome for person i associated with time h. Here Y_{ti}^* is the value that person i would have displayed if that person had been observed at time t, and m_{thi} is an indicator variable taking on a value of 1 if the h-th measurement for person i did occur at time t, 0 if not. Thus, Y_{ti}^*, $t = 1$, ..., T, represent the complete data for person i while Y_{hi}, $h = 1$, ..., T_i are the observed data, and the indicators m_{thi} tell us the pattern of missing data for person i.

To make this clear, consider $T = 5$ and a person who has data at occasions 1,2, and 4, but not at occasions 3 and 5. Then Equation 7.1 expands to

$$\begin{pmatrix} Y_{1i} \\ Y_{2i} \\ Y_{3i} \end{pmatrix} = \begin{pmatrix} 1 & 0 & 0 & 0 & 0 \\ 0 & 1 & 0 & 0 & 0 \\ 0 & 0 & 0 & 1 & 0 \end{pmatrix} \begin{pmatrix} Y_{1i}^* \\ Y_{2i}^* \\ Y_{3i}^* \\ Y_{4i}^* \\ Y_{5i}^* \end{pmatrix} \tag{7.2}$$

or, in matrix notation,

$$Y_i = M_i Y_i^*$$

(7.3)

This model says simply that the three observed data points for person i were observed at times 1, 2, and 4, so that data were missing at times 3 and 5. Although these data were missing, they do exist, in principle. Thus, every participant has a full 5×1 vector of "complete data" even though the $T_i \times 1$ vector of observed data will vary in length across persons.

We now pose a structural model for the within-person variation in Y^*:

$$Y_{ti}^* = \pi_{0i} + \sum_{p=1}^{P} \pi_{pi} a_{pt} + \varepsilon_{ti}$$

(7.4)

or, in matrix notation

$$Y_i^* = A\pi_i + \varepsilon_i,$$

(7.5)

where we assume that ε_i is multivariate normal in distribution with a mean vector of 0 and an arbitrary $T \times T$ covariance matrix Δ. In fact, Δ is not a "within-person" covariance. Rather, it captures all variation and covariation among the T repeated observations.

7.1.2 Level-2 model

The level-2 model includes covariates, X_i, that vary between persons:

$$\pi_{pi} = \beta_{p0} + \sum_{q=1}^{Q} \beta_{pq} X_{qi}$$

(7.6)

or in matrix notation

$$\pi_i = X_i \beta$$

(7.7)

Note there is no random variation between persons in the regression coefficients π_{pi} because all random variation has been absorbed into Δ (see the text below Equation 7.5).

7.1.3 Combined model

Substituting the level-2 model into the level-1 model gives the combined model for the complete data, in matrix form:

$$Y_i^* = AX_i\beta + \varepsilon_i, \qquad \varepsilon_i \sim N(0, \Delta) \tag{7.8}$$

Here the design matrix captures main effects of within-person covariates (the as), main effects of person-level covariates (Xs), and two-way interaction effects between them ($a \times X$ terms).

In sum, our reformulation poses a "multiple measures" model (Equation 7.3) that relates the observed data Y_i to the "complete data" Y_i^*, that is, the data that would have been observed if the researcher had been successful in obtaining outcome data at every time point. Our combined model is a standard multivariate normal regression model for the complete data.

Algebraically substituting the combined model expression for Y_i^* into the model for the observed data (Equation 7.3) yields the combined model

$$Y_i = M_i A X_i \beta + M_i \varepsilon_i. \tag{7.9}$$

Under the unrestricted model, the number of parameters estimated is $f + T(T+1)/2$, where f is the number of fixed effects and T is the number of observations intended for each person. The models below impose constraints on the unrestricted model, and therefore include fewer parameters. The fit of these simpler models to the data can be compared to the fit of the unrestricted model using a likelihood ratio test.

7.2   HLM with homogenous level-1 variance

Under the special case in which the within-person design is fixed[1], with T observations per person and randomly missing time points, the two-level HLM can be derived from the unrestricted model by imposing restrictions on the covariance matrix, Δ. (Note: regressors A_i having varying designs may be included in the level-1 model, but coefficients associated with such A_i values must not have random effects at level 2). The most frequently used assumption in the standard HLM is that the within-person residuals are independent with a constant variance, σ^2.

---

1 That is, $A_i = A$ for all i.

7.2.1 Level-1 model

The level-1 model has a similar form to that in the case of the unrestricted model

$$Y_i^* = A\pi_i + \varepsilon_i, \quad \varepsilon_i \sim N(0, \Sigma) \tag{7.10}$$

with $\Sigma = \sigma^2 I_T$.

7.2.2 Level-2 model

The level-2 model includes covariates, X_i, that vary between persons. Degrees of freedom are now available to estimate randomly varying intercepts and slopes across people:

$$\pi_{pi} = \beta_{p0} + \sum_{q=1}^{Q_p} X_{qi} \beta_{pq} + r_{qi} \tag{7.11}$$

or in matrix notation

$$\pi_i = X_i \beta + r_i \tag{7.12}$$

All of the usual forms are now available for the intercepts and slopes (fixed, randomly varying, non-randomly varying), provided T is large enough.

7.2.3 Combined model

Substituting the level-2 model into the level-1 model gives the combined model for the complete data, in matrix form:

$$\begin{aligned} Y_i^* &= AX_i\beta + A_i r_i + e_i \\ &= AX_i\beta + \varepsilon_i, \end{aligned} \tag{7.13}$$

where $\varepsilon_i = A r_i + e_i$ has variance-covariance matrix

$$\begin{aligned} Var(\varepsilon_i) &= Var(A r_i + e_i) \\ &= A\tau A' + \sigma^2 I_T = \Delta. \end{aligned} \tag{7.14}$$

Under the HLM with homogenous level-1 variance, the number of parameters estimated is $f + r(r+1)/2 + 1$, where r is the dimension of τ. Thus, r must be less than T.

7.3 HLM with varying level-1 variance

One can model heterogeneity of level-1 variance as a function of the occasion of measurement. Such a model is suitable when we suspect that the level-1 residual variance varies across occasions. The models that can be estimated are a subset of the models that can be estimated within the standard HLM2 (see Section 2.8.8.2 on the option for heterogeneity of level-1 variance). The level-1 model is the same as in the case of homogenous variances (equations 7.11 and 7.12) except that now

$$Var(e_i) = \Sigma = diag\left\{\sigma_t^2\right\},\tag{7.15}$$

that is, Σ is now diagonal with elements σ_t^2, the variance associated with occasion t, $t = 1, \ldots, T$.

The number of parameters estimated is $f + r(r+1)/2 + T$. Now r must be no larger than $T - 1$. When $r = T - 1$, the results will duplicate those based on the unrestricted model.

7.4 HLM with a log-linear model for the level-1 variance

The model with varying level-1 variance, described above, assumes a unique level-1 variance for every occasion. A more parsimonious model would specify a functional relationship between aspects of the occasion (*e.g.* time or age) and the variance. We would again have $\Sigma = diag\left\{\sigma_t^2\right\}$, but now

$$\log\left(\sigma_t^2\right) = \alpha_0 + \sum_{h=1}^{H} \alpha_h c_{ht}.\tag{7.16}$$

Thus, the natural log of the level-1 variance may be a linear or quadratic function of age. If the explanatory variables c_h are $T - 1$ dummy variables, each indicating the occasion of measurement, the results will duplicate those of the previous section.

The number of parameters estimated is now $f + r(r+1)/2 + H + 1$. Again, r must be no larger than $T - 1$ and H must be no larger than $T - 1$.

7.5 First-order auto-regressive model for the level-1 residuals

This model allows the level-1 residuals to be correlated under Markov assumptions (a level-1 residual depends on previous level-1 residuals only through the immediately preceding level-1 residuals).

This leads to the level-1 covariance structure

$$Cov(e_{ti}, e_{t'i}) = \sigma^2 \rho^{|t-t'|}. \tag{7.17}$$

Thus, the variance at each time point is σ^2 and each correlation diminishes with the distance between time points, so that the correlations are $\rho, \rho^2, \rho^3, \dots$ as the distance between occasions is 1, 2, 3, ...

The number of parameters estimated is now $f + r(r+1)/2 + 2$. Again, r must be no larger than $T-1$. Note that level-1 predictors are assumed to have the same values for all level-2 units of the complete data. This assumption can be relaxed. However, if the design for a_{pti} varies over i, its coefficient cannot vary randomly at level 2. In this regard, the standard 2-level model (See Chapters 2, 3) is more flexible than HMLM.

7.6   HMLM2: A multilevel, multivariate model

Suppose now that the persons yielding multiple outcomes are nested within higher-level units such as schools. We can embed the multivariate model for incomplete data within this multilevel structure.

7.6.1 Level-1 model

The level-1 model again relates the observed data, Y, to the complete data, Y^*. We simply add a subscript to the HMLM model to create the HMLM equation for the observed data:

$$Y_{hij} = \sum_{t=1}^{T} m_{thij} Y_{tij}^*. \tag{7.18}$$

Here individual i is nested within group j ($j = 1, \dots, J$) and we have Y_{hij}, the h-th outcome observed for person i in group j. Here Y_{tij}^* is the value that person i would have displayed if that person had been observed at time t, and m_{thij} is an indicator variable taking on a value of 1 if the h-th measurement for that person did occur at time t, 0 if not. Thus Y_{tij}^*, $t = 1, \dots, T$ represent the complete data for person i in group j while Y_{hij}, $h = 1, \dots, T_i$ are the observed data, and the indicators m_{thij} tell us the pattern of the missing data. Again, we pose a structural model for the within-person variation in Y^*:

$$Y_{tij}^* = \pi_{0ij} + \sum_{p=1}^{P} \pi_{pij} a_{pt} + e_{tij}, \tag{7.19}$$

or, in matrix notation

$$Y_{ij}^* = A\pi_{ij} + e_{ij},$$ (7.20)

where we assume that e_{ij} is multivariate normal in distribution with a mean vector of 0 and an arbitrary $T \times T$ covariance matrix Σ.

7.6.2 Level-2 model

The level-2 model includes covariates, X_{ij}, that vary between persons within groups:

$$\pi_{pij} = \beta_{p0j} + \sum_{q=1}^{Q_{pq}} \beta_{pqj} X_{qij}$$ (7.21)

or, in matrix notation

$$\pi_{ij} = X_{ij}\beta_j$$ (7.22)

7.6.3 Level-3 model

Now the coefficients defined on persons (in the level-2 model) are specified as possibly varying at level-3 over groups:

$$\beta_{pqj} = \gamma_{pq0} + \sum_{s=1}^{S_{pq}} \gamma_{pqs} W_{sqj} + u_{pqj}.$$ (7.23)

Here the vector u_j, composed of elements u_{pqj} is multivariate normal in distribution with a zero mean vector and covariance matrix τ_β.

7.6.4 The combined model

The combined model can then be written in matrix notation as

$$Y_{ij}^* = AX_{ij}W_j\gamma + AX_{ij}u_j + \varepsilon_{ij},$$ (7.24)

where

$$\varepsilon_{ij} = Ar_{ij} + e_{ij}$$ (7.25)

where ε_{ij} has a variance-covariance matrix

$$Var(\varepsilon_{ij}) = \Sigma \qquad (7.26)$$

and Σ is modeled just as in the case of HMLM, depending on which submodel is of interest. The next chapter provides an illustration.

Note that level-1 predictors a_{pt} are assumed to have the same values for all level-2 units of the complete data. This assumption can be relaxed. However, if the design for a_{ptij} varies over i and j, the coefficient for a_{ptij}, that is π_{ptij}, must have no random effect at level 2. In this regard, the standard three-level model (see Chapters 3 and 4) is more flexible than is HMLM2.

8 Working with HMLM/HMLM2

Like the other programs, HMLM and HMLM2 execute analyses using MDM (multivariate data matrix) files, which consist of the combined level-1 and level-2 data files.

The procedures for constructing the MDM file are similar to the ones for HLM2 and HLM3 with one major difference: the user has to create and input indicator variables for the outcome(s) while constructing the MDM file. Model specification for HMLM and HMLM2 involves the same mechanics as in HLM2 and HLM3 with an extra step of model covariance structure selection.

Below we provide two examples using data sets from the first cohort of the National Youth Survey (Elliot, Huizinga, & Menard, 1989, Raudenbush, 1999) and the time-series observations on 1,721 students nested within 60 public primary schools as described in Chapter 6. Windows mode execution is illustrated. See Appendix D for interactive and batch mode execution.

8.1 An analysis using HMLM via Windows mode

8.1.1 Constructing the MDM from raw data

The range of options for data input are the same as for HLM2 and HLM3. We will use SPSS file input in our example.

8.1.1.1   Level-1 file

The level-1 file, NYS1.SAV, has 1,079 observations collected from interviewing annually 239 eleven-year-old youths beginning at 1976 for five consecutive years. Therefore, $T = 5$. The variables and the T indicator variables are:

ATTIT   a 9-item scale assessing attitudes favorable to deviant behavior.

Subjects were asked how wrong (very wrong, wrong, a little bit wrong, not wrong at all) they believe it is for someone their age to, for example, damage and destroy property, use marijuana, use alcohol, sell hard drugs, or steal.

The measure was positively skewed, so a logarithmic transformation was performed to reduce the skewness.

	EXPO	Exposure to deviant peers.

EXPO   Exposure to deviant peers.

                          Subjects were asked how wrong their best friends thought the nine deviant behaviors surveyed in the ATTIT scale were.

AGE   age of the participant

AGE11   age of participant at a specific time minus 11

AGE13   age of participant at a specific time minus 13

AGE11s   AGE11* AGE11

AGE13s   AGE13* AGE13

IND1   indicator for measure at time 1

IND2   indicator for measure at time 2

IND3   indicator for measure at time 3

IND4   indicator for measure at time 4

IND5   indicator for measure at time 5

The five indicators were created to facilitate use of HMLM. Data for the first two children are shown in Fig. 8.1.

Child 15 had data at all five years. Child 33, however, did not have data for the fourth year.

Indicators for the repeated measures

	id	attit	age	age11	age13	age11s	age13s	ind1	ind2	ind3	ind4	ind5
16	15	.44	11.00	.00	-2.00	.00	4.00	1.0	.00	.00	.00	.00
17	15	.44	12.00	1.00	-1.00	1.00	1.00	.00	1.0	.00	.00	.00
18	15	.89	13.00	2.00	.00	4.00	.00	.00	.00	1.0	.00	.00
19	15	.75	14.00	3.00	1.00	9.00	1.00	.00	.00	.00	1.0	.00
20	15	.80	15.00	4.00	2.00	16.00	4.00	.00	.00	.00	.00	1.0
21	33	.20	11.00	.00	-2.00	.00	4.00	1.0	.00	.00	.00	.00
22	33	.64	12.00	1.00	-1.00	1.00	1.00	.00	1.0	.00	.00	.00
23	33	.69	13.00	2.00	.00	4.00	.00	.00	.00	1.0	.00	.00
24	33	.11	15.00	4.00	2.00	16.00	4.00	.00	.00	.00	.00	1.0

Figure 8.1   Two children in the NYS1.SAV data set

8.1.1.2   Level-2 file

The level-2 data file, NYSB.SAV, consists of three variables on 239 youths. The file has the same structure as that for HLM2. The variables are:

FEMALE   an indicator for gender (1 = female, 0 = male)
MINORITY   an indicator for ethnicity (1 = minority, 0 = other)
INCOME   income

The construction of the MDM involves three major steps:

1. Select type of input data.
2. Supply the program with the appropriate data-defining information.
3. Check whether the data have been properly read into the program.

The steps are very similar to the ones described in Section 2.5.1. Select **HMLM** as the **MDM** type at the **Select MDM type** dialog box (see Figure 2.4) and inform WHLM the type of data input.

While the structure of HMLM input files is almost the same as in HLM2, there is one important difference: the indicator variables. In order to create these, one first needs to know the maximum number of level-1 records per level-2 group; this determines the number of indicators. We shall call them the number of "occasions." (This is the number of time points in a repeated measures study or the number of outcome variables in a cross-sectional multivariate study. Also note that each person does not need to have this number of occasions.) Then create the indicator variables so that a given variable takes on the value of 1.0 if the given occasion is at this time point, 0.0 otherwise. Looking at Figure 8.1, we see that IND1 is 1 if AGE11 is 0, IND2 is 1 if AGE11 is 1, IND3 is 1 if AGE11 is 2, and so on. Fig 8.2 shows the **Choose variables – HMLM** dialog box where the indicator variables are checked before the MDM file is created. This dialog box can be opened from the **Level-1 specification** section in the **Make MDM – HMLM** dialog box.

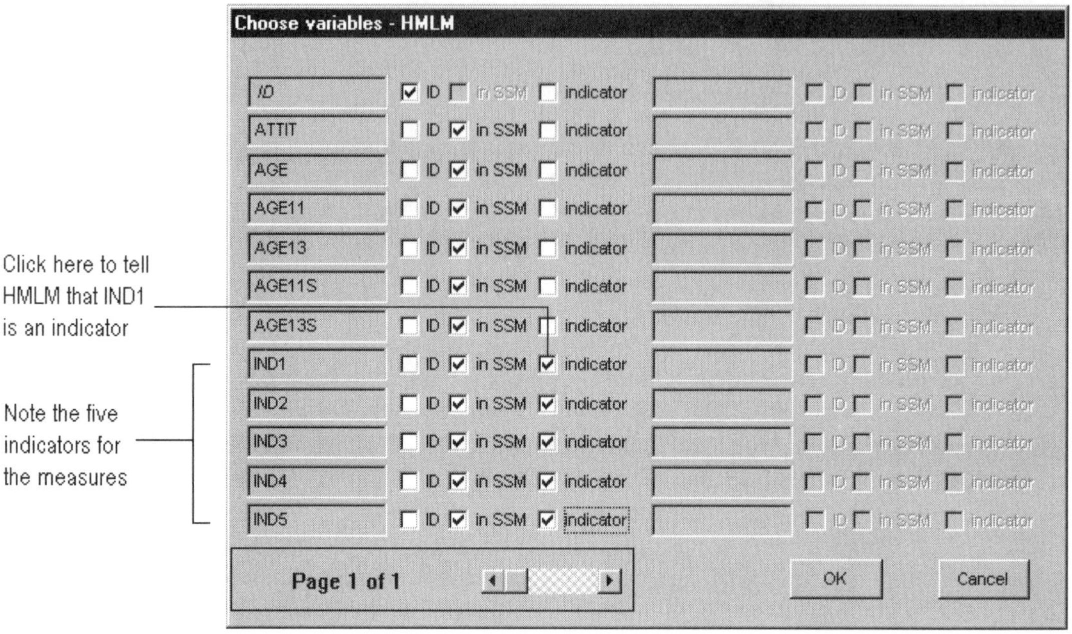

Figure 8.2   Choose variables – HMLM dialog box

8.2   Executing analyses based on the MDM file

The steps involved are similar to the ones for HLM2 as described on Section 2.5.2. It is necessary to specify

1. the level-1 model,
2. the level-2 structural model, and
3. the level-1 coefficients as random or non-random.

Under HMLM, level-1 predictors having random effects must have the same value for all participants at a given occasion. If the user specifies a predictor not fulfilling this condition to have a random effect, such coefficients will be automatically set as non-random by the program. Furthermore, an extra step for selecting the covariance structure for the models to be estimated is needed. Figure 8.3 displays the model specified for our example. Figure 8.4 shows the dialog box where the covariance structure is selected.

8.3 An annotated example of HMLM

In the example below (see NYS1.MLM) we specify AGE13 and AGE13S as predictors at level 1. At level 2, the model is unconditional. This is displayed in Fig. 8.3. We shall compare three alternative covariance structures:

- an unrestricted model,
- the homogeneous model, $\sigma_t^2 = \sigma^2$ for all t, and
- the heterogeneous model, which allows σ_t^2 to vary over time.

These three models are requested simply by checking the **Heterogeneous** option in the **Basic Model Specifications – HMLM** dialog box, as shown in Fig. 8.4.

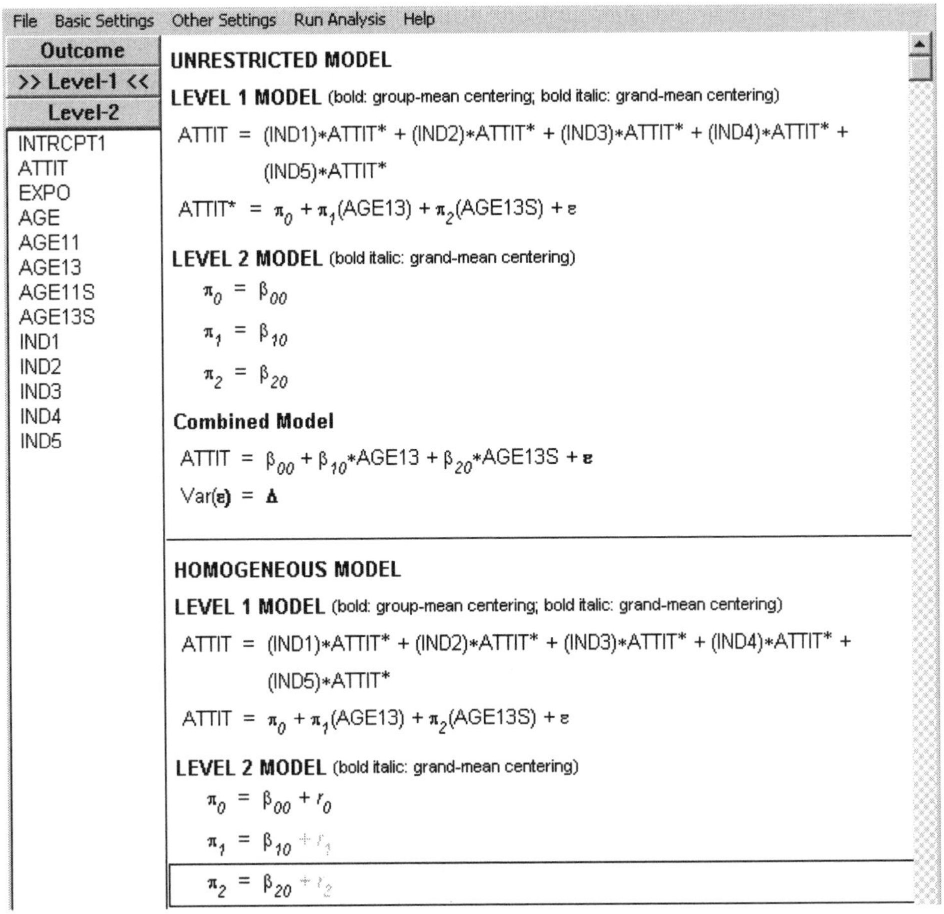

File   Basic Settings   Other Settings   Run Analysis   Help

Outcome
>> Level-1 <<
Level-2

INTRCPT1
ATTIT
EXPO
AGE
AGE11
AGE13
AGE11S
AGE13S
IND1
IND2
IND3
IND4
IND5

UNRESTRICTED MODEL

LEVEL 1 MODEL (bold: group-mean centering; bold italic: grand-mean centering)

$$\text{ATTIT} = (\text{IND1})*\text{ATTIT*} + (\text{IND2})*\text{ATTIT*} + (\text{IND3})*\text{ATTIT*} + (\text{IND4})*\text{ATTIT*} + (\text{IND5})*\text{ATTIT*}$$

$$\text{ATTIT*} = \pi_0 + \pi_1(\text{AGE13}) + \pi_2(\text{AGE13S}) + \varepsilon$$

LEVEL 2 MODEL (bold italic: grand-mean centering)

$$\pi_0 = \beta_{00}$$
$$\pi_1 = \beta_{10}$$
$$\pi_2 = \beta_{20}$$

Combined Model

$$\text{ATTIT} = \beta_{00} + \beta_{10}*\text{AGE13} + \beta_{20}*\text{AGE13S} + \varepsilon$$
$$\text{Var}(\varepsilon) = \Delta$$

HOMOGENEOUS MODEL

LEVEL 1 MODEL (bold: group-mean centering; bold italic: grand-mean centering)

$$\text{ATTIT} = (\text{IND1})*\text{ATTIT*} + (\text{IND2})*\text{ATTIT*} + (\text{IND3})*\text{ATTIT*} + (\text{IND4})*\text{ATTIT*} + (\text{IND5})*\text{ATTIT*}$$

$$\text{ATTIT} = \pi_0 + \pi_1(\text{AGE13}) + \pi_2(\text{AGE13S}) + \varepsilon$$

LEVEL 2 MODEL (bold italic: grand-mean centering)

$$\pi_0 = \beta_{00} + r_0$$
$$\pi_1 = \beta_{10} + r_1$$
$$\pi_2 = \beta_{20} + r_2$$

Figure 8.3   Model specification window for the NYS example

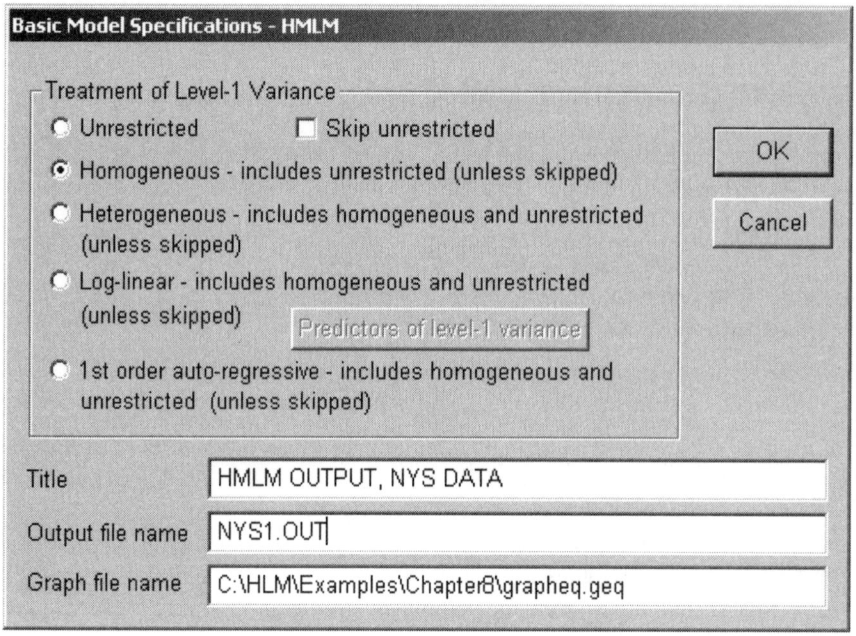

Figure 8.4   Basic Model Specifications - HMLM dialog box

Similarly, checking the **Log-linear** button will produce output on:

- the unrestricted model,
- the homogeneous model, and
- the log-linear model for σ_t^2.

In this case a modified model will be displayed, as shown in Fig. 8.5.

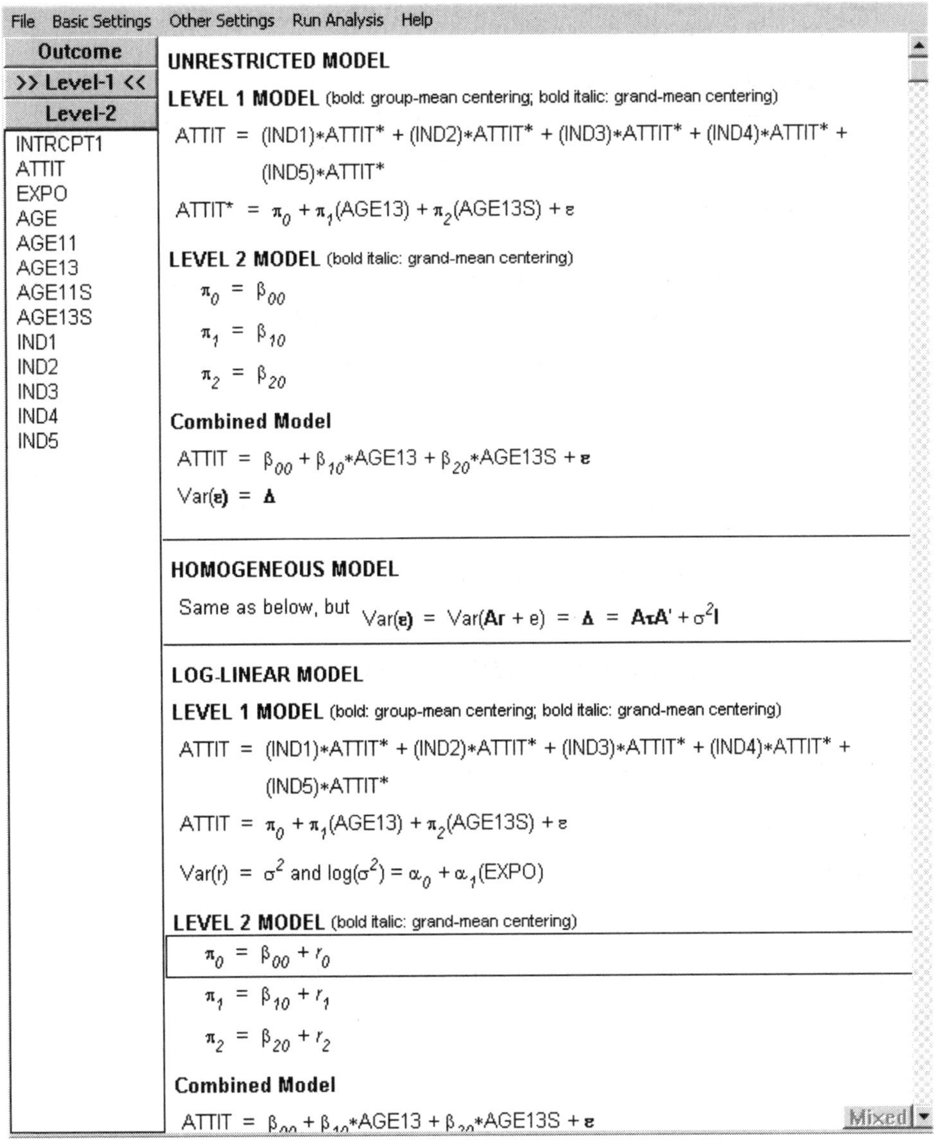

Outcome
>> Level-1 <<
Level-2

INTRCPT1
ATTIT
EXPO
AGE
AGE11
AGE13
AGE11S
AGE13S
IND1
IND2
IND3
IND4
IND5

UNRESTRICTED MODEL

LEVEL 1 MODEL (bold: group-mean centering; bold italic: grand-mean centering)

$$ATTIT = (IND1)*ATTIT^* + (IND2)*ATTIT^* + (IND3)*ATTIT^* + (IND4)*ATTIT^* +$$
$$(IND5)*ATTIT^*$$

$$ATTIT^* = \pi_0 + \pi_1(AGE13) + \pi_2(AGE13S) + \varepsilon$$

LEVEL 2 MODEL (bold italic: grand-mean centering)

$$\pi_0 = \beta_{00}$$

$$\pi_1 = \beta_{10}$$

$$\pi_2 = \beta_{20}$$

Combined Model

$$ATTIT = \beta_{00} + \beta_{10}*AGE13 + \beta_{20}*AGE13S + \varepsilon$$

$$Var(\varepsilon) = \Delta$$

HOMOGENEOUS MODEL

Same as below, but $Var(\varepsilon) = Var(Ar + e) = \Delta = A\tau A' + \sigma^2 I$

LOG-LINEAR MODEL

LEVEL 1 MODEL (bold: group-mean centering; bold italic: grand-mean centering)

$$ATTIT = (IND1)*ATTIT^* + (IND2)*ATTIT^* + (IND3)*ATTIT^* + (IND4)*ATTIT^* +$$
$$(IND5)*ATTIT^*$$

$$ATTIT = \pi_0 + \pi_1(AGE13) + \pi_2(AGE13S) + \varepsilon$$

$$Var(r) = \sigma^2 \text{ and } \log(\sigma^2) = \alpha_0 + \alpha_1(EXPO)$$

LEVEL 2 MODEL (bold italic: grand-mean centering)

$$\pi_0 = \beta_{00} + r_0$$

$$\pi_1 = \beta_{10} + r_1$$

$$\pi_2 = \beta_{20} + r_2$$

Combined Model

$$ATTIT = \beta_{00} + \beta_{10}*AGE13 + \beta_{20}*AGE13S + \varepsilon$$

Mixed ▾

Figure 8.5   Model specification window for the NYS example: loglinear model selection

And, again similarly, choosing the **1st order auto-regressive** option will produce unrestricted and homogeneous results in addition to first-order auto-regressive results.

```
Problem Title: HMLM Output, NYS Data

The data source for this run  = C:\HLM\NYS.MDM
The command file for this run = C:\HLM\NYS1.MLM
Output file name             = C:\HLM\NYS1.OUT
The maximum number of level-2 units = 239
The maximum number of iterations = 50


The outcome variable is    ATTIT

The model specified for the fixed effects was:
-----------------------------------------------------


   Level-1                  Level-2
   Coefficients             Predictors
   ---------------------    -----------------
         INTRCPT1, P0       INTRCPT2, B00
     AGE13 slope, P1        INTRCPT2, B10
    AGE13S slope, P2        INTRCPT2, B20

OUTPUT FOR UNRESTRICTED MODEL

Summary of the model specified (in equation format)
-----------------------------------------------------
```

Level-1 Model

```
   Y = IND1*Y1* + IND2*Y2* + IND3*Y3* + IND4*Y4* + IND5*Y5*
```

The level-1 model relates the observed data, Y, to the complete data, Y^*.


```
Y* = P0 + P1*(AGE13) + P2*(AGE13S) + e
```

Level-2 Model

```
   P0 = B00
   P1 = B10
   P2 = B20
```

For the restricted model, there is no random variation between persons in regression coefficient B0, B1, and B2 because all random variation has been absorbed into D.

```
Var(E) = D
```

```
Iterations stopped due to small change in likelihood function
```

```
******* ITERATION 8 *******

D
    IND1      0.03507      0.01671      0.01889      0.02149      0.02486
    IND2      0.01671      0.04458      0.02779      0.02468      0.02714
    IND3      0.01889      0.02779      0.07272      0.05303      0.04801
    IND4      0.02149      0.02468      0.05303      0.08574      0.06636
    IND5      0.02486      0.02714      0.04801      0.06636      0.08985
```

The 5×5 matrix "D" contains the maximum likelihood estimates of the five variances (one for each time point) and ten covariances (one for each pair of time points). The associated correlation matrix is printed below.

```
D (as correlations)
    IND1  1.000  0.423  0.374  0.392  0.443
    IND2  0.423  1.000  0.488  0.399  0.429
    IND3  0.374  0.488  1.000  0.672  0.594
    IND4  0.392  0.399  0.672  1.000  0.756
    IND5  0.443  0.429  0.594  0.756  1.000

Standard Errors of D
    IND1      0.00347      0.00304      0.00375      0.00413      0.00429
    IND2      0.00304      0.00434      0.00430      0.00457      0.00473
    IND3      0.00375      0.00430      0.00678      0.00631      0.00625
    IND4      0.00413      0.00457      0.00631      0.00811      0.00736
    IND5      0.00429      0.00473      0.00625      0.00736      0.00853
```

The 5×5 matrix above contains estimated standard errors for each element of D.

```
The value of the likelihood function at iteration 8 = 1.891335E+002

Final estimation of fixed effects:
-------------------------------------------------------------------
    Fixed Effect      Coefficient    Standard Error   T-ratio   P-value
-------------------------------------------------------------------
For          INTRCPT1, B0
    INTRCPT2, G00       0.320244       0.014981       21.377    0.000
For     AGE13 slope, B1
    INTRCPT2, G10       0.059335       0.004710       12.598    0.000
For     AGE13S slope, B2
    INTRCPT2, G20       0.000330       0.003146        0.105    0.917
```

The expected log attitude at age 13 is 0.320244. The mean linear growth rate of increase is estimated to be 0.059335, t = 12.598, indicating a highly significantly positive average rate of increase in deviant attitude at age 13. The quadratic rate is not statistically significant.

```
Statistics for current covariance components model
--------------------------------------------------
Deviance =   -378.26694
Number of estimated parameters =   18
```

There are 3 fixed effects ($f = 3$) and five observations in the "complete data" for each person ($T = 5$). Thus, there are a total of $f + T(T+1)/2 = 3 + 5(5+1)/2 = 18$ parameters. This is the end of the unrestricted model output.

Next follows the results for the homogeneous level-1 variance.

```
OUTPUT FOR RANDOM EFFECTS MODEL WITH HOMOGENEOUS LEVEL-1 VARIANCE

Summary of the model specified (in equation format)
----------------------------------------------------

Level-1 Model
Y = IND1*Y1* + IND2*Y2* + IND3*Y3* + IND4*Y4* + IND5*Y5*
Y* = P0 + P1*(AGE13) + P2*(AGE13S) + e

Level-2 Model
P0 = B00 + R0
P1 = B10 + R1
P2 = B20 + R2

Var(E) = Var(A*R + e) = D = A*Tau*A' + S     where S = sigma_squared*I
```

The above equation, written with subscripts and Greek letters, is

$$Var(Y^*) = \Delta = ATA' + \Sigma$$

where $\Sigma = \sigma^2 I_T$.

```
A
    IND1        1.00000       -2.00000       4.00000
    IND2        1.00000       -1.00000       1.00000
    IND3        1.00000        0.00000       0.00000
    IND4        1.00000        1.00000       1.00000
    IND5        1.00000        2.00000       4.00000
```

The above matrix describes the design matrix on occasions one through five.

```
Iterations stopped due to small change in likelihood function
```

Note: The results below duplicate exactly the results produced by a standard HLM2 run using homogeneous level-1 variance.

```
******* ITERATION 5 *******
                      Parameter       Standard Error
                    -------------     ----------------
   sigma_squared =      0.02421           0.001672

Tau
INTRCPT1          0.04200        0.00808       -0.00242
   AGE13          0.00808        0.00277       -0.00012
   AGE13S        -0.00242       -0.00012        0.00049

Tau (as correlations)
 INTRCPT1  1.000  0.749 -0.532
    AGE13  0.749  1.000 -0.101
   AGE13S -0.532 -0.101  1.000

Standard Errors of Tau
INTRCPT1          0.00513        0.00127        0.00089
   AGE13          0.00127        0.00054        0.00024
   AGE13S         0.00089        0.00024        0.00025

D
    IND1          0.03536        0.01388        0.01616        0.01801        0.01943
    IND2          0.01388        0.04870        0.03150        0.03488        0.03464
    IND3          0.01616        0.03150        0.06620        0.04766        0.04849
    IND4          0.01801        0.03488        0.04766        0.08056        0.06095
    IND5          0.01943        0.03464        0.04849        0.06095        0.09625
```

The 5×5 matrix above contains the five variance and ten covariance estimates implied by the "homogeneous level-1 variance" model.

```
D (as correlations)
    IND1  1.000  0.334  0.334  0.338  0.333
    IND2  0.334  1.000  0.555  0.557  0.506
    IND3  0.334  0.555  1.000  0.653  0.607
    IND4  0.338  0.557  0.653  1.000  0.692
    IND5  0.333  0.506  0.607  0.692  1.000

The value of the likelihood function at iteration 5 = 1.741132E+002
```

```
Final estimation of fixed effects:
-----------------------------------------------------------------
     Fixed Effect      Coefficient   Standard Error   T-ratio   P-value
-----------------------------------------------------------------
For         INTRCPT1,  B0
   INTRCPT2,  G00        0.327231       0.015306      21.379     0.000
For    AGE13 slope,  B1
   INTRCPT2,  G10        0.064704       0.004926      13.135     0.000
For    AGE13S slope,  B2
   INTRCPT2,  G20        0.000171       0.003218       0.053     0.958

Statistics for current covariance components model
------------------------------------------------------
Deviance =    -348.22643
Number of estimated parameters =    10
```

There are 3 fixed effects ($f = 3$); the dimension of τ is 3, and a common σ^2 is estimated at level-1. Thus, there are a total of $f + r(r+1)/2 + 1 = 3 + 3(3+1)/2 + 1 = 10$ parameters.

This is the end of the output for the "homogeneous level-1 variance" model. Finally, the heterogeneous level-1 variance solution is listed.

```
OUTPUT FOR RANDOM EFFECTS MODEL WITH HETEROGENEOUS LEVEL-1 VARIANCE

Summary of the model specified (in equation format)
-----------------------------------------------------

Level-1 Model

Y = IND1*Y1* + IND2*Y2* + IND3*Y3* + IND4*Y4* + IND5*Y5*
Y* = P0 + P1*(AGE13) + P2*(AGE13S) + e

Level-2 Model

   P0 = B00 + R0
   P1 = B10 + R1
   P2 = B20 + R2

Var(E) = Var(A*R + e) = D = A*Tau*A' + S,
where S = diag(sigma_squared(1),...,sigma_squared(5))
```

The above equation, written with subscripts and Greek letters, is

$$Var(Y^*) = ATA' + \Sigma$$

where $\Sigma = diag\{\sigma_t^2\}$, i.e. that is, Σ is now a diagonal matrix with diagonal elements σ_t^2, the variance associated with occasion t, $t = 1, 2, ..., T$.

```
A
      IND1      1.00000      -2.00000      4.00000
      IND2      1.00000      -1.00000      1.00000
      IND3      1.00000       0.00000      0.00000
      IND4      1.00000       1.00000      1.00000
      IND5      1.00000       2.00000      4.00000
```

Iterations stopped due to small change in likelihood function

******* ITERATION 8 *******

	sigma_squared	Standard Error
IND1	0.01373	0.005672
IND2	0.02600	0.003296
IND3	0.02685	0.003658
IND4	0.02602	0.003633
IND5	0.00275	0.007377

The five estimates above are the estimates of the level-1 variance for each time point.

Tau
INTRCPT1	0.04079	0.00736	-0.00241
AGE13	0.00736	0.00382	0.00025
AGE13S	-0.00241	0.00025	0.00106

Tau (as correlations)
INTRCPT1	1.000	0.590	-0.366
AGE13	0.590	1.000	0.124
AGE13S	-0.366	0.124	1.000

Standard Errors of Tau
INTRCPT1	0.00512	0.00124	0.00088
AGE13	0.00124	0.00066	0.00042
AGE13S	0.00088	0.00042	0.00030

D
IND1	0.03410	0.01707	0.01646	0.01851	0.02325
IND2	0.01707	0.05165	0.03103	0.03322	0.03223
IND3	0.01646	0.03103	0.06764	0.04574	0.04588
IND4	0.01851	0.03322	0.04574	0.08208	0.06421
IND5	0.02325	0.03223	0.04588	0.06421	0.08996

The 5×5 matrix above contains the estimates of five variances and ten covariances implied by the "heterogeneous level-1 variance" model.

D (as correlations)
IND1	1.000	0.407	0.343	0.350	0.420
IND2	0.407	1.000	0.525	0.510	0.473
IND3	0.343	0.525	1.000	0.614	0.588
IND4	0.350	0.510	0.614	1.000	0.747
IND5	0.420	0.473	0.588	0.747	1.000

The value of the likelihood function at iteration 8 = 1.816074E+002
The outcome variable is   ATTIT

Final estimation of fixed effects:

Fixed Effect	Coefficient	Standard Error	T-ratio	P-value

For   INTRCPT1, B0
| INTRCPT2, G00 | 0.327646 | 0.015252 | 21.482 | 0.000 |

For   AGE13 slope, B1
| INTRCPT2, G10 | 0.060864 | 0.004737 | 12.849 | 0.000 |

For   AGE13S slope, B2
| INTRCPT2, G20 | -0.000541 | 0.003178 | -0.170 | 0.865 |

```
Statistics for current covariance components model
-----------------------------------------------------
Deviance =    -363.21489
Number of estimated parameters =    14
```

There are 3 fixed effects ($f = 3$), the dimension of τ is 3, and there are five observations intended for each person, each associated with a unique level-1 variance. Thus, there are a total of $f + r(r+1)/2 + T = 3 + 3(4)/2 + 5 = 14$ parameters.

```
Summary of Model Fit
```

Model	Number of Parameters	Deviance
1. Unrestricted	18	-378.26694
2. Homogeneous sigma_squared	10	-348.22642
3. Heterogeneous sigma_squared	14	-363.21488

Model Comparison	Chi_square	df	P-value
Model 1 vs Model 2	30.04052	8	0.000
Model 1 vs Model 3	15.05206	4	0.005
Model 2 vs Model 3	14.98846	4	0.005

The model deviances are employed to evaluate the fits of the three models (unrestricted, homogeneous sigma_squared, and heterogeneous sigma_squared). Differences between deviances are distributed asymptotically as chi-square variates under the null hypothesis that the simpler model fits the data as well as the more complex model does. The results show that Model 1 fits better than does the homogeneous sigma_squared model $\chi^2 = 30.04052$, df = 8; it also fits better than does the heterogeneous sigma_squared model $\chi^2 = 15.05206$, df = 4.

In addition to the evaluation of models based on their fit to the data, the above results can be used to check the sensitivity of key inferences to alternative specifications of the variance-covariance structure. For instance, one could compare the mean and variance in the rate of changeat age 13 obtained in Model 2 and Model 3 to assess how robust the results are to alternative plausible covariance specifications. The mean rate, G10, for Model 2 is 0.064704 (s.e. = 0.004926), and the variance, τ_{22}, is 0.00277 (s.e. = 0.00054). The mean rate, G10, for Model 3 is 0.060864 (s.e. = 0.004737), and the variance, τ_{22}, is 0.00382 (s.e. = 0.00066). The results are basically similar. See Raudenbush (2001) for a more detailed analysis of alternative covariance structures for polynomial models of individual growth and change using the same NYS data sets employed here for the illustrations.

Below are partial outputs for two random effect models.

OUTPUT FOR RANDOM EFFECTS MODEL FOR LOG-LINEAR MODEL FOR LEVEL-1 VARIANCE

Summary of the model specified (in equation format)

Level-1 Model

Y = IND1*Y1* + IND2*Y2* + IND3*Y3* + IND4*Y4* + IND5*Y5*

Y* = P0 + P1*(AGE13) + P2*(AGE13S) + e

Level-2 Model

   P0 = B00
   P1 = B10
   P2 = B20

Var(E) = Var(A*R + e) = D = A*Tau*A' + S
where S = diag(sigma_squared(1),...,sigma_squared(5)),
and log(sigma_squared(t)) = alpha0 + alpha1(EXPO)

The above equation, written with subscripts and Greek letters, is

$$Var(Y^*) = ATA' + \Sigma$$

where $\Sigma = diag(\sigma_t^2)$, and

$$\log(\sigma_t^2) = \alpha_0 + \alpha_1\ (EXPO)_t.$$

A
IND1	1.00000	-2.00000	4.00000
IND2	1.00000	-1.00000	1.00000
IND3	1.00000	0.00000	0.00000
IND4	1.00000	1.00000	1.00000
IND5	1.00000	2.00000	4.00000

Iterations stopped due to small change in likelihood function

******* ITERATION 7 *******

		Parameter	Standard Error
alpha0	=	-3.72883	0.069238
alpha1	=	-1.43639	1.053241

The results suggest no linear association between AGE and the log σ_t^2, Z = − 1.436/1.053 = −1.36.

	sigma_squared
IND1	0.02690
IND2	0.02677
IND3	0.02419
IND4	0.02188
IND5	0.02136

Tau			
INTRCPT1	0.04255	0.00831	-0.00257
AGE13	0.00831	0.00277	-0.00005
AGE13S	-0.00257	-0.00005	0.00051

```
Tau (as correlations)
 INTRCPT1  1.000  0.766 -0.549
    AGE13  0.766  1.000 -0.042
   AGE13S -0.549 -0.042  1.000

Standard Errors of Tau
 INTRCPT1    0.00517       0.00128       0.00089
    AGE13    0.00128       0.00054       0.00025
   AGE13S    0.00089       0.00025       0.00025


D
     IND1    0.03576       0.01267       0.01566       0.01782       0.01917
     IND2    0.01267       0.05095       0.03168       0.03516       0.03464
     IND3    0.01566       0.03168       0.06674       0.04829       0.04889
     IND4    0.01782       0.03516       0.04829       0.07909       0.06192
     IND5    0.01917       0.03464       0.04889       0.06192       0.09510
```

The 5×5 matrix above contains the variance and covariance estimates implied by the "log-linear" model for the level-1 variance.

```
D (as correlations)
     IND1  1.000  0.297  0.320  0.335  0.329
     IND2  0.297  1.000  0.543  0.554  0.498
     IND3  0.320  0.543  1.000  0.665  0.614
     IND4  0.335  0.554  0.665  1.000  0.714
     IND5  0.329  0.498  0.614  0.714  1.000

The value of the likelihood function at iteration 7 = 1.749583E+002


The outcome variable is    ATTIT

Final estimation of fixed effects:
-------------------------------------------------------------------
   Fixed Effect    Coefficient   Standard Error   T-ratio   P-value
-------------------------------------------------------------------
For       INTRCPT1, B0
    INTRCPT2, G00      0.328946       0.015379     21.390     0.000
For    AGE13 slope, B1
    INTRCPT2, G10      0.064661       0.004923     13.135     0.000
For    AGE13S slope, B2
    INTRCPT2, G20     -0.000535       0.003222     -0.166     0.869

Statistics for current covariance components model
-------------------------------------------------
Deviance =   -349.91650
Number of estimated parameters =    11
```

There are 3 fixed effects ($f = 3$), the dimension of τ is 3 ($r = 3$), and there is 1 intercept and 1 explanatory ($H = 1$) variable. Thus, there are a total of $f + r(r+1)/2 + 1 + H = 3 + 3(3+1)/2 + 1 + 1 = 11$ parameters.

Next are the results for the first-order auto-regressive model (Example: NYS4.MLM)

OUTPUT FOR RANDOM EFFECTS MODEL FIRST-ORDER AUTOREGRESSIVE MODEL
FOR LEVEL-1 VARIANCE

Summary of the model specified (in equation format)

Level-1 Model

Y = IND1*Y1* + IND2*Y2* + IND3*Y3* + IND4*Y4* + IND5*Y5*

Y* = P0 + P1*(AGE13) + P2*(AGE13S) + e

Level-2 Model

    P0 = B00 + R0
    P1 = B10
    P2 = B20

Note that B1 and B2 are specified as non-random due to the fact that the time-series is relatively short and therefore the data do not allow the estimation of both random slopes and an autocorrelation parameter.

Var(E) = Var(A*R + e) = D = A*Tau*A' + S
where S = {sigma_squared*rho**|t - t'|}

The above equation, written with subscripts and Greek letters, is

$$Var(Y^*) = ATA' + \Sigma$$

where

$$\Sigma = \sigma^2 \rho^{|t-t'|}.$$

A
        IND1   1.00000
        IND2   1.00000
        IND3   1.00000
        IND4   1.00000
        IND5   1.00000

Iterations stopped due to small change in likelihood function

******* ITERATION 6 *******

                        Parameter   Standard Error
                        ---------   --------------
    rho   =   0.39675   0.053849
    sigma_squared =   0.04158   0.003582

Note that the mamimum-likelihood estimate of $\hat{\rho}$ = 0.397 is much larger than its standard error (0.054), suggesting a significantly positive autocorrelation.

Tau
 INTRCPT1   0.02427

Tau (as correlations)
 INTRCPT1   1.000

```
Standard Errors of Tau
INTRCPT1        0.00450

D
    IND1    0.06585     0.04077     0.03081     0.02686     0.02530
    IND2    0.04077     0.06585     0.04077     0.03081     0.02686
    IND3    0.03081     0.04077     0.06585     0.04077     0.03081
    IND4    0.02686     0.03081     0.04077     0.06585     0.04077
    IND5    0.02530     0.02686     0.03081     0.04077     0.06585
```

The 5×5 matrix above contains the variance and covariance estimates implied by the "auto-correlation" model for the level-1 variance.

```
D (as correlations)
    IND1  1.000  0.619  0.468  0.408  0.384
    IND2  0.619  1.000  0.619  0.468  0.408
    IND3  0.468  0.619  1.000  0.619  0.468
    IND4  0.408  0.468  0.619  1.000  0.619
    IND5  0.384  0.408  0.468  0.619  1.000
```

```
The value of the likelihood function at iteration 6 = 1.471600E+002
```

```
Final estimation of fixed effects:
-----------------------------------------------------------------
   Fixed Effect      Coefficient   Standard Error   T-ratio   P-value
-----------------------------------------------------------------
For       INTRCPT1, B0
   INTRCPT2, G00       0.327579       0.015265       21.459     0.000
For    AGE13 slope, B1
   INTRCPT2, G10       0.061428       0.004836       12.703     0.000
For    AGE13S slope, B2
   INTRCPT2, G20       0.000211       0.003373        0.062     0.951
```

```
Statistics for current covariance components model
--------------------------------------------------
Deviance =    -294.31992
Number of estimated parameters =    6
```

8.4   An analysis using HMLM2 via Windows mode

To illustrate how to use HMLM2, we use the data files from the public school example described in Section 4.1.1.1. We prepared six indicators for the measures of mathematics proficiency collected over the six years and put them in the level-1 file, EG1.SAV. The new level-1 file is called EG1HMLM2.SAV. The same level-2 and level-3 files, EG2.SAV and EG3.SAV are used. The MDM file created is EGHMLM2.MDM. Like in the case in HMLM, users need to tell the program what the indicator variables are while creating the MDM file (see Fig. 8.2).

8.5   Executing analyses based on the MDM file

The steps involved are similar to the ones for HMLM outlined previously and for HLM3 as described in Section 4.2. The user specifies

1. the level-1 model,
2. the level-2 structural model, and
3. the level-1 coefficients as random or non-random.

In addition, the user selects the covariance structure for the models to be estimated. Below is the output for the linear growth model specified in Section 4.2. As in the case for HMLM, the results allow us to compare model fit and assess sensitivity of inferences with alternative specification of variance-covariance structures.

```
Problem Title: HMLM2 OUTPUT, PUBLIC SCHOOL DATA
The data source for this run  = EGHMLM2.MDM
The command file for this run = C:\HLM\EGHMLM1.MLM
Output file name              = C:\HLM\EGHMLM2.OUT
The maximum number of level-2 units = 1721
The maximum number of level-3 units = 60
The maximum number of iterations = 50

The outcome variable is      MATH


The model specified for the fixed effects was:
-------------------------------------------------
  Level-1              Level-2            Level-3
--------------------   ---------------    -----------------
      INTRCPT1, P0     INTRCPT2, B00     INTRCPT3, G000
      YEAR slope, P1   INTRCPT2, B10     INTRCPT3, G100

OUTPUT FOR UNRESTRICTED MODEL

Summary of the model specified (in equation format)
-------------------------------------------------

Level-1 Model

Y = IND1*Y1* + IND2*Y2* + IND3*Y3* + IND4*Y4* + IND5*Y5* +
      IND6*Y6*
Y* = P0 + P1*(YEAR) + E

Level-2 Model

        P0 = B00
        P1 = B10

Level-3 Model

        B00 = G000 + U0
        B10 = G100 + U1

Var(E) = D
A
      IND1,P0       1.00000      -2.50000
      IND2,P1       1.00000      -1.50000
      IND3,P2       1.00000      -0.50000
      IND4,P3       1.00000       0.50000
      IND5,P4       1.00000       1.50000
      IND6,P5       1.00000       2.50000

X
        1.00000       0.00000
        0.00000       1.00000
```

166

```
Estimation of fixed effects
(Based on starting values of covariance components)
------------------------------------------------------------------
   Fixed Effect       Coefficient   Standard Error   T-ratio   P-value
------------------------------------------------------------------

For        INTRCPT1, P0
   For INTRCPT2, B00
      INTRCPT3, G000    -0.827685      0.012189      -67.906    0.000
For     YEAR slope, P1
   For INTRCPT2, B10
      INTRCPT3, G100     0.765828      0.008433       90.812    0.000


D(0)
   IND1,P0   0.04268   0.01233   0.01919   0.01968   0.01506   0.00898
   IND2,P1   0.01233   0.60634   0.35457   0.42101   0.31132   0.24927
   IND3,P2   0.01919   0.35457   0.76957   0.62363   0.42394   0.35205
   IND4,P3   0.01968   0.42101   0.62363   1.15453   0.67302   0.52773
   IND5,P4   0.01506   0.31132   0.42394   0.67302   0.81870   0.55086
   IND6,P5   0.00898   0.24927   0.35205   0.52773   0.55086   0.65701

Tau(beta)(0)
 INTRCPT1         YEAR
 INTRCPT2,B00 INTRCPT2,B10
   0.20128      0.01542
   0.01542      0.01608

Iterations stopped due to small change in likelihood function

******* ITERATION 32 *******

D
   IND1,P0   0.67340   0.31616   0.38755   0.52412   0.53030   0.38971
   IND2,P1   0.31616   0.77832   0.47127   0.56726   0.54171   0.50187
   IND3,P2   0.38755   0.47127   0.91072   0.76829   0.66199   0.64640
   IND4,P3   0.52412   0.56726   0.76829   1.24542   0.88364   0.81782
   IND5,P4   0.53030   0.54171   0.66199   0.88364   1.05646   0.84356
   IND6,P5   0.38971   0.50187   0.64640   0.81782   0.84356   0.98722




Standard Errors of D
   IND1,P0   0.08003   0.05328   0.07256   0.02999   0.02811   0.04341
   IND2,P1   0.05328   0.05757   0.06998   0.02542   0.03289   0.03656
   IND3,P2   0.07256   0.06998   0.07252   0.02966   0.03284   0.03565
   IND4,P3   0.02999   0.02542   0.02966   0.02844   0.03044   0.03913
   IND5,P4   0.02811   0.03289   0.03284   0.03044   0.03030   0.03518
   IND6,P5   0.04341   0.03656   0.03565   0.03913   0.03518   0.03859

D (as correlations)
   IND1,P0  1.000  0.437  0.495  0.572  0.629  0.478
   IND2,P1  0.437  1.000  0.560  0.576  0.597  0.573
   IND3,P2  0.495  0.560  1.000  0.721  0.675  0.682
   IND4,P3  0.572  0.576  0.721  1.000  0.770  0.738
   IND5,P4  0.629  0.597  0.675  0.770  1.000  0.826
   IND6,P5  0.478  0.573  0.682  0.738  0.826  1.000

Tau(beta)
 INTRCPT1         YEAR
 INTRCPT2,B00 INTRCPT2,B10
   0.14824      0.01268
   0.01268      0.00935
```

```
Standard Errors of Tau(beta)
 INTRCPT1        YEAR
 INTRCPT2,B00  INTRCPT2,B10
   0.03286       0.00626
   0.00626       0.00218

Tau(beta) (as correlations)
 INTRCPT1/INTRCPT2,B00  1.000  0.341
     YEAR/INTRCPT2,B10  0.341  1.000
```

The value of the likelihood function at iteration 32 = -7.980254E+003

The outcome variable is   MATH

Final estimation of fixed effects:

Fixed Effect	Coefficient	Standard Error	T-ratio	P-value
For INTRCPT1, P0				
For INTRCPT2, B00				
INTRCPT3, G000	-0.824938	0.054960	-15.010	0.000
For YEAR slope, P1				
For INTRCPT2, B10				
INTRCPT3, G100	0.755026	0.014229	53.062	0.000

Statistics for current covariance components model

Deviance = 15960.50740
Number of estimated parameters =   26

OUTPUT FOR RANDOM EFFECTS MODEL WITH HOMOGENEOUS LEVEL-1 VARIANCE
Summary of the model specified (in equation format)

Level-1 Model

```
Y = IND1*Y1* + IND2*Y2* + IND3*Y3* + IND4*Y4* + IND5*Y5* +
    IND6*Y6*
Y* = P0 + P1*(YEAR) + E
```

Level-2 Model

```
      P0 = B00 + R0
      P1 = B10 + R1
```

Level-3 Model

```
      B00 = G000 + U0
      B10 = G100 + U1
```

Var(E) = Var(A*R + e) = D = A*Tau(pi)*A' + S
where S = sigma_squared*I

A

IND1,P0	1.00000	-2.50000
IND2,P1	1.00000	-1.50000
IND3,P2	1.00000	-0.50000
IND4,P3	1.00000	0.50000
IND5,P4	1.00000	1.50000
IND6,P5	1.00000	2.50000

X

```
    1.00000      0.00000
    0.00000      1.00000
```

The value of the likelihood function at iteration 1 = -7.980254E+003
The value of the likelihood function at iteration 2 = -8.271230E+003
The value of the likelihood function at iteration 3 = -8.163134E+003
The value of the likelihood function at iteration 4 = -8.163116E+003

Iterations stopped due to small change in likelihood function

******* ITERATION 5 *******

	Parameter	Standard Error
sigma_squared =	0.30144	0.00660

Tau(pi)
```
  INTRCPT1,P0    0.64046      0.04679
     YEAR,P1     0.04679      0.01126
```

Tau(pi) (as correlations)
```
  INTRCPT1   1.000   0.551
     YEAR    0.551   1.000
```

Standard Errors of Tau(pi)
```
  INTRCPT1,P0      0.02515      0.00499
     YEAR,P1       0.00499      0.00197
```

D
IND1,P0	0.77832	0.49553	0.51417	0.53282	0.55146	0.57011
IND2,P1	0.49553	0.82687	0.55533	0.58523	0.61513	0.64503
IND3,P2	0.51417	0.55533	0.89793	0.63765	0.67880	0.71996
IND4,P3	0.53282	0.58523	0.63765	0.99150	0.74247	0.79489
IND5,P4	0.55146	0.61513	0.67880	0.74247	1.10758	0.86981
IND6,P5	0.57011	0.64503	0.71996	0.79489	0.86981	1.24618

D (as correlations)
IND1,P0	1.000	0.618	0.615	0.607	0.594	0.579
IND2,P1	0.618	1.000	0.644	0.646	0.643	0.635
IND3,P2	0.615	0.644	1.000	0.676	0.681	0.681
IND4,P3	0.607	0.646	0.676	1.000	0.709	0.715
IND5,P4	0.594	0.643	0.681	0.709	1.000	0.740
IND6,P5	0.579	0.635	0.681	0.715	0.740	1.000

Tau(beta)
```
  INTRCPT1          YEAR
  INTRCPT2,B00  INTRCPT2,B10
    0.16532        0.01705
    0.01705        0.01102
```

Standard Errors of Tau(beta)
```
  INTRCPT1          YEAR
  INTRCPT2,B00  INTRCPT2,B10
    0.03641        0.00720
    0.00720        0.00252
```

Tau(beta) (as correlations)
```
  INTRCPT1/INTRCPT2,B00   1.000   0.399
       YEAR/INTRCPT2,B10  0.399   1.000
```

The value of the likelihood function at iteration 5 = -8.163116E+003

Final estimation of fixed effects:
```
--------------------------------------------------------------------------------
     Fixed Effect          Coefficient    Standard Error   T-ratio   P-value
--------------------------------------------------------------------------------
For          INTRCPT1, P0
   For INTRCPT2, B00
      INTRCPT3, G000       -0.779305      0.057829         -13.476   0.000
For       YEAR slope, P1
   For INTRCPT2, B10
      INTRCPT3, G100        0.763028      0.015262          49.996   0.000
```

Statistics for current covariance components model
```
------------------------------------------------------
```
Deviance = 16326.23120
Number of estimated parameters =   9

OUTPUT FOR RANDOM EFFECTS MODEL WITH HETEROGENEOUS LEVEL-1 VARIANCE

Summary of the model specified (in equation format)
```
-------------------------------------------------------
```

Level-1 Model

$Y = IND1*Y1* + IND2*Y2* + IND3*Y3* + IND4*Y4* + IND5*Y5* + IND6*Y6*$
$Y* = P0 + P1*(YEAR) + E$

Level-2 Model

$P0 = B00 + R0$
$P1 = B10 + R1$

Level-3 Model

$B00 = G000 + U0$
$B10 = G100 + U1$

$Var(E) = Var(A*R + e) = D = A*Tau(pi)*A' + S$
where $S = diag(sigma\_squared(1),...,sigma\_squared(6))$

A
```
     IND1,P0      1.00000      -2.50000
     IND2,P1      1.00000      -1.50000
     IND3,P2      1.00000      -0.50000
     IND4,P3      1.00000       0.50000
     IND5,P4      1.00000       1.50000
     IND6,P5      1.00000       2.50000
```
X
```
     1.00000      0.00000
     0.00000      1.00000
```

Iterations stopped due to small change in likelihood function

******* ITERATION 7 *******

	sigma-squared	Standard Error
IND1	0.34891	0.05960
IND2	0.38314	0.02056
IND3	0.31846	0.01491
IND4	0.37849	0.01584
IND5	0.20344	0.01147
IND6	0.15546	0.01422

```
Tau(pi)
  INTRCPT1,P0      0.62722      0.04769
       YEAR,P1     0.04769      0.01386


Tau(pi) (as correlations)
  INTRCPT1   1.000  0.511
      YEAR   0.511  1.000

Standard Errors of Tau(pi)
  INTRCPT1,P0      0.02499      0.00495
       YEAR,P1     0.00495      0.00205

D
IND1,P0    0.82432     0.48844     0.50148     0.51451     0.52755     0.54058
IND2,P1    0.48844     0.89848     0.54224     0.56913     0.59603     0.62293
IND3,P2    0.50148     0.54224     0.90146     0.62376     0.66452     0.70528
IND4,P3    0.51451     0.56913     0.62376     1.05687     0.73300     0.78762
IND5,P4    0.52755     0.59603     0.66452     0.73300     1.00493     0.86997
IND6,P5    0.54058     0.62293     0.70528     0.78762     0.86997     1.10778


D (as correlations)
    IND1,P0  1.000  0.568  0.582  0.551  0.580  0.566
    IND2,P1  0.568  1.000  0.603  0.584  0.627  0.624
    IND3,P2  0.582  0.603  1.000  0.639  0.698  0.706
    IND4,P3  0.551  0.584  0.639  1.000  0.711  0.728
    IND5,P4  0.580  0.627  0.698  0.711  1.000  0.825
    IND6,P5  0.566  0.624  0.706  0.728  0.825  1.000

Tau(beta)
  INTRCPT1          YEAR
  INTRCPT2,B00 INTRCPT2,B10
    0.16531        0.01552
    0.01552        0.00971

Standard Errors of Tau(beta)
  INTRCPT1          YEAR
  INTRCPT2,B00 INTRCPT2,B10
    0.03637        0.00677
    0.00677        0.00225

Tau(beta) (as correlations)
  INTRCPT1/INTRCPT2,B00  1.000  0.387
      YEAR/INTRCPT2,B10  0.387  1.000

The value of the likelihood function at iteration 7 = -8.070079E+003

  Final estimation of fixed effects:
  -------------------------------------------------------------------
    Fixed Effect       Coefficient   Standard Error  T-ratio  P-value
  -------------------------------------------------------------------
  For        INTRCPT1, P0
    For INTRCPT2, B00
       INTRCPT3, G000    -0.781960      0.057792     -13.531   0.000
  For       YEAR slope, P1
    For INTRCPT2, B10
       INTRCPT3, G100     0.751231      0.014452      51.983   0.000

  Statistics for current covariance components model
  --------------------------------------------------
  Deviance =  16140.15899
  Number of estimated parameters =    14
```

171

Summary of Model Fit

```
--------------------------------------------------------
Model                            Number of      Deviance
                                 Parameters
--------------------------------------------------------
1. Unrestricted                      26       15960.50733
2. Homogeneous sigma-squared          9       16326.23111
3. Heterogeneous sigma-squared       14       16140.15892


--------------------------------------------------------
Model Comparison                 Chi-square    df    P-value
--------------------------------------------------------
Model 1 vs Model 2               365.72378     17    0.000
Model 1 vs Model 3               179.65159     12    0.000
Model 2 vs Model 3               186.07219      5    0.000
```

9 Special Features

9.1   Latent variable analysis

Researchers may be interested in studying the randomly varying coefficients not only as outcomes, but as predictors as well. For instance, in a two-level repeated measures study of adolescents' tolerance of deviant behaviors, a user may choose to use the level-1 coefficient capturing the level of tolerance at the beginning of the study to predict the coefficient tapping the linear growth rate.

Treating these coefficients as latent variables, the HLM2, HLM3, and HMLM modules allow researchers to study direct as well as indirect effects among them and to assess their impacts on coefficients associated with observed covariates in the model. Furthermore, using HMLM with unrestricted covariance structures, one may use latent variable analysis to run regressions with missing data.

Below are two examples of latent variable analysis via Windows mode. See Appendix E for batch and interactive modes.

9.1.1 A latent variable analysis using HMLM: Example 1

The first example employs the National Youth Survey data sets described in Section 8.1. The MDM file is NYS.MDM, the level-1 data file is NYS1.SAV, and the level-2 file is NYS2.SAV. Figure 9.1 displays a linear growth model with gender as a covariate. The command file that contains the model specification information is NYS2.MLM.

We use π_0, the level of tolerance at age 11, to predict π_1, the linear growth rate, controlling for gender. Note that FEMALE must be in the model for both π_0 and π_1 to control for gender fully. Note also that π_0 and π_1 are latent variables, that is, they are free of measurement error, which is contained in e. Furthermore, we assess whether the effect of gender on the linear growth rate may change after controlling for the initial status at age 11. We select the homogeneous level-1 variance option for this model. Thus, using HLM2 will yield identical results in this case.

Below are the steps for setting up a latent variable analysis.

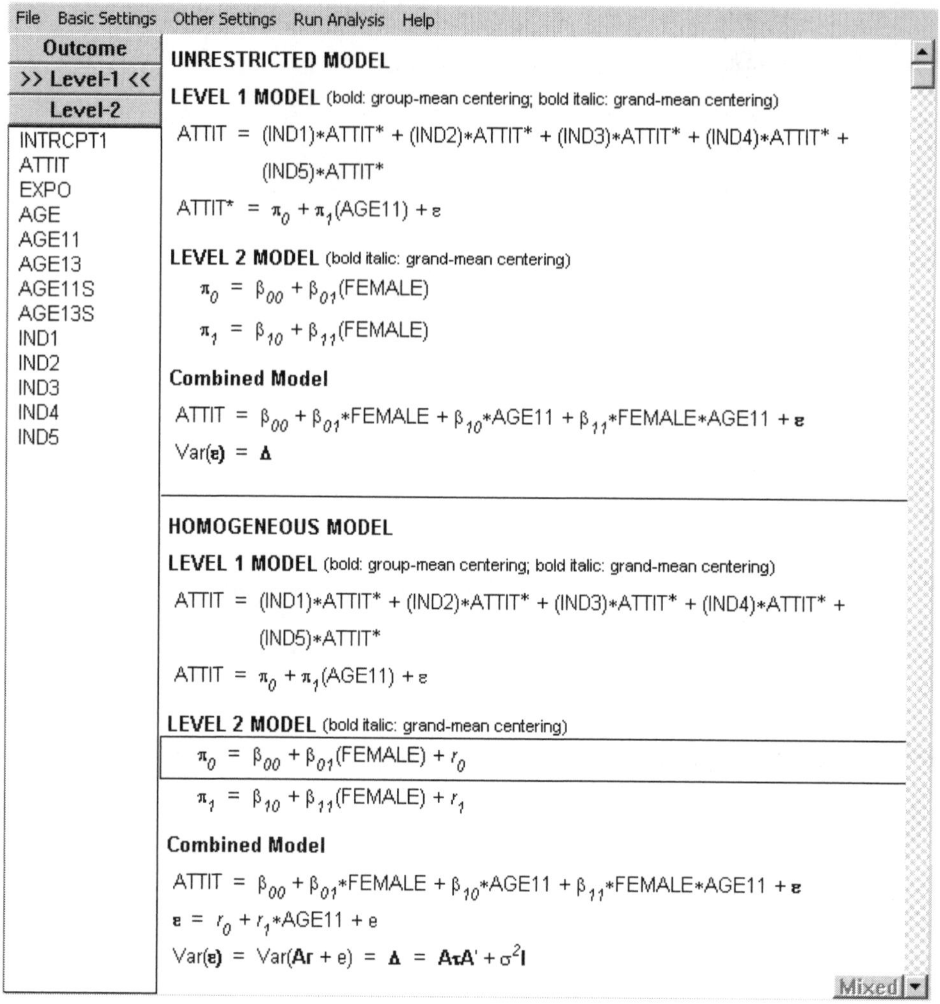

Figure 9.1   Model screen for the NYS example

To set up a latent variable analysis

1. After specifying the model, select the **Estimation Settings** option from the **Other Settings** menu.

2. Choose **Latent Variable Regression** to open the **Latent Variable Regression** dialog box (Figure 9.2 shows an example for the NYS example).

3. Select the predictor(s) and outcome(s) by clicking the selection buttons in front of them (for our example, select INTRCPT1, π_0, as the predictor and AGE11, π_1, as the outcome).

Select HMLM output to illustrate latent variable regression follows.

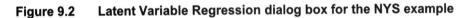

Figure 9.2   Latent Variable Regression dialog box for the NYS example

```
Final estimation of fixed effects:
-----------------------------------------------------------------------
    Fixed Effect      Coefficient   Standard Error   T-ratio   P-value
-----------------------------------------------------------------------
For        INTRCPT1, P0
    INTRCPT2, B00      0.221755       0.015961        13.894     0.000
      FEMALE, B01     -0.048274       0.022926        -2.106     0.035
For     AGE11 slope, P1
    INTRCPT2, B10      0.070432       0.006781        10.386     0.000
      FEMALE, B11     -0.012003       0.009826        -1.222     0.222
```

The results indicate that there is a significant linear growth rate in the attitude toward deviant behaviors (coefficient = 0.070432, s.e. = 0.006781) for males. Also, there is no gender effect on the linear growth rate.

```
Latent Variable Regression Results
The model specified (in equation format)

B1 = G10* + G11*(FEMALE) + G12*(B0) + U1*
```

```
  Outcome    Predictor     Estimated    Standard    T-ratio   P-value
                           Coefficient  Error
------------------------------------------------------------------------
  AGE11,B1  INTRCPT2,G10*    0.024765    0.024807    0.998     0.319
            FEMALE,G11*     -0.002062    0.013058   -0.158     0.875
            B0,G12*          0.205934    0.105410    1.954     0.050
------------------------------------------------------------------------
```

The results indicate that, controlling for gender, the initial status at age 11 has a marginally significant effect on the linear growth rate (coefficient = 0.205934, s.e. = 0.105410). There is no statistically significant partial gender effect, however. Indeed, the gender effect on π_1 appears somewhat reduced after controlling π_0.

```
Latent Variable Regression: Comparison of Original and Adjusted Coefficients
------------------------------------------------------------------------
  Outcome    Predictor     Original    Adjusted    Difference  Standard
                           Coefficient Coefficient             Error of
                                                               Difference
------------------------------------------------------------------------
  AGE11,B1  INTRCPT2         0.07043     0.02477     0.04567    0.024311
            FEMALE          -0.01200    -0.00206    -0.00994    0.006941
------------------------------------------------------------------------
```

This table lists the original coefficients, the adjusted coefficients, and the difference between the two for the intercept and the gender effect. For the variable FEMALE, the "original coefficient" describes the total association, the "adjusted coefficient" describes the direct association, and the "difference" is the indirect association between gender and the linear growth rate, respectively.

```
Var(u1*)
   AGE11        0.00196
```

An estimate of the variance of $u1*$, the residual variance in π_1, controlling both FEMALE and π_0, is also given.

As mentioned earlier, a latent variable analysis using HLM2 will reproduce identical results. The same procedures generalize to three-level applications (HMLM2, HLM3, & HGLM) to model randomly varying level-2 coefficients as outcome variables. See Raudenbush and Sampson (1999) for an example that implemented a latent variable analysis with a three-level model. In the study, they investigated the extent to which neighborhood social control mediated the association between neighborhood social composition and violence in Chicago.

9.1.2 A latent variable analysis using HMLM: Example 2

In this example, we illustrate how to use latent variable analysis to run regression with missing data with an artificial data set. We are interested in estimating regression coefficients that relate two predictors to the outcome. There are three intended measures, an outcome (OUTCOME) and two predictors (PRED1 and PRED2) for 15 participants in the data. Some participants are missing one or two measures. To use HMLM to run regression with missing data, we first re-organize the data and re-conceive the three measures for each participant j as "occasions of measurement." If the data are complete, each case has $R = 3$ occasions. If participant j is missing one value, there will only be 2 occasions for that participant, and if participant j is missing 2 values, there will be only 1 occasion for that case. The measure is then re-conceived as $MEASURE_{ij}$, that is, the value of the datum collected at occasion i for participant j, with $i = 1, 2, ..., n_j$, and with $n_j \leq R = 3$. If the data are complete for participant j, then:

$$MEASURE_{1j} = OUTCOME_j,$$
$$MEASURE_{2j} = PRED_{1j},$$
$$MEASURE_{3j} = PRED_{2j}.$$

Three indicators IND_{1j}, IND_{2j}, and IND_{3j} indicating whether $MEASURE_{ij}$ is $OUTCOME_j$, $PRED_{1j}$, or $PRED_{2j}$ are added to the data set.

Data for the first three participants are shown in Fig. 9.3.

	id	measures	ind1	ind2	ind3
1	1	48.92	1.00	.00	.00
2	1	41.86	.00	1.00	.00
3	1	60.41	.00	.00	1.00
4	2	56.06	.00	1.00	.00
5	2	52.99	.00	.00	1.00
6	3	59.49	1.00	.00	.00

Data View / Variable View

Figure 9.3   First three participants for Example 2

Note that Participant 1 has complete data, Participant 2 has data on PRED1 and PRED2 but not the outcome, and the Participant 3 has data only on OUTCOME.

Data on the measures and the three indicators constitute the level-1 data file, MISSING1.SAV, for the example. The level-2 file, MISSING2.SAV, contains a dummy variable, DUMMY, which is not to be used in the analysis. A MDM file, MISSING.MDM, is created. Figure 9.4 displays the model specified with unrestricted covariance structure for the missing data example. The file that contains the file specification information is MISSING1.MLM.

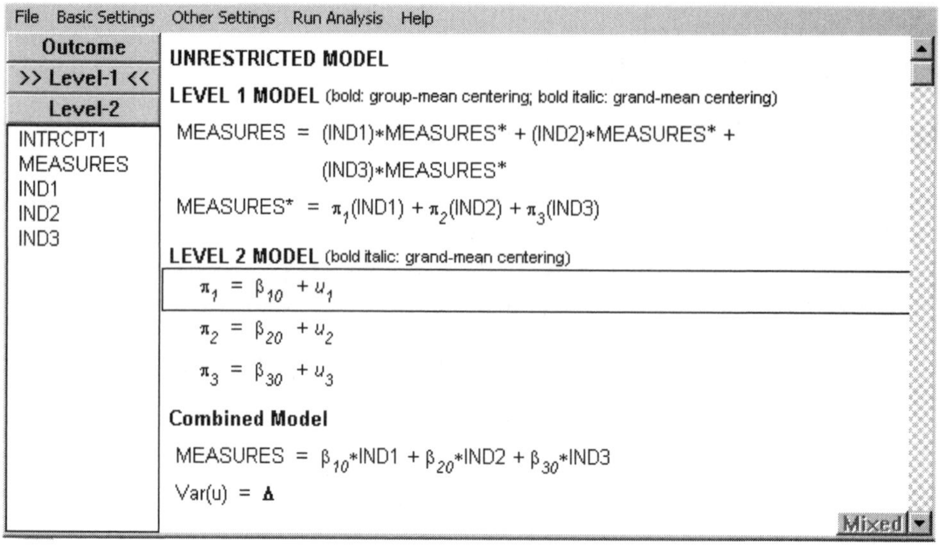

```
File   Basic Settings   Other Settings   Run Analysis   Help
```

| Outcome |
| >> Level-1 << |
| Level-2 |

INTRCPT1
MEASURES
IND1
IND2
IND3

UNRESTRICTED MODEL

LEVEL 1 MODEL (bold: group-mean centering; bold italic: grand-mean centering)

$$\text{MEASURES} = (\text{IND1}){*}\text{MEASURES}^{*} + (\text{IND2}){*}\text{MEASURES}^{*} + (\text{IND3}){*}\text{MEASURES}^{*}$$

$$\text{MEASURES}^{*} = \pi_1(\text{IND1}) + \pi_2(\text{IND2}) + \pi_3(\text{IND3})$$

LEVEL 2 MODEL (bold italic: grand-mean centering)

$$\pi_1 = \beta_{10} + u_1$$

$$\pi_2 = \beta_{20} + u_2$$

$$\pi_3 = \beta_{30} + u_3$$

Combined Model

$$\text{MEASURES} = \beta_{10}{*}\text{IND1} + \beta_{20}{*}\text{IND2} + \beta_{30}{*}\text{IND3}$$

$$\text{Var}(u) = \Lambda$$

Mixed

Figure 9.4   Model window for the missing data example

To regress OUTCOME (IND1) on PRED1 (IND2) and PRED2 (IND3), select IND1 as the outcome and IND2 and IND3 as predictors in the **Latent Variable Regression** dialog box.

The following selected output (example MISSING1.MLM) gives the latent variable regression results.

```
Latent Variable Regression Results
```

Outcome	Predictor	Estimated Coefficient	Standard Error	T-ratio	P-value
IND1,B1	INTRCPT2,G10*	-23.966161	14.173726	-1.691	0.116
	B2,G11*	0.879462	0.232665	3.780	0.003
	B3,G12*	0.544410	0.220194	2.472	0.030

```
Latent Variable Regression: Comparison of Original and Adjusted Coefficients
```

Outcome	Predictor	Original Coefficient	Adjusted Coefficient	Difference	Standard Error of Difference
IND1,B1	INTRCPT2	52.25565	-23.96616	76.22181	14.285875

```
Var(u1*)
     IND1        33.51134
```

The results indicate that π_2 (associated with IND2) and π_3 (associated with IND3) have statistically significant effects on IND1 (OUTCOME)[4].

9.2 Applying HLM to multiply-imputed data

A satisfactory solution to the missing data problem involves multiple, model-based imputation (Rubin, 1987, Little & Rubin, 1987, Schafer, 1997). A multiple imputation procedure produces M "complete" data sets. Users can apply HLM2 and HLM3 to these multiply-imputed data to produce appropriate estimates that incorporate the uncertainty resulting from imputation.

There can be multiply-imputed values for the outcome or one covariate, or for the outcome and/or covariates.

HLM has two methods to analyze multiply-imputed data. They both use the same equations to compute the averages, so the method chosen depends on the data you are analyzing.

"Plausible Values" as described in Sections 9.2.1 and 9.2.3. This method is usually preferable for data sets that have only one variable (outcome or predictor) for which you have several plausible values. In this case, you need to make one MDM file containing *all* of the plausible values, plus any other variables of interest.

"Multiple Imputation" as described in Section 9.2.4. This method is necessary if you have more than one variable for which you have multiply-imputed data. This method also requires a different way of setting up MDM files. Here, you have to create as many MDMs as you have plausible vales. When making these MDMs, you should use the same level-2 file (and level-3 file if using HLM3), but several level-1 files are needed.

Those variables that are not multiply imputed should be the same in all these level-1 files. The variables that *are* multiply imputed should be separated into the separate level-1 files, but they *must* have the same variable names across these level-1 files, since the same model is run on each of these MDMs.

9.2.1 Data with multiply-imputed values for the outcome or one covariate

HLM2 and HLM3 enable users to produce correct HLM estimates when using data sets that contain two or more values or plausible values for the outcome variable or one covariate. One such data set is the National Assessment of Educational Progress (NAEP), an U.S. Department of Education achievement test given to a national sample of fourth, eighth, and twelfth graders.

---

[4]Raudenbush and Bryk (*Hierarchical Linear Models*, 2002) have shown that using this approach with complete data replicated the results of SPSS regression analysis for the regression coefficients. As HMLM adopts the full maximum likelihood estimation approach and the SPSS uses the restricted maximum likelihood approach, the two sets of standard errors estimated differ by a factor of

$$\sqrt{\frac{J}{J-Q-1}}$$, where in this case $J = 15$ and $Q = 2$.

Due to the use of balanced incomplete block (BIB) spiraling in the administration of the NAEP assessment battery, special procedures and calculations are necessary when estimating any population parameters and their standard errors with data sets such as NAEP. Every student was not tested on the same items, so item response theory (IRT) was used to estimate proficiency scores for each individual student. This procedure estimated a range or distribution of plausible values for each student's proficiency rather than an individual observed score. NAEP drew five plausible values at random from the conditional distribution of proficiency scores for each student. The measurement error is due to the fact that these scores are estimated, rather than observed.

In general, these plausible values are used to produce parameter estimates in the following way.

- Each parameter is estimated for each of the five plausible values, and the five estimates are averaged.
- Then, the standard error for this average estimate is calculated using the approach recommended by Little & Schenker (1995).
- This formula essentially combines the average of the sampling error from the five estimates with the variance between the five estimates multiplied with a factor related to the number of plausible values. The result is the measurement error.

In an HLM analysis, with either two- or three-levels, the parameter estimates are based on the average parameter estimates from separate HLM analyses of the five plausible values. That is, a separate HLM analysis is conducted on each of the five plausible values.

Without HLM, these procedures could be performed by producing HLM estimates for each plausible value, and then averaging the estimates and calculating the standard errors using another computer program. These procedures are tedious and time-consuming, especially when performed on many models, grades, and dependent variables.

HLM takes the plausible values into account in generating the HLM estimates. For each HLM model, the program runs each of the five (or the number specified) plausible values internally, and produces their average value and the correct standard errors. There will seem to be one estimate, but the five HLM estimates from the five plausible values are produced and their average and measurement error calculated correctly, thus ensuring an accurate treatment of plausible value data. The output is similar to the standard HLM program output, except that all the components are averaged over estimates derived from the five plausible values. In addition, the output from the five plausible value runs is available in a separate output file.

9.2.2 Calculations performed

The program conducts a separate HLM analysis for each plausible value. The output of the separate HLM analyses is written to files with consecutive numbers, for example, OUT.1, OUT.2, OUT.3, etc. Then, HLM calculates the average of the parameter estimates from the separate analyses and computes the standard errors. The output of the average HLM parameter estimates and their standard errors is found in the output file with the extension AVG.

9.2.2.1   Average parameter estimates

The following parameter estimates are averaged by HLM:

- The fixed effects (gammas)
- The reliabilities
- The parameter variances (tau) and its correlations
- The chi-square values to test whether the parameter variance is zero
- The standard errors for the variance-covariance components (full maximum likelihood estimates)
- Multivariate hypothesis testing for fixed effects

9.2.2.2   Standard error of the gammas

The standard error of the averaged fixed effects (gammas) is estimated as described below. The Student's t-value is calculated by dividing the average gamma by its standard error, and the probability of the t-value is estimated from a standard t-distribution table.

The standard error of the gammas consists of two components – sampling error and measurement error. The following routine provided in the NAEP *Data Files User Guide* (Rogers, *et al.*, 1992) is used to approximate the component of error variance due to the error in imputations and to add it to the sampling error.

Let $\hat{\theta}_m$ $(m = 1,..., M)$ represent the m-th plausible value. Let $\hat{t}_m$ represent the parameter estimate based on the m-th plausible value. Let U_m represent the estimated variance of $\hat{t}_m$.

- Five HLM runs were conducted based on each plausible value $\hat{\theta}_m$. The parameter estimates from these runs were averaged:

$$t^* = \frac{\sum_{m=1}^{M} \hat{t}_m}{M}$$

(9.1)

- The variances of the parameters from these runs were averaged:

$$U^* = \frac{\sum_{m=1}^{M} U_m}{M} \qquad (9.2)$$

- The variance of the m estimates, $\hat{t}_m$, was estimated:

$$B_m = \frac{\sum_{m=1}^{M} \left(\hat{t}_m - t^* \right)}{(M-1)} \qquad (9.3)$$

- The final estimate of the variance of the parameter estimate is the sum of the two components:

$$V = U^* + \left(1 + M^{-1} \right) B_m \qquad (9.4)$$

where the degrees of freedom is computed:

$$d.f. = (M-1)(1+r)^2,$$

where

$$r = \frac{1 + U^*}{B \left(1 + \dfrac{1}{M} \right)}.$$

The square root of this variance is the standard error of the gamma, and it is used in a standard Student's t formula to evaluate the statistical significance of each gamma.

9.2.3 Working with plausible values in HLM

Below is the procedure for running a plausible value analysis via Windows mode:

To run a plausible value analysis

1. After specifying the model, select the **Estimation Settings** option from the **Other Settings** menu.
2. Choose **Plausible Values** to open the **Select Plausible Value Outcome Variables** dialog box (See Figure 9.5 for an example).

3. Select the first plausible value (either the outcome or a covariate) from the **Choose first variable from level 1 equation** drop-down menu.
4. Double-click the other plausible values from the **Possible choices** box.
5. Click **OK**.

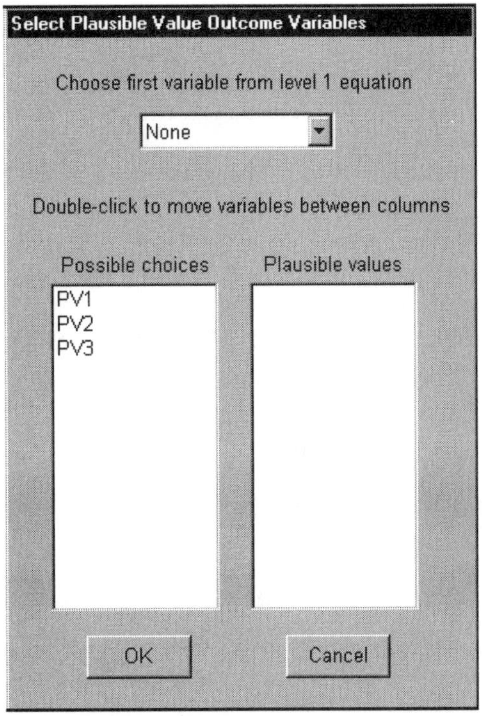

Figure 9.5   Select Plausible Value Outcome Variables dialog box

9.2.4 Data with multiply-imputed values for the outcome and covariates

There may be multiply-imputed values for both the outcome and the covariates. To apply HLM to such data, it is necessary to prepare as many MDM files as the number of imputed data sets. Thus, if there are five imputed data sets, five MDM files with identical variable labels need to be prepared. To run these models in batch mode, refer to Section E.3 in Appendix E.

Below are the commands for running an analysis with multiply-imputed data sets via Windows mode.

1. After specifying the model, select the **Estimation Settings** option from the **Other Settings** menu.
2. Choose **Multiple Imputation** to open the **Multiple Imputation MDM files** dialog box (See Figure 9.6 for an example).
3. Enter the names of the MDM files that contain the multiply-imputed data either by typing into the **File #** edit boxes or clicking **Browse** to open them.
4. Click **OK**. Model specification follows the usual format.

The calculations involved are very similar to the ones mentioned in Section 9.2.2.

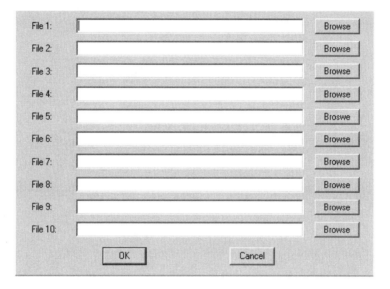

Figure 9.6   Multiple Imputation MDM files dialog box

9.3   "V-Known" models for HLM2

The V-known option in HLM2 is a general routine that can be used for applications where the level-1 variances (and covariances) are known. Included here are problems of meta-analysis (or research synthesis) and a wide range of other possible uses as discussed in Chapter 7 of *Hierarchical Linear Models*. The program input consists of Q random level-1 statistics for each group and their associated error variances and covariances.

We illustrate the use of the program with the following data from the meta-analysis of teacher expectancy effects described on pp. 210-216 of *Hierarchical Linear Models*. Here we show the process of V-known analysis in its most generic form, which requires using the interactive mode. See Section 9.3.4 for a alternative method for $Q = 1$ using the Windows interface.

1	0.030	0.016	2.000
2	0.120	0.022	3.000
3	-0.140	0.028	3.000
4	1.180	0.139	0.000
5	0.260	0.136	0.000
6	-0.060	0.011	3.000
7	-0.020	0.011	3.000
8	-0.320	0.048	3.000
9	0.270	0.027	0.000
10	0.800	0.063	1.000
11	0.540	0.091	0.000
12	0.180	0.050	0.000
13	-0.020	0.084	1.000
14	0.230	0.084	2.000
15	-0.180	0.025	3.000
16	-0.060	0.028	3.000
17	0.300	0.019	1.000
18	0.070	0.009	2.000
19	-0.070	0.030	3.000

9.3.1 Data input format

Unlike the standard HLM2 program, the V-known routine uses only a single data input file. It consists of the following information:

1. The first field is the unit ID in character format.

2. This is followed by the Q statistics from each unit. In the teacher expectancy effects meta-analysis, Q equals one, the experiment effect size. (The effect size estimate appears in the third column of Table 7.1 in *Hierarchical Linear Models.*)

3. Next are the $Q(Q+1)/2$ error variances and covariances associated with the set of Q statistics. These variance-covariance elements must be specified in row-column sequence from the lower triangle of the matrix, *i.e.*, $V_{11}, V_{21}, V_{22}, ..., V_{Q,Q-1}, V_{QQ}$. For the meta-analysis application only a single error variance is needed. (Note the values in the third column above are the squares of the standard errors that appear in the fourth column of Table 7.1.)

4. Last are the potential level-2 predictor variables. In the teacher expectancy effects meta-analysis, there was only one predictor, the number of weeks of prior contact. (See column 2 of Table 7.1).

The Q statistics, their error variances and covariances, and the level-2 predictors must be ordered as described above and have a numeric format.

9.3.2 Creating the MDM file

The V-known program must be implemented in batch or interactive mode; it is not available in Windows mode.

We present below an example of an HLM2 session that creates a multivariate data matrix file using the V-known routine on the teacher expectancy effects data.

```
C:\HLM>HLM2

Will you be starting with raw data?  y
Is the input file a v-known file? y
How many level-1 statistics are there? 1
How many level-2 predictors are there? 1
 Enter 8 character name for level-1 variable number 1: EFFSIZE

 Enter 8 character name for level-2 variable number 1: WEEKS
 Input format of raw data file (the first field must be the character ID)
 format: (a2,3f12.3)
 What file contains the data? expect.dat

Enter name of MDM file: expect.MDM
      19 groups have been processed
```

The file, EXPECT.DAT, contains the input data displayed above and the resulting multivariate data matrix are saved in the EXPECT.MDM file. Note that the input format has been specified for the character ID, the level-1 statistic (EFFSIZE), the associated variance, and the level-2 predictor (WEEKS).

9.3.3 Estimating a V-known model

Once the MDM file has been created, it can be used to specify and estimate a variety of models as in any other HLM2 application. The example below illustrates interactive use of the V-known program (example EXPECT.HLM).

```
C:\HLM>hlm2 expect.MDM

                    SPECIFYING AN HLM MODEL

Level-1 predictor variable specification

Which level-1 predictors do you wish to use?
 The choices are:
 For  EFFSIZE enter  1

    level-1 predictor? (Enter 0 to end)  1

Level-2 predictor variable specification

Which level-2 variables do you wish to use?
```

```
The choices are:
For    WEEKS enter  1

Which level-2 predictors to model  EFFSIZE?

      Level-2 predictor? (Enter 0 to end)  1

                  ADDITIONAL PROGRAM FEATURES

Select the level-2 variables that you might consider for
inclusion as predictors in subsequent models.
 The choices are:
For    WEEKS enter  1

Which level-2 variables to model  EFFSIZE?
      Level-2 variable? (Enter 0 to end)  0

Do you want to run this analysis with a heterogeneous sigma^2? n
Do you wish to use any of the optional hypothesis testing procedures? n
                  OUTPUT SPECIFICATION
Do you want a residual file? n
How many iterations do you want to do? 10000
Do you want to see OLS estimates for all of the level-2 units? n
 Enter a problem title: Teacher expectancy meta-analysis
      Enter name of output file: expect.lis
Computing . . ., please wait


----------------------------------------------


  Problem Title: Teacher expectancy meta-analysis

  The data source for this run  = expect.MDM
  The command file for this run =
  Output file name              = expect.lis
  The maximum number of level-2 units = 19
  The maximum number of iterations = 10000
  Method of estimation: restricted maximum likelihood
  Note: this is a v-known analysis

  The outcome variable is INTRCPT1

  The model specified for the fixed effects was:

  ----------------------------------------------------
  Level-1                  Level-2
  Effects                  Predictors
  ---------------------    ---------------
        EFFSIZE, B1          INTRCPT2, G10
                             WEEKS, G11


The model specified for the covariance components was:
-----------------------------------------------------------

        Variance(s and covariances) at level-1 externally specified


        Tau dimensions
           EFFSIZE slope
```

187

Summary of the model specified (in equation format)

Level-1 Model

Y1 = B1 + E1

Level-2 Model

B1 = G10 + G11*(WEEKS) + U1

 STARTING VALUES

 Tau(0)
  EFFSIZE,B(null)   0.02004

 Estimation of fixed effects
 (Based on starting values of covariance components)

                                    Standard   Approx.
     Fixed Effect   Coefficient Error   T-ratio d.f.   P-value
 ----
 For   EFFSIZE, B1
    INTRCPT2, G10   0.433737   0.109700   3.954   17   0.001
        WEEKS, G11   -0.168572   0.046563 -3.620   17   0.002

The value of the likelihood function at iteration 1 = -3.414348E+001
The value of the likelihood function at iteration 2 = -3.350241E+001
The value of the likelihood function at iteration 3 = -3.301695E+001
The value of the likelihood function at iteration 4 = -3.263749E+001
The value of the likelihood function at iteration 5 = -3.121675E+001

                                                  .
                                                  .
The value of the likelihood function at iteration 7849 = -2.979898E+001
The value of the likelihood function at iteration 7850 = -2.979898E+001
The value of the likelihood function at iteration 7851 = -2.979897E+001
The value of the likelihood function at iteration 7852 = -2.979897E+001

Iterations stopped due to small change in likelihood function

******* ITERATION 7853 *******

Tau
  EFFSIZE,B   0.00001

Tau (as correlations)
  EFFSIZE,B   1.000

  Random level-1 coefficient   Reliability estimate

   EFFSIZE, B   0.000

The value of the likelihood function at iteration 7853 = -2.979897E+001

```
Final estimation of fixed effects:
------------------------------------------------------------------------
                                     Standard           Approx.
     Fixed Effect       Coefficient  Error     T-ratio  d.f.    P-value
------------------------------------------------------------------------
For       EFFSIZE, B1
    INTRCPT2, G10          0.408572  0.087146   4.688     17    0.000
      WEEKS, G11          -0.157963  0.035943  -4.395     17    0.000
------------------------------------------------------------------------

Final estimation of variance components:
------------------------------------------------------------------------
Random Effect           Standard    Variance    df   Chi-square  P-value
                        Deviation   Component
------------------------------------------------------------------------
 EFFSIZE,      U          0.00283    0.00001     17   16.53614    >.500
------------------------------------------------------------------------

Statistics for current covariance components model
--------------------------------------------------
Deviance =        59.59795
Number of estimated parameters =     2
```

In general, the HLM2 results for this example closely approximate the more traditional results that would be obtained from a graphical examination of the likelihood function. (For this particular model, the likelihood mode is at zero.) Note that the value of the likelihood was still changing after 7850 iterations. Often, HLM2 converges after a relatively small number of iterations. When the number of iterations required is large, as in this case, this indicates that the estimation is moving toward a boundary condition (in this example it is a variance estimate of zero for Tau). This can be seen by comparing the starting value estimate for Tau, 0.02004, with the final estimate of 0.00001. (For a further discussion see p. 202 of *Hierarchical Linear Models*.)

9.3.4 V-known analyses where Q = 1

There is an alternative and appealing method for analysis for V-known analyses when $Q = 1$. This may be accomplished as follows:

1. Select the **Estimation Settings** option from the **Other Settings** menu.
2. Use the pull down menus to select the variable that represents the known level-1 variance.

This may be accomplished in either the two-level or the three-level HLM programs.

10 Conceptual and Statistical Background for Cross-classified Random Effect Models (HCM2)

All of the applications discussed thus far have involved a strictly hierarchical data structure. For example, in Chapter 4, the three-level hierarchical model formulated to investigate the contextual effects on children's growth in academic achievement applies only to those students who remained in a single school during the course of the investigation. The students and their academic records in this study design could belong to one and only one school. If there were changes in school memberships among the students over time, the students who moved to other schools and their achievement scores would belong to more than one school. This would result in a more complex data structure in which the lower-level units (repeated measures on achievement) are cross-classified by two higher-level units (students and schools). To model school and student contribution to academic growth requires the use of cross-classified random effects models (HCM2).

Chapter 12 of *Hierarchical Linear Models* discusses two applications of a cross-classified random effects model. The first is from a study of neighborhood and school effects on educational attainment in Scotland (Garner & Raudenbush, 1991). As there were students who resided in a specific neighborhood and enrolled in schools located in a different neighborhood, the data collected did not have a strictly hierarchical data structure. Here the attainment data of students were cross-classified by neighborhoods and schools. The second case is an assessment of the effects of classrooms on children's cognitive growth during the primary years. This latter example is from the Immersion Study. As there were changes in classroom memberships among the students during the course of the investigation, the achievement data were cross-classified by students and classrooms.

10.1 The general cross-classified random effects models

A general random cross-classified model consists of two sub-models: level-1 or within-cell and level-2 or between-cell models. The cells refer to the cross-classifications by the two higher-level units. For example, if the research problem consists of data on students cross-classified by schools and neighborhoods, the level-1 or within-cell model will represent the relationships among the student-level variables, the level-2 or between-cell model will capture the influence of school- and neighborhood-level factors. Formally, there are $i = 1, 2, ..., n_{jk}$ level-1 units (*e.g.*, students) nested within cells cross-classified by $= 1, ..., J$ first level-2 units (*e.g.*, neighborhoods), designated as rows, and $k = 1, ..., K$ second level-2 units (e.g., schools), designated as columns.

10.1.1   Level-1 or "within-cell" model

We represent in the level-1 or within-cell model the outcome for case i in individual cells cross-classified by level-2 units j and k.

$$Y_{ijk} = \pi_{0jk} + \pi_{1jk}a_{1ijk} + \pi_{2jk}a_{2ijk} + \cdots + \pi_{pjk}a_{pijk} + e_{ijk}$$

$$= \pi_{0jk} + \sum_{p=1}^{P} \pi_{pjk}a_{pijk} + e_{ijk} \qquad (10.1)$$

where

π_{pjk} $(p=1,2,\ldots,P)$ are *level-1 coefficients,*

a_{pijk} is the level-1 predictor p for case i in cell jk,

e_{ijk} is the *level-1 or within-cell random effect,* and

σ^2 is the variance of e_{ijk}, that is the *level-1* or *within-cell variance.* Here we assume that the random term $e_{ijk} \sim N(0,\sigma^2)$.

10.1.2   Level-2 or "between-cell" model

Each of the π_{pjk} coefficients in the level-1 or within-cell model becomes an outcome variable in the level-2 or between-cell model:

$$\pi_{pjk} = \theta_p + \left(\beta_{p1} + b_{p1j}\right)X_{1k} + \left(\beta_{p2} + b_{p2j}\right)X_{2k} + \cdots + \left(\beta_{pQ_p} + b_{pQ_p j}\right)X_{Q_p k} +$$

$$\left(\gamma_{p1} + c_{p1k}\right)W_{1j} + \left(\gamma_{p2} + c_{p2k}\right)W_{2j} + \cdots + \left(\gamma_{pR_p} + c_{pR_p k}\right)W_{R_p j} +$$

$$\delta_{p1jk}Z_{1jk} + \cdots + \delta_{pS_p jk}Z_{S_p jk} +$$

$$b_{p0j} + c_{p0k} + d_{p0jk}$$

$$= \theta_p + \sum_{q=1}^{Q_p}\left(\beta_{pq} + b_{pqj}\right)X_{qk} + \sum_{r=1}^{R_p}\left(\gamma_{pr} + c_{prk}\right)W_{rj} + \sum_{s=1}^{S_p}\delta_{psjk}Z_{sjk} + b_{p0j} + c_{p0k} + d_{p0jk} \qquad (10.2)$$

where

θ_{p00} is the model intercept, the expected value of π_{pjk} when all explanatory variables are set to zero;

β_{pq} are the fixed effects of column-specific predictors $X_{qk}, q = 1,\ldots,Q_p$;

b_{pqj} are the random effects associated with column-specific predictors X_{qk}. They vary randomly over rows $j = 1,\ldots, J$;

γ_{pr} are the fixed effects of row-specific predictors $W_{rj}, r = 1, ..., R_p$;

c_{prk} are the random effects associated with row-specific predictors W_{rj}. They vary randomly over columns $k = 1, ..., K$;

δ_{psjk} are the fixed effects of cell-specific predictors Z_{sjk}, which are the interaction terms created as the products of X_{qk} and $W_{rj}, s = 1, ..., S_p$ and $S_p \leq R_p \times Q_p$; and

b_{p0j}, c_{p0k}, and d_{p0jk} are residual row, column, and cell-specific random effects, respectively, on π_{pjk}, after taking into account X_{qk}, W_{rj}, and Z_{sjk}. We assume that $b_{p0j} \sim N\left(0, \tau_{pb00}\right)$, $c_{p0k} \sim N\left(0, \tau_{pc00}\right)$, and that the effects are independent of each other.

However, the vector containing elements b_{pqj} is assumed multivariate normal with a mean zero and a full covariance matrix τ. Similarly the vector with elements c_{prk} is assumed multivariate normal with mean vector zero and full covariance matrix Δ.

10.2 Parameter estimation

Three kinds of parameter estimates are available in HCM2: empirical Bayes estimates of randomly varying effects of level-1 or within-cell and row- and column-specific coefficients; maximum-likelihood estimates of the level-2 or row-, column- and cell-specific coefficients; and maximum likelihood estimate of the level-1 or within-cell and level-2 or between-cell variance-covariance components. The estimation procedure uses a full maximum likelihood approach (Kang, 1992; Raudenbush, 1993).

10.3 Hypothesis testing

As in the case of HLM2, HCM2 routinely prints standard errors and t-tests for each of the level-2 coefficients (the "fixed effects") as well as a chi-square test of homogeneity for each random effect. In addition, optional "multivariate hypothesis tests" are available in HCM2. Multivariate tests for the level-2 coefficients enable both omnibus tests and specific comparisons of the parameter estimates just as described in the section *Multivariate hypothesis tests for fixed effects* in Chapter 2. Multivariate tests regarding alternative variance-covariance structures at level 2 proceed just as described in the section *Multivariate tests of variance-covariance components specification* in Section 2.8.8.1.

11 Working with HCM2

11.1 An example using HCM2 in Windows mode

HCM2 analyses can be executed in Windows, interactive, and batch modes. We describe a Windows execution below. We consider interactive and batch execution in Appendix F. A number of special options are presented at the end of the chapter.

Chapter 12 in *Hierarchical Linear Models* presents a series of analyses of data from a study of neighborhood and school contribution to educational attainment in Scotland (Garner & Raudenbush, 1991). We use the data from the study, provided along with the HLM software, to illustrate the operation of the HCM2 program.

11.1.1 Constructing the MDM file from raw data

In constructing the MDM file, there are the same range of options for data input as for HLM2. Similar to HLM3, HCM2 requires two IDs, one for each higher-level unit, and the IDs have to be sorted. The two higher-level units in our example are neighborhoods and schools. Whereas the user can choose either higher-level unit as the row or column factor, we adopt the convention that the data are arranged such that the level with more units becomes the row factor and the level with fewer units becomes the column factor. Thus, we will designate the neighborhood ($N = 542$) as the row factor and school ($N = 17$) as the column factor.

11.1.2 SPSS input

Data input requires a level-1 file (student-level file), a level-2 row-factor (neighborhood-level) file, and a level-2 column-factor (school-level) file.

Level-1 file. The level-1 or within-cell file, ATTAINW.SAV has 2,310 students and 8 variables. The two IDs are NEIGHID for neighborhoods and SCHID for schools. The variables are:

- ATTAIN (a measure of educational attainment)
- P7VRQ (Primary 7 verbal reasoning quotient)
- P7READ (Primary 7 reading test scores)
- DADOCC (father's occupation scaled on the Hope-Goldthorpe scale in conjunction with the Registrar General's social-class index (Willms, 1986));
- DADUNEMP, an indicator for father's unemployment status (1 if unemployed, 0 otherwise)

193

- DADED, an indicator for father's educational level (1 if schooling past the age of 15, 0 otherwise)
- MOMED, an indicator for mother's educational level (1 if schooling past the age of 15, 0 otherwise)
- MALE, an indicator for student gender (1 if male, 0 if female)

Data for the first 15 observations are shown in Figure 11.1. Note that five students from Neighborhood 26 and one from Neighborhood 27 attended School 20. These first six observations provided information about two neighborhood-by-school combinations or cells. One of the next nine students living in Neighborhood 29 attended School 18 and the other eight went to School 20. They provided data for two cross-classified neighborhood-by-school cells (see Table 12.1 in *Hierarchical Linear Models*, p. 374, for a display of the organization of the data by counts in each neighborhood-by-school cell).

	neighid	schid	attain	p7vrq	p7read	dadocc	dadunemp	daded	momed	male
1	26.00	20.00	-1.33	-1.03	-.87	-3.45	.00	.00	.00	1.00
2	26.00	20.00	-1.33	-10.03	-27.87	-3.45	.00	.00	.00	.00
3	26.00	20.00	1.52	1.97	11.13	-9.09	.00	.00	.00	.00
4	26.00	20.00	.56	2.97	6.13	2.32	.00	.00	.00	.00
5	26.00	20.00	1.52	17.97	17.13	16.20	.00	.00	.00	1.00
6	27.00	20.00	-.13	3.97	-.87	-3.45	.00	.00	1.00	.00
7	29.00	18.00	.03	8.97	6.13	16.20	.00	1.00	1.00	1.00
8	29.00	20.00	-1.33	-17.03	-23.87	-3.45	.00	.00	.00	1.00
9	29.00	20.00	-1.33	-8.03	-4.87	-3.45	.00	.00	.00	.00
10	29.00	20.00	.16	1.97	-4.87	-11.49	.00	.00	.00	.00
11	29.00	20.00	.56	-.03	-5.87	-3.45	.00	.00	.00	.00
12	29.00	20.00	.16	4.97	11.13	-11.49	.00	.00	.00	1.00
13	29.00	20.00	.74	-4.03	.13	-3.45	.00	.00	.00	1.00
14	29.00	20.00	-1.33	-15.03	-25.87	-3.45	.00	.00	.00	.00
15	29.00	20.00	-.36	-8.03	-13.87	-3.45	.00	.00	.00	.00

Figure 11.1   First 16 cases in the ATTAINW.SAV dataset

11.1.3   Level-2 row-factor file

For our neighborhood example, the level-2 row-factor (neighborhood) level file, ATTAINR.SAV, consists data on 1 variable for 542 neighborhoods. The variable is DEPRIVE (a scale measuring social deprivation, which incorporates information on the poverty concentration, health, and housing stock of a local community).

Figure 11.2 shows data from the first 4 neighborhoods.

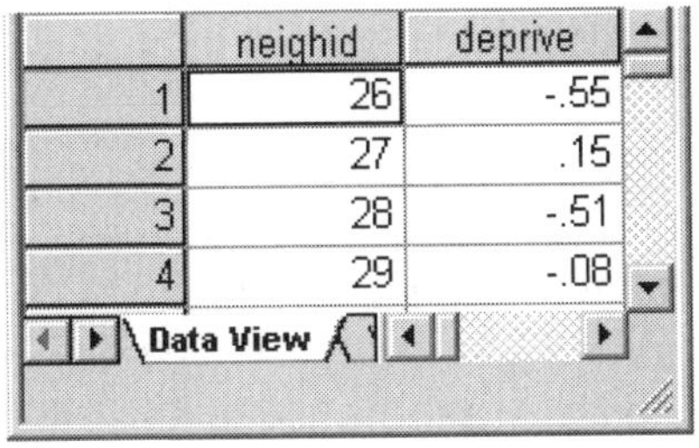

	neighid	deprive
1	26	-.55
2	27	.15
3	28	-.51
4	29	-.08

Figure 11.2 First 4 cases in the ATTAINR.SAV data set

11.1.4 Level-2 column-factor file

The level-2 column-factor (neighborhood) file, ATTAINCO.SAV, has 17 schools and 1 variable. The variable is DUMMY, a dummy variable.

Figure 11.3 shows data for the first 4 schools.

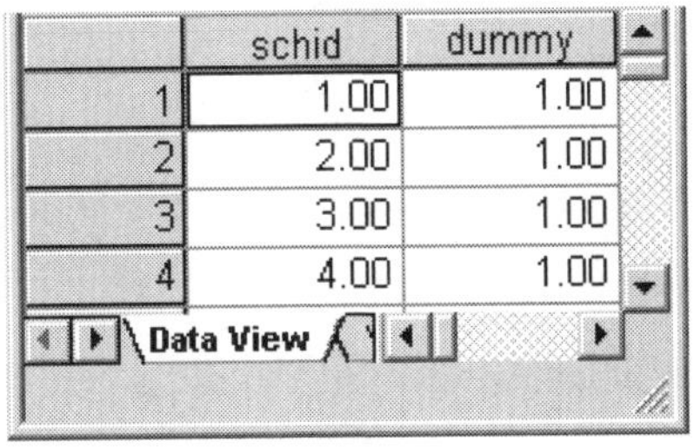

	schid	dummy
1	1.00	1.00
2	2.00	1.00
3	3.00	1.00
4	4.00	1.00

Figure 11.3 First 4 cases in the ATTAINCO.SAV data set

The steps for the construction of the MDM for HCM2 are similar to the ones described earlier. Select **HCM2** in the **Select MDM type** dialog box (see Figure 2.5). Note that the program can handle missing data at level 1 or within-cell only. The MDM template file, ATTAIN.MDMT, contains a log of the input responses used to create the MDM file, ATTAIN.MDM, using ATTAINW.SAV, ATTAINR.SAV, and ATTAINCO.SAV. Figure 11.4 displays the dialog box used to create the MDM file. Figures 11.5 to 11.7 show the dialog boxes for the within-cell file, ATTAINW.SAV, the row-factor file, ATTAINR.SAV, and the column-factor file, ATTAINCO.SAV.

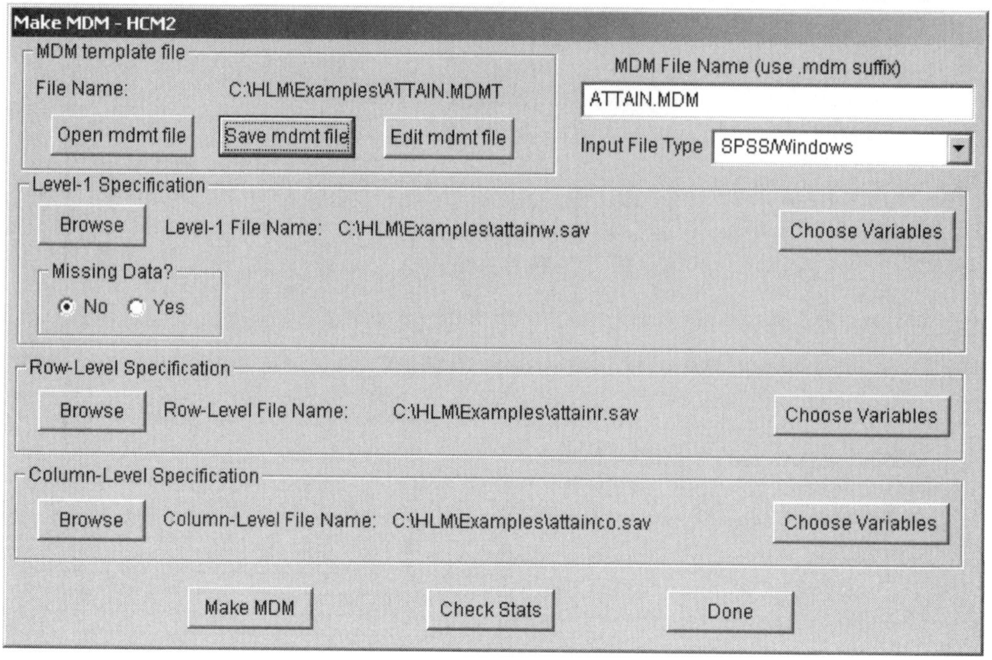

Make MDM – HCM2

- MDM template file
  - File Name: C:\HLM\Examples\ATTAIN.MDMT
  - [Open mdmt file] [Save mdmt file] [Edit mdmt file]
- MDM File Name (use .mdm suffix)
  - ATTAIN.MDM
  - Input File Type: SPSS/Windows

- Level-1 Specification
  - [Browse] Level-1 File Name: C:\HLM\Examples\attainw.sav [Choose Variables]
  - Missing Data?
    - ⦿ No ○ Yes

- Row-Level Specification
  - [Browse] Row-Level File Name: C:\HLM\Examples\attainr.sav [Choose Variables]

- Column-Level Specification
  - [Browse] Column-Level File Name: C:\HLM\Examples\attainco.sav [Choose Variables]

[Make MDM] [Check Stats] [Done]

Figure 11.4   Make MDM – HCM2 dialog box for ATTAIN.MDMT

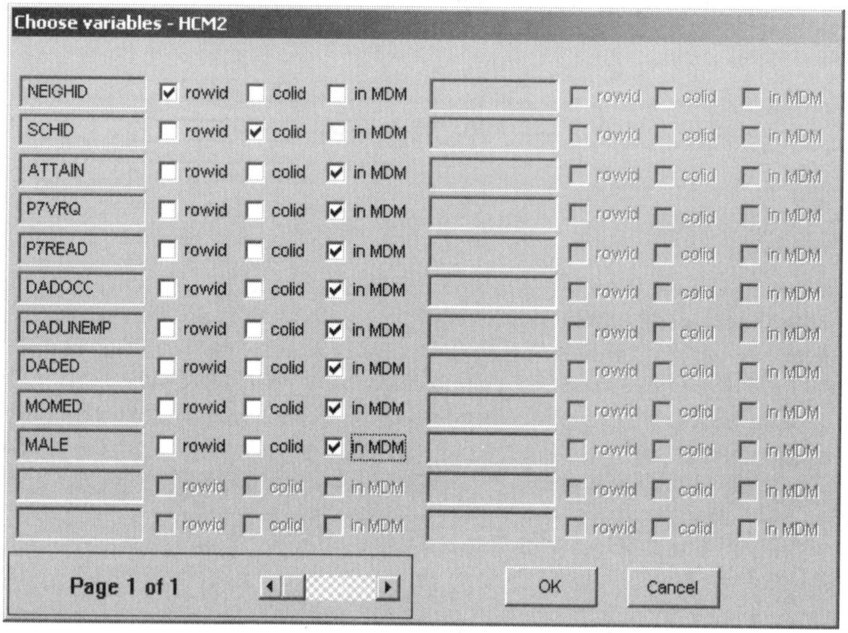

Choose variables - HCM2

NEIGHID	☑ rowid ☐ colid ☐ in MDM
SCHID	☐ rowid ☑ colid ☐ in MDM
ATTAIN	☐ rowid ☐ colid ☑ in MDM
P7VRQ	☐ rowid ☐ colid ☑ in MDM
P7READ	☐ rowid ☐ colid ☑ in MDM
DADOCC	☐ rowid ☐ colid ☑ in MDM
DADUNEMP	☐ rowid ☐ colid ☑ in MDM
DADED	☐ rowid ☐ colid ☑ in MDM
MOMED	☐ rowid ☐ colid ☑ in MDM
MALE	☐ rowid ☐ colid ☑ in MDM

Page 1 of 1   [OK] [Cancel]

Figure 11.5   Choose variables – HCM2 dialog box for level-1 or within-cell file, ATTAINW.SAV

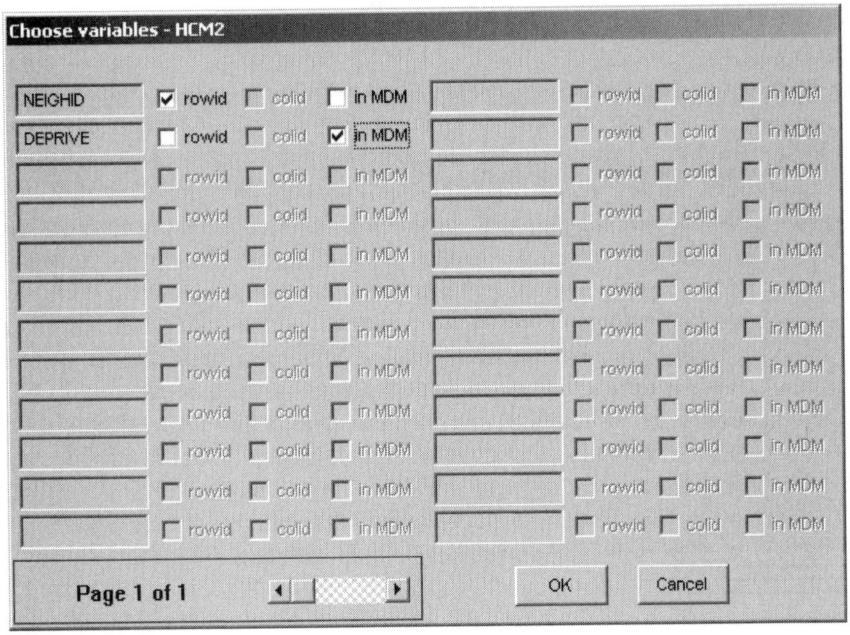

Figure 11.6   Choose variables – HCM2 dialog box for level-1 or row-factor file, ATTAINR.SAV

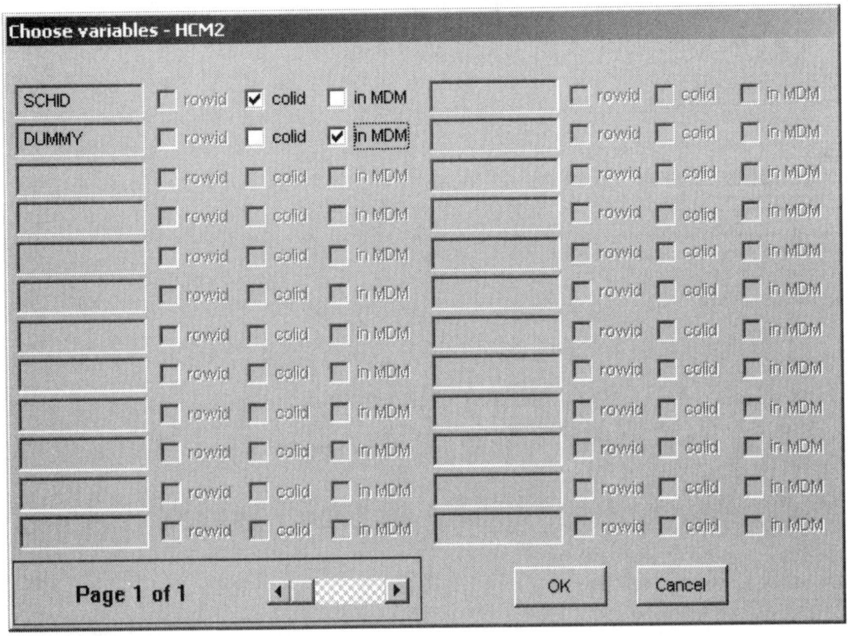

Figure 11.7   Choose variables – HCM2 dialog box for level-1 or column-factor file, ATTAINCO.SAV

197

11.2 Executing analyses based on the MDM file

Once the MDM file is constructed, it can be used as input for the analysis. Model specification has three steps:

1. Specification of the level-1 or within-cell model. In our example, we shall model educational attainment (ATTAIN) as the outcome. We first formulate an unconditional model that includes no predictor variables at any level. In the second or conditional model, we use prior measures of cognitive skill, verbal reasoning quotient and reading achievement, father's employment status and occupation and father's and mother's education to predict attainment.

2. Specification of the row- or column-factor prediction model. In the second or conditional model, we shall predict each student's intercept with social deprivation.

3. Specification of the residual row, column, and cell-specific effects as random or non-random, the effects associated with row-specific predictors as varying randomly or fixed over columns, and the effects associated with column-specific predictors as varying randomly or fixed over rows. We shall test whether the association between social deprivation (a row-specific predictor) and attainment varies over schools in the third model.

Following the three steps above, we first specify a model with no student-, neighborhood-, or school-level predictors. The purpose is to estimate the components of variation that lie between neighborhoods, between schools, and within cells.

1. From the **WHLM** window, open the **File** menu.

2. Choose **Create a new model using an existing MDM file** to open an **Open MDM File** dialog box. Open the existing MDM file (ATTAIN.MDM in our example).

3. Click on the name of the outcome variable (ATTAIN in our example). Click **Outcome variable**. The specified model will appear in equation format (see Figure 11.8).

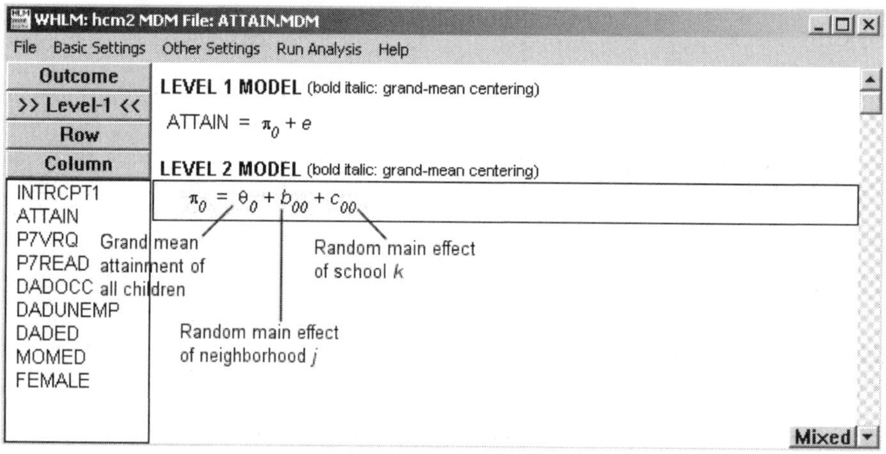

Figure 11.8   Unconditional model for the attainment example

The results of the analysis are given below.

```
Problem Title: Unconditional Model

  The data source for this run  = C:\HLM\ATTAIN.MDM
  The command file for this run = C:\HLM\attain1.hlm
  Output file name              = C:\HLM\attain1.txt
  The maximum number of level-1 units     = 2310
  The maximum number of row-level units   = 524
  The maximum number of column-level units = 17
  The maximum number of iterations = 100
  Method of estimation: full maximum likelihood
  The maximum number of iterations = 100
  Z-structure: independent

  The outcome variable is   ATTAIN

  The model specified for the fixed effects was:
-------------------------------------------------------
```

Level-1 Model

   Y = P0 + e

Level-2 Model

  P0 = theta(0) + b00 + c00

For starting values, data from 2310 level-1 and 524 level-2 records were used

Iterations stopped due to small change in likelihood function

****** ITERATION 21 ******

Sigma_squared =   0.79909

Tau(rows)
 INTRCPT1
  ICPTROW,b00
   0.14105

Tau(rows) (as correlations)
 INTRCPT1/ ICPTROW,b00 1.000

Tau(columns)
 INTRCPT1
  ICPTCOL,c00
   0.07546

Tau(columns) (as correlations)
 INTRCPT1/ ICPTCOL,c00 1.000

The intra-neighborhood correlation, the correlation between outcomes of two students who live in the same neighborhood but attend different schools, is estimated to be:

$$\widehat{Corr}\left(Y_{ijk}, Y_{ijk'\varepsilon}\right) = \frac{\hat{\tau}_{b00}}{\hat{\tau}_{b00} + \hat{\tau}_{c00} + \hat{\sigma}^2}$$

$$= \frac{0.141}{0.141 + 0.075 + 0.799}$$

$$= 0.139.$$

Thus, about 13.9% of the total variance lies between neighborhoods.

The intra-school correlation is the correlation between outcomes of two students who attend the same school but live in different neighborhoods:

$$\widehat{Corr}\left(Y_{ijk}, Y_{i'j'k}\right) = \frac{\hat{\tau}_{c00}}{\hat{\tau}_{b00} + \hat{\tau}_{c00} + \hat{\sigma}^2}$$

$$= \frac{0.075}{0.141 + 0.075 + 0.799}$$

$$= 0.074.$$

That is, about 7.4% of the variation lies between schools.

The intra-cell correlation is the correlation between outcomes of two students who live in the same neighborhood and attend the same school:

$$\widehat{Corr}\left(Y_{ijk}, Y_{ijk'\varepsilon}\right) = \frac{\hat{\tau}_{b00} + \hat{\tau}_{c00}}{\hat{\tau}_{b00} + \hat{\tau}_{c00} + \hat{\sigma}^2}$$

$$= \frac{0.141 + 0.075}{0.141 + 0.075 + 0.799}$$

$$= 0.212.$$

Thus, according to the fitted model, about 22% of the variance lies between cells.

```
The value of the likelihood function at iteration 26 = -2.938490E+003
The value of the likelihood function at iteration 21 = -3.178356E+003

The outcome variable is    ATTAIN

Final estimation of fixed effects:
------------------------------------------------------------------------
                                  Standard           Approx.
     Fixed Effect     Coefficient  Error    T-ratio   d.f.   P-value
------------------------------------------------------------------------
For INTRCPT1, P0
   INTERCEPT,theta0    0.075357   0.072226   1.043    2309    0.297
------------------------------------------------------------------------
```

11.3 Specification of a conditional model with the effect associated with a row-specific predictor fixed

The above example involves a model that is unconditional at all levels. In this model we set up a level-1 and a row-factor prediction model.

To set up the level-1 model:

At the model specification dialog box, select P7VCR, P7READ, DADOCC, DADUNEMP, DADED, MOMED, and MALE and grand-mean center all the predictors. Figure 11.9 shows the models with the level-1 predictors. In the interest of parsimony, given the small cell sizes and within-neighborhood sizes, all level-1 coefficients are fixed. (To specify any of them as randomly varying, select the equation containing a specific regression coefficient, π_p, and click on b_{p0}).

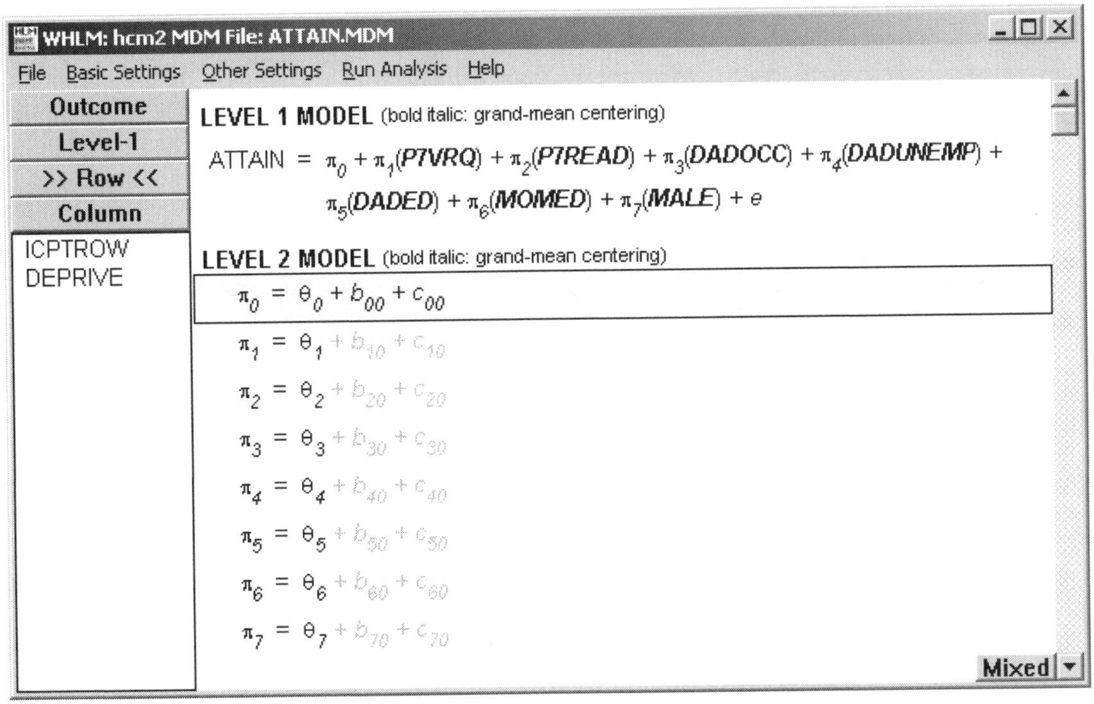

WHLM: hcm2 MDM File: ATTAIN.MDM

File   Basic Settings   Other Settings   Run Analysis   Help

| Outcome |
| Level-1 |
| >> Row << |
| Column |

ICPTROW
DEPRIVE

LEVEL 1 MODEL (bold italic: grand-mean centering)

$$\text{ATTAIN} = \pi_0 + \pi_1(P7VRQ) + \pi_2(P7READ) + \pi_3(DADOCC) + \pi_4(DADUNEMP) + \pi_5(DADED) + \pi_6(MOMED) + \pi_7(MALE) + e$$

LEVEL 2 MODEL (bold italic: grand-mean centering)

$$\pi_0 = \theta_0 + b_{00} + c_{00}$$

$$\pi_1 = \theta_1 + b_{10} + c_{10}$$

$$\pi_2 = \theta_2 + b_{20} + c_{20}$$

$$\pi_3 = \theta_3 + b_{30} + c_{30}$$

$$\pi_4 = \theta_4 + b_{40} + c_{40}$$

$$\pi_5 = \theta_5 + b_{50} + c_{50}$$

$$\pi_6 = \theta_6 + b_{60} + c_{60}$$

$$\pi_7 = \theta_7 + b_{70} + c_{70}$$

Mixed

Figure 11.9   Level-1 Prediction Model for the Attainment Study

To set up the level-2 row-factor prediction model:

Select the equation containing π_0. A listbox for row-factor variables (>>**Row**<<) will appear. Click DEPRIVE and apply the grand-mean centering scheme. In the level-2 model, we treated the association between social deprivation and educational attainment as fixed across all schools. Note that c_{01} is disabled. We relax this assumption in our next model. Figure 11.10 displays the conditional model.

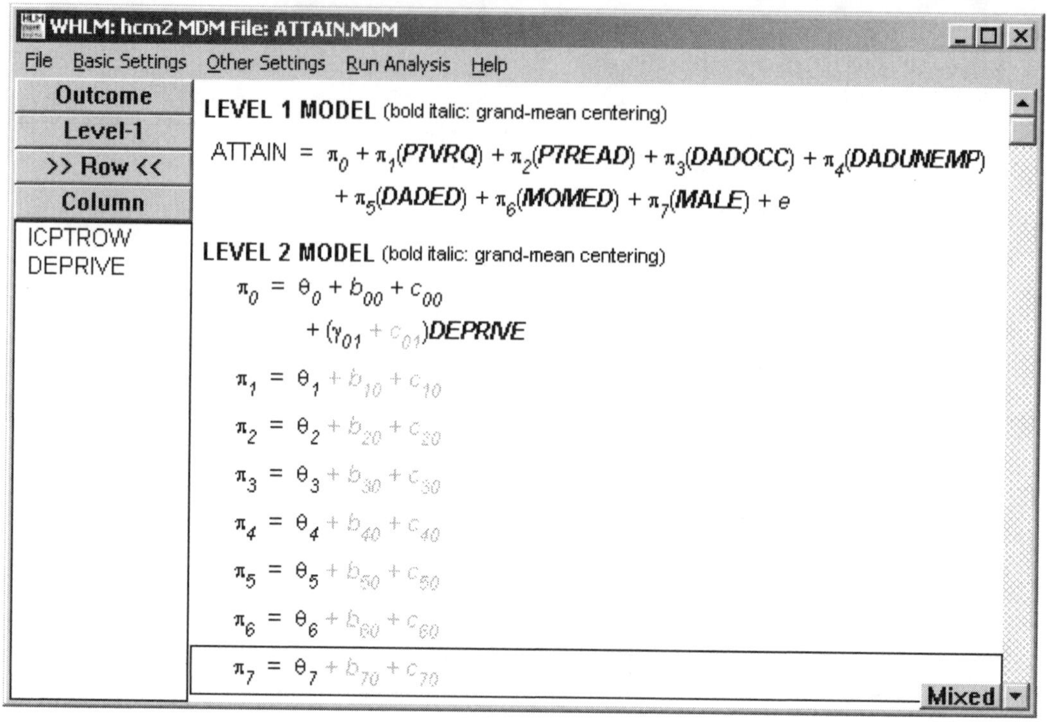

File Basic Settings Other Settings Run Analysis Help

| Outcome |
| Level-1 |
| >> Row << |
| Column |

ICPTROW
DEPRIVE

LEVEL 1 MODEL (bold italic: grand-mean centering)

$$ATTAIN = \pi_0 + \pi_1(\textbf{\textit{P7VRQ}}) + \pi_2(\textbf{\textit{P7READ}}) + \pi_3(\textbf{\textit{DADOCC}}) + \pi_4(\textbf{\textit{DADUNEMP}})$$
$$+ \pi_5(\textbf{\textit{DADED}}) + \pi_6(\textbf{\textit{MOMED}}) + \pi_7(\textbf{\textit{MALE}}) + e$$

LEVEL 2 MODEL (bold italic: grand-mean centering)

$$\pi_0 = \theta_0 + b_{00} + c_{00}$$
$$+ (\gamma_{01} + c_{01})\textbf{\textit{DEPRIVE}}$$

$$\pi_1 = \theta_1 + b_{10} + c_{10}$$

$$\pi_2 = \theta_2 + b_{20} + c_{20}$$

$$\pi_3 = \theta_3 + b_{30} + c_{30}$$

$$\pi_4 = \theta_4 + b_{40} + c_{40}$$

$$\pi_5 = \theta_5 + b_{50} + c_{50}$$

$$\pi_6 = \theta_6 + b_{60} + c_{60}$$

$$\pi_7 = \theta_7 + b_{70} + c_{70}$$

Mixed

Figure 11.10   Conditional Model for the Attainment Study, with Social Deprivation Effect Fixed

The results of the analysis are given below.

```
Problem Title: Conditional Model, with social deprivation effect fixed

    The data source for this run  = C:\HLM\ATTAIN.MDM
    The command file for this run = C:\HLM\attain2.hlm
    Output file name             = C:\HLM\attain2.txt
    The maximum number of level-1 units    = 2310
    The maximum number of row-level units   = 524
    The maximum number of column-level units = 17
    The maximum number of iterations = 100
    Method of estimation: full maximum likelihood
    The maximum number of iterations = 100
    Z-structure: independent

    The outcome variable is    ATTAIN

    The model specified for the fixed effects was:
    --------------------------------------------------

Level-1 Model
    Y = P0 + P1*(P7VRQ) + P2*(P7READ) + P3*(DADOCC) + P4*(DADUNEMP)
            + P5*(DADED) + P6*(MOMED) + P7*(MALE) + e


Level-2 Model

    P0 = theta(0) + b00 + c00
                + (G01)*DEPRIVE
    P1 = theta(1)
    P2 = theta(2)
```

```
        P3 = theta(3)
        P4 = theta(4)
        P5 = theta(5)
        P6 = theta(6)
        P7 = theta(7)
```

P7VRQ P7READ DADOCC DADUNEMP DADED MOMED MALE have been centered around the grand mean.

For starting values, data from 2310 level-1 and 524 level-2 records were used

Iterations stopped due to small change in likelihood function

******* ITERATION 34 *******

Sigma_squared =   0.45891

Tau(rows)
 INTRCPT1
  ICPTROW,b00
     0.00014

Tau(rows) (as correlations)
 INTRCPT1/ ICPTROW,b00 1.000

Tau(columns)
 INTRCPT1
  ICPTCOL,c00
     0.00389

Tau(columns) (as correlations)
 INTRCPT1/ ICPTCOL,c00 1.000

The value of the likelihood function at iteration 34 = -2.384802E+003

Final estimation of fixed effects:

Fixed Effect	Coefficient	Standard Error	T-ratio	Approx. d.f.	P-value
For INTRCPT1, P0					
INTERCEPT,theta0	0.100561	0.021142	4.756	2301	0.000
DEPRIVE, G01	-0.156676	0.025178	-6.223	2301	0.000
For P7VRQ, P1					
INTERCEPT,theta1	0.027556	0.002263	12.176	2301	0.000
For P7READ, P2					
INTERCEPT,theta2	0.026291	0.001749	15.028	2301	0.000
For DADOCC, P3					
INTERCEPT,theta3	0.008165	0.001359	6.008	2301	0.000
For DADUNEMP, P4					
INTERCEPT,theta4	-0.120771	0.046779	-2.582	2301	0.010
For DADED, P5					
INTERCEPT,theta5	0.144426	0.040782	3.541	2301	0.001
For MOMED, P6					
INTERCEPT,theta6	0.059440	0.037381	1.590	2301	0.112
For MALE, P7					
INTERCEPT,theta7	-0.056058	0.028401	-1.974	2301	0.048

Several features of the results are remarkable:

- Several level-1 covariates are significantly related to educational attainment, with especially large effects for P7READ and P7VRQ.
- The residual level-1 variance is estimated to be 0.459, implying that 43% of the unconditional level-1 variance (estimated at 0.799) is accounted for by the covariates.
- Controlling these level-1 effects, a highly significant negative effect of social deprivation appears ($\hat{\gamma}_{01} = -0.157$, $t = -6.22$).
- The residual variation between neighborhoods, τ_{b00}, (estimated at 0.000), and between schools, τ_{c00} (estimated at 0.004) are close to zero; compare to the unconditional variance estimates (0.141 and 0.075). The level-2 neighborhood variance component was substantially reduced.

Specification of a conditional model with the effect associated with the row-specific predictor random

In the next model, the relationship between social deprivation and attainment was assumed invariant across schools. Now we test the tenability of the assumption.

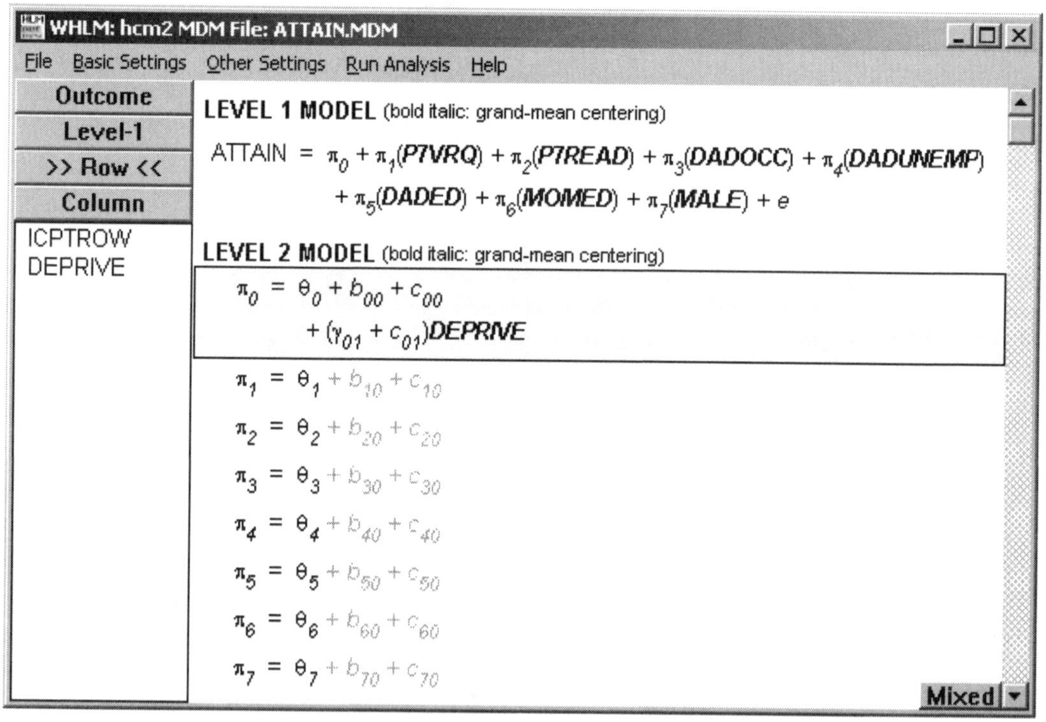

LEVEL 1 MODEL (bold italic: grand-mean centering)

$$ATTAIN = \pi_0 + \pi_1(P7VRQ) + \pi_2(P7READ) + \pi_3(DADOCC) + \pi_4(DADUNEMP)$$
$$+ \pi_5(DADED) + \pi_6(MOMED) + \pi_7(MALE) + e$$

LEVEL 2 MODEL (bold italic: grand-mean centering)

$$\pi_0 = \theta_0 + b_{00} + c_{00}$$
$$+ (\gamma_{01} + c_{01})DEPRIVE$$

$$\pi_1 = \theta_1 + b_{10} + c_{10}$$
$$\pi_2 = \theta_2 + b_{20} + c_{20}$$
$$\pi_3 = \theta_3 + b_{30} + c_{30}$$
$$\pi_4 = \theta_4 + b_{40} + c_{40}$$
$$\pi_5 = \theta_5 + b_{50} + c_{50}$$
$$\pi_6 = \theta_6 + b_{60} + c_{60}$$
$$\pi_7 = \theta_7 + b_{70} + c_{70}$$

Figure 11.11 Conditional Model for the Attainment Study, with Social Deprivation Effect Random

To specify the effect of the row-specific predictor random, select the equation containing π_0. Click on c_{01}. Figure 11.11 displays the conditional model with the social deprivation effect specified as random. To test the assumption, we compare the model deviance of this model against the one estimated in the last analysis. The procedure is the same as described in Section 2.9.6.

The results of the analysis are given below.

```
Sigma_squared =      0.45519

Tau(rows)
 INTRCPT1
  ICPTROW,b00
    0.00370

Tau(rows) (as correlations)
 INTRCPT1/ ICPTROW,b00   1.000

Tau(columns)
 INTRCPT1        INTRCPT1
  ICPTCOL,c00  DEPRIVE,c01
    0.00380      0.00156
    0.00156      0.00066
```

The point estimate of the variance of the unique contribution of school k to the association between social deprivation and attainment is .001 and that of the covariance between the effect with the school random effect is .002.

```
Tau(columns) (as correlations)
 INTRCPT1/ ICPTCOL,c00   1.000   0.983
 INTRCPT1/ DEPRIVE,c01   0.983   1.000

The value of the likelihood function at iteration 955 = -2.384254E+003

The outcome variable is   ATTAIN

Final estimation of fixed effects:
```

Fixed Effect	Coefficient	Standard Error	T-ratio	Approx. d.f.	P-value
For INTRCPT1, P0					
INTERCEPT,theta0	0.098355	0.021179	4.644	2301	0.000
DEPRIVE, G01	-0.159041	0.026754	-5.945	2301	0.000
For P7VRQ, P1					
INTERCEPT,theta1	0.027635	0.002263	12.210	2301	0.000
For P7READ, P2					
INTERCEPT,theta2	0.026242	0.001750	14.993	2301	0.000
For DADOCC, P3					
INTERCEPT,theta3	0.008112	0.001360	5.964	2301	0.000
For DADUNEMP, P4					
INTERCEPT,theta4	-0.120311	0.046759	-2.573	2301	0.010
For DADED, P5					
INTERCEPT,theta5	0.142630	0.040753	3.500	2301	0.001
For MOMED, P6					
INTERCEPT,theta6	0.060862	0.037358	1.629	2301	0.103
For MALE, P7					
INTERCEPT,theta7	-0.056139	0.028383	-1.978	2301	0.048

```
Statistics for current covariance components model
---------------------------------------------------
Deviance                      = 4768.508345
Number of estimated parameters = 14

Model comparison test
--------------------------------
Chi-square statistic      =     1.09165
Number of degrees of freedom =   2
P-value                   = >.500
```

The result of the deviance test is not significant. There is no evidence that the social deprivation varies over schools. Not surprisingly, the standard error for $\hat{\gamma}_{01}$, the social deprivation effect, remains nearly unchanged, as do all inferences about the fixed effects.

11.4 Other program features

HCM models provide options for multivariate hypothesis tests for the fixed effects and the variance-covariance components. A "no-intercept" model is available for the level-1, level-2 and between-cell models. Figure 11.12 displays the **Basic Model Specifications - HCM2** dialog box.

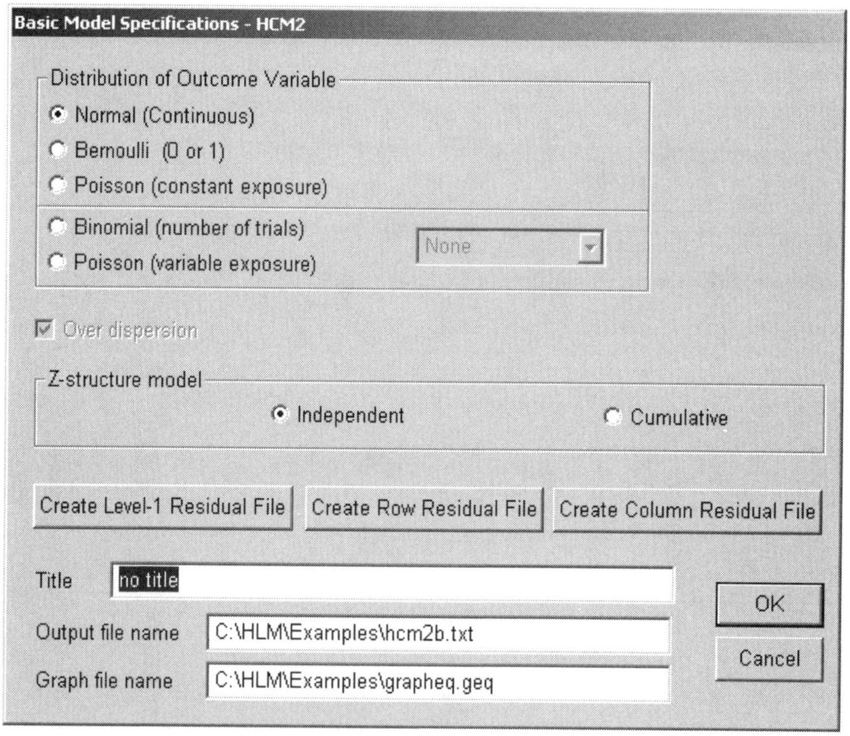

Fig 11.12   **The Basic Model Specifications – HCM2 dialog box**

206

The options are similar to the corresponding dialog box for HLM2 (see Section 2.5.2). Unlike HLM2, there is the option to create level-1, row and column residual files. There is also another option unique to HCM2. When modeling longitudinal, repeated measures, it is possible to select a cumulative effect model to allow carry-over treatment effects by specifying a cumulative Z-structure model. See *Hierarchical Linear Models*, p. 390, for an example.

12 Graphing Data and Models

HLM2 and HLM3 provide the ability to make data-based and model-based graphs. Data-based graphs allow examination of univariate and bivariate distributions. Model-based graphs, which can be produced by ALL the modules of WHLM, facilitate visualization and presentation of analytic results for the whole or a subset of the population of interest. They also enable users to check the tenability of underlying model assumptions.

12.1 Data – based graphs – two level analyses

12.1.1 Box and whisker plots

We first illustrate how to use box-and-whisker plots to display univariate distributions of level-1 variables for each level-2 unit, with and without a level-2 classification variable. Using the HS&B data (see Section 2.5.1.1), we display graphical summaries of the mathematics achievement variable, MATHACH, and simultaneously show differences in the student scores within a school and among schools.

To prepare box-and-whisker plots

1. From the **HLM** window open the **File** menu.
2. Choose **Create a new model using an existing MDM file** to open an **Open MDM File** dialog box. Open HSB.MDM.
3. Open the **File** menu, choose **Graph Data ... box-whisker plots** to open an **Choose Y for box plot** dialog box (see Figure 12.1).

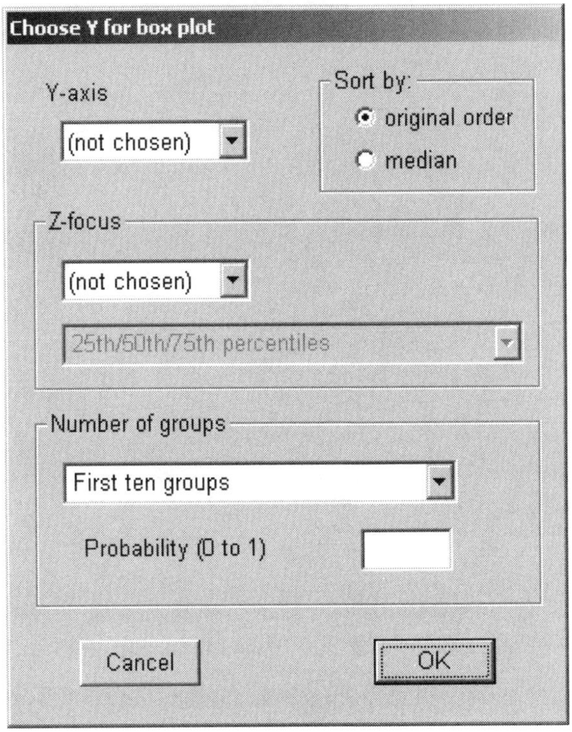

Figure 12.1   Choose Y for box plot dialog box

4. Select MATHACH in the **Y-axis** drop-down listbox.
5. Choose the number of groups to be used for graphing. There are three options: (a) **First ten groups**; (b) **Random sample of spec'd prob** (specified probability) and (c) **All groups** (n = total number of groups) for users to choose from in the **Number of groups** drop-down list box. The selection of option (b) requires the user to specify the proportion or percent of the level-2 units to be included. to do so, enter a probability into the text box for **Probability (0 to 1)**. In our example, we randomly select 10 percent of the schools to illustrate. we select **Random sample of spec'd prob** from the **Number of groups** drop-down list box. Enter 0.1 into the text box for **Probability (0 to 1)** to indicate that 10 percent or a proportion of .1 of the schools will be used.
6. Specify the arrangement of the plots by either (a) the original order of the groups as appeared in the data set or (b) the median in an ascending order. Click on the selection button for **median** in the **Sort by** section to arrange the box-and-whisker plots of MATHACH by median in an ascending order (see Figure 12.2).

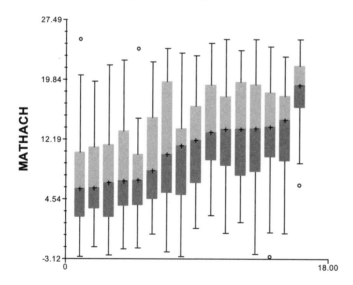

Figure 12.2   Choose Y for box plot dialog box for the MATHACH example

7. Click **OK** to display the plots (see Figure 12.3).

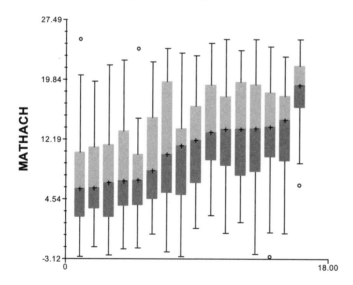

Figure 12.3   Box and whisker plot for MATHACH

The figure gives side-by-side graphical summaries of the distributions of MATHACH for the sixteen schools sorted by median. The x-axis denotes number of schools in the display and the y-axis mathematics achievement. The plot tells us that the first school from the left has a median score of about 6.05, which is the lowest school median in this group. The distribution of the scores of the students in this school is positively skewed and there is an outlier at the upper end.

The third and the fourth schools from the left have similar distributions of mathematics scores. Compared to the distribution of the scores of the adjacent school on the right, however, the scores of these two schools display greater variability, as defined by the lengths of the boxes or interquartile ranges. In addition, there is an outlier at the upper end of the distribution for the fifth school. The highest median mathematics score among the 16 schools was 19.08.

8. (Optional) WHLM allows users to list the raw data of a specific group that is graphically summarized in one of the box-and-whisker plots as well. To see the data of a specific level-2 unit, click on one of the box-and-whisker plots (near the median is usually a good place) in Figure 12.3, which brings up the following dialog box:

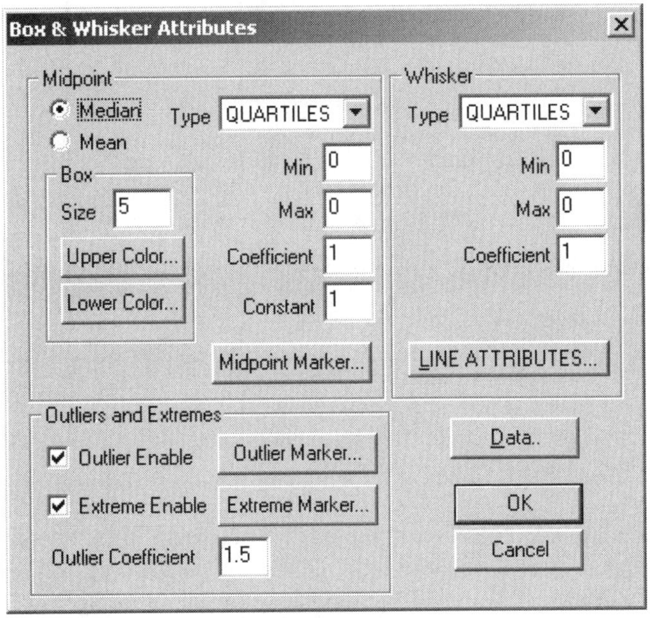

Figure 12.4   **Box & Whisker Attributes dialog box**

For a description of the options, see Table 12.1.

Table 12.1 Definitions and options in the Box & Whisker Attributes dialog box

	Key terms	Function	Option	Definition
1	Midpoint	Specify the type of average used	2 choices	1. Median 2. Mode
2	Box Size	Specify the width in units of the axis that the box width is parallel to.		
3	Min, Max, and Coefficient for box or whisker and Constant for box	Min and Max specify the box percentage minimum and maximum when the box or whisker Type is PERCENT. The coefficient is the box or whisker coefficient by which the selected range value will be multiplied. The Constant is the box constant, valid when the box Type is CONSTANT.		
4	Midpoint marker	Display a **Marker Attributes** dialog box that allows the user to specify the shape, color, size, and style of the midpoint marker.		
5	Line attributes	Display a **Line Parameters** dialog box that allows the user to specify the thickness, color, and style of the whisker.		

Click **Data** and then a a dialog box containing the data of a specific group will appear. In our example, we examine the raw scores of the school with the highest median (see Figure 12.5). The title bar of Figure 12.5 tells us the level-2 ID of the box-and-whisker plot we selected is 3427. # is a zero-based counter for group plots.

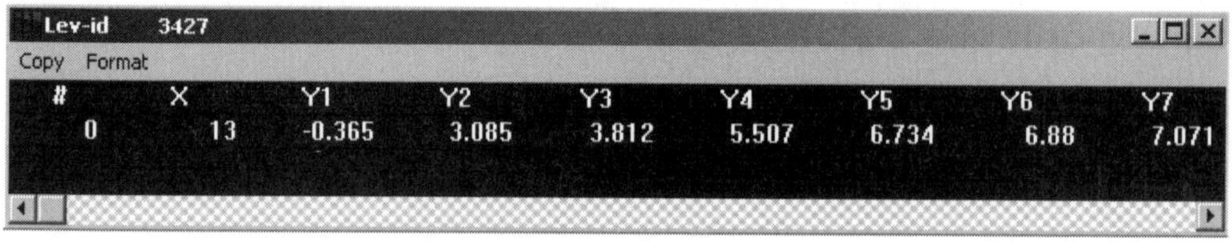

Lev-id 3427							_ □ ✕
Copy Format							
#	**X**	**Y1**	**Y2**	**Y3**	**Y4**	**Y5**	**Y6** **Y7**
0	13	-0.365	3.085	3.812	5.507	6.734	6.88 7.071

Figure 12.5   Data for School 3427 dialog box

As the box-and-whisker plots are plotted individually in the example, it is 0. X tells us that the data are from the thirteenth school displayed on the plot. Y1 to Y11 list the mathematics scores for the first eleven students in School 3427. Move the bottom scroll box to the left to display more scores for the other students.

9. (Optional) To edit the graph, open the **Edit** menu and choose **Graph Parameters...**. The user can change attributes such as size and color of the graph, border, and plotting area. By choosing **Copy graph** or **Copy current page** (when there are more than one pages of graphs), users can directly copy and paste the graph or current page into a word processing or graphics document.

10. (Optional) To print the graph, open the **File** menu, select **Print current page** or **Print selected graph** when there are more than one graph. Users can choose **Printing Options...** to change printing parameters such as choice of background, border type, aspect ratio (the ratio of the x-axis length to the y-axis length, the default is 5/3), and printing style.

11. To save the graph for future use by opening the **File** menu and choose **Save as metafile**. A **Save as** dialog box will open. Enter a filename for the file and click **OK**. The file can be saved as an Enhanced Metafile (.emf) (default and preferred as it holds more information than the other option) or Windows Metafile (.wmf). Users can use word processing programs to insert the graph file into the text. For example, to insert the saved .emf file into Word, choose **Insert-...Picture-...From File** from Word's main menu.

12. (Optional) To make modifications to the specifications, select **Graph Settings**. The **Equation Graphing** dialog box will appear. We are going to illustrate this by adding a level-2 classification variable next.

To include a level-2 classification variable

13. After choosing the the **Y-Axis** variable, select the level-2 classification variable in the **Z-focus** drop-down listbox. There are two types of level-2 classification variables, categorical and continuous. For categorical variables, WHLM will classify the plots with the levels of the variables. For continous variables, users can choose either to dichotomize them using median splits, or trichotomize them into three groups: (a) 0 to 24th percentile; (b) 25th to 75th percentile; and (c) 76th percentile and above. These two options, available when a continuous classification variable is chosen, can be found in the lower **Z-focus** drop-down listbox. In our example, we will choose school sector, Catholic vs. public school, as the classification variable. To continue working on the plot we have just made, click **Graph Settings** to open the **Equation Graphing** dialog box. Select SECTOR in the **Z-focus** dialog box. The following graph will be displayed (see Figure 12.6).

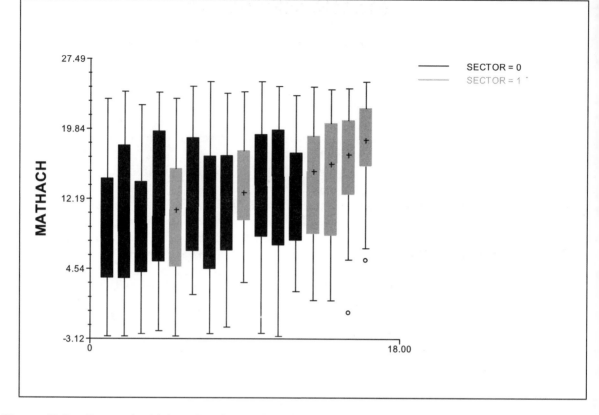

Figure 12.6   Box-and-whisker plots for MATHACH for a random sample of schools as classified by school sector

In the graph, the box-and-whisker plots for Catholic and public schools are coded differently (red for Catholic and blue for public schools). The colored graphs (not showed here) suggest that the three schools that have the highest median mathematics scores are Catholic schools. The school with the lowest average belongs to the public sector.

Users can edit the legends by clicking on them in the graph above to open the **Legend Parameters** dialog box (see Figure 12.7), which allows them to make changes in the titles of the legends, their sizes and font types, and the display of the legend box. For example, one may like to change SECTOR = 0 in the text box of Figure 12.7 to PUBLIC = 0 and SECTOR = 1 to CATHOLIC = 1.

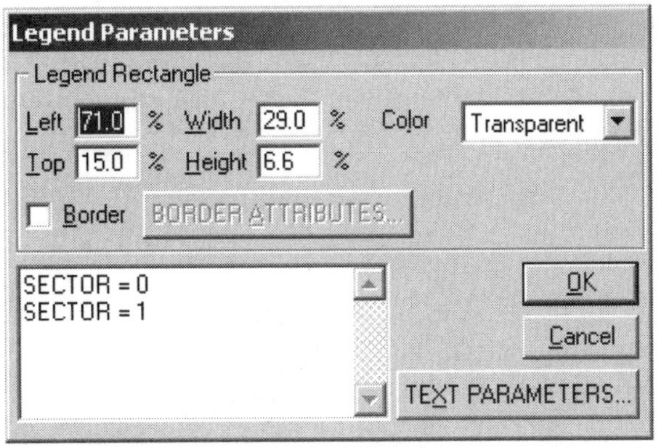

Figure 12.7 Legend Parameters dialog box

12.1.2 Scatter plots

In the previous section, we illustrated how to graphically summarize and compare univariate distributions of level-1 variables, with and without a level-2 classification variable. Now we demonstrate how to use data-based scatter plots to explore bivariate relationships between level-1 variables for individual or a group of level-2 units, with and without controlling level-2 variables. We will continue to use the HS&B data set and we are going examine the relationships between MATHACH and SES for a group or individual schools, with and without controlling for the sector of the school.

To prepare a scatter plot
1. From the HLM window, open the **File** menu.
2. Choose **Create a new model using an existing MDM file** to open an **Open MDM File** dialog box. Open HSB.MDM.
3. Open the **File** menu, choose **Graph Data …. line plots, scatter plots** to open a **Choose X and Y variables** dialog box (see Figure 12.8).

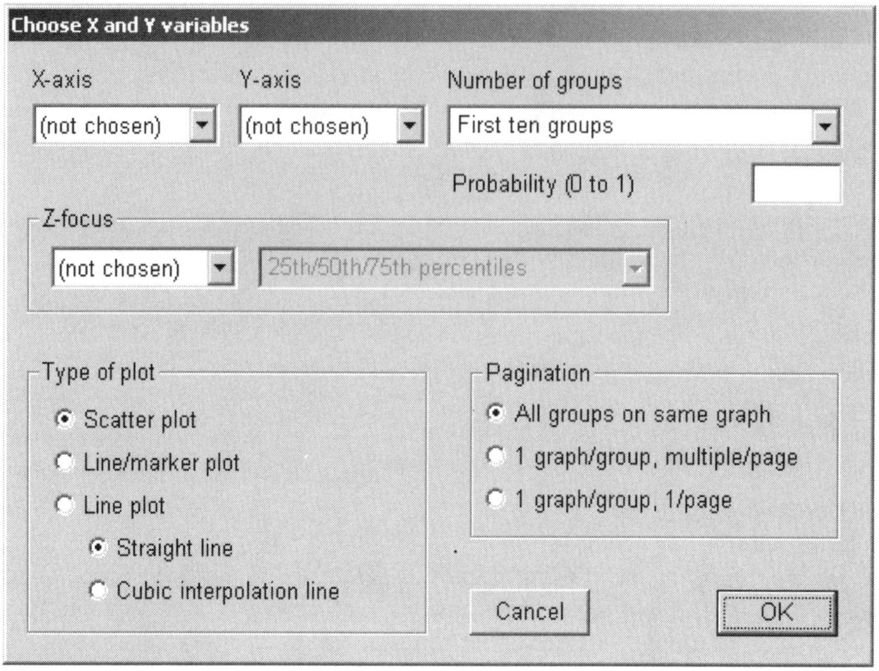

Figure 12.8   Choose X and Y variables dialog box

4. Select SES from the **X-axis** drop-down listbox.
5. Select MATHACH from the **Y-axis** drop-down listbox.
6. Select number of groups. In this example, select **Random sample of spec'd prob** and enter .2 into the textbox to select 20 percent of the schools.
7. Select type of plot. Users can select one of the two major types of plots: (a) scatter plot; and (b) line plot with and without markers or asterisks showing where the data points are. Click the selection button for **Scatter plot** (default) for this example.
8. Select type of pagination. There are three options: (a) all groups on the same graph (default); (b) one graph per groups and to display a maximum of eight graphs on one page, and (c) 1 graph per group and to be displayed on multiple pages. In this example, we will display the bivariate relationship between SES and MATHACH for all the selected schools on a single graph. We choose the option **All groups on same graph** accordingly.
9. Click **OK** to make the scatter plot. This gives us the following graph (see Figure 12.9), indicating a moderate positive association between SES and MATHACH, and suggesting that both variables have "ceilings" (upper limits).

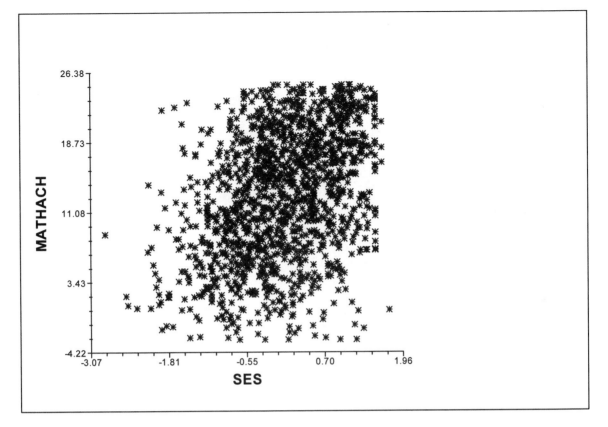

Figure 12.9   Scatter plot for the 20% random sample of cases

10. For more information on the editing, printing, saving and modification options, see Steps 11 to 13 in Section 12.1.1.

To include a level-2 classification variable

11. After specifying the variables for the x- and y-axis, select the controlling variable from the **Z-focus** drop-down listbox. As in the case for the box-and-whisker plots, users can choose either a categorical and continuous controlling variable (see Step 14 in Section 12.1.1). In our example, we will choose school sector, Catholic vs. public school, as the controlling variable. To continue working on the scatter plot we have just made, click **Graph Settings** to open the **Equation Graphing** dialog box. Select SECTOR in the **Z-focus** dialog box. The following graph will be displayed (see Figure 12.10).

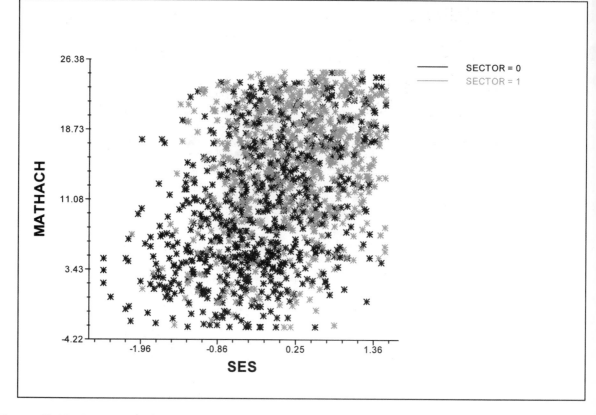

Figure 12.10 Scatter plot for random sample by SECTOR

The color-coded scatter plot shows that there is not in general a radical difference in the SES-MATCHACH relationship for the two types of schools.

It may be helpful to use a different pagination option to help us to discern the relationships for these two groups of school. Instead of having all the groups on the same graph, we select the **1 graph/group, multiple/page** pagination option. This gives us Figure 12.11, where we see how the two groups of schools vary in their SES and MATHACH distributions. Note, for example, that school 8946 has high levels of SES and that in school 4325, the association between SES and MATHACH appears a bit stronger than in several of the other schools. WHLM puts a maximum of 8 groups in a window. We can page back and forth using the **->** and **<-** buttons in the lower right corner of the window to display the scatter plots for other schools.

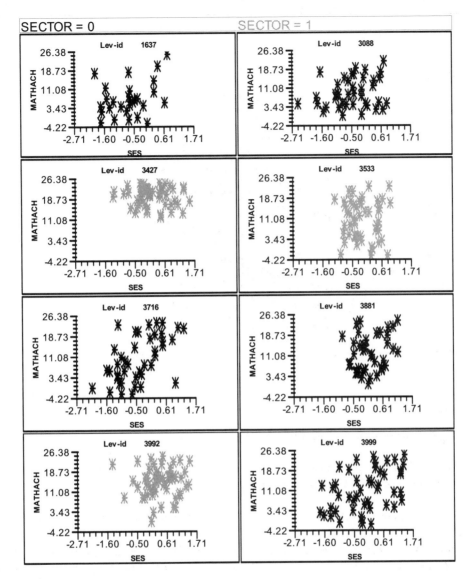

Figure 12.11 Scatter plots for individual schools on one page

As an elaboration of this, we can also choose on the **Graph Settings** dialog box to have each group's plot in a separate graph by choosing **1 graph/group, 1/page**, as shown below:

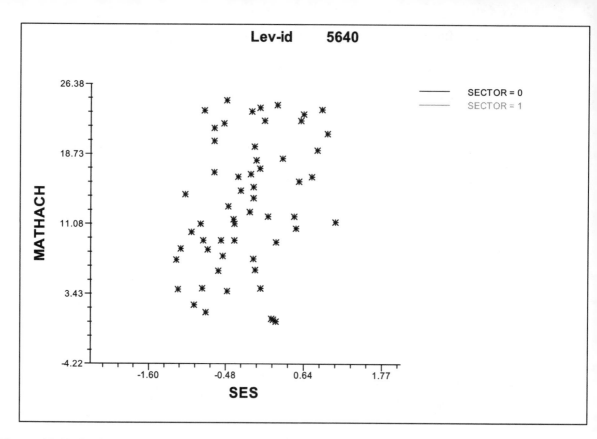

Figure 12.12 Individual scatter plot for school 7697

12.1.3 Line plots – two-level analyses

In scatter plots, observations on a pair of level-1 variables are plotted to examine their association, with and without a level-2 controlling variable. In line plots, level-1 repeated measures observations are joined by lines to describe changes or developments over time during the course of the research study. We illustrate this type of plot with data from two studies of children's vocabulary development (Huttenlocher, Haight, Bryk, and Seltzer, 1991, see also *Hierarchical Linear Models*, pp. 170-179). Twenty-two children were observed in the home on three to seven occasions at 2 to 4-month intervals during their second year of birth. A measure of the child's vocabulary size at each measurement occasion was derived from these observations. In this example, the level-1 file, VOCABI1.SAV has

- AGE   Age in months
- VOCAB   Vocabulary size
- AGE12   Age in months minus 12
- AGE12Q   AGE12*AGE12

The level-2 data file, VOCABL2.SAV, consists of 22 children and an indicator variable for gender

- MALE   An indicator for gender (1 = male, 0 = female)

To prepare a line plot

1. From the HLM window, open the **File** menu.
2. Choose **Create a new model using an existing MDM file** to open an **Open MDM File** dialog box. Open VOCAB.MDM.
3. Open the **File** menu, choose **Graph Data...line plots, scatter plots** to open an **Choose X and Y variables** dialog box (see Figure 12.8).
4. Select AGE from the **X-axis** drop-down listbox.
5. Select VOCAB from the **Y-axis** drop-down listbox.
6. Select number of groups. In this example, we include all the children in the display by selecting **All groups (n = 22)** in **Number of groups** drop-down list box.
7. Select type of line plot and method of interpolation. Users can select line plots with and without markers or asterisks showing where the data points are. The two types of interpolation are linear and cubic. In linear interpolations, the data points are simply joined by straight line segments. Cubic interpolations may be chosen to provide a smoother function and more continuity between the segments. For our example, suppose we want a line plot with no markers that is graphed with the linear interpolation method. Click the selection button for **Straight line**.
8. Select type of pagination. In this example, we want to have the trajectories for all children on the same graph and select **All groups on same graph pagination** option accordingly. When all the choices are made, the **Choose X and Y variables** dialog box should look like the one shown in Figure 12.13.

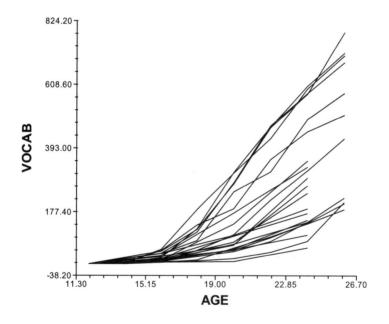

Figure 12.13 Choose X and Y variables dialog box for line plot of VOCAB and AGE

9. Click **OK** to make the line plot. The following graph will appear.

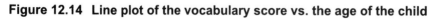

Figure 12.14 Line plot of the vocabulary score vs. the age of the child

We see that, for all children, vocabulary size is near zero at around a year of age (12 – 15 months) and that for each child, vocabulary size increases, typically quite rapidly during the second year of life.

To include a classifying level-2 variable

Now we want to look at the difference between boys and girls. On the menu of the graph dialog box, click **Graph Settings**. Here we choose the level-2 variable FEMALE as a **Z-focus** variable. For illustrative purposes, we will use the cubic interpolation method this time by clicking the selection button for **Cubic interpolation line**. The colored version of the following graph shows that girls' vocabulary tends to grow more rapidly than that of boys, on average.

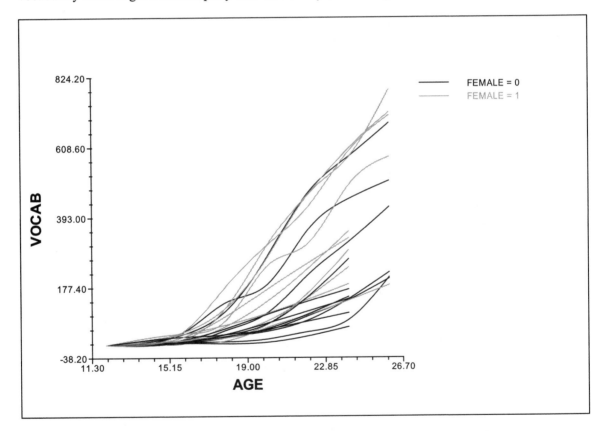

Figure 12.15 Cubic interpolation line plot of the difference between boys and girls

12.2 Model-based graphs – two level

12.2.1 Model graphs

WHLM provides graphing options to display the relationships between the outcome and the predictor(s) based on the final analytic results. The options allow us to visually represent the results of the models for the whole or a subset of population, and to graphically examine underlying model assumptions as well. Below we provide a 2-level example of a growth curve analysis of pro-deviant attitude for fourteen-year-old youth over a period of five years with data from the National Youth Survey (Elliot, Huizinga, & Menard, 1989; Raudenbush & Chan, 1993). In our example, the level-1 file, NYSW2.SAV, has 1,066 observations collected from interviewing annually fourteen-years-old youths beginning at 1976:

- ATTIT A nine-item scale assessing attitudes favorable to deviant behavior

  Subjects were asked how wrong (very wrong, wrong, a little bit wrong, not wrong at all) they believe it is for someone their age, for example, to damage and destroy property, use marijuana, use alcohol, sell hard drugs, or steal.

  The measure was positively skewed; so a logarithmic transformation was performed to reduce the skewness.

- AGE16 Age of participant at a specific time minus 16

- AGE16S = AGE16 * AGE16

The level-2 data file, NYSB2.SAV, consists of 241 youths and three variables per participant.

- FEMALE An indicator for gender (1 = female, 0 = male)
- MINORITY An indicator for ethnicity (1 = minority, 0 = other)
- INCOME Income

At level-1, we formulate a polynomial model of order 2 using AGE16 and AGE16S (see Figure 12.16) with FEMALE and MINORITY as covariates at level-2 modeling π_0, the expected pro-deviant attitude score at age 16 for subject j; π_1 and π_2, which are the expected average linear and quadratic growth rate for pro-deviant attitude score respectively. The procedure for setting up the model is given in 2.5.2. We will ask WHLM to graph the predicted values of pro-deviant attitude scores at different ages for different gender-by-ethnicity groups.

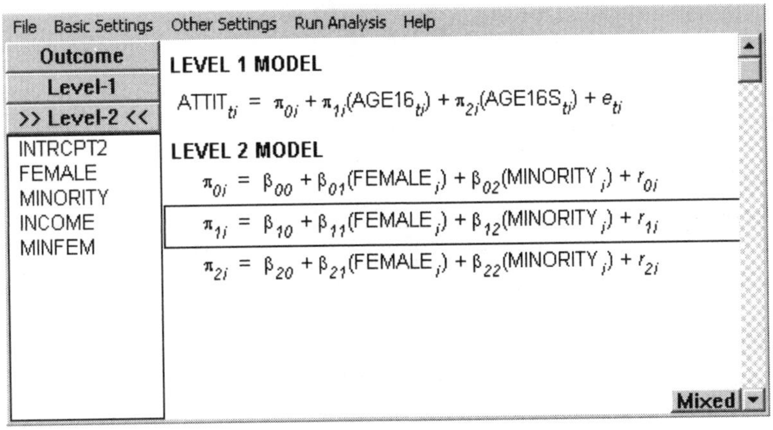

Figure 12.16 A polynomial model of order 2 with FEMALE and MINORITY as level-2 covariates

To prepare the graph

1. After running the model, select **Basic Settings** to open the **Basic Model Specifications – HLM2** dialog box.
2. Enter a name for the graphics file. The default name is graphequ.geq.
3. Enter a title and name the output filename, save the command file, and run the analysis as described in section 2.5.2.
4. Open the **File** menu and choose **Graph Equations**. An **Equation Graphing dialog** box will open (see Figure 12.17). Table 12.2 lists the definitions and options in the **Equation Graphing** dialog box.

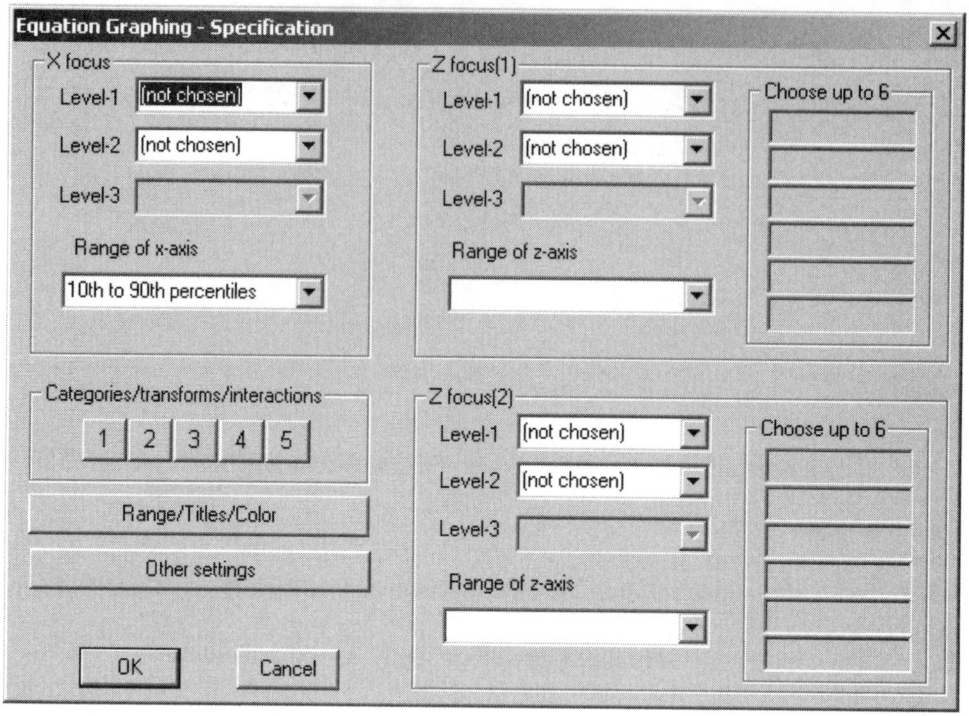

Figure 12.17 Equation Graphing – Specification dialog box

Table 12.2 Definitions and options in the Equation Graphing dialog box

	Key terms	Function	Option	Definition
1	X focus	Specify the variable to be displayed on x-axis	2 choices	1. Level-1 predictor 2. Level-2 predictor
2	Range of x-axis	Specify the maximum and minimum values of X to be displayed	5 choices	1. 10th to 90th percentiles 2. 5th to 95th percentiles 3. 25th to 75the percentiles 4. +/- 2 s.e.'s 5. Entire range
3	Categories/ transforms/ interactions	Define the reference category for categorical variables with more than two levels, and specify the relationship between the transformed\interaction and the original variables	5 choices	1. define categorical variable (for variable with more than two levels) 2. interaction 3. power of x/z 4. square root 5. natural log

	Key terms	Function	Option	Definition
4	Range/ Titles/ Color	Specify the maximum and minimum values of X and Y to be displayed (defaults are values computed). Enter legend titles for X and Y. Enter graph title. Select screen color	2 choices	1. Black and white 2. Color
5	Other Settings	Specify graphing function	2 choices	1. rough – original points 2. smooth – smoothed data
		Predictors not in graph	2 choices	1. constant at grand mean (default) 2. constant at zero.
		Use fixed effects from These are only available for HGLM models, and Laplace is only available if Laplace was asked for in HGLM2/HGLM3 Bernoulli runs	3 choices	1. unit-specific PQL estimates 2. population-average estimates 3. unit-specific Laplace estimates
6	Z focus(1 or 2)	Specify the first or second classification variable for X	3 choices	1. Level-1 predictor 2. Level-2 predictor
7	Range of z-axis	Specify the specific values of Z focus to be included.	4 choices for continuous variables	1. 25th and 75th percentiles 2. 25th/50th/75th percentiles 3. Averaged lower/upper quartiles 4. Choose up to 6 values (enter the six values into the textboxes)
			2 choices for categorical variables	1. Use the two actual values 2. Choose one or two values

We now proceed to select the predictor variables and specify their ranges or values, and choose the graphing functions and the various attributes of the plot for the polynomial model represented in Figure 12.16, as described in Steps 5 to 14 below.

5. Select AGE16 in the **X focus Level 1** drop-down listbox to graph pro-deviant attitude score as a function of age.
6. Select **Entire range** in the **Range of x-axis** drop-down listbox to include the entire range of age on the x axis in the graph.
7. Click 1 in the **Categories/transforms/interactions** section and select **power of x/z** for Polynomial relationships. An **Equation Graphing - power** dialog box will open (see Figure 12.18).

227

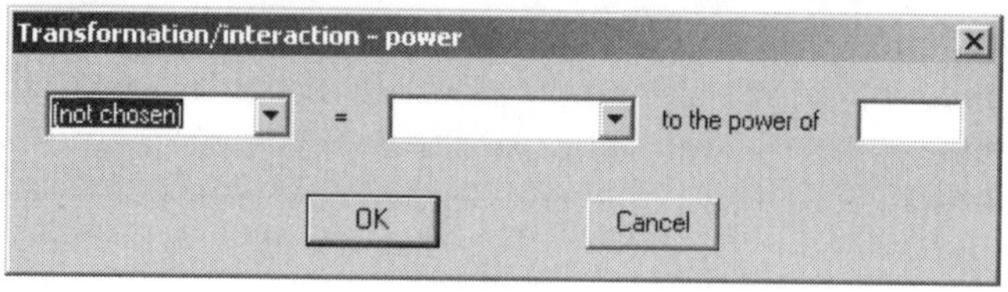

Figure 12.18 Equation Graphing – power dialog box

8. The textbox to the left of the equal sign is for the entry of the transformed variable. Select AGE16S in the drop-down listbox (see Figure 12.19). The textbox to the right is for the entry of the original variable. AGE16 will appear in the drop-down listbox as it is the only level-1 variable left. Enter 2 in the textbox for the **power** to be raised. Click **OK**.

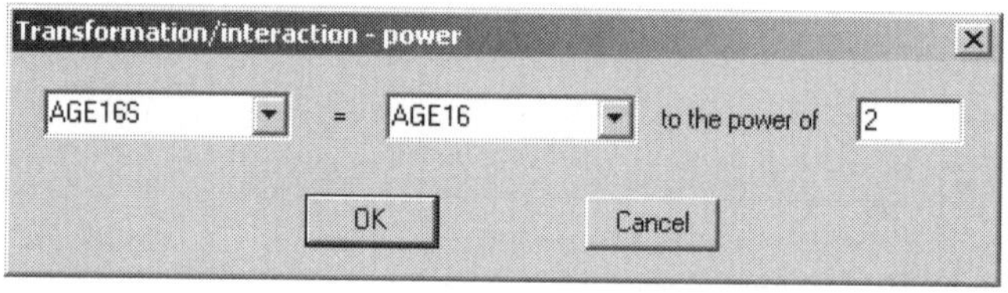

Figure 12.19 Equation for the transformed variable AGE16S

9. Click **Range/Legend/Color** to specify the ranges for x- and y-axis (the default values are those computed from the data), to enter legend and graph titles, and to select screen color (see Figure 12.20). Enter **Pro-deviant attitude score as a function of age, gender and ethnicity** in the textbox for **Graph title**. Click **OK**.

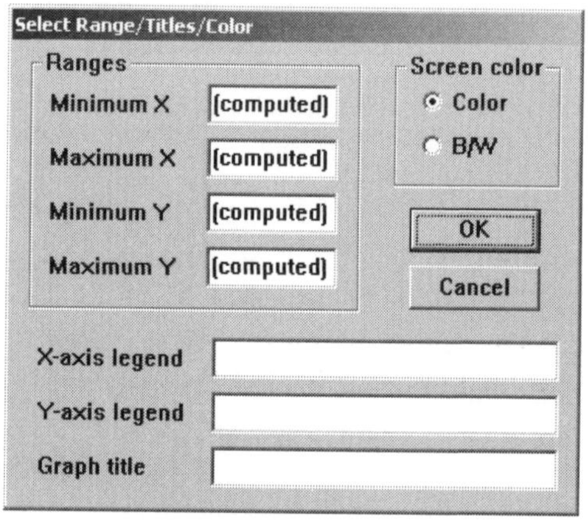

Figure 12.20 Select Range/Legend/Color dialog box

10. Click the **Other settings** button and click the selection button for **Smooth** in **For continuous x** section to display a set of smooth curves.
11. Select FEMALE in the **Z focus(1)** drop-down listbox to graph pro-deviant attitude score as a function of age for male and female youths. **Use the two actual values** will appear in the textbox for the **Range of z-axis** as FEMALE is an indicator variable. We will use this default option.

228

12. Select MINORITY in the **Z focus(2)** drop-down listbox to graph pro-deviant attitude score as a function of age for minority and non-minority male and female youths. **Use the two actual values** will appear in the textbox for the **Range of z-axis** as MINORITY again is an indicator variable. We will use this default option. See Figure 12.21 for the specifications for this growth curve analysis example.

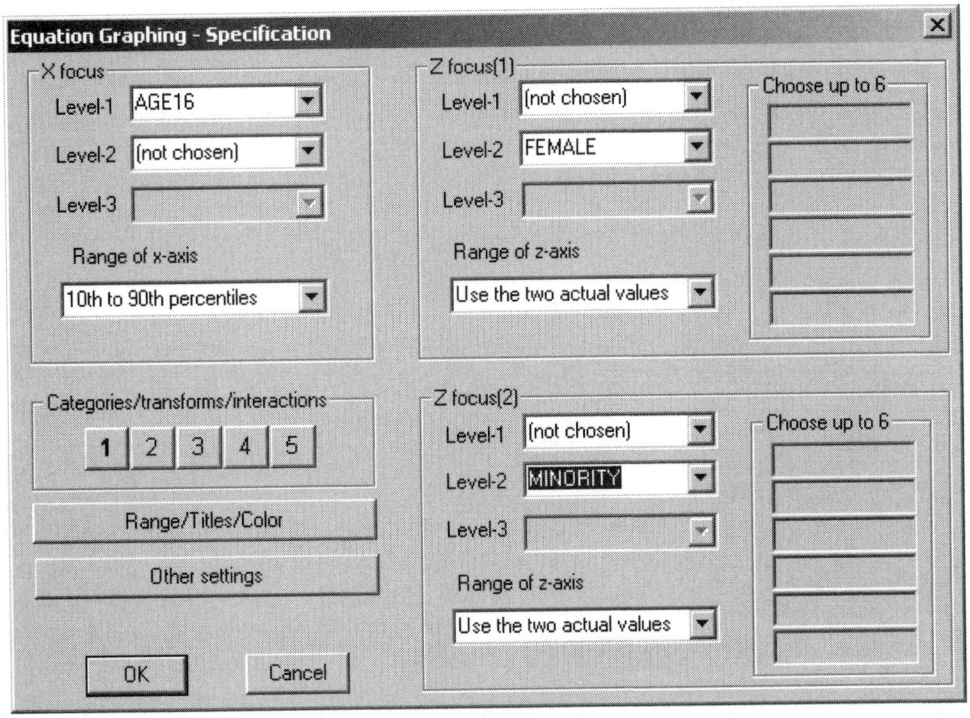

Figure 12.21 Specifications for the Growth Curve Analysis Example

13. Click **OK**. A colored version of the plot (not displayed here) showing the relationship between pro-deviant attitude score and age for different gender-by-ethnicity groups will appear (see Figure 12.22). The curves indicate that there is a nonmonotonic and nonlinear relationship between pro-deviant attitude scores and age for minority and non-minority male youths over the five year period. Such a relationship, however, does not exist for minority and non-minority female youths.

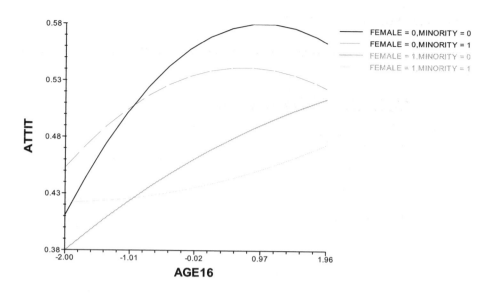

Figure 12.22 Plot showing the relationship between pro-deviant attitude score and age for different gender-by-ethnicity groups

14. For information on the editing, printing, saving, and modification options, see Steps 11 to 13 in section 12.1.1.

12.2.2 Level-1 equation modeling

WHLM will also let us examine plots for individual level-2 units by just using the level-1 equation instead of the entire model. For this example, we will be using the vocabulary data, VOCAB.MDM described in section 12.1.2, and have run the following model:

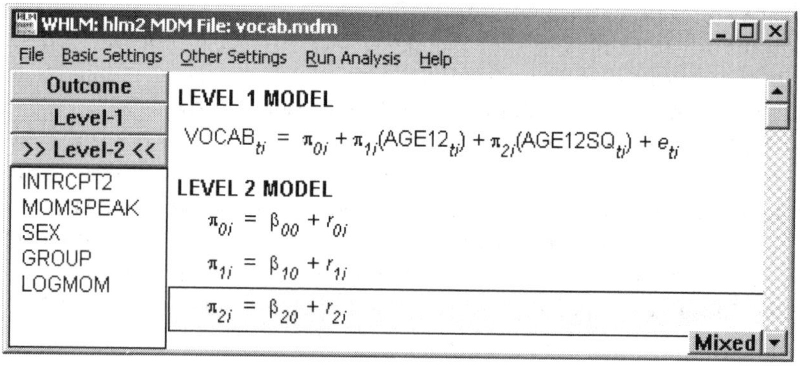

Figure 12.23 Model specification window for the vocabulary data

To perform the level-1 equation graphing

1. After the model is run, select **Graph Equations...Level-1 equation graphing** from the **File** menu, which will give us the following dialog box.

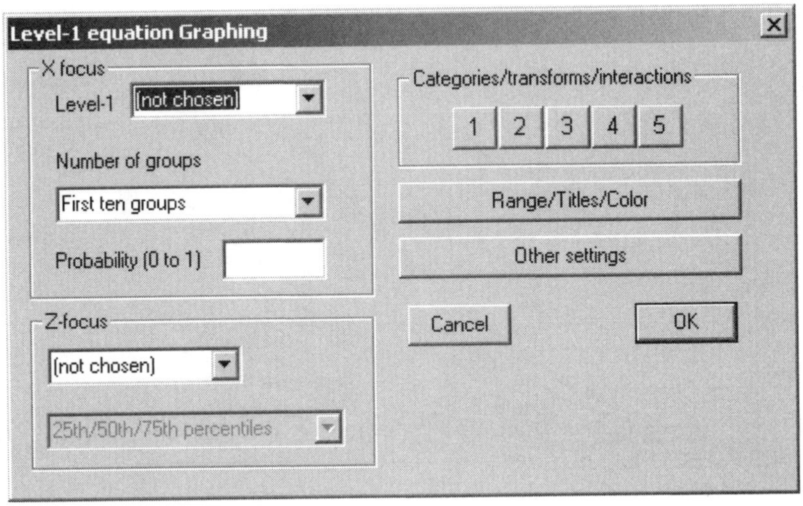

Figure 12.24   Level-1 equation Graphing dialog box

For the definition of **Number of groups**, see step 5 in section 12.1. Table 12.2 describes and explains the other options in the dialog box.

2. Select an **X focus** variable. In our example, we want the age of the child in months minus 12 to be the **X focus**. Choose AGE12 from the **X focus** drop-down listbox.
3. Select number of groups. We will include all the children. Choose **All groups (n=22)** in the **Number of groups** drop-down listbox.
4. Specify the relationship between the transformed and the original variable. The transformed variable is AGE12S and the original variable is AGE12. Click 1 in the **Categories/ transforms/interactions** section and select **power of x/z** for Polynomial relationships. A **Equation Graphing - power** dialog box will open. Select AGE12S from the drop-down listbox to the left of the equal sign. AGE12 will appear in the drop-down listbox as it is the only level-1 variable left. Enter 2 in the textbox for the **power** to be raised. Click **OK**.
5. (Optional) click **Range/Legend/Color** to specify the ranges for x- and y-axis (the default values are those computed from the data), to enter legend and graph titles, and to select screen color.
6. Click the **Other settings** button and click the selection button for **Smooth** in **For continuous x** section to display a set of smooth curves. Click **OK**.
7. Click **OK** and we get the following figure that shows vocabulary size accelerates during the second year of life. Note that the individual trajectories, as expected, are "smoother" than in the comparable data-based graphs in Figure 12.14 in Section 12.1.3.

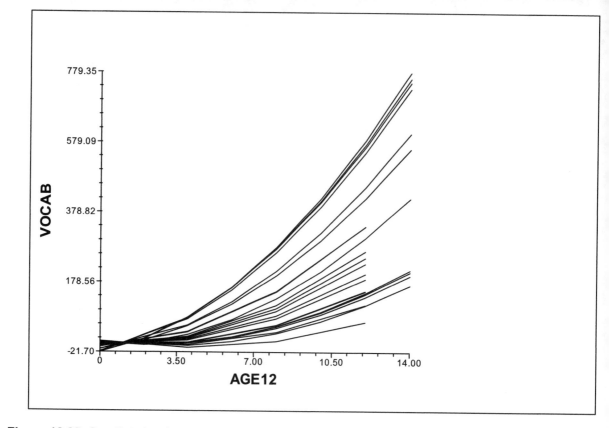

Figure 12.25 Predicted trajectories of vocabulary growth for individual children

To include a level-2 classification variable

8. Click **Graph Settings** on the menu bar to open the **Level-1 equation Graphing** dialog box.

9. Choose MALE from the **Z-focus** drop-down listbox as the level-2 classification variable.

10. Click **OK**. The following figure will appear. A colored version of the graph (not shown here) indicates that girls on average have a greater acceleration rate in vocabulary growth over the course of the study.

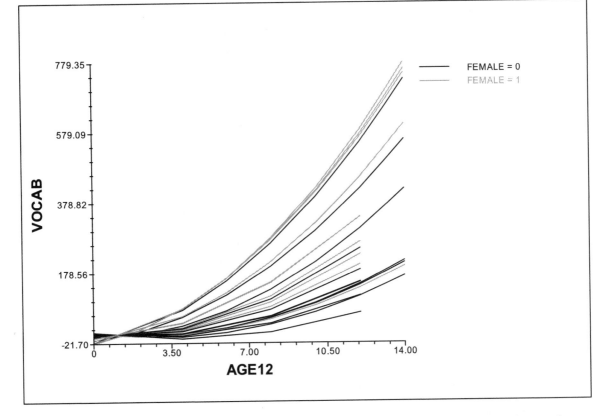

Figure 12.26 Predicted trajectories of vocabulary growth of individual children grouped by gender

12.2.3 Level-1 residual box-and-whisker plots

In addition to plotting predicted values for individual level-2 units using level-1 equations, users can also examine the distributions of the level-1 errors or residuals (see Equation 3.63 on p. 50 in *Hierarchical Linear Models*). The plots allow users to graphically examine the assumptions about the level-1 residuals and to identify cases for which the model provides a particularly poor fit. We continue to use VOCAB.MDM to illustrate this graphing procedure.

To prepare level-1 residual box-and-whisker plots

1. After the model is run, select **Graph Equations...Level-1 box whisker** from the **File** menu, which will give us the following dialog box.

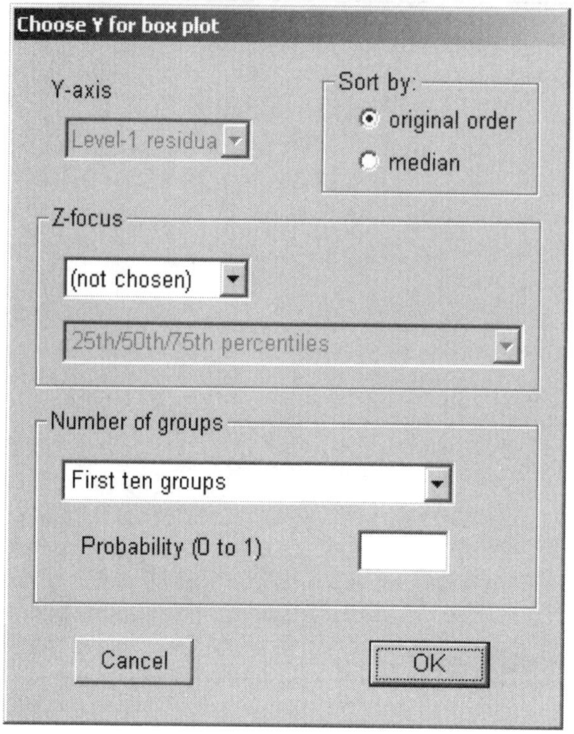

Figure 12.27 Choose Y for box plot dialog box

For definitions of the options in the dialog box, see Section 12.1.1. Note that the variable for Y-axis, level-1 residual has been pre-selected.

2. Select **All groups (n=22)** in the **Number of groups** to include all the 22 children in the display.
3. Click the selection button for **median** in the **Sort by** section to arrange the plots by median order.
4. Click **OK**. The following graph will appear.

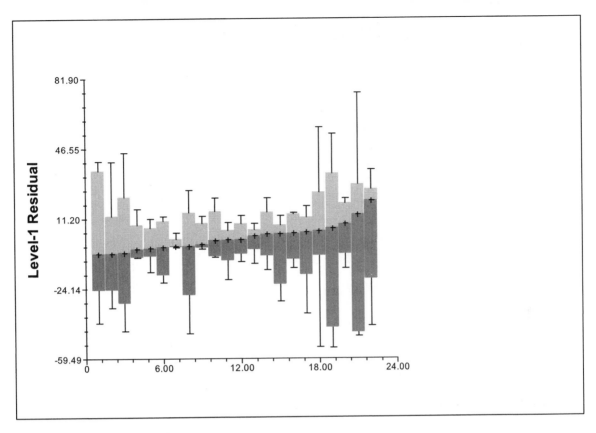

Figure 12.28 Box-and-whisker plots of the level-1 residuals

The box-and-whisker plots provide side-by-side graphical summaries of the level-1 residuals for each level-2 units. The plots suggests that the underlying model assumptions may not be tenable. First, quite a number of the distributions are highly asymmetric, such as the last one from the left. Thus, the normality assumption may not hold. There seems to be heterogeneity of variance as well, judging from the wide disparities in the box lengths. The nonconstant residual spread may suggest an omission of important effects from the model. However, there are no extreme values or outliers in any of the 22 plots. Note that this graphical analysis of level-1 residuals differs from the one performed in Section 2.5.4.1.2 in that it does not pool the residuals across level-2 units. In addition, WHLM has a statistical test for evaluating the adequacy of the homogeneity of level-1 variance assumption (see Section 2.8.8.2). See *Hierarchical Linear Models* pp. 263-267 for a discussion of the examination of assumptions about level-1 random effects.

5. (Optional) Users can look at the EB estimates for any child by clicking on the corresponding box-and-whisker plot. See Step 9 in Section 2.1.1.

6. (Optional) Users can choose to include a level-2 classification variable when examining the level-1 residuals. See Step 14 in Section 2.1.1.

12.2.4 Level-1 residual vs predicted value

Users can graphically assess the assumptions of constant error variance and linearity and probe for outlying cases by examining a scatter plot of level-1 residuals and predicted values. Using the same data and model of the previous two sections, we now plot the level-1 residual against its predicted value.

To prepare a level-1 residuals by predicted values scatter plot

1. After the model is run, select **Graph Equations...Level-1 residual vs predicted value** from the **File** menu, which will give us the following dialog box.

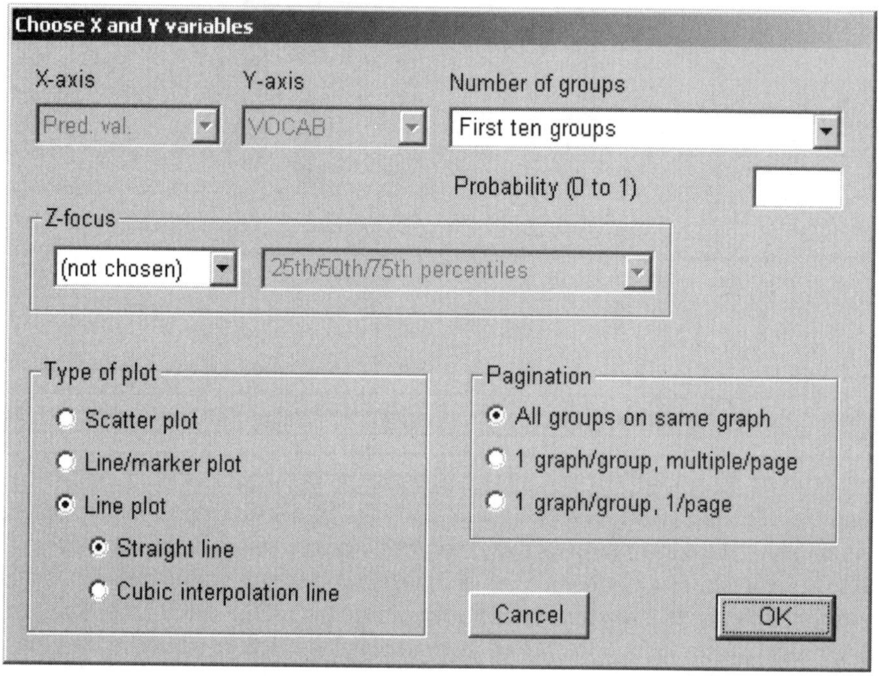

Figure 12.29 Choose X and Y variables

For definitions of the various options in the dialog box, see Section 12.1.2. Note that the **X-axis** variable, **Pred. val.** and **Y-axis** variable, **Level-1 residuals** have been pre-selected.

2. Select **All groups (n=22)** in the **Number of groups** to include all the 22 children in the display.

3. Click the selection button for **Scatter plot** in the **Type of plot** section to request a scatter plot of the predicted values by level-1 residuals.

4. Select **All groups on same graph** in the **Pagination** section to display all the residuals pooled across the level-2 units. To examine the residuals for individual children, choose either of the other pagination options.

5. Click **OK**.

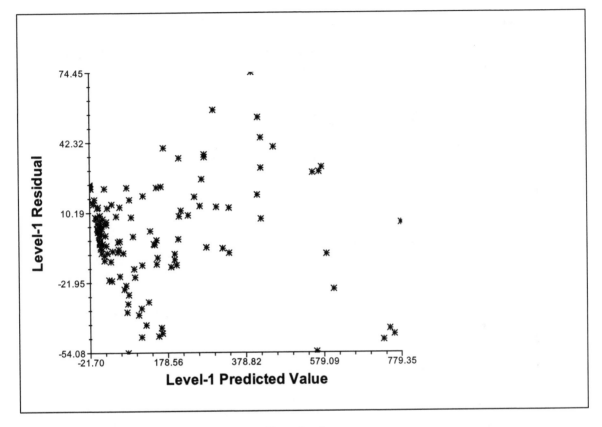

Figure 12.30   Plot of level-1 residuals by predicted values

The plot suggests that there is a tendency for the residual scatter to get narrower at the smallest predicted values and to get wider around the interval between 150 and 170. The residuals seem to follow a slightly curvilinear trend as well. They may suggest that there is a specification error in the model.

6. (Optional) Users can choose to include a level-2 classification variable when examining the level-1 residuals. See Step 14 in Section 2.1.1.

12.2.5   Level-1 EB/OLS coefficient confidence intervals

We can also look at graphs of the estimated empirical Bayes (EB) or OLS estimates of randomly varying level-1 coefficient (see Section 1.3 and *Hierarchical Linear Models*, p. 47 and p. 49 for their computational formulae). This enables us to compare level-2 units with respect to these two types of estimates.

To prepare level-2 EB estimates of randomly varying level-1 coefficient confidence intervals

1. After the model is run, select **Graph Equations...Level-2 EB/OLS coefficient confidence intervals** from the **File** menu, which will give us the following dialog box:

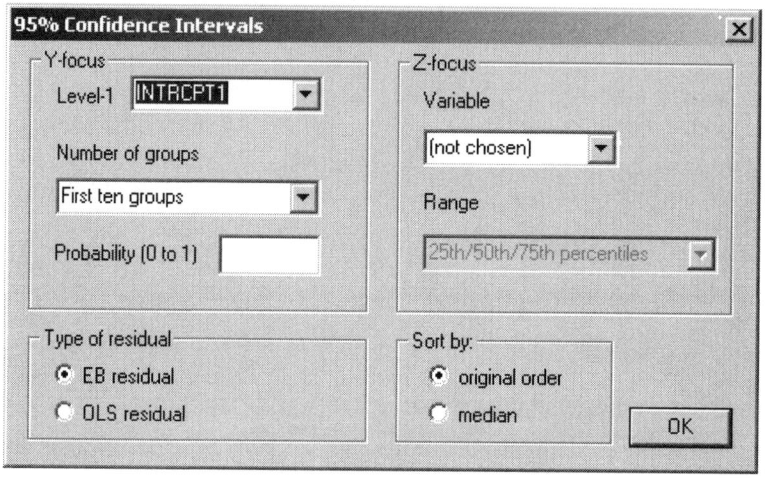

Figure 12.31   95% Confidence Intervals dialog box

For definitions about the various options regarding Y- and Z-focus and sorting, see Section 12.1.1.

2. Choose the randomly varying level-1 coefficient of interest. We will look at the coefficient for the quadratic term or acceleration rate of vocabulary growth in this example. Choose AGE12S from the **Y-focus** drop-down listbox.
3. Select **All groups (n=22)** in the **Number of groups** to include all the 22 children in the display.
4. Click the **EB residual** button in the **Type of residual** section to select the empirical Bayes estimates.
5. Click **OK**. The following graph will appear.

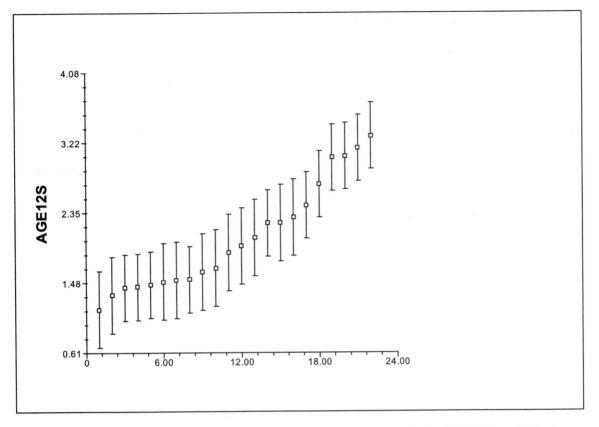

Figure 12.32 Confidence intervals of empirical Bayes estimates of the AGE12S coefficients

The graph suggests that there is significant variation in the rate of acceleration in vocabulary growth in children during the second year of life. For instance, the confidence intervals of the EB estimates of the AGE12S coefficients for the last four children from the left did not overlap with those of the first eleven children.

6. Users can look at the actual empirical Bayes estimates and their 95% confidence intervals of individual level-2 units by clicking on the confidence interval plots.

7. (Optional) Users can choose to include a level-2 classification variable when examining the confidence interval plots. See Step 14 in Section 2.1.1.

12.2.6   Graphing categorical predictors

Model graphs can be displayed in which predictor variables are categorical. Suppose, for example, that the variable ETHNICITY has three possible values: BLACK, HISPANIC, and WHITE and that this variable is represented by indicator variables for BLACK and HISPANIC, with WHITE serving as the reference category. To represent ethnicity as a predictor, click the first box under **Categories/ transformations/interactions**. Next, click on **define categorical variable**. Then four boxes will appear:

1. Under the box **Choose first category from foci** click on the variable that is the first of the indicator variables in the model. In our example, this will be BLACK.
2. Under the box **Possible choices** click on any other indicators in the model that represent the categorical variable of interest; in our case, there is only one : HISPANIC.
3. Under **Name of reference** category, type in the name of the reference group; in our case, this will be WHITE.
4. Under **Category Name**, type the name of the categorical variable; in our case, this will be ETHNICITY.

Now click **OK** to continue.

12.3 Three-level applications

Graphing with 3-level data is very similar to the 2-level graphing. The only two differences are that users can (a) group the plots at either level 2 or 3, and (b) choose exclusively a level-2 or level-3 classifying or conditioning variable. To illustrate these two differences, we will use the EG.MDM as describe in Section 4.1. We will prepare line plots of the mathematics test score, MATH, to detect trends over the course of the six-year study, grouped by the level-3 units, schools, and classified by a level-3 variable, the socioeconomic composition of schools. The same logic applies to the sets of three-level model-based graphing procedure.

To prepare line plots with level-3 grouping

1. From the HLM window, open the **File** menu.
2. Choose **Create a new model using an existing MDM file** to open an **Open MDM File** dialog box. Open EG.MDM.
3. Open the **File** menu, choose **Graph Data...line plots, scatter plots** to open an **Choose X and Y variables** dialog box (see Figure 12.33).

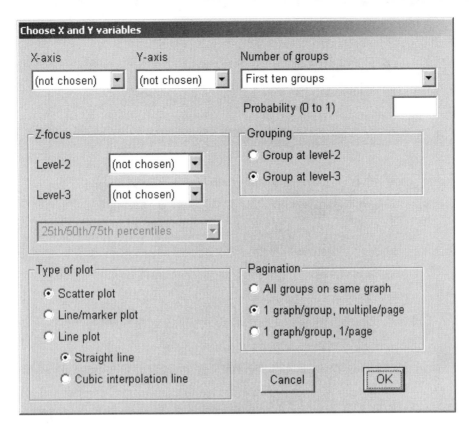

Figure 12.33 Choose X and Y variables dialog box

4. Select YEAR from the **X-axis** drop-down listbox.
5. Select MATH from the **Y-axis** drop-down listbox.
6. Select number of groups. In this example, we want to include a random sample of 20 percent of the schools in the display. Select **Random sample of spec'd prob** from the **Number of groups** drop-down listbox. Enter 0.2 into the textbox for **Probability (0 to 1)** to indicate that 10 percent or a proportion of .1 of the schools will be used.
7. Select type of plot and method of interpolation (see Step 7 in Section 12.1.3 for explanations). For our example, we want a line plot with no markers that is graphed with the linear interpolation method. Click the selection button for **Straight line**.
8. Select type of grouping at level 2 or level 3. In this example, we want to have the trajectories for individual schools (**Group at level 3**). Click **Group at level-3** selection button (default) in the **Grouping** section.
9. Select type of pagination. We want separate plots for individual schools and choose **1 graph/group, multiple page** option accordingly.
10. Click **OK**. The following graph will appear.

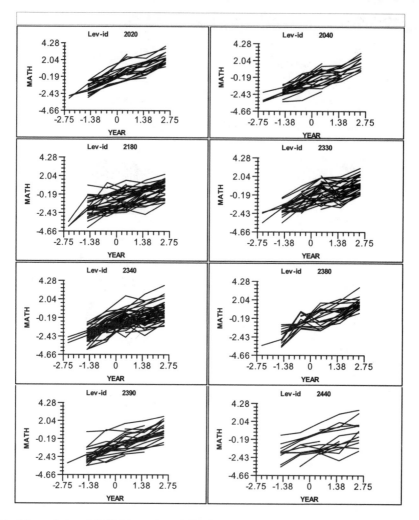

Figure 12.34 Line plots of MATH against YEAR for eight schools

The eight line plots indicate the collection of students' growth trajectories of mathematics achievement within individual schools. The schools varied in their number of students. There was a generally positive average rate of growth across all schools.

To include a level-3 classification variable

11. Now we want to look at the trajectories as classified by the socioeconomic composition of the study body of a school. On the menu of the graph dialog box, click **Graph Settings**. Choose the level-3 variable LOWINC, the percent of students from low income families, as a **Z-focus** variable. As LOWINC is a non-dichotomous variable we have an additional choice that was not needed for our earlier dichotomous z-foci. In this case, we choose **Above/Below 50th percentile** from the combo box immediately below where we chose the LOWINC as the grouping variable.
12. Click **OK**. The following graph will appear.

242

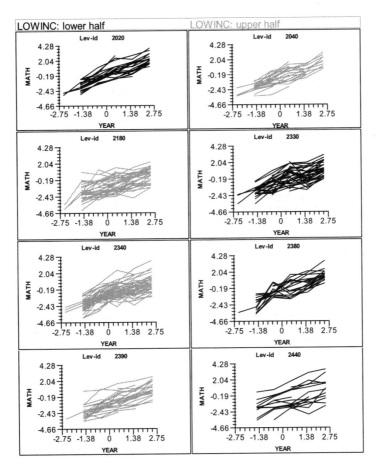

Figure 12.35 Line plots of MATHACH against YEAR for eight schools by LOWINC

This shows us that schools with a greater percent of students from low income families (upper high) tend to have lower mathematics achievement than do schools with less percent of poor students. Compared to their peers in School 2020, for instance, students in School 2330 generally have lower achievement across the six years.

A Using HLM2 in interactive and batch mode

This appendix describes and illustrates how to use HLM2 in interactive and batch mode to construct MDM files, to execute analyses based on the MDM file, and to specify a residual file to evaluate model fit. It also lists and describes command keywords and options. References are made to appropriate sections in the manual where the procedures are described in greater details.

A.1 Using HLM2 in interactive mode

A.1.1 Example: constructing an MDM file for the HS&B data using SPSS file input

In the computer session that follows, all responses entered by the user are typed in boldface. All text presented in *italics* represents additional commentary we have added to help the user understand what is happening in the program at that moment.

```
C:\HLM> HLM2                          (type the program name at the system prompt to start)

Will you be starting with raw data?  Y
Is the input file a v-known file? N
Are your data measures within persons? N
Enter type of raw data:
     for ASCII input                    enter 1
     for SYSTAT .SYS file               enter 2
     for SAS V5 transport file          enter 3
     for SPSS file (UNIX or windows)    enter 4
     for STATA .dta file                enter 5
     for anything DBMSCOPY reads        enter 6
     for anything Stat/Transfer reads   enter 7
Type? 4
```

The "anything DBMSCOPY reads" and "anything Stat/Transfer reads" prompts are only present on PC versions of HLM.

```
Input name of level-1 file: HSB1.SAV
Input name of level-2 file: HSB2.SAV
```

(See Section 2.5 for a description of the variables in HSB1.SAV and HSB2.SAV)

```
The available level-1 variables are:
For      ID enter  1    For MINORITY enter  2    For    FEMALE enter  3
For     SES enter  4    For  MATHACH enter  5
What variable is the group ID? 1
Please specify level-1 variable # 1 (enter 0 to end): 2
Please specify level-1 variable # 2 (enter 0 to end): 3
```

244

```
Please specify level-1 variable # 3 (enter 0 to end): 4
Please specify level-1 variable # 4 (enter 0 to end): 5

The available level-2 variables are:
For      ID  enter  1    For     SIZE  enter  2    For    SECTOR  enter  3
For   PRACAD  enter  4    For  DISCLIM  enter  5    For    HIMNTY  enter  6
For  MEANSES  enter  7
What variable is the group ID? 1

Please specify level-2 variable # 1 (enter 0 to end): 2
Please specify level-2 variable # 2 (enter 0 to end): 3
Please specify level-2 variable # 3 (enter 0 to end): 4
Please specify level-2 variable # 4 (enter 0 to end): 5
Please specify level-2 variable # 5 (enter 0 to end): 6
Please specify level-2 variable # 6 (enter 0 to end): 7
Are there missing data in the level-1 file? N
```

Note, had we indicated that missing data were present in the level-1 file, the following additional prompts would have come to the screen:

```
Do you want to delete the missing data now, or at analysis time? Now
(Enter "now" or "analysis")
```

See Section 2.6 on how HLM2 handles missing data.

```
Enter name of MDM file: HSB.MDM
```

HLM2 will now proceed to create a multivariate data matrix file.

HLM2 will always write out a file named CREATMDM.MDMT that contains a log of the input responses given to create the MDM file. Should the MDM file appear incorrect for some reason, inspection of the log may provide a clue. Also, this file may be edited, renamed, and used as input to create a new MDM file. At the system prompt simply type, for example,

```
HLM2 -R CREATMDM.NEW
```

where CREATMDM.NEW is the edited, renamed input file. The interactive prompts will be quickly sent to the screen and "answered" (by responses read from the file CREATMDM.NEW), and the program will proceed automatically to recreate the MDM file.

A.1.2 Example: constructing an MDM file for the HS&B data using ASCII file input

```
C:\HLM> HLM2

Will you be starting with raw data?  Y (type the program name at the system prompt to
start)
Is the input file a v-known file? N


Enter type of raw data:
    for ASCII input                 enter 1
```

```
for SYSTAT .SYS file              enter 2
for SAS V5 transport file         enter 3
for SPSS file (UNIX or windows)   enter 4
for STATA .dta file               enter 5
for anything DBMSCOPY reads       enter 6
for anything Stat/Transfer reads  enter 7
```

Type? **1**

Input number of level-1 variables (not including the character ID): **4**
Input format of level-1 file (the ID must be read as character data)

format:(A4,8X,4F12.3)   (*See Section A.2 for rules for format statements*)
Input name of level-1 file: **HSB1.DAT**

Input number of level-2 variables (not including the character ID): **6**
Input format of level-2 file (the ID must be read as character data)

format: **(A2,8X,6F12.3)**
Input name of level-2 file: **HSB2.DAT**

Enter 8 character name for level-1 variable number 1: **MINORITY**
Enter 8 character name for level-1 variable number 2: **FEMALE**
Enter 8 character name for level-1 variable number 3: **SES**
Enter 8 character name for level-1 variable number 4: **MATHACH**

Enter 8 character name for level-2 variable number 1: **SIZE**
Enter 8 character name for level-2 variable number 2: **SECTOR**
Enter 8 character name for level-2 variable number 3: **PRACAD**
Enter 8 character name for level-2 variable number 4: **DISCLIM**
Enter 8 character name for level-2 variable number 5: **HIMINTY**
Enter 8 character name for level-2 variable number 6: **MEANSES**

Are there missing data in the level-1 file? **N**

Note, had we indicated that missing data were present in the level-1 file, the following additional prompts would have come to the screen:

Is the missing value the same for all variables? **Y**

HLM2 allows for the possibility of a different missing value code for each variable. An answer of "N" causes HLM2 to ask the user to enter value for missing variable for each level-1 variable.

Enter the number that represents missing data. **-99.0**

Do you want to delete the missing data now, or at analysis time? **Now**
(Enter "now" or "analysis")

Enter name of MDM file: **HSB.MDM**

HLM2 will now proceed to create a multivariate data matrix file.

A.2 Rules for format statements

While the input format statement for HLM resembles FORTRAN, only a subset of format options are acceptable. The user may specify:

1. The A format descriptor to read in the ID variable. This is followed by a number of columns that the ID occupies.
2. The F format descriptor (and the E, used to read in numbers with exponents). This may be preceded with a number specifying a repeat value, and needs to be followed by a decimal number specifying both the number of columns that variable occupies and the places to the right of the decimal.
3. For example, 4F12.3 tells HLM that there are four variables in a row occupying 12 columns and that each value has three numbers to the right of the decimal point.
4. The X format descriptor. This is used to skip over a number of columns. For example, 8X skips over eight columns when reading the data.
5. The / (forward slash) format descriptor. This tells HLM to go to the next line of the input file to read data. It is used when each case takes more than one line in the raw data file.
6. Commas have to be inserted to separate each of the descriptors.
7. Unlike FORTRAN, HLM does not allow nesting of parentheses is not allowed (*e.g.*, (4A,4(1X,F12.3)) will not be read properly by HLM programs).

A.2.1 Example: Executing an analysis using HSB.MDM

Here is an example of an HLM2 session in the interactive mode. At the system command line prompt, we first type the program name – HLM2 – followed by the name of the multivariate data matrix file – HSB.MDM. The program now takes the user directly into the model specification process.

```
C:\HLM> HLM2 HSB.MDM
Do you want to do a non-linear analysis? N      (See Appendix 3 for non-linear analysis)

                SPECIFYING A LEVEL-1 OUTCOME VARIABLE

Please specify a level-1 outcome variable
 The choices are:
 For MINORITY enter  1    For   FEMALE enter  2    For      SES enter  3
 For  MATHACH enter  4

What is the outcome variable: 4

Do you wish to:

   Examine means,variances,chi-squared, etc? Enter 1
   Specify an HLM model?                      Enter 2
   Define a new outcome variable?             Enter 3
   Exit?                                      Enter 4
What do you want to do? 2
```

Option 1 is detailed in section A1.7 "Preliminary exploratory analysis with HLM2"

```
                    SPECIFYING AN HLM MODEL
Level-1 predictor variable specification

Which level-1 predictors do you wish to use?
 The choices are:
 For MINORITY enter  1     For   FEMALE enter  2     For      SES enter  3

  level-1 predictor? (Enter 0 to end)  3
  level-1 predictor? (Enter 0 to end)  0

 Do you want to center any level-1 predictors? Y
 (Enter 0 for no centering, enter 1 for group-mean, 2 for grand-mean)
 How do you want to center     SES? 1
```

Note: we have selected group-mean centering for the level-1 predictor, SES.

```
Do you want to set the level-1 intercept to zero in this analysis? N
```

An answer of "Y" here specifies a level-1 model without an intercept or constant term (see Section 2.9.6).

```
Level-2 predictor variable specification

Which level-2 variables do you wish to use?

 The choices are:
 For       SIZE enter  1     For    SECTOR enter  2     For    PRACAD enter  3
 For   DISCLIM enter  4     For    HIMNTY enter  5     For   MEANSES enter  6

 Which level-2 predictors to model INTRCPT1?
  Level-2 predictor? (Enter 0 to end)  2
  Level-2 predictor? (Enter 0 to end)  6
  Level-2 predictor? (Enter 0 to end)  0

 Which level-2 predictors to model     SES slope?
  Level-2 predictor? (Enter 0 to end)  2
  Level-2 predictor? (Enter 0 to end)  6
  Level-2 predictor? (Enter 0 to end)  0

Do you want to constrain the variances in any of the level-2 random
 effects to zero? N
```

An answer of "Y" here causes HLM2 to list out the level-1 coefficients and asks the user whether the corresponding random effect should be set to zero. An answer of "Y" to one of these probes is equivalent to specifying that level-1 coefficient as a fixed (or non-randomly varying) effect.

```
 Do you want to center any level-2 predictors? N
```

Note: the user has the option of selecting grand-mean centering for each of the level-2 predictors.

```
                    ADDITIONAL PROGRAM FEATURES

Select the level-2 variables that you might consider for
inclusion as predictors in subsequent models.
```

```
The choices are:

For      SIZE enter   1      For    SECTOR enter   2      For    PRACAD enter   3
For   DISCLIM enter   4      For    HIMNTY enter   5      For   MEANSES enter   6

Which level-2 variables to model INTRCPT1?
 Level-2 variable? (Enter 0 to end)  1
 Level-2 variable? (Enter 0 to end)  3
 Level-2 variable? (Enter 0 to end)  4
 Level-2 variable? (Enter 0 to end)  5
 Level-2 variable? (Enter 0 to end)  0
Which level-2 variables to model      SES slope?
 Level-2 variable? (Enter 0 to end)  -1
```

For all of the level-2 predictors selected here, HLM2 will compute approximate "t-to-enter statistics" that can be used to guide specification of subsequent HLM2 models. Note, the code "-1" tells HLM2 to use for the SES slope model the same set of level-2 predictors as selected for the previous level-2 equation (i.e., the model for INTRCPT1).

```
Do you want to run this analysis with a heterogeneous sigma^2? N
```

An answer of "Y" here causes HLM2 to ask which variables to be included in modeling sigma^2 (See Section 2.9.3 for details) and the number of macro- and micro-iterations. See Table A1.5.1.
```
Do you want to constrain any (more) of the gammas? N
```

An answer of "Y" here causes HLM2 to ask the user which gamma is to constrained (See Section 2.9.8 and Table A1.5.1).

```
Do you wish to use any of the optional hypothesis testing procedures? N
```

HLM2 allows multivariate hypothesis tests among the fixed effects and of variance-covariance components specification. The first example below illustrates how a multivariate hypothesis test for fixed effects are implemented (See Section 2.9.2 for details):

```
Do you wish to use any of the optional hypothesis testing procedures?  Y
Do you wish to specify a multivariate hypothesis for the fixed effects?  Y
Enter contrast value for INTRCPT1/INTRCPT2 (0 to ignore) 0
Enter contrast value for           / SECTOR (0 to ignore) 1
Enter contrast value for           / MEANSES (0 to ignore) 0
Enter contrast value for        SES/INTRCPT2 (0 to ignore) 0
Enter contrast value for           / SECTOR (0 to ignore) 0
Enter contrast value for           / MEANSES (0 to ignore) 0

Do you wish to specify another contrast as part of this hypothesis? Y
Enter contrast value for INTRCPT1/INTRCPT2 (0 to ignore)  0
Enter contrast value for           / SECTOR (0 to ignore)  0
Enter contrast value for           / MEANSES (0 to ignore)  0
Enter contrast value for        SES/INTRCPT2 (0 to ignore)  0
Enter contrast value for           / SECTOR (0 to ignore)  1
Enter contrast value for           / MEANSES (0 to ignore)  0

Do you wish to specify another contrast as part of this hypothesis?  N
Do you wish to specify another hypothesis?  N
```

The second example illustrates how a multivariate test of variance-covariance components is specified:

```
Do you wish to test the specification for the variance-covariance components against an
alternative model?(Note: the same fixed effects must be specified in both models)  Y
Enter the deviance statistic value  46512.978
Enter the number of variance-covariance parameters  4

Do you want to do a latent variable regression? N

                           OUTPUT SPECIFICATION

Do you want a residual file? N
```

Had we answered yes, we would be prompted:

```
Enter type of stat package you will use:
    for SYSTAT      enter 1
    for SAS         enter 2
    for SPSS        enter 3
Type? 3

Enter additional variables to go in residual file
  The choices are:
For      SIZE enter  1    For    SECTOR enter  2    For    PRACAD enter  3
For  DISCLIM enter  4    For    HIMNTY enter  5    For  MEANSES enter  6

  Level-2 variable? (Enter 0 to end)  1
  Level-2 variable? (Enter 0 to end)  3
  Level-2 variable? (Enter 0 to end)  5
  Level-2 variable? (Enter 0 to end)  0
```

A SPSS syntax file, RESFIL2.SPS, will be written out as the HLM2 runs. See Sections 2.5.4.1 and 2.5.4.2 on structure of the residual file and possible residual analyses.

```
How many iterations do you want to do? 100
Do you want to see OLS estimates for all of the level-2 units? N
  Enter a problem title: Intercept and Slopes-as-Outcomes Model
  Enter name of output file: HSB1.OUT

Computing . . ., please wait

Starting values computed.  Iterations begun.
```

While the program is running, HLM2 sends the value of the likelihood function computed for each iteration to the screen. We have printed below just the first and last three. Because the change between the 60th and 61st iterations was very small, the program automatically terminated before the requested 100 iterations were computed. The sensitivity of this "automatic stopping value" can be controlled by the user. See Section A1.5 for details.

Produced along with the output file is a file called "NEWCMD.HLM" which is a command file constructed by HLM based on the interactive session just completed.

```
Should you wish to terminate the iterations prior to convergence, enter cntl-c
The value of the likelihood function at iteration 1 = -2.325291E+004
The value of the likelihood function at iteration 2 = -2.325274E+004
The value of the likelihood function at iteration 3 = -2.325266E+004
```

```
The value of the likelihood function at iteration 59 = -2.325186E+004
The value of the likelihood function at iteration 60 = -2.325186E+004
The value of the likelihood function at iteration 61 = -2.325186E+004
```

See Section 2.5.3 for an annotated example of the output for this model.

A.3 Using HLM in batch and/or interactive mode

HLM users can control which questions come to the screen by means of a command file. At one extreme, the command file is virtually empty and questions regarding every possible optional procedure or output will come to the screen. At the other extreme, the command file specifies the answer to every question that might arise, in which case the analysis is performed completely in batch mode. In between the two extremes are a large number of possibilities in which various questions are answered in the command file while other questions come to the screen. Hence, the execution can be partly batch and partly interactive.

The file presented below is produced along with output file by HLM for the *Intercept and Slopes-as-Outcomes* Model for the HS&B data specified in Section A.2.1. The italicized comments provide a brief description of each command function. A complete overview of each of the keywords and related options in this command file appears in the Section A.4.

```
#This command file was run with HSB.MDM          Indicates which MDM was used.
NUMIT:100                                    Sets the maximum number of iterations.
STOPVAL:0.0000010000      Sets the criteria for automatically stopping the iterations.
NONLIN:N                                        Switch to do a non-linear analysis.
LEVEL1:MATHACH=INTRCPT1+SES,1+RANDOM              Specifies the level-1 model.
LEVEL2:INTRCPT1=INTRCPT2+SECTOR+MEANSES+RANDOM/SIZE,PRACAD,DISCLIM,HIMNTY
LEVEL2:SES=INTRCPT2+SECTOR+MEANSES+RANDOM/SIZE,PRACAD,DISCLIM,HIMNTY
                    Specifies the level-2 model and other level-2 predictors for
           possible inclusion in subsequent models for both intrcpt1 and the ses slope.
LEVEL1WEIGHT: NONE                              Specifies level-1 weight variable.
LEVEL2WEIGHT: NONE                              Specifies level-2 weight variable.
RESFIL:N                                  Controls whether a residual file is created.
HETEROL1VAR:N                       Specifies an analysis with a heterogeneous sigma2.
ACCEL:5                                  Controls frequency of use of accelerator.
LVR:N                              Specifies a latent varible regression model.
LEV1OLS:10               Controls the number of level-1 OLS regressions printed out.
MLF: N                                     Specifies restricted maximum likelihood.
HYPOTH:N                        Disables some optional hypothesis testing procedures.
FIXTAU:3                        Alternative options for generating starting values.
CONSTRAIN:N                  Estimates a model with constrained level-2 coefficients.
OUTPUT:HSB1.OUT                          File where HLM2 output will be saved.
FULLOUTPUT: Y                          Controls amount of output in output file.
TITLE:Intercept and Slopes-as-Outcome Model              Title on page 1 of output.
```

An user can rename the file with or without modification with a plain text (ASCII) editor for subsequent batch-mode application. For instance, he or she may request the program to print out all the level-1 OLS regressions by changing the LEV1OLS:10 to LEV1OLS:160 and rename the file to HSB2.MLM. The user can execute the analysis by typing:

at the system prompt. As the run is fully specified in the command file HSB2.MLM, no questions will come to the screen during its execution. This is full batch mode. The user may choose a fully interactive execution mode or an execution mode that is partly interactive and partly batch. With partly interactive, partly batch mode, some specification occurs in the command file; the program prompts the user with questions for the remaining program features. Some users may find this a useful way to suppress some the questions relating to less often used features of the programs. Fully interactive mode is invoked when one of the programs is invoked without a second argument, *i.e.*,

HLM2 HSB.MDM

In this case, all of the possible questions will be asked with the exception relating to type of estimation used. (mlf:y must be specified in the command file).

A.4 Using HLM2 in batch mode

A command file consists of a series of lines. Each line begins with a keyword followed by a colon, after the colon is the option chosen by the user, *i.e.*,

KEYWORD:OPTION

For example, HLM2 provides several optional hypothesis-testing procedures, described in detail in the Sections 2.9.2 to 2.9.4. Suppose the user does not wish to use these optional procedures in a given analysis. Then the following line would be included in the command file:

HYPOTH:N

The keyword hypoth concerns the optional hypothesis testing procedures; the option chosen, 'N', indicates that the user does not wish to employ these procedures. Alternatively, the user might include the line:

HYPOTH:Y

This prompts HLM2 to activate the optional hypothesis testing menu during model specification in the interactive mode. Lines beginning with a pound (#; also called hash mark) are ignored and may be used to put comments in the command file.

HLM2, by default, has set up the following options unless the user specifies an alternative command file.

```
STOPVAL:0.0000010000           Sets convergence criterion to be 0.000001.
ACCEL:5                        Use accelerator once after five iterations.
FIXTAU:3 Use the "standard" computer-generated values for the variances and covariances.
MLF:N                          Use the restricted maximum likelihood approach.
```

Table A.1 presents the list of keywords and options recognized by HLM2. Examples with detailed explanation follow.

252

Table A.1 Keywords and options for the HLM2 command file

Keyword	Function	Option	Definition
LEVEL1	Level-1 model specification	INTRCPT1	Level-1 intercept
		+VARNAME	Level-1 predictor (no centering)
		+VARNAME,1	Level-1 predictor centered around group (or level-2 unit) mean
		+VARNAME,2	Level-1 predictor centered around grand mean
LEVEL2	Level-2 model specification	INTRCPT2	Level-2 intercept
		+VARNAME	Level-2 predictor (no centering)
		+VARNAME,2	Level-2 predictor centered around grand mean
		+/VARLIST	List after the slash level-2 variables for exploratory analysis and "t-t-enter" statistics on subsequent runs
NUMIT	Maximum number of iterations	POSITIVE INTEGER	
ACCEL	Controls iteration acceleration	INTEGER $\geq$ 3	Selects how often the accelerator is used. Default is 5.
LEV1OLS	Number of units for which OL equations should be printed	POSITIVE INTEGER	Default is 10.
CONSTRAIN	Constraining of gammas	N	No constraining
		Y	Yes: two or more gammas will be constrained

The program will prompt the user interactively to set the constraints. Alternatively, constraints can be set in the command file. For example, suppose the following

coefficients were estimated: $\gamma_{01}, \gamma_{11}, \gamma_{20}, \gamma_{21}$ and we wish to specify $\gamma_{20} = \gamma_{21}$, we add the following command line: **CONSTRAIN: 0,0,1,1**.

For the following coefficients: $\gamma_{00}, \gamma_{01}, \gamma_{02}, \gamma_{10}, \gamma_{11}, \gamma_{12}$, the command line: CONSTRAIN: **0,1,2,0,1,2** will have the following result: $\gamma_{01} = \gamma_{11}$ *and* $\gamma_{02} = \gamma_{12}$.

Note that all coefficients sharing the value "0" are free to be estimated independently.

		Y	Yes: send optional hypothesis testing menu to the screen during interactive mode use.
HYPOTH	Select optional hypothesis testing menu	N	No. (Note, during batch execution, HYPOTH:N should be selected to suppress screen prompt. Select desired options through keywords below.
GAMMA#	Specifies a particular multivariate contrast to be tested.		In any single run, HLM2 will test up to 5 multivariate hypotheses. Each hypothesis may consist of up to 5 contrasts.

Each contrast is specified by its own line in the command file. The contrast associated with the first hypothesis is specified with the keyword GAMMA1. For example, the contrast shown in Fig 2.37 can be specified by adding the following lines:

```
GAMMA1:0.0,1.0,0.0,0.0,0.0,0.0
GAMMA1:0.0,0.0,0.0,0.0,1.0,0.0
```

For the second hypothesis, the keyword is GAMMA2 and for the third it is GAMMA3 (See Section 2.9.2 for further discussion and illustration.)

HOMVAR	Test homogeneity of level-1 variance	N	No
		Y	Yes
DEVIANCE	Deviance statistic from prior analysis	POSITIVE REAL NUMBER	-2 * log-likelihood at maximum-likelihood estimate
DF	Degrees of freedom associated with deviance statistics from prior analsis (use only if "DEVIANCE" has been specified)	POSITIVE INTEGER	
FIXTAU	Method of correcting unacceptable starting values	1	Set all off-diagonal elements to 0
		2	Manually reset starting values
			Automatic fix-up (default)
		3	Terminate run
		4	Stop program even if starting values are acceptable; display starting values and then allow user to manually reset them.
		5	
HETERO1VAR		N	No
		VARLIST	Variable list
FIXSIGMA2	Controls σ^2	N	Default: does not restrict σ^2.
		REAL NUMBER >0	Fixes σ^2 to the specified value.
LEVEL1WEIGHT LEVEL2WEIGHT	Specifies design weights	Variable name	Allows specification of design weights at the respective levels. Example level1weight:weight1
LEVEL1DELETION	Level-1 deletion list	VARLIST	This keyword only comes into play when the user has opted for deleting data at analysis time while making the MDM file. By default in such cases, deletion is done on the variables in the model. See section 2.9.2.2 for more details.
STOPVAL	Convergence criterion for maximum likelihood estimation	POSITIVE REAL NUMBER	Example: 0.000001. Can be specified to be more (or less) restrictive.

MLF	Controls maximum likelihood estimation method	N	No
		Y	Yes, full maximum likelihood.
			Produces standard errors of **T** and σ^2
RESFIL1	Create level-1 residual file	N	No
		Y/[vl1]/[vl2]	Yes – this may be followed by two '/'s denoting the two levels that can be in the residual file. By default, all the variables in the model will be present in the residual file, this can be added to put additional variables. Vl1 and vl2 are lists of comma-separated variables
RESFIL2	Create a residual file	Y	Yes
		N	No
		/VARLIST	List after the slash additional level-2 variables to be included in the residual file.
RESFIL1NAME, RESFIL2NAME	Name of residual file	FILENAME	The names, respectively of the level-1 and level-2 residual files.
RESFILTYPE	Type of residual file	SYSTAT SAS SPSS STATA FREEFORMAT	Selects program type to be used in subsequent analysis of residual file. SPSS and Stata residual files are written out as .sav and .dta files. Freeformat files are written out in ASCII format with the first line of the file being the variable names
PRINTVARIANCE-COVARIANCE	Output files containing the variance-covariance matrices of Tau and Gammas	N	No
		Y	Yes
		A	Append the files in consecutive runs.
TITLE			Program label up to 64 characters.
OUTPUT	Filename of file that contains output	FILENAME	Will be written to disk; output will overwrite a file of same name.
FULLOUTPUT	Amount of desired output	Y	Full (traditional) output
		N	Reduced output only containing header page and final results

The following keywords are specific to nonlinear, latent variable, and multiply imputed data analysis:

NONLIN	Selects a nonlinear analysis	BERNOULLI POISSON BINOMIAL, COUNTVAR POISSON, COUNTVAR MULTINOMIAL, COUNTVAR ORDINAL, COUNTVAR	These options are explained in detail in Chapter 6.
MACROIT	Maximum number of macro iterations	POSITIVE INTEGER	Used in non-linear models
MICROIT	Maximum number of micro iterations	POSITIVE INTEGER	Used in non-linear models
STOPMACRO	Convergence criterion for change in parameters across macro iterations	POSITIVE INTEGER	

Table A.1 Keywords and options for the HLM2 command file (continued)

STOPMICRO	Convergence criterion for micro iterations	POSITIVE INTEGER	Note same function as STOPVAL in a linear analysis.
LAPLACE	Requests Laplace-6 iterations	N	No
		Y, # where '#' is the maximum number of iterations desired	Yes, with # iterations; uses a sixth order approximation to the likelihood based on a Laplace transform for Bernoulli models. See Sections 5.6.3 and 6.8.2 for details.
EMLAPLACE	Requests EM-Laplace iterations	N	*No*
		Y, # where '#' is the maximum number of iterations desired	Yes, with # iterations. Uses third order approximation.
LVR	Performs a latent variable regression	N	No
		I	Ignore
		P	Predictor
			Outcome
		O	(See Section 9.1 for details)
PLAUSVALS	Selects a list of plausible values for multiple imputation application	VARLIST	See Section 9.2.1 for details.

A.5 Printing of variance and covariance matrices for fixed effects and level-2 variances

The variance-covariance matrices of estimates of fixed effects and variance-covariance parameters based on HLM2 or HLM3 can be saved by checking the "print variance-covariance matrices" in the **Output Settings** dialog box accessed via the **Other Settings** menu. The keyword PRINTVARIANCE-COVARIANCE facilitates the same purpose in batch mode.

The following gives a description of the files containing critical statistics and their variances that are provided by the program upon request.

Let r = number of random effects at level-1.

f = number of fixed effects

p = number of outcomes in a latent variable run

pm = number of alphas in a latent variable run

1. For HLM2:

TAUVC.DAT contains tau in r columns of r rows and then the inverse of the information matrix (the standard errors of tau are the square roots of the diagonals). The dimensions of this matrix are $r*(r+1)/2 \times r*(r+1)/2$.

GAMVC.DAT contains the gammas and the gamma variance-covariance matrix. After the gammas, there are f more rows of f entries containing the variance-covariance matrix.

GAMVCR.DAT contains the gamma and the gamma variance-covariance matrix used to compute the robust standard errors. After the gammas, there are f rows of f entries containing the variance-covariance matrix.

2. For HGLM:

TAUVC.DAT contains tau for the final unit-specific results in r columns of r rows and then the inverse of the information matrix (the standard errors of tau are the square roots of the diagonals). The dimensions of this matrix are $r*(r+1)/2 \times r*(r+1)/2$.

GAMVCUS.DAT contains the final unit-specific gammas and the gamma variance-covariance matrix. The gammas are in the first line and this line has f entries. Then there are f more rows of f entries containing the variance and covariance matrix.

GAMVCPA.DAT contains the final unit-specific gammas and the gamma variance-covariance matrix. The gammas are in the first line and this line has f entries. Then there are f more rows of f entries containing the variance and covariance matrix.

GAMVCPAR.DAT contains the final unit-specific gammas and the gamma variance-covariance matrix used to compute the population-averaged robust standard errors. The gammas are in the first line and this line has f entries. Then there are f more rows of f entries containing the variance and covariance matrix.

3. For Bernoulli models, if Laplace iterations are requested:

GAMVCL.DAT contains the gammas and the variance-covariance matrix used to compute the Laplace standard errors. There are f rows of f entries containing the variance and covariance matrix.

4. For latent variable regression:

LVRALPHA.DAT contains pm lines each containing an alpha and its standard error. The order is the same as in the output table. The final p lines of p columns contain the $Var(u^*)$ matrix printed in the output.

5. For plausible values analysis:

GAMVC.DAT (and GAMVCR.DAT and TAUVC.DAT) are from the last run and TAUVCPC.DAT, GAMVCPV.DAT, and GAMVCPVR.DAT are the PV average files.

All of the above files are created with an n(F15.7 1X) format. That is, each entry is fifteen characters wide withs even decimal places, followed by a space (blank character).

If the value of r or $r*(r+1)/2$ exceeds 60, the line is split into two or more pieces.

A.6 Preliminary exploratory analysis with HLM2

The first option in the basic HLM2 menu "Examine means, variances, chi-squared, etc.?" provides a variety of statistics useful as we begin to formulate HLM problems. The use of this option is available only in interactive mode and a description of the output appears below.

HLM2 HSB.MDM

```
            SPECIFYING A LEVEL-1 OUTCOME VARIABLE
Please specify a level-1 outcome variable

The choices are:
For MINORITY enter  1    For   FEMALE enter  2    For       SES enter  3
For  MATHACH enter   4 What is the outcome variable:  4

Do you wish to:

Examine means,variances,chi-squared, etc? Enter 1
Specify an HLM model?                       Enter 2
Define a new outcome variable?              Enter 3
Exit?                                       Enter 4

What do you want to do?  1
```

Below is the output that HLM2 sends to the screen.

```
The outcome variable is  MATHACH
```

potential level-1 predictors	mean univariate regression coefficient	ANOVA estimate of variance in regression coefficient	reliability	chi-squared	j
MEANS	12.74785	8.76642	0.90192	1618.70998	160
MINORITY	-2.72109	5.60227	0.30517	228.41290	136
FEMALE	-0.94302	0.27533	0.05944	143.41090	123
SES	2.10355	0.46634	0.17531	212.38315	160

```
0 level-2 units were deleted because of no variance in  MATHACH
```

The display above presents information from a series of univariate regressions conducted separately on each unit. The outcome variable selected for these regressions is displayed at the top (MATHACH). The row entitled "MEANS" provides the statistics from a one-way ANOVA on the outcome variable in the 160 schools. The remaining lines summarize the result from the respective univariate regressions estimated separately in each school. The mean univariate coefficient averaged across the J schools is reported in the first column. Column 2 provides an ANOVA-type estimate of the parameter variability in these univariate coefficients. The average reliability and chi-squared test statistics for homogeneity among the univariate regressions are reported in the third and fourth columns.

These data provide our first information about which level-1 coefficients might be specified as random. Though very preliminary results, they suggest that both MINORITY and SES coefficients might be specified as random. Note, these are just univariate regression coefficients and are not adjusted for any other level-1 effects as they would be in a full level-1 model.

```
Hit return to continue < HRt >

Do you wish to:

Examine correlations among univariate
coefficients and level-2 variables?          Enter 1
Specify an HLM model?                         Enter 2
Define a new outcome variable?                Enter 3
Exit?                                         Enter 4

What do you want to do?  1
```

At this point, the user identifies which of the univariate regression coefficients computed above are to be considered further. In this instance we will chose all three. (The unit mean is automatically included.)

```
Please enter the level-1 univariate slopes you wish to estimate

The choices are:
For MINORITY enter  1   For    FEMALE enter  2   For        SES enter  3
level-1 predictor? (Enter 0 to end)  1
level-1 predictor? (Enter 0 to end)  2
level-1 predictor? (Enter 0 to end)  3
```

Next, we select the level-2 predictors that might be used to model the means and univariate regression slopes.

```
Please enter the level-2 predictors you wish to estimate

The choices are:
For    SIZE enter  1    For    SECTOR enter  2    For    PRACAD enter  3
For  DISCLIM enter  4    For   HIMINTY enter  5    For   MEANSES enter  6

level-2 predictor? (Enter 0 to end)  1
level-2 predictor? (Enter 0 to end)  2
level-2 predictor? (Enter 0 to end)  3
level-2 predictor? (Enter 0 to end)  4
level-2 predictor? (Enter 0 to end)  5
level-2 predictor? (Enter 0 to end)  6
```

The correlation matrix among level-1 univariate coefficients (Diagonal elements are standard deviations)

Predictors	MEANS	MINORITY	FEMALE	SES
MEANS	3.1177			
MINORITY	0.1238	4.2846		
FEMALE	-0.0639	0.0978	2.1522	
SES	0.0135	-0.5121	-0.2078	1.6310

Hit return to continue < **HRt** >

These are simple correlations and standard deviations among the univariate regression coefficients estimated in the 160 schools.

The correlation matrix among level-2 predictors
(Diagonal elements are standard deviations)

Predictors	SIZE	SECTOR	PRACAD	DISCLIM	HIMINTY	MEANSES
SIZE	629.5064					
SECTOR	-0.4519	0.4976				
PRACAD	-0.3150	0.6724	0.2559			
DISCLIM	0.3554	-0.7125	-0.6119	0.9770		
HIMINTY	0.1150	0.0494	-0.0792	0.0373	0.4479	
MEANSES	-0.1296	0.3553	0.6491	-0.3493	-0.4056	0.4140

Hit return to continue < **HRt** >

These are simple correlations among the level-2 predictors.

Correlations between level-2 predictors and level-1 univariate coefficients

Level-2 Predictors	Level-1 univariate coefficients			
	MEANS	MINORITY	FEMALE	SES
SIZE	-0.0982	-0.1862	-0.2591	0.2008
SECTOR	0.4492	0.3680	0.1199	-0.3977
PRACAD	0.6821	0.2152	0.0612	-0.2017
DISCLIM	-0.4678	-0.4343	-0.1038	0.3355
HIMINTY	-0.3752	0.0790	-0.0004	-0.1964
MEANSES	0.7847	0.0626	0.0576	0.0496

Hit return to continue < **HRt** >

The display above contains our first cross-level information. It presents information on the level-2 predictors that might be associated with the unit means and univariate regression coefficients. It suggests a list of candidate variables that might be included in the level-2 model for each level-1 coefficient. Again, this too is preliminary because the level-2 coefficients used here are univariate. Nonetheless they are informative.

Do you wish to:

Specify an HLM model?	Enter 1
Define a new outcome variable?	Enter 2
Exit?	Enter 3

What do you want to do? **3**

B Using HLM3 in Interactive and Batch Mode

This appendix describes and illustrates how to use HLM3 in interactive and batch mode to construct MDM files, and to execute analyses based on the MDM file. It also lists and defines command keywords and options unique to HLM3. References are made to appropriate sections in the manual where the procedures are described in greater details.

As in the case of HLM2, formulation, estimation, and testing of models using HLM3 in several ways: Windows mode (PC users only), interactive mode, or batch mode. Interactive execution guides the user through the steps of the analysis by posing questions and providing a menu of options. However, batch mode can be considerably faster once the user becomes skilled in working with the program. In between the two extremes – fully interactive and fully batch – is a range of execution modes that are partly interactive and partly batch. The degree to which the execution is automated (via batch mode) is controlled by the command file, as in the case of HLM2.

B.1 Using HLM3 in interactive mode

B.1.1 Example: constructing an MDM file for the public school data using SPSS file input

```
C:\HLM>HLM3                          (type the program name at the system prompt to start)

Will you be starting with raw data?  Y
Enter type of raw data:
     for ASCII input                enter 1
     for SYSTAT .SYS file           enter 2
     for SAS V5 transport file      enter 3
     for SPSS file (UNIX or windows) enter 4
     for STATA .dta file            enter 5
     for anything DBMSCOPY reads    enter 6
     for anything Stat/Transfer reads enter 7
Type? 4
```

The "anything Stat/Transfer reads" prompt is only present on PC versions.

```
Input name of level-1 file: EG1.SAV
Input name of level-2 file: EG2.SAV
Input name of level-3 file: EG3.SAV        (see Section 4.1.1.1 for a description of the
                                                    variables  in the data files).

The available level-1 variables are:
For      GID enter  1    For      PLID enter  2    For      YEAR enter  3
For    GRADE enter  4    For      MATH enter  5    For RETAINED enter  6
What variable is the level-3 ID? 1
What variable is the level-2 ID? 2
```

Note: there are two linking ID's in the level-1 data file.

```
Please specify level-1 variable # 1 (enter 0 to end): 3
Please specify level-1 variable # 2 (enter 0 to end): 4
Please specify level-1 variable # 3 (enter 0 to end): 5
Please specify level-1 variable # 4 (enter 0 to end): 6

The available level-2 variables are:

For     GID enter  1    For     PLID enter  2    For   FEMALE  enter  3
For   BLACK enter  4    For HISPANIC enter  5
What variable is the level-3 ID? 1
What variable is the level-2 ID? 2
```

Note: there are two linking ID's in the level-2 data file.

```
Please specify level-2 variable # 1 (enter 0 to end): 3
Please specify level-2 variable # 2 (enter 0 to end): 4
Please specify level-2 variable # 3 (enter 0 to end): 5

The available level-3 variables are:

For     GID enter  1    For     SIZE enter  2    For   LOWINC  enter  3
For MOBILITY enter  4
What variable is the level-3 ID? 1
```

Note: there is only one linking ID in the level-3 data file.

```
Please specify level-3 variable # 1 (enter 0 to end): 2
Please specify level-3 variable # 2 (enter 0 to end): 3
Please specify level-3 variable # 3 (enter 0 to end): 4

Are there missing data in the level-1 file? N
```

Note: had we indicated that missing data were present in the level-1 file, the following additional prompts would have come to the screen:

```
Is the missing value the same for all variables?  Y

Do you want to delete the missing data now, or at analysis time? Now
(Enter "now" or "analysis")
```

See Section 2.6 on how HLM2 handles missing data.

```
Enter name of MDM file: EG.MDM
```

*After the MDM file is computed, descriptive statistics for each file are sent to the screen. **It is important to examine these carefully to guarantee that no errors were made in specifying the format of the data.** HLM3 will save these statistics in a file named HLM3MDM.STS. These results are helpful as a reference and when constructing a descriptive table about the data for a written report.*

B.1.2 Example: constructing an MDM file for the HS&B data using ASCII file input

```
C:\HLM> HLM3

Will you be starting with raw data?  Enter type of raw data:
    for ASCII input              enter 1
    for SYSTAT .SYS file         enter 2
    for SAS V5 transport file    enter 3
    for SPSS file (UNIX or windows) enter 4
    for anything DBMSCOPY reads  enter 5

Type? 1

Input number of level-1 variables (not including the character ID):4
The first A field must be a character level-3 id, the second, the level-2 id
Input format of level-1 file: (A4,1X,A9,1X,2F5.1,F7.3,F2.0)
(see A1.3 for rules for format statements)
Input name of level-1 file: EG1.DAT

Input number of level-2 variables (not including the character ID): 3
The first A field must be a character level-3 id, the second, the level-2 id
 Input format of level-2 file: (A4,1X,A9,3F2.0)
Input name of level-2 file: EG2.DAT

Input number of level-3 variables (not including the character ID): 3
The first A field must be a character level-3 id
 Input format of level-3 file: (A4,1X,3F7.1)
Input name of level-3 file: EG3.DAT

Enter 8 character name for level-1 variable number 1: YEAR
Enter 8 character name for level-1 variable number 2: GRADE
Enter 8 character name for level-1 variable number 3: MATH
Enter 8 character name for level-1 variable number 4: RETAINED

Enter 8 character name for level-2 variable number 1: GENDER
Enter 8 character name for level-2 variable number 2: BLACK
Enter 8 character name for level-2 variable number 3: HISPANIC

Enter 8 character name for level-3 variable number 1: SIZE
Enter 8 character name for level-3 variable number 2: LOWINC
Enter 8 character name for level-3 variable number 3: MOBILE

Are there missing data in the level-1 file? N

Enter name of MDM file: EG.MDM
```

HLM3 automatically creates a file named CREATMDM.MDMT that lists the stream of responses typed by the user while creating the MDM file. The CREATMDM.MDMT file has several uses. It can help the user discover errors in the format or variable name specification. Once these are identified, CREATMDM.MDMT can be copied, for example, to NEWSS.MDMT, and then edited. Alternatively, if the user wishes to delete or add variables, the copy of CREATMDM.MDMT can be edited. To reconstruct the MDM file using this new set of commands, simply type:

B.1.3 Example: Executing an analysis using EG.MDM

C:\HLM> **HLM3 EG.MDM**

As in HLM2, the first argument, HLM3, tells the computer to execute the three-level HLM program; the second argument specifies the MDM file to be analyzed. An optional third argument specifies a command file that can be used to automate aspects of model specification via batch-mode .

Do you want to do a non-linear analysis? **N**

SPECIFYING A LEVEL-1 OUTCOME VARIABLE

Please specify a level-1 outcome variable
The choices are:
 For   YEAR enter 1   For   GRADE enter 2   For   MATH enter 3
 For RETAINED enter 4

What is the outcome variable: **3**

SPECIFYING AN HLM MODEL

Level-1 predictor variable specification

Which level-1 predictors do you wish to use?
The choices are:
 For   YEAR enter 1   For   GRADE enter 2
 For RETAINED enter 4

level-1 predictor? (Enter 0 to end) **1**
level-1 predictor? (Enter 0 to end) **0**

Do you want to set the level-1 intercept to zero in this analysis? **N**

This allows you to formulate a model with no intercept term at level 1.

Do you want to center any level-1 predictors? **N**

If you answer "Y" here, the program will offer the option of centering each predictor around the unit mean, a_{jk}, or the grand mean, $a_{...}$

Level-2 predictor variable specification

Which level-2 variables do you wish to use?

The choices are:
 For   FEMALE enter 1   For   BLACK enter 2   For HISPANIC enter 3

Which level-2 predictor to model INTRCPT1, P0?
  Level-2 predictor? (Enter 0 to end) **0**
Which level-2 predictor to model   YEAR, P1 slope?
  Level-2 predictor? (Enter 0 to end) **0**
Do you want to set the level-2 intercept to zero for INTRCPT1, P0? **N**

This allows you to formulate a model with no intercept term at level 2.

Do you want to set the level-2 intercept to zero for   YEAR, P1? **N**

264

```
Do you want to constrain the variances in any of the level-2 random
  effect to zero? N
```

If you answer "Y" here, HLM3 will allow you to fix one or more level-2 variances (and associated covariances) to zero. Through this process the corresponding level-2 outcome is specified as fixed (no predictors) or non-randomly varying (some predictors included.) Notice that the model above contains no level-2 predictors. Had level-2 predictors been included, the user would have been prompted about possible centering options. The choices are: centering around the group mean, $X_{.k}$, centering around the grand mean, $X_{..}$, or no centering.

```
Level-3 predictor variable specification

Which level-3 predictors do you wish to use?

The choices are:
  For     SIZE enter  1    For    LOWINC enter  2    For MOBILITY enter  3

Which level-3 predictors to model INTRCPT1/INTRCPT2, B00?
Level-3 predictor? (Enter 0 to end)  0
Which level-3 predictors to model     YEAR/INTRCPT2, B10 slope?
Level-3 predictor? (Enter 0 to end)  0
```

Notice also that this model contains no level-3 predictors. Had level-3 predictors been included, the user would have been prompted about possible centering options. The choices are: centering around the grand mean, W, or no centering.

```
Do you want to constrain the variances in any of the level-3 random
  effect to zero? N
```

By answering "Y" here, you can specify level-3 outcomes as fixed or non-randomly varying.

ADDITIONAL PROGRAM FEATURES

```
Select the level-2 variables that you might consider for
inclusion as predictors in subsequent models.
The choices are:
  For   FEMALE enter  1    For     BLACK enter  2    For HISPANIC enter  3

Which level-2 variables to model INTRCPT1, P0?
Level-2 predictor? (Enter 0 to end)  1
Level-2 predictor? (Enter 0 to end)  2
Level-2 predictor? (Enter 0 to end)  3
Which level-2 variables to model     YEAR, P1 slope?
Level-2 predictor? (Enter 0 to end)  -1
```

As in HLM2, HLM3 will interpret the response of "-1" to repeat the selections made for the previous prompt, i.e., 1, 2, 3.

```
Select the level-3 predictor variables that you might consider for
inclusion as predictors in subsequent models.
```

The choices are:
For   SIZE enter 1   For   LOWINC enter 2   For MOBILITY enter 3

Which level-3 variables to model INTRCPT1/INTRCPT2, B00?
  Level-3 predictor? (Enter 0 to end) **1**
  Level-3 predictor? (Enter 0 to end) **2**
  Level-3 predictor? (Enter 0 to end) **3**
Which level-3 variables to model   YEAR/INTRCPT2, B10 slope?
  Level-3 predictor? (Enter 0 to end) **1**
  Level-3 predictor? (Enter 0 to end) **2**
  Level-3 predictor? (Enter 0 to end) **3**
Do you want to constrain any (more) of the gammas? **N**
Do you wish to use any of the optional hypothesis testing procedures? **N**

The options available here are a multivariate hypothesis test for the fixed effects and Likelihood Ratio Test for comparison of nested models.

Do you want to do a latent variable regression on tau(beta)? **N**

                        OUTPUT SPECIFICATION

Do you want a level-2 residual file? **Y**

Enter additional variables to go in residual file
The choices are:
For   FEMALE enter 1   For   BLACK enter 2   For HISPANIC enter 3

  Level-2 variable? (Enter 0 to end) **0**
Do you want a level-3 residual file? **Y**

Enter additional variables to go in residual file
The choices are:
For   SIZE enter 1   For   LOWINC enter 2   For MOBILITY enter 3

  Level-3 variable? (Enter 0 to end) **0**
Enter type of stat package you will use:
     for SYSTAT   enter 1
     for SAS   enter 2
     for SPSS   enter 3
     for Stata   enter 4
     for Free Format   enter 5
Type? **3**
How many iterations do you want to do? **100**
Enter a problem title: **Unconditional Linear Growth Model**
Enter name of output file: **EG1.OUT**

Computing . . ., please wait
Starting values computed. Iterations begun.
Should you wish to terminate the iterations prior to convergence, enter cntl-c
The value of the likelihood function at iteration 1 = -8.169527E+003
The value of the likelihood function at iteration 2 = -8.165377E+003
...
The value of the likelihood function at iteration 5 = -8.164748E+003
The value of the likelihood function at iteration 6 = -8.163118E+003
The value of the likelihood function at iteration 7 = -8.163116E+003
The value of the likelihood function at iteration 8 = -8.163116E+003
The value of the likelihood function at iteration 9 = -8.163116E+003

See Section 4.2.1 for an annotated output of EG1.OUT.

B.2 Using HLM3 in batch mode

The command file structure for HLM3 closely parallels that of HLM2. Each line begins with a keyword followed by a colon. After the colon is the option chosen by the user, *i.e.*,

```
KEYWORD:OPTION
```

As with HLM2, a pound sign ("#") as the first character of a line can be used to introduce a comment into the command file.

The following keywords have the same definitions and options in HLM3 as in HLM2 (Table A.1)

```
ACCEL        CONSTRAIN    DEVIANCE      DF        FIXTAU     FIXSIGMA2   GAMMA#
HYPOTH       LAPLACE      MACROIT       MICROIT   NONLIN     NUMIT       OUTPUT
PLAUSVALS PRINTVARIANCE-COVARIANCE      RESFIL1   RESFIL1NAME            RESFIL2
RESFIL2NAME               RESFILTYPE    FIXSIGMA2 STOPMACRO STOPMICRO    STOPVAL
TITLE                     LEVEL1DELETION          FULLOUTPUT
```

The following keywords are available only for HLM2:

```
LEV1OLS   HOMVAR    HETERO1VAR     MLF    LVR
```

B.2.1 Table of keywords and options

Table B.1 presents the list of keywords and options unique to HLM3.

Table B.1 Keywords and options unique to the HLM3 command file

Keyword	Function	Option	Definition
		INTRCPT1	Level-1 intercept
		+VARNAME	Level-1 predictor (no centering)
		+VARNAME,1	Level-1 predictor centered around unit mean a_{jk}
LEVEL1	Level-1 model specification	+VARNAME, 2	Level-1 predictor centered around grand mean $a...$
		(Note: variable names may be specified in either upper or lower case.)	
		INTRCPT2	Level-2 intercept
		+VARNAME	Level-2 predictor (no centering)
		+VARNAME,1	Level-2 predictor centered around group mean, $X_{.k}$
LEVEL2	Level-2 model specification	+VARNAME, 2	Level-2 predictor centered around grand mean, $X_{..}$
			Comma separated list after the slash level-2 variables for exploratory analysis and "t-to-enter" statistics on subsequent runs. A slash without a subsequent variable suppresses the interactive prompt.
		/VARLIST	

LEVEL3	Level-3 model specification	INTRCPT2	Level-3 intercept (must be included in the level-2 model)
		+ VARNAME	Level-3 predictor (no centering)
		+ VARNAME, 2	Level-3 predictor centered around grand mean, W.
		/VARLIST	List after the slash level-3 variables for exploratory analysis and "t-to-enter" statistics on subsequent runs.
			A slash without a subsequent variable suppresses the interactive prompt.
RESFIL3	Create a level-3 residual file	Y	Yes
		N	No
		/ VARLIST	List after the slash additional level-3 variables to be included in the residual file. Works just like RESFIL2
RESFIL3NAME	Name of residual file	FILENAME	Changes the default
FIXTAU2	Method of correcting unacceptable starting values for $\mathbf{T}_\pi$	1	Set all off-diagonal elements to 0
		2	Manually reset starting values
		3	Automatic fix-up (default)
		4	Terminate run
		5	Stop program even if the starting values are acceptable; display starting values and then allow user to manually reset them.
FIXTAU3	Method of correcting unacceptable starting values for $\mathbf{T}_\beta$	1	Set all off-diagonal elements to 0
		2	Manually reset starting values
		3	Automatic fix-up (default)
		4	Terminate run
		5	Stop program even if the starting values are acceptable; display starting values and then allow user to manually reset them.
LVR-BETA	Performs a latent variable regression	N	No
		P,O	P for predictor(s); O for outcomes (s)
			See Section 9.1 for details.
DOFISHER	Turns on/off Fisher estimation	Y	Use Fisher
		N	Do not use Fisher
FISHERTYPE	Controls type of Fisher acceleration	0	Same as DOFISHER:N
		1	Use 1st derivate Fisher
		2	Use 2nd derivative Fisher(default)
			See section 4.5

B.3 Printing of variance and covariance matrices

Besides the files described in Section A.5, HLM3 can provide the following files upon request.

Note that adding the command line

`PRINTVARIANCE-COVARIANCE:Y`

to the command file will request HLM3 to print out statistics for both tau(pi) as well as tau(beta).

Let r = number of random effects at level-1
$r2$ = number of random effects at level-2

1. For HLM3:

TAUVC.DAT contains tau (tau(pi)) in r columns of r rows, the next $r2$ lines are the tau(beta), and then the inverse of the information matrix (the standard errors of tau[s] are the square roots of the diagonals). The dimensions of this matrix are
$$(r*(r+1)/2+r2*(r2+1)/2)\times(r*(r+1)/2+r2*(r2+1)/2).$$

2. For three-level HGLM:

TAUVC.DAT has the same format as the one for HLM3. The tau(s) are the final unit-specific results. The files for the gammas have the identical structure as those for two-level models (see Section A.5)

All files are created with an n(F15.7,1X) format. That is, each entry is fifteen characters wide with seven decimal places, followed by a space (blank character).

If the value of r or f or $(r*(r+1)/2+r2*(r2+1)/2$ exceeds 60, the line is split into two or more pieces.

C Using HGLM in Interactive and Batch Mode

This appendix describes and illustrates how to use HGLM in interactive and batch mode to execute analyses based on the MDM files. References are made to appropriate sections in the manual where the procedures are described in greater details.

C.1 Example: Executing an analysis using THAIUGRP.MDM

Here is an example of an HLM2 session in the interactive mode. At the system command line prompt, we first type the program name – HLM2 – followed by the name of the multivariate data matrix file – THAIUGRP.MDM. The program now takes the user directly into the model specification process.

```
C:\HLM> HLM2 THAIUGRP.MDM

Do you want to do a non-linear analysis? Y

Enter type of non-linear analysis:
```

See Chapter 5 for details regarding type of non-linear analysis.

```
1) Bernoulli (0 or 1)
2) Binomial (count)
3) Poisson  (constant exposure)
4) Poisson  (variable exposure)
5) Multinomial
6) Ordinal

type of analysis: 1
```

As mentioned, with one binary outcome per level-1 unit, the model choice is "1" (Bernoulli).

If "2"(Binomial) is chosen, the user will be asked:

```
For the non-linear analysis, which variable indicates the number of trials?
```

If "4"(Poisson (variable exposure)) is chosen, the user will be asked:

```
For the non-linear analysis, which variable indicates the exposure?
```

If "5"(Multinomial) or "6"(Ordinal) is chosen, the user will be asked:

```
How many categories does the "OUTCOME" have?
```

```
Enter maximum number of macro iterations: 25
Enter maximum number of micro iterations: 20
```

Specifying 25 macro iterations sets an upper limit; if, after the 25th iteration the algorithm has not converged. The program will nonetheless terminate and print the results at that iteration. Similarly, setting 20 as the number of micro iterations insures that, after 20 micro iterations, the current macro iteration will terminate even if the micro iteration convergence criterion has not been met.

```
Do you wish to allow over-dispersion at level 1? N
```

An answer of "Y" here allows a user to estimate a level-1 dispersion parameter σ^2. If the assumption of no dispersion holds, $\sigma^2 = 1.0$. If the data are over-dispersed, $\sigma^2 > 1.0$; if the data are under-dispersed, $\sigma^2 < 1.0$.

```
Do you want to do the Laplace-6 iterations? N
Do you want to do the Laplace-8 iterations? N
```

An answer of "Y" here allows use to obtain highly accurate Laplace approximation to maximum likelihood. See Sections 5.6.3 and 6.9.2. The user will be prompted to enter maximum number of Laplace macro iterations.

```
                   SPECIFYING A LEVEL-1 OUTCOME VARIABLE

Please specify a level-1 outcome variable
  The choices are:
  For      MALE enter  1     For       PPED enter  2     For        REP1 enter  3

What is the outcome variable: 3

Do you wish to:

     Examine means,variances,chi-squared, etc? Enter 1
     Specify an HLM model?                      Enter 2
     Define a new outcome variable?             Enter 3
     Exit?                                      Enter 4
What do you want to do? 2

                      SPECIFYING AN HLM MODEL
Level-1 predictor variable specification

Which level-1 predictors do you wish to use?
  The choices are:
  For      MALE enter  1     For       PPED enter  2
  level-1 predictor? (Enter 0 to end)  1
  level-1 predictor? (Enter 0 to end)  2
```

Thus, we have set up a level-1 model with repetition (REP1) as the outcome and with gender (MALE) and pre-primary experience (PPED) as predictors.

```
 Do you want to center any level-1 predictors? N

Do you want to set the level-1 intercept to zero in this analysis? N
```

Level-2 predictor variable specification

Which level-2 variables do you wish to use?

The choices are:
For   MSESC enter 1

Which level-2 predictors to model INTRCPT1?
  Level-2 predictor? (Enter 0 to end) **1**
Which level-2 predictors to model   MALE slope?
  Level-2 predictor? (Enter 0 to end) **0**
Which level-2 predictors to model   PPED slope?
  Level-2 predictor? (Enter 0 to end) **0**

Thus we have modeled the level-1 intercept as depending on the mean SES (MSESC) of the school. The coefficients associated with gender and pre-primary experience are fixed. Mean SES has been centered around its grand mean.

Do you want to constrain the variances in any of the level-2 random
effects to zero? **Y**
Do you want to fix INTRCPT1? **N**
Do you want to fix   MALE? **Y**
Do you want to fix   PPED? **Y**

Do you want to center any level-2 predictors? **Y**
(Enter 0 for no centering, 2 for grand-mean)
How do you want to center   MSESC? **2**

ADDITIONAL PROGRAM FEATURES

Select the level-2 variables that you might consider for
inclusion as predictors in subsequent models.
The choices are:
For   MSESC enter 1

Which level-2 variables to model INTRCPT1?
  Level-2 variable? (Enter 0 to end) **0**
Do you want to constrain any (more) of the gammas? **N**
Do you wish to use any of the optional hypothesis testing procedures? **N**
Do you want to do a latent variable regression? **Y**
Setting method of estimation to full.

Enter o for outcome, p for predictor, or i to ignore
How do you want to model INTRCPT1? **P**

OUTPUT SPECIFICATION

Do you want a level-1 residual file? **Y**

Enter additional variables to go in residual file
The choices are:
For   MALE enter 1   For PPED enter 2   For REP1 enter 3

Level-1 variable? (Enter 0 to end) **1**
Level-1 variable? (Enter 0 to end) **2**
Level-1 variable? (Enter 0 to end) **3**

Enter additional variables to go in residual file
The choices are:
Level-1 variable? (Enter 0 to end) **1**
For   MSESC enter 1

Level-2 variable? (Enter 0 to end)   **1**

Do you want a level-2 residual file? **Y**

Enter additional variables to go in residual file
The choices are:
Level-1 variable? (Enter 0 to end) **1**
For   MSESC enter 1

Level-2 variable? (Enter 0 to end)   **1**

Enter type of stat package you will use:
     for SYSTAT   enter 1
     for SAS   enter 2
     for SPSS   enter 3
     for Stata   enter 4
     for Free Format enter 5
Type? **3**

Do you want to see OLS estimates for all of the level-2 units? **N**
 Enter a problem title: Bernoulli output, Thailand data
 Enter name of output file: **THAIBERN.OUT**

                    MACRO ITERATION 1

Starting values computed. Iterations begun.
Should you wish to terminate the iterations prior to convergence, enter cntl-c
The value of the likelihood function at iteration 1 = -2.400265E+003
The value of the likelihood function at iteration 2 = -2.399651E+003
The value of the likelihood function at iteration 3 = -2.399620E+003
The value of the likelihood function at iteration 4 = -2.399614E+003
The value of the likelihood function at iteration 5 = -2.399612E+003
The value of the likelihood function at iteration 6 = -2.399612E+003
The value of the likelihood function at iteration 7 = -2.399612E+003

Macro iteration number 1 has converged after six micro iterations. This macro iteration actually computes the linear-model estimates (using the identity link function as if the level-1 errors were assumed normal).
These results are then transformed and input to start macro iteration 2, which is, in fact, the first non-linear iteration.

                    MACRO ITERATION 2

Starting values computed. Iterations begun.
Should you wish to terminate the iterations prior to convergence, enter cntl-c
The value of the likelihood function at iteration 1 = -1.067218E+004
The value of the likelihood function at iteration 2 = -1.013726E+004
The value of the likelihood function at iteration 3 = -1.011008E+004
The value of the likelihood function at iteration 4 = -1.010428E+004
The value of the likelihood function at iteration 5 = -1.010265E+004
The value of the likelihood function at iteration 6 = -1.010193E+004
The value of the likelihood function at iteration 7 = -1.010188E+004
The value of the likelihood function at iteration 8 = -1.010188E+004
The value of the likelihood function at iteration 9 = -1.010187E+004
The value of the likelihood function at iteration 10 = -1.010187E+004

```
The value of the likelihood function at iteration 11 = -1.010187E+004
The value of the likelihood function at iteration 12 = -1.010187E+004
```

Macro interaction 2, the first non-linear macro iteration, converged after twelve micro iterations.

MACRO ITERATION 3

```
Starting values computed.  Iterations begun.
Should you wish to terminate the iterations prior to convergence, enter cntl-c
The value of the likelihood function at iteration 1 = -9.954836E+003
The value of the likelihood function at iteration 2 = -9.954596E+003
The value of the likelihood function at iteration 3 = -9.954567E+003
The value of the likelihood function at iteration 4 = -9.954558E+003
The value of the likelihood function at iteration 5 = -9.954555E+003
The value of the likelihood function at iteration 6 = -9.954554E+003
The value of the likelihood function at iteration 7 = -9.954553E+003
```

MACRO ITERATION 4

```
Starting values computed.  Iterations begun.
Should you wish to terminate the iterations prior to convergence, enter cntl-c
The value of the likelihood function at iteration 1 = -1.000019E+004
The value of the likelihood function at iteration 2 = -1.000018E+004
The value of the likelihood function at iteration 3 = -1.000018E+004
The value of the likelihood function at iteration 4 = -1.000017E+004
The value of the likelihood function at iteration 5 = -1.000017E+004
The value of the likelihood function at iteration 6 = -1.000017E+004
The value of the likelihood function at iteration 7 = -1.000017E+004
```

MACRO ITERATION 5

```
Starting values computed.  Iterations begun.
Should you wish to terminate the iterations prior to convergence, enter cntl-c
The value of the likelihood function at iteration 1 = -1.000347E+004
The value of the likelihood function at iteration 2 = -1.000347E+004
The value of the likelihood function at iteration 3 = -1.000347E+004
```

MACRO ITERATION 6

```
Starting values computed.  Iterations begun.
Should you wish to terminate the iterations prior to convergence, enter cntl-c
The value of the likelihood function at iteration 1 = -1.000375E+004
The value of the likelihood function at iteration 2 = -1.000375E+004
```

MACRO ITERATION 7

```
Starting values computed.  Iterations begun.
Should you wish to terminate the iterations prior to convergence, enter cntl-c
The value of the likelihood function at iteration 1 = -1.000375E+004
The value of the likelihood function at iteration 2 = -1.000375E+004
```

Note that macro iteration 7 converged with just 2 micro iterations. Also, the change in parameter estimates between macro iterations 6 and 7 was found negligible (less than the criterion for convergence) so that macro iteration 8 was the final "unit-specific" macro iteration. One final "population average" iteration is computed, and screen output for that is given below.

MACRO ITERATION 8

```
Starting values computed.  Iterations begun.
Should you wish to terminate the iterations prior to convergence, enter cntl-c
The value of the likelihood function at iteration 1 = -1.000374E+004
```

The value of the likelihood function at iteration 2 = -1.000374E+004

Thus concludes the interactive terminal session. See Section 6.2 for an annotated output for this run.

The interactive session annotated above produced the following command file (NEWCMD.HLM).

```
#This command file was run with thaiugr.mdm
STOPMICRO:0.0000010000
STOPMACRO:0.0001000000
MACROIT:25
MICROIT:20
NONLIN:BERNOULLI
LAPLACE:n,50
LAPLACE8:n,50
LEVEL1:REP1=INTRCPT1+MALE+PPED+RANDOM
LEVEL2:INTRCPT1=INTRCPT2+MSESC,2+RANDOM/
LEVEL2:MALE=INTRCPT2/
LEVEL2:PPED=INTRCPT2/
LEVEL1WEIGHT:NONE
LEVEL2WEIGHT:NONE
RESFILTYPE:SPSS
RESFIL1:Y/MALE,PPED,REP1/MSESC
RESFIL1NAME:resfil1.sav
RESFIL2:Y/MSESC
RESFIL2NAME:resfil2.sav
HETEROL1VAR:n
ACCEL:5
LVR:P
LEV1OLS:10
MLF:y
HYPOTH:n
FIXSIGMA2:1.000000
FIXTAU:3
CONSTRAIN:N
OUTPUT:nnn
FULLOUTPUT:Y
TITLE:Bernoulli output, Thailand data
```

If one types at the system prompt:

```
HLM2 THAIUGRP.MDM NEWCMD.HLM
```

the output above would be reproduced. It is a good idea to rename the NEWCMD.HLM file if it is to be edited and re-used. Each execution of the program will produce a NEWCMD.MLM file that will overwrite the old one.

Note that the "NEWCMD.HLM" file above is similar to the same file produced by a linear-model analysis, with the addition of the following lines:

```
STOPMICRO:0.000010        (default convergence criterion for micro iterations)
STOPMACRO:0.000100        (default convergence criterion for micro iterations)
MACROIT:25                       (maximum number if macro iterations)
MICROIT:20         (maximum number if micro iterations per macro iteration)
NONLIN:BERNOULLI                        (type of non-linear model)
```

See Tables A.1 and B.1 for a description of the keywords and options.

D Using HMLM in Interactive and Batch Mode

This appendix describes prompts and commands for creating MDM files and executing analyses based on the MDM files. References are made to appropriate sections in the manual where the procedures are described in greater details. To start HMLM or HMLM2, type HMLM or HMLM2 at the system prompt.

D.1 Constructing an MDM file

The procedure for MDM creation is similar to the one for MDM (see Sections A1.1 and A1.2). The only difference is that the user will be prompted with questions regarding the number of occasions contained in the data and which the indicator variables. To create a MDM file using the NYS data sets described in Section 8.1.1, for example, HMLM will display the following prompts to request the needed information:

```
How many occasions are contained in the data? 5

Please select the 5 indicator variables:
Is     ATTIT     an indicator variable?  N
Is      AGE      an indicator variable?  N
Is     AGE11     an indicator variable?  N
Is     AGE13     an indicator variable?  N
Is    AGE11S     an indicator variable?  N
Is    AGE13S     an indicator variable?  N
Is     IND1      an indicator variable?  Y
Is     IND2      an indicator variable?  Y
Is     IND3      an indicator variable?  Y
Is     IND4      an indicator variable?  Y
Is     IND5      an indicator variable?  Y
```

D.2 Executing analyses based on MDM files

The procedure for executing analyses based on MDM files is similar to the one based on MDM files. A major difference is that only coefficients associate with variables that are invariant across all level-1 units, *i.e.*, their values do not vary across the units, can be specified as random. Otherwise, the coefficients will be automatically set as non-random by the program. The following displays prompts unique to HMLM and HMLM2 for the NYS example described in Section 8.2.

```
C:\HLM> HMLM NYS.MDM

Enter type HMLM analysis:
```

See Chapter 7 for details regarding type of HMLM analysis.

```
1) Unrestricted
2) Random effects model with homogeneous level-1 variance
3) Random effects model with heterogeneous level-1 variance
4) Random effects model with log-linear model for level-1 variance
5) Random effects model with first-order autoregressive level-1 variance
```

```
type of analysis: 3
```

For choices 2 to 5, the user will be prompted.

```
Do you want to skip the unrestricted iterations? N
```

If "4"(log-linear model for level-1 variance) is chosen, HMLM will ask the user to enter variables to model sigma^2, for example:

```
Should VAR1 be in C?
```

An interactive session will output a command file NEWCMD.MLM. An example for one of the analyses discussed in Section 8.2 is given below.

```
#This command file was run with nys.mdm
LEVEL1:ATTIT=INTRCPT1+AGE13+AGE13S+RANDOM
LEVEL2:INTRCPT1=INTRCPT2+RANDOM
LEVEL2:AGE13=INTRCPT2+RANDOM
LEVEL2:AGE13S=INTRCPT2+RANDOM
NUMIT:50
STOPVAL:0.0000010000
FIXTAU:3
OUTPUT:nys1.out
FULLOUTPUT:Y
TITLE:HMLM OUPUT, NYS DATA
ACCEL:5
R_E_MODEL:UNRESTRICTED
LVR:N
```

If one types at the system prompt:

```
HMLM NYS.MDM NEWCMD.MLM
```

the result will be the output for a model with an unrestricted covariance structure given in Section 8.3. It is a good idea to rename the NEWCMD.MLM file if it is to be edited and re-used. Each execution of the program will produce a NEWCMD.MLM file that will overwrite the old one.

The following keywords have the same definitions and options in HMLM as in HLM2 (Table A.1)

```
ACCEL     DEVIANCE   DF                      FIXTAU
LEVEL1    LEVEL2     GAMMA#                  HYPOTH
NUMIT     OUTPUT     PRINTVARIANCE-COVARIANCE
STOPVAL   TITLE      FULLOUTPUT   LVR
```

The following keywords are not available in HMLM:

```
LEV1OLS    HOMVAR       HETERO1VAR   MLF        LEVEL1DELETION
CONSTRAIN  FIXSIGMA2    HYPOTH       LAPLACE    MACROIT
MICROIT    NONLIN       PLAUSVALS    RESFIL1    RESFIL1NAME
RESFIL2    RESFIL2NAME  RESFILTYPE   STOPMACRO  STOPMICRO
```

D.2.1 Table of keywords and options

Table D.1 Keywords and options unique to the HMLM command file

Keyword	Function	Option	Definition
R_E_MODEL	Choose type of model	UNRESTRICTED	Do only unrestricted iterations
		HOMOL1VAR	Do homogeneous model
		HETL1VAR	Do homogeneous and heterogeneous model
		AUTOREG	Do homogeneous and auto-regressive model
		LOGLIN/var	Do homogeneous and log-linear model
UNRESTRICTED	Possible suppression of unrestricted	Y	Do unrestricted iterations
		N	Don't do unrestricted iterations. Only possible it R_E_MODEL is not UNRESTRICTED

The following keywords have the same definitions and options in HMLM2 as in HLM3 (Table B.1)

```
ACCEL     DEVIANCE    DF      FIXTAU2       FIXTAU3
LEVEL1    LEVEL2      LEVEL3  GAMMA#        HYPOTH
NUMIT     OUTPUT      PRINTVARIANCE-COVARIANCE
STOPVAL   TITLE       FULLOUTPUT           LVR
```

The following HLM3 keywords are not available in HMLM2:

```
LEV1OLS    HOMVAR      LEVEL1DELETION
CONSTRAIN  FIXSIGMA2   HYPOTH       LAPLACE      MACROIT
MICROIT    NONLIN      PLAUSVALS    RESFIL1      RESFIL1NAME
RESFIL2    RESFIL2NAME RESFIL3      RESFIL3NAME  RESFILTYPE
STOPMACRO  STOPMICRO   LVR-BETA
```

D.2.2 Table of HMLM2 keywords and options

Table D.1 Keywords and options unique to the HMLM2 command file

Keyword	Function	Option	Definition
R_E_MODEL	Choose type of model	UNRESTRICTED	Do only unrestricted iterations
		HOMOL1VAR	Do homogeneous model
		HETL1VAR	Do homogeneous and heterogeneous model
		AUTOREG	Do homogeneous and auto-regressive model
		LOGLIN/var	Do homogeneous and log-linear model
UNRESTRICTED	Possible suppression of unrestricted	Y	Do unrestricted iterations
		N	Don't do unrestricted iterations. Only possible it R_E_MODEL is not UNRESTRICTED

Note that HMLM and HMLM2 do not allow non-linear outcomes, use of plausible values and multiply-imputed values, constraints of gammas, and they do not write out any residual files.

E Using Special Features in Interactive and Batch Mode

This appendix describes and illustrates how to use the special features in interactive and batch mode to execute analyses. References are made to appropriate sections in the manual where the procedures are described in greater details.

E.1 Example: Latent variable analysis using the National Youth Study data sets

The following interactive session illustrates a latent variable analysis example using the National Youth Study (NYS) data sets. A description of the data files and the model specification can be found in Sections 8.1.1 and 9.1.1.

```
C:\HLM> HMLM NYS.MDM
Enter type HMLM analysis:

   1) Unrestricted
   2) Random effects model with homogeneous level-1 variance
   3) Random effects model with heterogeneous level-1 variance
   4) Random effects model with log-linear model for level-1 variance
   5) Random effects model with first-order autoregressive level-1 variance

type of analysis: 2
```

We select the homogeneous level-1 variance option for this model. Thus, using HLM2 will yield identical results in this case.

```
Do you want to skip the unrestricted iterations? Y

                 SPECIFYING A LEVEL-1 OUTCOME VARIABLE

Please specify a level-1 outcome variable
  The choices are:
  For     ATTIT enter  1    For       AGE enter  2    For     AGE11 enter  3
  For     AGE13 enter  4    For    AGE11S enter  5    For    AGE13S enter  6
  For      IND1 enter  7    For      IND2 enter  8    For      IND3 enter  9
  For      IND4 enter 10    For      IND5 enter 11
What is the outcome variable: 1
```

The outcome is tolerance towards deviant behavior.

```
                        SPECIFYING AN HMLM MODEL
Level-1 predictor variable specification

Which level-1 predictors do you wish to use?
  The choices are:
                     For       AGE enter  2    For     AGE11 enter  3
  For     AGE13 enter  4    For    AGE11S enter  5    For    AGE13S enter  6
```

280

```
For     IND1 enter  7    For     IND2 enter  8    For     IND3 enter  9
For     IND4 enter 10    For     IND5 enter 11

level-1 predictor? (Enter 0 to end)  3
level-1 predictor? (Enter 0 to end)  0
```

AGE11 is the age of participant at a specific time minus 11.

```
Do you want to center any level-1 predictors? N

Do you want to set the level-1 intercept to zero in this analysis? N

Level-2 predictor variable specification

Which level-2 variables do you wish to use?

  The choices are:
  For    FEMALE enter  1    For MINORITY enter  2    For    INCOME enter  3

  Which level-2 predictors to model INTRCPT1?
    Level-2 predictor? (Enter 0 to end)  1
    Level-2 predictor? (Enter 0 to end)  0

  Which level-2 predictors to model    AGE11 slope?
    Level-2 predictor? (Enter 0 to end)  1
    Level-2 predictor? (Enter 0 to end)  0

Do you want to constrain the variances in any of the level-2 random
  effects to zero? N

Do you want to center any level-2 predictors? N

                    ADDITIONAL PROGRAM FEATURES
Do you want to do a latent variable regression? Y

Enter o for outcome, p for predictor, or i to ignore
How do you want to handle INTRCPT1? P
How do you want to handle    AGE11? O
```

INTRCPT1, the level of tolerance at age 11, is used as a predictor to model the outcome, AGE11, the linear growth rate. Note that INTRCPT1 and AGE11 are latent variables, that is, they are free of measurement error.

```
Do you want to specify a multivariate hypothesis for the fixed effects? N

                       OUTPUT SPECIFICATION
How many iterations do you want to do? 50
Enter a problem title: Latent variable regression, NYS Data
Enter name of output file: NYS2.OUT

Computing . . ., please wait
```

Partial output for this analysis is given in Section 9.1.1.

E.2 A latent variable analysis to run regression with missing data

The following interactive session illustrates a latent variable analysis to run regression with missing data with an artificial data set. A description of the data files and the model specification can be found in Section 9.1.2.

```
C:\HLM> HMLM MISSING.MDM
```

Enter type HMLM analysis:

```
1) Unrestricted
2) Random effects model with homogeneous level-1 variance
3) Random effects model with heterogeneous level-1 variance
4) Random effects model with log-linear model for level-1 variance
5) Random effects model with first-order autoregressive level-1 variance
```

type of analysis: **1**

```
                SPECIFYING A LEVEL-1 OUTCOME VARIABLE
```

Please specify a level-1 outcome variable

```
The choices are:
For MEASURES enter  1    For     IND1 enter  2    For     IND2 enter  3
For     IND3 enter  4
```

What is the outcome variable: **1**

```
                SPECIFYING AN HMLM MODEL
```

Level-1 predictor variable specification

Which level-1 predictors do you wish to use?

```
The choices are:
For     IND1 enter  2    For     IND2 enter  3    For     IND3 enter  4

level-1 predictor? (Enter 0 to end)  1
That is the outcome variable!
level-1 predictor? (Enter 0 to end)  2
level-1 predictor? (Enter 0 to end)  3
level-1 predictor? (Enter 0 to end)  4
```

Do you want to center any level-1 predictors? **N**

Do you want to set the level-1 intercept to zero in this analysis? **Y**

Note that a no-intercept model is formulated (see Section 2.9.6).

Level-2 predictor variable specification

Which level-2 variables do you wish to use?

```
The choices are:
For     DUMMY enter  1

Which level-2 predictors to model      IND1 slope?
  Level-2 predictor? (Enter 0 to end)  0
Which level-2 predictors to model      IND2 slope?
```

282

```
Level-2 predictor? (Enter 0 to end)  0

Which level-2 predictors to model     IND3 slope?
  Level-2 predictor? (Enter 0 to end)  0
```

IND2 and IND3 are selected to predict IND1.

```
Do you want to constrain the variances in any of the level-2 random
 effects to zero? N

                  ADDITIONAL PROGRAM FEATURES

Do you want to do a latent variable regression? Y

Enter o for outcome, p for predictor, or i to ignore
How do you want to handle     IND1? O
How do you want to handle     IND2? P
How do you want to handle     IND3? P

Do you want to specify a multivariate hypothesis for the fixed effects? N

                    OUTPUT SPECIFICATION
How many iterations do you want to do? 50
  Enter a problem title: Latent variable analysis, Missing data example
  Enter name of output file: MISSING1.OUT
```

Partial output for this analysis is given in Section 9.1.2.

E.3 Commands to apply HLM to multiply-imputed data

To analyze data with multiply-imputed values for the outcome variable or only one covariate, the user needs to manually add the following line into the command file:

```
PLAUSVALS: VARLIST
```

where VARLIST lists variables containing the multiply-imputed values.

To analyze data with multiply-imputed values for the outcome and/or covariates, the user needs to prepare multiple MDM files. After setting up the multiple MDM files, the user have to submit the command files to HLM2 and HLM3 as many times as the number of multiple MDM files with an extra flag, -MI#, where # is the sequence number, starting from 0. On the last run, you also need the -E flag, (E for estimate).

Suppose there are 4 sets of multiply-imputed data for a two-level model, called MDATA1.MDM, MDATA2.MDM, MDATA3.MDM, and MDATA4.MDM and the command file is ANALYSE.MLM; the following commands need to be typed in at the system prompt:

```
HLM2 -MI0 MDATA1.MDM ANALYSE.MLM
```

```
HLM2 -MI1 MDATA2.MDM ANALYSE.MLM
HLM2 -MI2 MDATA3.MDM ANALYSE.MLM
HLM2 -MI3 -E MDATA.4MDM ANALYSE.MLM
```

F Using HCM2 in Interactive and Batch Mode

This appendix describes and illustrates how to use HCM2 in interactive construct MDM files, and in both interactive and batch mode to execute analyses based on the MDM file. It also lists and defines command keywords and options unique to HCM2. References are made to appropriate sections in the manual where the procedures are described in greater details.

F.1 Using HCM2 in interactive mode

F.1.1 Example: constructing an MDM file for the educational attainment data as described in Chapter 11 using SPSS file input

```
C:\HLM>HCM2                    (type the program name at the system prompt to start)

Will you be starting with raw data? Y
Enter type of raw data:
    for ASCII input              enter 1
    for SYSTAT .SYS file         enter 2
    for SAS V5 transport file    enter 3
    for SPSS file (UNIX or windows) enter 4
    for STATA .dta file          enter 5
    for anything DBMSCOPY reads  enter 6
    for anything Stat/Transfer reads enter 7
Type? 4
```

The "anything DBMSCOPY reads" prompt is only present on PC versions.

```
Input name of level-1 file: ATTAINW.SAV
Input name of row file: ATTAINR.SAV
Input name of column file: ATTAINCO.SAV
```

See Section 11.1.2 for a description of variables in the data files.

```
The available level-1 variables are:
For   NEIGHID  enter  1    For    SCHID  enter  2    For    ATTAIN  enter  3
For    P7VRQ   enter  4    For   P7READ  enter  5    For    DADOCC  enter  6
For DADUNEMP   enter  7    For    DADED  enter  8    For    MOMED   enter  9
For    MALE    enter 10
What variable is the row ID? 1
What variable is the column ID? 2
```

Note there are two linking ID's in the level-1 or within-cell file.

```
Please specify level-1 variable # 1 (enter 0 to end): 3

Please specify level-1 variable # 2            (enter 0 to end): 4
```

```
Please specify level-1 variable # 3 (enter 0 to end): 5
Please specify level-1 variable # 4 (enter 0 to end): 6
Please specify level-1 variable # 5 (enter 0 to end): 7
Please specify level-1 variable # 6 (enter 0 to end): 8
Please specify level-1 variable # 7 (enter 0 to end): 9
Please specify level-1 variable # 8 (enter 0 to end): 10
```

```
The available row-level variables are:

 For  NEIGHID  enter  1    For  DEPRIVE  enter  2
 What variable is the row ID? 1
```

Note there is one row ID the level-2 row factor file.

```
 Please specify row-level variable # 1 (enter 0 to end): 2

 The available column-level variables are:
 For    SCHID  enter  1    For    DUMMY  enter  2
 What variable is the column ID? 1
```

Note there is one column ID the level-2 column factor file.

```
 Please specify column-level variable # 1 (enter 0 to end): 2
```

```
Are there missing data in the level-1 file? y
```

```
Enter name of MDM file: ATTAIN.MDM
```

HCM2 save send the descriptive statistics of variables for each file to the screen. It is important to examine these carefully to ensure that no errors were made. The program will save these statistics in a file name HCM2MDM.STS.

LEVEL-1 DESCRIPTIVE STATISTICS

VARIABLE NAME	N	MEAN	SD	MINIMUM	MAXIMUM
ATTAIN	2310	0.09	1.00	-1.33	2.42
P7VRQ	2310	0.51	10.65	-27.03	42.97
P7READ	2310	-0.04	13.89	-31.87	28.13
DADOCC	2310	-0.46	11.78	-23.45	29.23
DADUNEMP	2310	0.11	0.31	0.00	1.00
DADED	2310	0.22	0.41	0.00	1.00
MOMED	2310	0.25	0.43	0.00	1.00
MALE	2310	0.48	0.50	0.00	1.00

ROW LEVEL DESCRIPTIVE STATISTICS

VARIABLE NAME	N	MEAN	SD	MINIMUM	MAXIMUM
DEPRIVE	524	0.04	0.62	-1.08	2.96

COLUMN LEVEL DESCRIPTIVE STATISTICS

VARIABLE NAME	N	MEAN	SD	MINIMUM	MAXIMUM
DUMMY	17	2.41	1.18	1.00	4.00

```
2310 level-1 records have been processed
524 row-level records have been processed
17 column-level records have been processed
```

F.1.2 Example: Executing an unconditional model analysis using ATTAIN.MDM

```
C:\HLM> HCM2 ATTAIN.MDM
```

Do you want to do a non-linear analysis? **N**

                 SPECIFYING A LEVEL-1 OUTCOME VARIABLE

Please specify a level-1 outcome variable
  The choices are:
  For   ATTAIN enter 1   For   P7VRQ enter 2   For   P7READ enter 3
  For   DADOCC enter 4   For DADUNEMP enter 5   For   DADED enter 6
  For   MOMED enter 7   For   MALE enter 8
What is the outcome variable: **1**

We shall model educational attainment with an unconditional model and specific the residual row, column, and cell-specific effects as random. See Section 11.2 .

                      SPECIFYING AN HCM2 MODEL

Level-1 predictor variable specification

Which level-1 predictors do you wish to use?
  The choices are:
                          For   P7VRQ enter 2   For   P7READ enter 3
  For   DADOCC enter 4   For DADUNEMP enter 5   For   DADED enter 6
  For   MOMED enter 7   For   MALE enter 8
level-1 predictor? (Enter 0 to end) **0**

Do you want to set the level-1 intercept to zero in this analysis? **N**

Level-1/row predictor variable specification

Which row variables do you wish to use?

  The choices are:
  For   DEPRIVE enter 1

Which row-level predictor to model INTRCPT1, P0?
  Row-level predictor? (Enter 0 to end) **0**

Column-level predictor variable specification

Which column-level variables do you wish to use?

  The choices are:
  For   DUMMY enter 1

Which column-level predictor to model INTRCPT1, P0?
  Column-level predictor? (Enter 0 to end) **0**

Do you want to constrain the variances in any of the row-level random
  effect to zero? **N**

Do you want to constrain the variances in any of the column-level random
  effect to zero? n

```
Enter type of deflection:
for independent(default) enter 1
for cumulative           enter 2
Type? 1
```

Select 2 if to define a cumulative effect model.

```
                    OUTPUT SPECIFICATION

Do you want a row-level residual file? N
Do you want a column-level residual file? N
How many iterations do you want to do? 100
Enter a problem title: UNCONDITIONAL MODEL
Enter name of output file: ATTAIN1.TXT


Computing . . . ., please wait
The value of the likelihood function at iteration 1 = -3.208601E+003
The value of the likelihood function at iteration 2 = -3.207263E+003
The value of the likelihood function at iteration 3 = -3.205187E+003
The value of the likelihood function at iteration 4 = -3.201693E+003
The value of the likelihood function at iteration 5 = -3.196031E+003
The value of the likelihood function at iteration 6 = -3.188714E+003
The value of the likelihood function at iteration 7 = -3.182922E+003
The value of the likelihood function at iteration 8 = -3.180439E+003
The value of the likelihood function at iteration 9 = -3.179676E+003
The value of the likelihood function at iteration 10 = -3.179379E+003
The value of the likelihood function at iteration 11 = -3.179212E+003
The value of the likelihood function at iteration 12 = -3.179104E+003
The value of the likelihood function at iteration 13 = -3.179032E+003
The value of the likelihood function at iteration 14 = -3.178984E+003
The value of the likelihood function at iteration 15 = -3.178881E+003
The value of the likelihood function at iteration 16 = -3.178879E+003
The value of the likelihood function at iteration 17 = -3.178878E+003
The value of the likelihood function at iteration 18 = -3.178877E+003
The value of the likelihood function at iteration 19 = -3.178876E+003
The value of the likelihood function at iteration 20 = -3.178874E+003
The value of the likelihood function at iteration 21 = -3.178874E+003
```

See Section 11.2 for a discussion of the results of this unconditional model.

F.1.3 Example: Executing a conditional model analysis using ATTAIN.MDM

```
C:\HLM> HCM2 ATTAIN.MDM

Do you want to do a non-linear analysis? N

                SPECIFYING A LEVEL-1 OUTCOME VARIABLE

Please specify a level-1 outcome variable
 The choices are:
 For    ATTAIN enter  1    For      P7VRQ enter  2    For    P7READ enter  3
 For    DADOCC enter  4    For  DADUNEMP enter  5    For     DADED enter  6
 For     MOMED enter  7    For       MALE enter  8
What is the outcome variable: 1
```

We shall model educational attainment with all the level-1 predictor variables. All the level-1 coefficients associated with the predictors are fixed. See Section 11.3.

Level-1 predictor variable specification

Which level-1 predictors do you wish to use?
 The choices are:
```
                          For    P7VRQ enter  2    For   P7READ enter  3
 For   DADOCC enter  4    For DADUNEMP enter  5    For    DADED enter  6
 For    MOMED enter  7    For     MALE enter  8
 level-1 predictor? (Enter 0 to end)  2
 level-1 predictor? (Enter 0 to end)  3
 level-1 predictor? (Enter 0 to end)  4
 level-1 predictor? (Enter 0 to end)  5
 level-1 predictor? (Enter 0 to end)  6
 level-1 predictor? (Enter 0 to end)  7
 level-1 predictor? (Enter 0 to end)  8
 level-1 predictor? (Enter 0 to end)  0
```

```
Do you want to center any level-1 predictors? y
 Enter 0 for no centering, 2 for grand-mean
 How do you want to center      P7VRQ? 2
 How do you want to center      P7READ? 2
 How do you want to center      DADOCC? 2
 How do you want to center DADUNEMP? 2
 How do you want to center      DADED? 2
 How do you want to center      MOMED? 2
 How do you want to center       MALE? 2
```

Do you want to set the level-1 intercept to zero in this analysis? N

Level-1/row predictor variable specification

Which row variables do you wish to use?

 The choices are:
 For   DEPRIVE enter 1

We shall use DEPRIVE to model the level-1 intercept.


```
Which row-level predictor to model INTRCPT1, P0?
 Row-level predictor? (Enter 0 to end)  1
Which row-level predictor to model      P7VRQ, P2 slope?
 Row-level predictor? (Enter 0 to end)  0
Which row-level predictor to model      P7READ, P3 slope?
 Row-level predictor? (Enter 0 to end)  0
Which row-level predictor to model      DADOCC, P4 slope?
 Row-level predictor? (Enter 0 to end)  0
Which row-level predictor to model DADUNEMP, P5 slope?
 Row-level predictor? (Enter 0 to end)  0
Which row-level predictor to model      DADED, P6 slope?
 Row-level predictor? (Enter 0 to end)  0
Which row-level predictor to model      MOMED, P7 slope?
 Row-level predictor? (Enter 0 to end)  0
Which row-level predictor to model       MALE, P8 slope?
 Row-level predictor? (Enter 0 to end)  0
```

Column-level predictor variable specification

Which column-level variables do you wish to use?

The choices are:

For   DUMMY enter 1

Which column-level predictor to model INTRCPT1, P0?
 Column-level predictor? (Enter 0 to end) **0**
Which column-level predictor to model   P7VRQ, P2 slope?
 Column-level predictor? (Enter 0 to end) **0**
Which column-level predictor to model   P7READ, P3 slope?
 Column-level predictor? (Enter 0 to end) **0**
Which column-level predictor to model   DADOCC, P4 slope?
 Column-level predictor? (Enter 0 to end) **0**
Which column-level predictor to model DADUNEMP, P5 slope?
 Column-level predictor? (Enter 0 to end) **0**
Which column-level predictor to model   DADED, P6 slope?
 Column-level predictor? (Enter 0 to end) **0**
Which column-level predictor to model   MOMED, P7 slope?
 Column-level predictor? (Enter 0 to end) **0**
Which column-level predictor to model   MALE, P8 slope?
 Column-level predictor? (Enter 0 to end) **0**

Do you want to center any row-level predictors? **y**
 Enter 0 for no centering, 2 for grand-mean
How do you want to center DEPRIVE? **2**

Do you want to constrain the variances in any of the row-level random
 effect to zero? **y**
Do you want to fix INTRCPT1/ICPTROW? **N**
Do you want to fix P7VRQ/ICPTROW? **Y**
Do you want to fix P7READ/ICPTROW? **Y**
Do you want to fix DADOCC/ICPTROW? **Y**
Do you want to fix DADUNEMP/ICPTROW? **Y**
Do you want to fix DADED/ICPTROW? **Y**
Do you want to fix MOMED/ICPTROW? **Y**
Do you want to fix MALE/ICPTROW? **Y**

Do you want to constrain the variances in any of the column-level random
 effect to zero? **Y**

*We shall treat the association between social deprivation and educational attainment as fixed across
all schools. See Section 11.2 .*

Do you want to fix INTRCPT1/DEPRIVE? **Y**
Do you want to fix INTRCPT1/ICPTCOL? **N**
Do you want to fix P7VRQ/ICPTCOL? **Y**
Do you want to fix P7READ/ICPTCOL? **Y**
Do you want to fix DADOCC/ICPTCOL? **Y**
Do you want to fix DADUNEMP/ICPTCOL? **Y**

290

```
Do you want to fix DADED/ICPTCOL? Y
Do you want to fix MOMED/ICPTCOL? Y
Do you want to fix MALE/ICPTCOL? Y
 Enter type of deflection:
 for independent(default) enter 1
 for cumulative          enter 2
Type? 1


                    OUTPUT SPECIFICATION


Do you want a row-level residual file? N
Do you want a column-level residual file? N


How many iterations do you want to do? 100
Enter a problem title: CONDITIONAL MODEL WITH THE EFFECT ASSOCIATED WITH A ROW-SPECIFIC
PREDICTOR FIXED
Enter name of output file: ATTAIN2.TXT


Computing . . ., please wait

The value of the likelihood function at iteration 1 = -2.391226E+003
The value of the likelihood function at iteration 2 = -2.390450E+003
The value of the likelihood function at iteration 3 = -2.390158E+003
The value of the likelihood function at iteration 4 = -2.389892E+003
The value of the likelihood function at iteration 5 = -2.389646E+003
The value of the likelihood function at iteration 6 = -2.389417E+003
The value of the likelihood function at iteration 7 = -2.389201E+003
The value of the likelihood function at iteration 8 = -2.388996E+003
The value of the likelihood function at iteration 9 = -2.388800E+003
The value of the likelihood function at iteration 10 = -2.388610E+003
The value of the likelihood function at iteration 11 = -2.388424E+003
The value of the likelihood function at iteration 12 = -2.388243E+003
The value of the likelihood function at iteration 13 = -2.388064E+003
The value of the likelihood function at iteration 14 = -2.387888E+003
The value of the likelihood function at iteration 15 = -2.387714E+003
The value of the likelihood function at iteration 16 = -2.387543E+003
The value of the likelihood function at iteration 17 = -2.387376E+003
The value of the likelihood function at iteration 18 = -2.387214E+003
The value of the likelihood function at iteration 19 = -2.387060E+003
The value of the likelihood function at iteration 20 = -2.386663E+003
The value of the likelihood function at iteration 21 = -2.385279E+003
The value of the likelihood function at iteration 22 = -2.384992E+003
The value of the likelihood function at iteration 23 = -2.384887E+003
The value of the likelihood function at iteration 24 = -2.384842E+003
The value of the likelihood function at iteration 25 = -2.384816E+003
The value of the likelihood function at iteration 26 = -2.384809E+003
The value of the likelihood function at iteration 27 = -2.384806E+003
The value of the likelihood function at iteration 28 = -2.384804E+003
The value of the likelihood function at iteration 29 = -2.384803E+003
The value of the likelihood function at iteration 30 = -2.384803E+003
The value of the likelihood function at iteration 31 = -2.384802E+003
The value of the likelihood function at iteration 32 = -2.384802E+003
The value of the likelihood function at iteration 33 = -2.384802E+003
The value of the likelihood function at iteration 34 = -2.384802E+003
```

See Section 11.2 for a discussion of the results of this conditional model.

F.2 Using HCM2 in batch mode

The interactive session in F.1.1 produced the following command file, NEWCMD.HLM

```
#WHLM CMD FILE FOR C:\HLM\ATTAIN.MDM
NUMIT:100
STOPVAL:0.0000010000
LEVEL1:ATTAIN=INTRCPT1+RANDOM
ROWCOL:INTRCPT1=THETA+RANDOMB+RANDOMC
FIXTAU:3
FIXDELTA:3
ACCEL:5
DEFLECTION:INDEPENDENT
TITLE:UNCONDITIONAL MODEL
OUTPUT:C:\HLM\ATTAIN1.TXT
FULLOUTPUT:N
```

If one types at the system prompt:

```
HCM2 ATTAIN.MDM NEWCMD.HLM
```

the result will be the output for the unconditional model. Note that each execution of the progam will produce a NEWCMD.HLM file that will overwrite the old one.

For the conditional model, the command file is

```
#WHLM CMD FILE FOR C:\HLM\ATTAIN.MDM
NUMIT:100
STOPVAL:0.0000010000
LEVEL1:ATTAIN=INTRCPT1+P7VRQ,2+P7READ,2+DADOCC,2+DADUNEMP,2+DADED,2+MOMED,2+
MALE,2+RANDOM
ROWCOL:INTRCPT1=THETA+DEPRIVE(FIXED),2+RANDOMB+RANDOMC
ROWCOL:P7VRQ=THETA
ROWCOL:P7READ=THETA
ROWCOL:DADOCC=THETA
ROWCOL:DADUNEMP=THETA
ROWCOL:DADED=THETA
ROWCOL:MOMED=THETA
ROWCOL:MALE=THETA
FIXTAU:3
FIXDELTA:3
ACCEL:5
DEFLECTION:INDEPENDENT
TITLE:CONDITIONAL MODEL, WITH SOCIAL DEPRIVATION EFFECT FIXED
OUTPUT:C:\HLM\ATTAIN2.TXT
FULLOUTPUT:N
```

The following keywords in the above command files have the same definition and options in HCM2 as in HLM2 and HLM3 (Tables A.1 and B.1)

```
ACCEL DOFISHER   FULLOUTPUT FIXTAU NONLIN   NUMIT OUTPUT    STOPVAL    TITLE
```

Had we requested residual level-1, and row and column files during the interaction session, the command files would contain the following additional command lines specifying the type (SPSS system file) and the names for each of the files (RESFIL1.SAV, RESROW.SAV, and RESCOL.SAV):

```
RESFILTYPE:SPSS
RESFIL1NAME:RESFIL1.SAV
RESFIL1:Y

RESROWNAME:RESROW.SAV
RESROW:Y
RESCOLNAME:RESCOL.SAV
RESCOL:Y
```

Table F.1 Keywords and options unique for HCM2 command file

Keyword	Function	Option	Definition
LEVEL1	Level-1 or within-cell model specification	INTRCPT1 +VARNAME +VARNAME,1 +VARNAME,2	Level-1 intercept Level-1 predictor (no centering) Level-1 predictor (group-mean centering) Level-1 predictor (grand-mean centering)
ROWCOL: INTRCPT1 or L-1 VARNAME	Level-2 or between-cell model specification	THETA +VARNAME(FIXED) +VARNAME(FIXED),2 +VARNAME(RANDOM),2 +VARNAME(RANDOM),2 +RANDOMB +RANDOMC	Level-2 intercept + Level-2 predictor (fixed and grand-mean centering) + Level-2 predictor (fixed and no centering) + Level-2 predictor (random and grand-mean centering) + Level-2 predictor (random and no centering) + Random main effect of the row factor + Random main effect of the column factor
DEFLECTION	Define the use of a cumulative effect model	1 2	Independent Cumulative

References

Barnett, R. C., Brennan, R. T., Raudenbush, S. W., & Marshall, N. L. (1993). Gender and the relationship between marital role-quality and psychological distress: A study of dual-earner couples. *Journal of Personality and Social Psychology, 64,* 794-806.

Bock, R. (1975). *Multivariate Statistical Methods in Behavioral Research.* New York: McGraw-Hill.

Breslow, N., & Clayton, D. (1993). Approximate inference in generalized linear mixed models. *Journal of the American Statistical Association, 88,* 9-25.

Bryk, A., & Raudenbush, S. W. (1992). *Hierarchical Linear Models for Social and Behavioral Research: Applications and Data Analysis Methods.* Newbury Park, CA: Sage.

Cheong, Y. F., Fotiu, R. P., & Raudenbush, S. W. (2001). Efficiency and robustness of alternative estimators for 2- and 3-level models: The case of NAEP. *Journal of Educational and Behavioral Statistics, 26,* 411-429.

Dempster, A., Laird, N., & Rubin, D. (1977). Maximum likelihood from incomplete data via the EM algorithm. *Journal of the Royal Statistical Society, Series B*(39), 1-8.

Elliot, D., Huizinga, D., & Menard, S. (1989). *Multiple Problem Youth: Delinquency, Substance Use, and Mental Health Problems.* New York: Springer-Verlag.

Garner, C., & Raudenbush, S. (1991). Neighborhood effects on educational attainment: A multi-level analysis of the influence of pupil ability, family, school, and neighborhood. *Sociology of Education,* 64(4), 251-262.

Goldstein, H. (1991). Non-linear multilevel models with an application to discrete response data. *Biometrika, 78,* 45-51.

Hedeker, D., & Gibbons, R. (1994). A random-effects ordinal regression model for multilevel analysis. *Biometrics,* pp. 993-944.

Huttenlocher, J.E., Haight, W., Bryk, A.S., & Seltzer, M. (1991). Early vocabulary growth: Relations to language input and gender. *Developmental Psychology*, 22(2), 236-249.

Jennrich, R., & Schluchter, M. (1986). Unbalanced repeated-measures models with structured covariance matrices. *Biometrics, 42,* 805-820.

Kang, S.J. (1992). A mixed linear model for unbalanced two-way crossed multilevel data with estimation via the EM algorithm. Unpublished doctoral dissertation, Michigan State University, East Lansing.

Little, R., & Rubin, D. (1987). *Statistical analysis with missing data.* New York: Wiley.

Little, R., & Schenker, N. (1995). Missing data. In G. Arminger, C. C. Clogg & M. E. Sobel (Eds.), *Handbook of Statistical Modeling for the Social and Behavioral Sciences* (pp. 39-76). New York: Plenum Press.

Longford, N. (1993). *Random Coefficient Models.* Oxford: Clarendon Press.

McCullagh, P., & Nelder, J. (1989). *Generalized Linear Models, 2nd Edition.* London: Chapman and Hill.

Pfefferman, D., Skinner, C.J., Homes, D.J., Goldstein, H., and Rasbash, J. (1998). Weighting for unequal selection models in multilevel models. *Journal of the Royal Statistical Society, Series B*, 60,1,23-40.

Raudenbush, S. (1993). A crossed random effects model for unbalanced data with applications in cross-sectional and longitudinal research. *Journal of Educational Statistics*, 18(4), 321-349.

Raudenbush, S. W. (1999). Hierarchical models. In S. Kotz (Ed.), *Encyclopedia of Statistical Sciences, Update Volume 3* (pp. 318-323). New York: John Wiley & Sons, Inc.

Raudenbush, S. W. (2001). Toward a coherent framework for comparing trajectories of individual change. Collins, L., & Sayer, A. (Eds.), *Best Methods for Studying Change* (pp. 33-64). Washington, DC: The American Psychological Association.

Raudenbush, S. W., & Bhumirat, C. (1992). The distribution of resources for primary education and its consequences for educational achievement in Thailand. *International Journal of Educational Research,* pp. 143-164.

Raudenbush, S. W., & Bryk, A. S. (2002). *Hierarchical Linear Models: Applications and Data Analysis Methods, Second Edition.* Newbury Park, CA: Sage.

Raudenbush, S. W., & Chan, W.S. (1993). Application of hierarchical linear models to study adolescent deviance in an overlapping cohort design. *Journal of Clinical and Consulting Psychology, 61*(6), 941-951.

Raudenbush, S. W., Yang, M.-l., & Yosef, M. (2000). Maximum likelihood for hierarchical models via high-order, multivariate LaPlace approximation. *Journal of Computational and Graphical Statistics, 9*(1), 141-157.

Raudenbush, S. W., & Sampson, R. (1999). Assessing direct and indirect associations in multilevel designs with latent variables *Sociological Methods and Research, 28*(2), 123-153.

Rodriguez, G., & Goldman, N. (1995). An asseMDMent of estimation procedures for multilevel models with binary responses. *Journal of the royal Statistical Society, A, 158,* 73-89.

Rogers, A., & *et. al.* (1992). *National AsseMDMent of Educational Progress: 1990 Secondary-use Data Files User Guide.* Princeton, New Jersey: Educational Testing Service.

Rowan, B., Raudenbush, S., & Cheong, Y. (1993). Teaching as a non-routine task: Implications for the organizational design of schools. *Educational Administration Quarterly, 29*(4), 479-500.

Rowan, R., Raudenbush, & Kang, S. (1991). Organizational design in high schools: A multilevel analysis. *American Journal of Education, 99*(2), 238-266.

Rubin, D. (1987). *Multiple Imputation for Nonresponse in Surveys.* New York: Wiley.

Schafer, J. (1997). *Analysis of Incomplete Multivariate Data.* London: Chapman & Hall.

Schall, R. (1991). Estimation in generalized linear models with random effects. *Biometrika, 40,* 719-727.

Stiratelli, R., Laird, N., & Ware, J. (1984). Random effects models for serial observations with binary response. *Biometrics, 40,* 961-971.

Wong, G., & Mason, W. (1985). The hierarchical logistic regression model for multilevel analysis. *Journal of the American Statistical Association, 80*(391), 513-524.

Yang, M. (1995). *A simulation study for the assessment of the non-linear hierarchical model estimation via approximate maximum likelihood*. Unpublished apprenticeship paper, College of Education, Michigan State University.

Yang, M.L. (1998). Increasing the efficiency in estimating multilevel Bernoulli models [Diss], East Lansing, MI: Michigan State University.

Zeger, S., Liang, K.Y., & Albert, P. (1988). Models for longitudinal data: A likelihood approach. *Biometrics, 44,* 1049-60.

Zeger, S., & Liang, L. (1986). Longitudinal data analysis using generalized linear models. *Biometrika, 73,* 13-22.

Subject Index

M

T

Tau, 10, 34, 49, 144, 148, 257
  average estimates, 181
TAUVC.DAT file, 257-8, 269
TAUVCPC.DAT file, 258
Template file
  for MDM, 19, 245, 263
  for model, 275, 277
Test statistic
  chi-square, 12, 71, 192
  likelihood ratio, 11, 12, 60, 62, 71, 141, 143
Thailand data, 115
Threshold, 103
t-ratio, 12, 71
t-to-enter statistic for potential predictor, 64-5, 84, 249

U

Under-dispersion, 111, 138, 271
Unit-specific
  differences from population-average, 111
  iteration, 274
  model and multinomial outcome, 133
  model and ordinal outcome, 133
  models, 109-11, 117, 119, 121, 125, 128, 132, 136, 139, 257, 269, 274
Univariate regressions per unit, 259
Unrestricted model, 141

V

Var-cov matrix
  printing gamma to file, 257-8, 269
Variable exposure, 126, 270

Variance
  combined model, 148
  first order AR at level-1, 141, 146, 155, 163
  heterogeneity at level-1, 16, 52, 140, 145
  homogeneity of level-1, 59, 60, 62, 143, 157, 158, 159, 173, 254, 276, 280, 282
  hypothesis tests, 12, 112
  matrix, 34, 144, 148, 257
  matrix for fixed effects, 139
  multivariate tests, 60
  level-1, 7-8, 52-4, 68, 81, 111, 119, 125-7, 140, 145, 159-1, 163, 165, 184, 191, 204, 276, 277, 280, 282
  level-2, 9, 69, 82-3, 91, 108, 265
  log-linear at level-1, 140, 145, 277
  posterior, 16, 41, 85-6
  printing to file, 256
  test for components, 60
  unrestricted structure, 140-5, 153-4, 157, 173, 177, 277
  within-cell, 191
Variance and covariance components, 9, 10, 11, 15, 35, 36, 61, 83, 91, 112, 121, 133, 137, 189
  average estimates, 181
  chi-square test, 15
V-known model, 42, 184-7
  estimating in interactive mode, 185-6

W

Weighting, 55-7, 76, 254
Within-cell
  data file, 193, 195, 196
  model, 190, 191, 198
  random effect, 191
  variance, 191
Within-person variation, 142